Frederic Pincott

Analytical index to Sir John W. Kaye's History of the Sepoy war and Col. G.B. Malleson's History of the Indian mutiny

Frederic Pincott

Analytical index to Sir John W. Kaye's History of the Sepoy war and Col. G.B. Malleson's History of the Indian mutiny

ISBN/EAN: 9783337303631

Printed in Europe, USA, Canada, Australia, Japan

Cover: Foto ©ninafisch / pixelio.de

More available books at **www.hansebooks.com**

ANALYTICAL INDEX

TO

SIR JOHN W. KAYE'S
HISTORY OF THE SEPOY WAR,

AND

COL. G. B. MALLESON'S
HISTORY OF THE INDIAN MUTINY.

(Combined in One Volume.)

BY

FREDERIC PINCOTT,
MEMBER OF THE ROYAL ASIATIC SOCIETY.

LONDON:
W. H. ALLEN & CO., 13 WATERLOO PLACE,
PALL MALL, S.W.

1880.

PREFACE.

This Index gives a summary of all the occurrences which took place in any town or district, and of all the actions recorded of any person, mentioned in the "History of the Sepoy War," by Sir John Kaye, and the "History of the Indian Mutiny," by Col. G. B. Malleson. In most cases the events are necessarily classified, but without losing sight of chronological arrangement; dates being given for all actions of particular significance, or of such as, it is supposed, those who use the book might desire to know, without referring to the volumes themselves. It is hoped that the method adopted will enable this Index to be of use to anyone who wishes to ascertain the extent to which any person or place was concerned in the great Mutiny, so far as mentioned in the volumes specified. For facilitating reference, the longer articles have been provided with italic side-heads, so that particular periods of the history may be readily found; examples of this are to be seen under the articles "Dehlí," "Lakhnau," &c. The method of arrangement enables the progress of the

Mutiny to be traced with remarkable distinctness, especially under the article "Mutiny" itself. This article, read with a map of Northern India, will show the fearful rapidity with which the outbreak spread, and the districts successively involved in it. The progress of the Mutiny can, thus, be traced from day to day with clearness and brevity.

With regard to the spelling of proper names, it must be remarked that the two authors indexed followed two diametrically opposite systems; there remained, therefore, a fair field for the Indexer to follow the bent of his own inclination, while supplying abundant cross-references for the varying spellings found in the volumes themselves. It need scarcely be remarked that, in the references, the letter K. refers to Sir John Kaye's volumes, and the latter M. to those of Col. Malleson. Where no year is specified, the year of the Mutiny (1857) is to be understood.

ANALYTICAL INDEX

OF THE

HISTORIES OF THE INDIAN MUTINY.

A.

Abbás Alí, bravely defends Lieut. Conolly, M. ii. 594; offers his life to preserve the English at Írinpúra, M. ii. 560; offers to desert rebels, but is refused pardon, M. ii. 562; becomes an active leader of the rebels, M. ii. 562; pardoned by Lord Canning, M. ii. 568.

Abbott, Capt., tides over first threat of mutiny at Aurangábád, M. iii. 12; reconnoitres Morár, M. iii. 215; his gallantry in the Málwá campaign, M. iii. 87.

Abbott, Col. Augustus, Inspector-General of Ordnance in 1857, K. i. 513.

Abbott, James, his character, K. i. 31.

Abd-ul-Alí, bravely defends Lieut. Conolly, M. ii. 594; offers his life to preserve the English at Írinpúra, M. ii. 560.

Aberdeen, Lord, writes letter of sympathy to Lord Canning, M. iii. 257.

Aboo Zuffer, see Abú Zafr.

Abú Zafr, becomes Emperor of Dehli, as Baháḍur Sháh, K. ii. 10.

Activity, the one thing needful for the English, at the outbreak of the Mutiny, K. ii. 152.

Admiralty, extraordinary decision of High Court of, M. iii. 202.

Adoption, right of, K. i. 70; of heir to property, K. i. 70; of heir to sovereignty, K. i. 70; the right necessary for the Hindú, M. iii. 23; effect produced by refusal of right, M. iii. 24; denial of this right, one cause of the Mutiny, M. iii. 388.

Afghan war of 1838, K. i. 274; its effect on the Sepoy, K. i. 274.

Afghanistan, terms of alliance with in 1856, K. i. 440, 442.

Afzul-ud-Daula, the Nizám, M. iii. 118.

1

A'grá, its importance, K. iii.
197; peculiar dangers of, K.
iii. 199; European cantonments at, K. iii. 198; military
force at, K. iii. 198; civil servants at, in May, K. iii. 199.
Almost cut off from Calcutta, K. iii. 181; occupants
of Fort resolve to assume the
offensive, K. iii. 110; council
of war (May 14), K. iii. 199,
M. i. 148; Mr. Colvin proposes retirement into Fort,
M. i. 149; proposal protested
against, M. i. 149; noisy character of council, K. iii. 200.
Trepidation shown by some
British officials (May 14), K.
iii. 200; company of Europeans ordered into Fort, K.
iii. 198; Mr. Drummond, the
magistrate at, disbelieves in
danger, K. iii. 202; his opinion changed by the mutiny
at Mathurá, M. i. 166; Col.
Hugh Fraser, Chief Engineer
at, K. iii. 203; Engineer officers at, deprecate over-confidence, K. iii. 202; Mr. Colvin
advised by Col. Fraser to distrust Sepoys, M. i. 151;
prompt precautionary measures recommended by Engineers, K. iii. 204; advice of Engineers not taken, K. iii. 205.
Troops at, addressed by
Mr. J. Colvin (May 15), K. iii.
205; the Sepoys scowl on Mr.
Colvin after his address, K.
iii. 206, M. i. 150; Mr. G. Harvey sent with escort towards
Dehlí (May 20), K. iii. 207.
Native Contingents in vicinity of, K. iii. 208; Mr. Colvin applies to Sindhiá and
Bharatpúr for aid, K. iii.
209, M. i. 153; Sindhiá sends
troops to protect (May 16),
K. iii. 209; and his body-

A'grá—*cont.*
guard (May 31), M. i. 169;
formation of Volunteer Cavalry Corps at, K. iii. 210, M.
i. 167; Major Prendergast
receives command of Volunteers, M. i. 263.
Panic at (May 22), K. iii.
227; critical position of, M.
i. 168; Mr. Colvin's hopes
destroyed by mutiny at Mathurá, M. i. 165; preparations
for defence of, K. iii. 228,
229; Mr. Colvin's proclamation of May 25, K. iii. 232,
M. i. 163, his proclamation
disapproved by Government of
India, M. i. 164; and superseded by Lord Canning, K.
iii. 233; Mr. Colvin defends
his proclamation, K. iii. 237;
Lord Canning's proclamation,
K. iii. 235.
Mr. Colvin disarms Sepoys
at (May 31), K. iii. 243, M. i.
167; departure of disbanded
Sepoys, K. iii. 359; the police
obstruct the victualling of
the Fort, M. i. 263; Mr. J.
Colvin forbids the removal of
property into Fort, M. i. 264;
great unpopularity of Mr.
Colvin, K. iii. 377.
Mr. Colvin authorises retirement into Fort, M. i. 264;
Mr. J. Colvin removes into
Fort, July 4, K. iii. 381; complete isolation of English, M.
i. 262; approach of Nímach
mutineers, K. iii. 378, M. i.
264; the troops in garrison,
M. i. 265; disposition of
troops to check advance of
Nímach mutineers, M. i. 265;
officers beg Brig. Polwhele to
go out to meet mutineers, K.
iii. 382.
Dangerous illness of Mr
Colvin, M. i. 266; resigns his

Ágrá—cont.
power to Commission, July 3, M. i. 266; the Commission to whom Mr. Colvin entrusted his powers, M. i. 266; measures of defence taken by Commission, M. i. 267; Kiraulí troops are induced to surrender their two guns, M. i. 267; Mr. Colvin resumes authority, M. i. 268; mutiny of Kotá Contingent at (July 4), M. i. 268; Kiraulí troops ordered home, M. i. 268. Nímach mutineers reach Sháhganj, M. i. 269; Brig. Polwhele resolves to go out to meet them (July 5), M. i. 270; Nímach mutineers secure best position for attack, through vacillation of Brig. Polwhele, K. iii. 383; strength of Nímach mutineers, K. iii. 383, M. i. 270; advance of Brig. Polwhele against them, M. i. 271; meets them at Sassiah near Sháhganj, M. i. 271; battle of Sháhganj, July 5, K. iii. 384; Brig. Polwhele has an artillery duel with mutineers, M. i. 272; he hesitates to order a charge, M. i. 272; Sepoy cavalry charge Brig. Polwhele's guns, M. i. 273; who orders advance when too late, M. i. 274; gallant charge of Capt. Prendergast's Volunteers, M. i. 274; the British capture village near Sháhganj, M. i. 275; defeat of the English, K. iii. 390; the British retreat, M. i. 276, 277; the mutineers destroy the city and cantonments, K. iii. 392, M. i. 277; Mr. Reade saves the revenue records, M. i. 277; bravery of Mr. E. A. Reade, K. iii. 398; Brig. Polwhele removed

Ágrá—cont.
from command (Aug. 5), M. i. 285; Col. Cotton succeeds Brig. Polwhele in command, M. i. 285. The King of Dehlí proclaimed at Ágrá (July 6), M. i. 277; slaughter of Christians during riots in, M. i. 279; Nímach mutineers march in triumph to Dehlí, M. i. 276; Rájá Rám induces Mr. Drummond to restore order, M. i. 278; Mr. Drummond does so, July 7, M. i. 278. Residents in Fort, M. i. 280; number shut up in the Fort, K. iii. 394, M. i. 283. Overcrowded state of Fort, K. iii. 404; quarters in, M. i. 282; Fort made defensible, K. iii. 396; difficulties in protecting magazines at, K. iii. 397; Mr. W. Muir made chief of Intelligence Department, K. iii. 406; Eurasian fugitives converted into gunners by Capt. Pearson, M. ii. 102; bravery and good service of Volunteers, M. i. 296; Mr. E. A. Reade, with assistance of Jotí Parsád, victuals the Fort, K. iii. 399, M. i. 286; native servants in, K. iii. 395; bázár established, K. iii. 400, M. i. 283; establishment of hospitals, M. i. 281; hospital duties discharged by ladies, M. i. 284; kindly ministrations of ladies in, K. iii. 393, 400, 403 n.; daily life in the Fort, K. iii. 405; reserved conduct of Roman Catholic community, K. iii. 402. Party sent against Alígarh, K. iii. 411; defeat of rebels at Alígarh (Aug. 24), K. iii. 413; Mr. Colvin's health broken by anxiety, M. i. 288;

Ágrá—cont.
he is improperly treated by his subordinates, K. iii. 415; death of Mr. Colvin at, Sept. 9, K. iii. 416, M. i. 290; Mr. E. A. Reade becomes chief civil officer in, M. ii. 94; Mr. Reade recommends to Government military rule at, M. ii. 94.

Constantly liable to attack from Gwáliár Contingent, M. i. 286, M. ii. 95; appeals urgently to Col. Greathed for help, M. ii. 97; Major Hennessy warns authorities of approach of mutineers (Oct. 10), M. ii. 98 n.; but is disbelieved, M. ii. 99 n.; Col. Greathed is informed that Sepoys have retreated, M. ii. 98 n.; dispute about encamping Col. Greathed's force, M. ii. 99; encamps on the parade ground, M. ii. 100; Sepoys surprise Col. Greathed's force, Oct. 10, M. ii. 101; Pearson's battery flies to help Col. Greathed's force, M. ii. 102; Cavalry charge puts Sepoys to flight, M. ii. 103; Col. Greathed's great victory (Oct. 10), M. ii. 104.

Meade's Horse raised at (Dec.), M. iii. 312; excellent service rendered by Meade's Horse, M. iii. 314; Játs from Rohtak; offer their services, M. iii. 313.

Lord Canning abolishes Chief Commissionership of (Feb. 9, 1858), M. ii. 418; state of, during first half of 1858, M. iii. 311; Brig. Showers sent to command at, M. iii. 310; Sindhiá flies to, for refuge (June 1, 1858), M. iii. 209; the Queen's Proclamation read with ceremony

Ágrá—cont.
at (Nov. 1, 1858), M. iii. 395.

Ahern, Mrs., revenges her husband's death by fighting at Fathgarh, K. iii. 298.

Ahmad Sháh, a name of the Maulaví, M. ii. 344.

Ahmad Ulláh of Faizábád, or the Maulaví, q.v.

Ahmad Ulláh, leading Waháhí of Patná, M. i. 52; fondled by the Government, K. iii. 168; arrested, condemned, and transported for treason, K. iii. 169.

Aikman, Lieut., captures the Selimgarh, Dehlí, M. ii. 68; gallantly defeats Mansab Alí, M. ii. 336.

Ainslie, Brig., leads force from Jháusí to Ránod, M. iii. 364.

Aislabie, Lieut., his guns do much execution in street-fighting in Dehlí, M. iii. 501.

Aitken, Lieut., captures Farid Bakhsh palace, M. ii. 152; his gallantry at Lakhnau, M. i. 485.

Ajhit Singh, see Ajít Singh.

Ajítmal occupied by Rúp Singh, M. iii. 309.

Ajít Singh, uncle of Mán Singh, joins in the revolt, M. iii. 334; evacuates Paurí, M. iii. 335; surprised and defeated near Bíjapúr, M. iii. 336; eludes Capt. Meade, and escapes to Sironj, M. iii. 376.

Ajmír, made head-quarters by Col. G. Lawrence, M. i. 256; dangerous guardianship of arsenal at, M. i. 248; Col. G. Lawrence summons British troops from Dísá to protect, M. i. 249; Col. Dixon brings Mairwárá battalion to, M. i. 250; the fort occupied by Mairs, and arsenal saved, M. i. 250; smaller fort, faithfully

Ajmír—cont.
guarded by Muhammadans of the shrine, M. i. 255 n.; regular garrison sent back to Nasírábád, M. i. 250; the fort repaired and provisioned, M. i. 255; European troops reinforce Mairs, M. i. 255; outbreak at (Aug. 9), M. ii. 553; Gen. Lawrence pursues and cuts up rioters at, M. ii. 553; routine of civil duties strictly preserved, M. i. 256 n., ii. 552.

Ajúdhiá, see Ayodhya.

Akalpúra, the village, refuses to pay tribute, M. iii. 435; Mr. Dunlop storms and captures, exacting his revenue, M. iii. 435.

Akbarpúr, Capt. Rattray defeats rebels at (Oct. 7), M. ii. 446; Major Sutherland watches the fords at, M. iii. 348.

A'khúnd of Swát communicates with Sepoy regiments, K. ii. 496.

Akyab to Chittagong, nature of road between in '56, K. i. 463.

A'lambágh, at Lakhnau, description of, M. ii. 343; Major McIntyre commands at, Sept., M. ii. 153; its garrison and defensible condition, M. ii. 152; ably defended by Major McIntyre, M. ii. 169.

Gen. Outram left in command of (Nov. 26), M. ii. 342; strength of force left with Gen. Outram, M. ii. 342 n.; the Maulaví's plan for driving Gen. Outram from, M. ii. 344; Gen. Outram attacked by the Maulaví (Dec. 22), M. ii. 345; Gen. Outram defeats the Maulaví, M. ii. 346; Gen. Outram attacked (Jan. 12, '58), M. ii. 347; attack re-

A'lambágh—cont.
pulsed, M. ii. 349; renewed attack on Gen. Outram (Jan. 16), M. ii. 351; another attack upon (Feb. 15), M. ii. 353; determined attack upon, Feb. 21, repulsed, M. ii. 354; despairing attack of rebels (Feb. 25), M. ii. 356.

Brig. Franklyn commands at (Mar. 16, '58), M. ii. 401; garrison of, M. ii. 401; rebels attack in force, M. ii. 402; Brig. Franklyn defeats the rebel attack (Mar. 16), M. ii. 402; Jang Bahádur clears its front of rebels, M. ii. 403; list of defenders of, M. ii. 361, 362.

Albert, Prince, amends the Queen's proclamation of 1858, M. iii. 390.

Alexander, Lieut., killed while charging on guns at Alláhábád, K. ii. 251.

Alford, Sergt.-Major, greatly distinguishes himself at Bándá, M. iii. 197.

Alíganj, strong force of rebels at, April '58, M. ii. 500.

Alígarh, its description and garrison, M. i. 154; Major Percy Eld commands at, K. iii. 211; Sepoys incited to mutiny by populace, K. iii. 212, M. i. 155; plot to seize the treasure, K. iii. 213; the plot disclosed by Sepoys, K. iii. 213; the Brahman who instigated robbery of treasury seized and hanged, K. iii. 213, M. i. 155.

Mutiny at (May 20), K. ii. 126, iii. 211, 213, 221, M. i. 3, 154, 156; the treasury plundered, K. iii. 216; Europeans spared, K. iii. 214; escape of Lady Outram, K. iii. 214.

Head-quarters of rebel

Alígarh—*cont.*
Ghussa Khán (Aug.), K. iii. 411; attacked by Major Montgomery, M. i. 287; desperate courage of Gházís at (Aug. 20), K. iii. 412, M. i. 287, 288; gallantry of De Kantzow, M. i. 287.
Captured by Col. Greathed, (Oct.), M. ii. 93; Brig. Seaton joins Col. Farquhar at, M. ii. 287.

Aligurh, *see* Alígarh.

Alí Karím, implicated in Patná plots, M. i. 54; Mr. Lowis's amusing attempt to arrest, M. i. 55; escapes from Patná, K. iii. 80.

Alí Khán Mewátí threatens Pílíbhít, M. iii. 275; repulsed at Núriá by Lieut. Craigie, M. iii. 276.

Ali Kureem, *see* Alí Karím.

Alí Nakí Khán accompanies King of Oudh on his arrest, M. i. 28.

Alípúr, junction of Mírat and Dehlí Field forces at, K. ii. 190.

Alláhábád, its situation and description, K. ii. 240; its military importance, K. ii. 241, M. ii. 447; its sanctity, K. ii. 260; military force at, K. ii. 242; Mr. Chester, Commissioner of, M. iii. 438; Mr. Court, Magistrate of, M. iii. 438.
Alarming tales circulated among Sepoys, K. ii. 244; volunteer guard formed, May 22, K. ii. 245; European population fly to the Fort, K. ii. 245; dispositions made to save the town from Banáras mutineers, K. ii. 247.
The 6th Regiment firmly believed in by all its officers, K. ii. 243; this Regiment

Alláhábád—*cont.*
thanked by Lord Canning for loyalty, K. ii. 248; Col. Simpson orders guns into Fort, K. ii. 249; disarmament of Sepoys within the Fort, K. ii. 255; revolt of the 6th Regiment (June 6), K. ii. 250, M. i. 12, iii. 438; massacre of officers at, K. ii. 252; Col. Simpson escapes amidst a shower of bullets, K. ii. 251; Bangálís at, robbed and ill-treated, K. ii. 258; frightful tortures inflicted on Christian population, K. ii. 257 and *n.*; murder and rapine rampant, K. ii. 256; Sikhs aid in disarming Sepoys, K. ii. 254; uprising in the city, K. ii. 256; Russell of the Artillery prepares to blow up the Fort, K. ii. 255; Sepoys rob the Treasury (June 7), K. ii. 259; amount of plunder in Treasury, K. ii. 259; Sepoys at first resolve to carry treasure to Dehlí, K. ii. 258; the Maulaví appears (June 7), K. ii. 261; re-inforcements arrive and the town is saved, K. ii. 262, iii. 3.
Rebellion in rural districts around, K. ii. 259, M. iii. 440; Col. Neill arrives at (June 11), K. ii. 263, M. iii. 439; he begins offensive operations, K. ii. 264; clears the villages on river bank, K. ii. 266; sends women and children to Calcutta, K. ii. 266; the town deserted by natives for fear of bombardment, K. ii. 267; recovery of possession of the city (June 18), K. ii. 267; Sikhs indulge in plunder, K. ii. 265; European volunteers assist in general plunder, K. ii. 265; Col. Neill

THE HISTORIES OF THE INDIAN MUTINY. 7

Alláhábád—*cont.*
stops plunder of Sikhs and volunteers, K. ii. 265; and removes Sikhs from Fort, K. ii. 266.
Retributive measures, K. ii. 268; punishment inflicted on, K. ii. 668; an advance from, causes consternation to Náná Sáhib, K. ii. 351.
Bullock train to, organised by Sir Colin Campbell, M. ii. 123; line of communication exposed, M. ii. 125; Col. Powell starts with detachment from, M. ii. 143.
Brig. Campbell commands at, M. ii. 447; Lord Canning arrives at, M. ii. 417; Gen. Franks establishes order around (Feb. '58), M. ii. 329; the Queen's proclamation read with ceremony at, Nov. 1, '58, M. iii. 395.
Alláhganj, Gen. Walpole sent against, M. ii. 311.
Alláhu-Bakhsh, gallant trooper who stood by Lieut. Conolly at Trinpúra, M. ii. 594.
Alláh-ud-Dín, Maulaví, leading insurgent at Haidarábád, transported to Andamán Islands, M. iii. 122.
Allan, Mr., pursues and scatters Rúp Singh's party at Kuwárí, M. iii. 310.
Allen, Mr., his bold assumption of responsibility at Silhat, M. ii. 425; sends Major Byng to stop Chatgáon mutineers, M. ii. 423.
Alwar, one of Rájpút states, M. i. 245 *n.*
Alwar, Rájá of, places a contingent at service of the English, M. i. 259.
Amain, a poor Muhammadan of, conceals Lieut. Tómkinson for four months, M. iii. 468.

Amar Singh, a gallant old Rájpút at Lakhnau, M. ii. 156 *n.*
Amar Singh, brother of Kunwar Singh, M. ii. 444; succeeds Kunwar Singh in command, M. ii. 478; defeated by Col. Lugard, M. ii. 480; his troops disperse as freebooters, M. ii. 480; and harry Sháhábád, M. ii. 481; raises revolt in Gayá, M. ii. 483; Brig. Douglas succeeds Col. Lugard in opposing, M. ii. 483; Brig. Douglas's method of rooting out his adherents, M. ii. 483; reoccupies Jagadíspúr, M. ii. 484; escapes from Jagadíspúr by default of Col. Walter, M. ii. 487; Major H. Havelock's plan for rooting out his adherents, M. ii. 487; escapes the slaughter of his rearguard, M. ii. 489; severe loss inflicted on him by Mounted Infantry, M. ii. 491; complete collapse of his rebellion, M. ii. 492.
Ambálá, a depôt of rifle instruction, K. i. 552; ominous fires at, in April 1857, K. i. 562; state of Native regiments at, early in May, K. ii. 142; Sir John Lawrence advocates disarmament of, K. ii. 142; the storm rises there, K. i. 552; consternation among Sepoys at, K. i. 553, 554; death of Gen. Anson at (May 27), K. ii. 164, M. i. 10.
Ambapání Nawáb, rebel leader in the Sironj jungle (April '59), M. iii. 378.
Ambarpúr, the Nipálese troops capture fort of (Feb. 25, '58), M. ii. 324.
Ámethí, *see* Amíthí.
Amíthí, Oudh rebels retreat to (Aug. '58), M. iii. 273; surrounded by the British, M.

Amíthí—*cont.*
iii. 290; the Rájá surrenders to Sir Colin Campbell, M. iii. 291.
Amjherá, mercenary troops of, plunder Bhúpáwar and Sirdárpúr, M. iii. 69; the fort recaptured by Lieut. Hutchinson, M. iii. 74.
Ammar Singh, *see* Amar Singh.
Ammunition of two-grooved rifles, its composition, K. i. 655.
Amorhá, fugitives from Faizábád reach, M. i. 401; Major Cox attacks and defeats rebels at (June 9, '58), M. iii. 282.
Amráo Singh, Chaudrí of Sherkot, compelled to fly from Bíjnúr (July), M. iii. 410.
Amrat Ráo, his agreement with the British (1818), M. iii. 199.
Amritsar, its religious associations, K. ii. 434.
Anádra, Jodhpúr troops at, try to assassinate English at Mount Abú (Aug. 21), M. ii. 556.
A'naud Ráo Púár, a lad, rules Dhár, M. iii. 68.
Anárkalí, in the Panjáb, Council at (May 12), K. ii. 427.
Anarkullee, *see* Anárkalí.
Anár Singh, commander of Jodhpúr troops at Pálí, M. ii. 563; quits his entrenchments to advance against rebels, M. ii. 565; defeated by rebels and killed, M. ii. 565.
Anderson, Capt., death of, at Lakhnau, M. ii. 374.
Anderson's post, a post at Lakhnau Residency, M. i. 443.
Anderson, Lieut., sent to Múltán, K. i. 20; murdered there, K. i. 21.
Angad, the trusty spy of Lakhnau, K. ii. 415 *n.*; his history, M. i. 454; brings news to

Angad—*cont.*
Lakhnau, July 22, M. i. 454; brings a letter from Col. Tytler to Lakhnau, July 25, M. i. 454; again brings news, Aug. 15, K. iii. 528; the spy narrowly escapes death, and refuses again to leave Residency, K. iii. 541.
Annexation, disadvantages of, K. ii. 291; cordially promoted by numerous English officers, K. i. 357; its effect on the Sepoy, K. i. 277.
of Sindh, 1843, K. i. 276; treatment of mutinies arising out of, K. i. 301.
of the Panjáb, K. i. 47.
of Pegu, K. i. 66.
of Sitárá, K. i. 74.
of Nágpúr, K. i. 83.
of Jhánsí, K. i. 91.
of Sambhalpúr, K. i. 98.
of Jethpúr, K. i. 111 *n.*
of Oudh, authorised by the Court of Directors, the Board of Control, and the British Cabinet, K. i. 146, 148; approved by Lord Canning, K. i. 381; its bad effects, M. i. 348; injurious to the Sepoys, M. i. 349; one cause of the Mutiny, M. iii. 388.
Anson, Capt. H. A., his conspicuous daring at the Sikandar Bágh, M. ii. 197.
Anson, Gen. Hon. George, Commander-in-Chief in India, K. i. 392; appointed, K. i. 393; his appointment a surprise, K. i. 393; his character, M. i. 10; unsuited to Indian climate, K. i. 393; personally esteemed by Lord Canning, K. i. 394 *n.*; combats fears of troops at Ambálá, K. i. 554; refuses to disarm Ambálá regiments, K. ii. 142; visits

Anson—*cont.*
Simla in April 1857, K. i. 561; one reason for his going there, K. ii. 105; receives intelligence of the mutiny at Mírat, K. ii. 137; orders Court-martial on 3rd Cavalry mutineers, K. ii. 48; fears the loss of great British magazines, K. ii. 139; orders 75th Foot to Ambálá, K. ii. 138; orders two fusilier regiments to Ambálá, K. ii. 139; seeks to secure Firozpúr, Govindgarh, and Phillaur, K. ii. 139; leaves Simla for Ambálá, May 14, K. ii. 140; uncertain how to act, K. ii. 141; issues a conciliatory address to the Native Army, May 19, K. ii. 242 *n.*; appoints Lieut. Hodson to Intelligence Department, K. ii. 182; Lord Canning urges him to detach troops for service in the field, M. i. 4; on the impossibility of immediate advance on Dehlí, K. ii. 148; explains delay in advance, K. ii. 157; the force with which he advanced, K. ii. 158; his death at Karnál (May 27), K. ii. 164, M. i. 10; his supposed plan of campaign, K. ii. 149 *n.*; estimate of his course of action, K. ii. 166.

Antrí, Gen. R. Napier induced to stop at, and allows Firoz Sháh to escape (Dec. '58), M. iii. 361.

Anúká Singh, gallant Sikh at Lakhnau, M. ii. 157 *n.*

Aon, battle of, July 15, defeat of Náná Sáhib's troops, K. ii. 369.

Appá Sáhib, Rájá of Sitárá, dies (1848), K. i. 72.

Apthorp, Col., his gallantry at Bándá, M. iii. 197; turns

Apthorp—*cont.*
right of Nawáb of Bándá's position, M. iii. 197.

Ará, out-station of Patná, K. iii. 71, M. i. 40; European residents at, M. i. 81 *n.*; Mr. Wake reports desertion of railway officials, M. i. 48; treasure removed to Patná, by Mr. W. Tayler, M. i. 49. Mr. Boyle's house at, K. iii. 125; made defensible, M. i. 80; the civilian garrison of, K. iii. 124; Europeans resolve to hold the house, K. iii. 126; they prepare for attack, M. i. 80; Mr. Tayler's prescience provides fifty Sikhs to assist them, K. iii. 125, M. i. 81; Mr. Wake takes command of the Sikhs, K. iii. 127.

Dánápúr mutineers attack and plunder town, K. iii. 101, 126; mutineers surround Mr. Boyle's house, July 27, K. iii. 127; the siege commences, M. i. 82; effort to stifle garrison, K. iii. 128, 129, M. i. 90. Kunwar Singh prepares to revolt, M. i. 49; he heads attack, K. iii. 130; digs up two guns for attack of, K. iii. 130, M. i. 83; mutineers improvise gun ammunition, K. iii. 130; the garrison summoned nightly to surrender, M. i. 83; besiegers tempt Sikhs in garrison, but fail, K. iii. 128, M. i. 82, 83; the garrison dig a well, and cast bullets, K. iii. 132; they capture four sheep, K. iii. 132; mutineers resort to mining, K. iii. 133, M. i. 91; the garrison make successful sorties, M. i. 91.

Capt. Dunbar advances to relieve, M. iii. 84; relieving party repulsed, M. i. 84; re-

Árá—cont.
treat of Capt. Dunbar's force, K. iii. 131, M. i. 86; a wounded Sikh tells the garrison of Capt. Dunbar's disaster, K. iii. 131, M. i. 89; the garrison resolve to resist to the last, M. i. 90; they are given up for lost, M. i. 105.

Major Eyre advances from Baksar to relieve, M. i. 96; his relieving force, K. iii. 137, M. i. 97 and n.; civilians eager to accompany, K. iii. 110; Major Eyre's great feat of arms at, M. i. 116; relieves the garrison (Aug. 2), K. iii. 134, M. i. 92; Major Eyre enters, M. i. 102; the city disarmed, M. i. 127; the great importance of Major Eyre's victory, M. i. 125.

Sepoys fly to Jagadíspúr, M. i. 102; rebels again attack (May '58), M. ii. 479; Col. Lugard's plan for relieving, M. ii. 479.

Arah, see Árá.
Árangábád, see Aurangábád.
Arcot, attempt to stir up sedition in, K. i. 262.
Armenians at Calcutta, Government declines their offer to raise volunteers, M. i. 2.
Arms Act, produces angry feelings in Calcutta, K. iii. 177.
Army of Retribution in Afghanistan (1842), K. i. 275.
Arrah, see Árá.
Arrest of the King of Oudh, at Calcutta, K. iii. 38–41.
Artistic hanging of criminals, K. ii. 236.
Ashburnham, Gen. T., suggests Naval Brigade to keep open communications with Alláhábád, M. i. 141; Lord Elphinstone suggests that he offer the China expeditionary

Ashburnham—cont.
force to Lord Canning, M. iii. 4.
Ashe, the gunner, works his gun with ceaseless enthusiasm at Káhnpúr, K. ii. 320.
Asírgarh, its situation and importance, M. iii. 57; the garrison of, M. iii. 57; Col. Le Mesurier commands at, M. iii. 58; Lieut. Gordon raises a body of Volunteers, M. iii. 58; Gordon's Volunteers occupy fort, M. iii. 59; Capt. Keatinge fortifies a post 14 miles from, M. iii. 59; Capt. Blair arrives at, and disarms Gwáliár Contingent, M. iii. 59; held by Brig. Hill against Tántia Topí, M. iii. 346.
Assault of Dehlí, first project for, K. ii. 526; revised scheme of, K. ii. 529, 530.
Aták, the fort of, secured by Pathán guard, May 13, K. ii. 460.
Atrauliá, Kunwar Singh concentrates his force upon, M. ii. 455; Col. Milman marches against, M. ii. 455; Col. Milman is forced back on Ázamgarh, M. ii. 456.
Attila, his address to his commanders at Chalons, M. i. 543 n.
Attock, see Aták.
Aurangábád, its situation, M. iii. 10; its Sepoy garrison, M. iii. 11; reason for disaffection in, M. iii. 11; fugitives from Sháhjahánpúr and Mohamdí, overtaken and butchered near, K. iii. 459, 460, M. i. 387.

Native cavalry openly threaten mutiny, June 13, M. iii. 12; Capt. Abbott appeases Native Cavalry, M. iii. 12; Gen. Woodburn enters with his column (June 23), M. iii.

THE HISTORIES OF THE INDIAN MUTINY. 11

Aurangábád—*cont.*
13; disarmament of Sepoys, M. iii. 13; Major Follett succeeds Gen. Woodburn in command at, M. iii. 16; and offers to advance from, M. iii. 17; Col. Stuart arrives at, and leads troops to Asírgarh, M. iii. 17.
A'wah, the Thákur of, hesitates to join the rebels, M. ii. 563; Capt. Monck-Mason not permitted to negotiate with him, M. ii. 564; joins rebels, and marches on Pálí, M. ii. 564. Trinpúra mutineers entrench themselves in A'wah, M. ii. 566; Gen. G. Lawrence advances against, but retires after reconnaissance, M. ii. 567; the Thákur gets rid of Trinpúra mutineers, M. ii. 567; he evacuates A'wah (Jan. 24, '58), M. ii. 573.
Awakening to a sense of danger by the Government (June), M. i. 8.
Ayodhya, Rájá of Porahát, proclaimed ruler of Singhbhúm at, M. ii. 438; Gen. Hope Grant destroys rebel boats at, M. iii. 271.
A'zamgarh, its situation and garrison, K. ii. 213; Major Burroughs commands at, K. ii. 213; outbreak at, M. i. 33; mutiny at (June 3), K. ii. 213, M. iii. 449; Sepoys rob a treasure-escort, K. ii. 214; they murder two, and protect the rest of their officers, K. ii. 215; some show romantic courtesy to their officers, K. ii. 215 n.
Placed under martial law, by Major J. Holmes (June 19), K. iii. 103; Mr. Venables repulses the rebels at, M. ii. 316; Nipálese troops occupy

A'zamgarh—*cont.*
(Aug.), M. ii. 317; threatened by rebels (Sept.), M. ii. 317; Nipálese troops drive rebels away, M. ii. 318; force sent by Sir Colin Campbell to clear, M. ii. 146.
The English force at (Mar. '58), M. ii. 455; Col. Milman commands at, M. ii. 455; he moves out to attack Kunwar Singh, Mar. 22, M. ii. 456; he is forced back upon, M. ii. 457; reinforcements arrive, and Col. Dames assumes command, Mar. 27, M. ii. 458; blockade of English force in, M. ii. 465; Sir E. Lugard sent from Lakhnau to relieve, M. ii. 468; Lord Mark Kerr sent to relieve (Mar. 31, '58), M. ii. 459; and succeeds in relieving (April 6, '58), M. ii. 463; pursuit of Kunwar Singh from, M. ii. 472; Brig. Douglas sent to strengthen pursuit of Kunwar Singh, M. ii. 472.
Azígarh, the Rání of, generous to fugitives from Naogáon, M. i. 196.
Azimgurh, *see* A'zamgarh.
Azim-ulláh Khán, agent of Nána Sáhib, K. i. 648; assists Nána Sáhib at Káhnpúr, K. ii. 312.

B.

Bábá Bhatt, brother of Nána Sáhib, K. ii. 312.
Bábá Gangádhar Ráo, Rájá of Jhánsí, M. i. 180.
Bad Faith, the prime cause of the Mutiny, M. iii. 472.
Badámí, Thákur Singh sent to command at (July), M. iii. 32.
Badáon, in charge of a single European, K. iii. 281; Mr.

Badáon—cont.
Edwards magistrate and collector of, M. i. 321; excited meeting at the I'd Festival, K. iii. 282; Mr. Edwards sends his wife and child to Nainí Tál, and remains the sole Englishman at, M. i. 322; Mr. Phillipps rides into, in search of help, M. i. 322; Mr. Phillipps leaves the place, M. i. 323; three Europeans join Mr. Edwards, M. i. 323; mutiny at (June 1), K. iii. 286, M. i. 323; Mr. Edwards reduces loss by refusing to receive revenue from landholders, M. i. 325; flight of Mr. Edwards, and his three companions, M. i. 324; Mr. Edwards reaches Dharampúr, M. i. 324; Mr. Edwards reaches Káhnpúr in safety, M. i. 325.

Authority of Khán Bahádur Khán proclaimed at, K. iii. 287; the seat of civil war, after departure of English, M. i. 333; Gen. Penny marches on, M. ii. 501; Gen. Penny is attacked and killed (Ap. '58), M. ii. 501.

Badjee Rao, see Báji Ráo.
Badlee-ka-Serai, see Badlí-kí-Saráí.
Badlí-kí-Saráí, battle of (June 8), K. ii. 191; defeat of mutineers, K. ii. 192.
Bádsháhganj, rebels concentrate at, M. ii. 332.
Bághpút, Brig. Wilson crosses Jamná at, K. ii. 188.
Báh, Brig. Showers scatters rebels at, M. iii. 311.
Bahádur Sháh, King of Dehli, K. ii. 3; becomes Emperor in 1837, K. ii. 10; his character, K. ii. 10, M. ii. 72; palace intrigues of, K. ii. 24, 33;

Bahádur Sháh—cont.
his wife Zínat Mahal interferes with succession to title, K. ii. 24; he protests against succession of Fikrud-Dín, K. ii. 24; and desires the succession of Jawán Bakht, K. ii. 28; Lord Canning's terms with respect to successor to, K. ii. 32.

Intrigues with Persia, K. ii. 37–39; becomes a Shí'ah, K. ii. 39; in the hands of the mutineers (May 11), K. ii. 80; separates from the Sepoys (Sept. 20), M. ii. 74; captured by Capt. Hodson, K. iii. 645–647; his trial, M. iii. 387; sentenced to transportation for life, M. iii. 387.

See also Dehlí, King of.
Bahádurpúr, Sir Hugh Rose arrives at, M. iii. 215.
Baháwalpúr, the chief of, assists Edwardes to attack Múltán, K. i. 29.
Bahwulpore, see Baháwalpúr.
Bahráich, description of, M. i. 389; Mr. C. Wingfield, Commissioner at, K. iii. 472, M. i. 389; Lieut. L. Clarke commands at, M. i. 394; Englishmen escape from, K. iii. 477; the three officers at, ride to Nánpárá, but are refused protection, M. i. 394; they return and attempt to cross Ghághrá at Bairámghát, M. i. 394; but are recognised and murdered, K. iii. 478, M. i. 395.
Bailey Guard, a post at Lakhnau Residency, M. i. 361 n., 442.
Bairám Ghát, on Ghághrá, murder of fugitives from Bahráich at, K. iii. 478.
Bairpúr, Brig. Berkeley captures fort of, M. iii. 281.

Baitúl, part of Ságar territory, M. iii. 88.
Bájí Ráo, the last Peshwá, compact made with him, M. iii. 482; retires to Bithúr, K. i. 99; advances five lákhs of rupees to the Company, K. i. 100; offers to raise and maintain troops to serve the Company, K. i. 100; his personal estate, K. i. 102 n.; terms of his will conferring *gaddi* on Dhundu Pant, K. i. 101 n.
Bajrúl, Zamíndár of, harries Barauth, M. iii. 430.
Bakht Khán, Súbádár of Artillery at Barailí, his effusive loyalty (May 14), M. i. 303 n.; leads Sepoys from Barailí to Dehlí (June 11), K. iii. 277, M. i. 317; becomes the Sepoy General at Dehlí, K. ii. 566; urges the King of Dehlí to fly with him, M. ii. 71.
Balamgarh, Rájá of, submits to British, M. ii. 108.
Bálá Ráo, brother of Náná Sáhib, K. ii. 312; pursued by Gen. Hope Grant, M. iii. 293; defeated by Col. Rowcroft at Tulsípúr, M. iii. 293; and his army driven into Nipál, M. iii. 293.
Bálábet, Major Gaussen captures fort of, M. iii. 99.
Balandshahr, mutiny at (May 20), M. i. 3, 156; battle of (Sept. 28), M. ii. 90.
Baldeo Singh, Thákur of Jhárá, raises body of horse for the English, M. iii. 313.
Balgáon, Mr. Seton-Karr, Collector and Magistrate of, M. iii. 20.
Balrámpúr, Gen. Hope Grant arrives at, M. iii. 292.
Balrámpúr, Rájá of, undertakes to protect refugees from Sikrorá, K. iii. 475 n., M. i. 391;

Balrámpúr—*cont.*
protects English refugees, and sends them to Gorakhpúr, M. i. 394.
Banáras, its situation and description, K. ii. 198; number of population, K. ii. 200 n.; number of temples, K. ii. 199 n.; many State prisoners resident at, K. ii. 200; leading Englishmen at (May 1857), K. ii. 201, 202.
Held by moral force, in May, K. ii. 205; Captains Olpherts and Watson propose the abandonment of, K. ii. 202; arms issued to European residents at, K. ii. 209; the Commissioner allows first reinforcements to pass on to Káhnpúr, K. ii. 205; the Mint made the rallying point, K. ii. 229; the Europeans fly to the Mint (June 4), K. ii. 232; missionaries fly to Rámnagar, K. ii. 229.
Government neglects to disarm Sepoys at, M. i. 5; disarmament of Sepoys resolved on, K. ii. 218; difficulties in the way of their disarmament, K. ii. 220; disarmament of 37th Regiment attempted, June 4, K. ii. 221; the disarmament mismanaged, K. ii. 226; resistance of Sepoys, K. ii. 222; mutiny at, M. i. 12; Sikhs appear to join in the revolt, K. ii. 223; they are fired into and dispersed, K. ii. 224; firing on Sikhs at, causes mutiny at Jánpúr, K. ii. 238; treasure at, saved by help of Súrat Singh, K. ii. 230; native gentlemen in, nobly assist the English, K. ii. 230, 231; indiscriminate executions at, after June 4, K. ii. 236; pri-

Banáras—*cont.*
sons overflowing with criminals, K. ii. 237; saved by succours from Calcutta, K. iii. 3.
Arrival of Col. Neill at (June 4), K. ii. 216; Brig. Ponsonby makes over command to him, K. ii. 225; the town remains tranquil after disarmament of Sepoys, K. ii. 233; uprising of rural population around, K. ii. 234; martial law proclaimed in district around, K. ii. 235.
Banáras, Rájá of, ably assists the English, K. ii. 231.
Banáras Rájás, the question of their loyalty, K. ii. 681.
Bándá, mutiny at, June 14, M. i. 197; occupied by the rebels, M. i. 34; Rájá of Rewá sends troops to, M. iii. 112; captured by Gen. Whitlock (Ap. 16, '58), M. iii. 197.
Bándá, the Nawáb of, generous to fugitives from Naogáon, M. i. 196; and to those from Hamírpúr and Fathpúr, M. i. 197; lays excellent trap for Gen. Whitlock, M. iii. 195; surprises Gen. Whitlock, but is defeated, M. iii. 196; marches into Kálpí, M. iii. 181; attacks English left at Kálpí (May 22, '58), M. iii. 184; flies from Bandelkhand, M. iii. 201; joins in attempt on Indúr, M. iii. 327; surrenders to the British, M. iii. 354.
Bándah, *see* Bándá.
Banda Husain, commands rebels at Chánda, M. ii. 330.
Bandelkhand, popular feeling antagonistic to English, M. iii. 345; rebellion restrained by Lieut. W. Osborne, M. iii. 112; rebellion gains no foot-

Bandelkhand—*cont.*
ing in, M. iii. 112; Gen. Whitlock ordered to subdue, M. iii. 194; the Nawáb of Bándá flies from, M. iii. 201.
Bangáon, strong force of rebels at, M. ii. 500; Gújádar Singh completely defeated at, M. iii. 296.
Bánkí, final defeat of Náná Sáhib at (Dec. '58), M. iii. 294.
Banks, Major, his antecedents, M. i. 414; sent by Lord Dalhousie to arrange the annexation of Oudh, K. iii. 496; Commissioner of Lakhnau, K. iii. 497; recommended by Sir H. Lawrence as his successor, K. iii. 495, M. i. 413; his death at Lakhnau (July 21), K. iii. 524, M. i. 452.
Banks's House, *see* Lakhnau.
Banswárá, one of Rájpút states, M. i. 245 *n.*; Tántiá Topí enters jungles of, M. iii. 355; positions of British troops around, M. iii. 355.
Báosí, Sepoy garrison of, M. ii. 130; Col. Burney commands at, M. ii. 133; he wins the confidence of his Sepoys, M. ii. 133; and drives away approaching mutineers, M. ii. 134.
Bánpúr, rebels evacuate fort, M. iii. 150.
Bánpúr, Rájá of, receives European officers escaping from Lallatpúr, M. iii. 98; attacks Lallatpúr mutineers, and is repulsed, M. iii. 98; openly bids for, and wins, Major Gaussen's Sepoys, M. iii. 99; entrenches himself at Niraulí, M. iii. 106; repulses Col. Dalyell there, M. iii. 107; attempts to raise the siege of Rathgarh, M. iii. 141; defeated by Sir Hugh Rose, on

THE HISTORIES OF THE INDIAN MUTINY. 15

Bánpúr, Rájá of—*cont.*
the banks of the Bína, M. iii. 143; attacked and defeated by Major Orr, M. iii. 174; ordered by Tántiá Topí to concentrate on Gwáliár, M. iii. 210.

Banqueting hall, a post at Lakhnau Residency, M. i. 442.

Bárá, Rájá of, sides with the English, K. ii. 260.

Barailí, its defensive position, M. ii. 523; nature of population, K. iii. 265; insurrection at, in 1816, K. iii. 265; its garrison and Christian residents, K. iii. 266; Sepoy garrison of, M. i. 302; Brig. Sibbald commands at, M. i. 302.

Excited state of Sepoys at, K. iii. 267; Brig Sibbald addresses the Sepoys, K. iii. 268; Sepoys at, use new cartridge reluctantly, M. i. 303; mutineers from Firozpúr arrive, K. iii. 269; return of Brig. Sibbald to, M. i. 307; accidental change in position of guns, M. i. 303; excitement caused by change of position of guns, M. i. 304; Col. Troup tries persuasive measures with Sepoys, M. i. 305; guns replaced in former position to satisfy Sepoys, M. i. 307; concerted rising of May 29 baulked, M. i. 308; loyal conduct of 8th Irreg. Cavalry on May 29, M. i. 308; former good conduct of 8th Irreg. Cavalry, M. i. 305; Col. Troup has especial confidence in this regiment, M. i. 305, 306; mutiny breaks out, M. i. 310; Capt. Mackenzie permitted to charge the guns, M. i. 313; Capt. Mackenzie finds

Barailí—*cont.*
that his men will not act, M. i. 315; attempt to lead Irreg. Cavalry against mutineers, K. iii. 272, M. i. 312; devotion of Capt. Mackenzie's native orderly, M. i. 316 *n.*; mutiny and massacre at (May 31), K. iii. 260, 270, M. i. 310; details of the massacre, K. iii. 273; Col. Troup orders retreat to Naini Tál, M. i. 312; fugitives from, reach Nainí Tál, M. i. 316.

Mutiny instigated by Khán Bahádur Khán, M. i. 307; two claimants for supremacy at, K. iii. 274; Khán Bahádur Khán elected ruler of, K. iii. 275, M. i. 316; he slaughters all the English found in, M. i. 317; and destroys Mr. Thomason's tomb, M. i. 317; Bakht Khán leads Sepoys of, to Delhí, M. i. 317.

Khán Bahádur Khán's force at, M. ii. 522; he resolves to oppose the English, M. ii. 523; Sir Colin Campbell arrives at, M. ii. 524; he drives rebels across Natiá rivulet, M. ii. 525; fierce attack of Ghází̇s at, M. ii. 526; the Highlanders annihilate the Ghází̇s, M. ii. 526; Khán Bahádur Khán evacuates, M. ii. 529.

Bárákpúr, chief cantonment in Bengal, K. i. 494; favourite retreat of officials, K. i. 494; mutiny at (1824), K. i. 266, 268.

Native regiments at, K. i. 495; mutinous spirit in, at beginning of 1857, M. i. 43; ominous fires at, K. i. 497; Sepoys fear overwhelming attack of Europeans, K. i. 526;

Bárákpúr—*cont.*
open mutiny at (March 1857), K. i. 538; disbandment of some Sepoys at, M. i. 6. Sepoys at, desire Enfield rifles, K. iii. 26; Sepoys demand to be led against the mutineers, K. iii. 26; Government neglects to disarm Sepoys, M. i. 5; Sepoys manifest mutinous intentions, K. iii. 27; Sepoys resolve to mutiny, M. i. 26; disarmament of Sepoys (June 14), K. iii. 28, M. i. 27.
Bárákpúr Sepoys, report of their mutiny causes "Panic Sunday," M. i. 26.
Barber (Lieut.) dies during retreat from Naogáon, M. i. 196.
Bareilly, *see* Barailí.
Bareitch, *see* Bahráich.
Barhámpúr, its situation and suitability for seditious purposes, K. i. 498; Sepoy garrison of, M. ii. 130; troops at, show their suspicions openly, K. i. 501, M, i. 43; suspicions of Sepoys at, confirmed by injudicious anger of Col. Mitchell, K. i. 502; rising of troops at, Feb. 27, K. i. 503; excitement at, suddenly subsides, K. i. 507; story of greased cartridges readily believed in, K. i. 500; mutinous incident at (June), M. i. 39; outbreak, not promptly or vigorously suppressed, M. i. 17; this delay a source of danger at Bárákpúr, K. i. 527; Sepoys at, disarmed (Aug. 2), M. ii. 139.
Barhí on the Chambal, seized by Rúp Singh, M. iii. 309; captured by Capt. Gordon, M. iii. 310.
Barká, Mr. Dunlop's fight with Bagdá at (July), M. iii. 433.

Barker, Col., clears the villages around Fathpúr, M. ii. 447.
Barker, Brig., defeats rebels at Pannú, after desperate battle, M. iii. 287; captures fort of Bírwá, M. iii. 287.
Barlow, Sir George, his policy towards the Rájpúts, M. ii. 576.
Barnard, Gen. Sir Henry, General of the Sirhind Division, K. i. 563; his indecision of character, K. ii. 532; his kindness of heart, K. ii. 542; his ceaseless activity, K. ii. 541, 558; loved by his troops, K. ii. 559; Col. Baird Smith's opinion of him, K. ii. 568; Brig. N. Chamberlain's opinion of him, K. ii. 569; Sir John Lawrence's opinion of him, K. ii. 568; Mr. Greathed's opinion of him, K. ii. 569.

Succeeds Gen. Anson in command of troops (May 27), K. ii. 164, M. i. 11; defends Gen. Anson from charge of dilatoriness, K. ii. 165; on the unpreparedness of the Army in May, K. ii. 148 *n.*; moves promptly on Dehli, K. ii. 169, 190; defeats mutineers at Badlí-kí-Saráí (June 8), K. ii. 192; chases mutineers into Dehlí, K. ii. 193; captures "the Ridge," at Dehlí, K. ii. 193; beats the rebels at Dehlí (June 8), M. i. 33.

His estimate of the strength of Dehlí, K. ii. 529; his opinion of immediate assault of Dehlí, K. ii. 537; resolves to assault Dehlí, June 16, K. ii. 528; again consents to a *coup-de-main*, June 28, K. ii. 558; urgently needs reinforcements, M. i. 33; his last letter to Lord Canning, K. ii.

Barnard, Gen. Sir Henry—*cont.* 678; his death, by cholera (July 5), K. ii. 567.
Barnes, Mr. George C., Commissioner of Cis-Satlaj States, energetically collects transport for Gen. Anson's army, K. ii. 160; preserves communication with Dehlí, K. ii. 511.
Baroch, *see* Barúch.
Barod, Tántiá Topí put to flight by Major Somerset, M. iii. 358.
Barodá, native state in Bombay Presidency, M. iii. 2; Tántiá Topí hopefully marches on, M. iii. 351.
Barodiá, fort captured by Sir Hugh Rose (Feb. 27, '58), M. iii. 148.
Barrackpore, *see* Bárákpúr.
Bárrákpúr, *see* Bárákpúr.
Barrett, Major, protests against disarmament of Sepoys at Banáras, K. ii. 219; stands with the Sepoys, when they revolt (June 4), K. ii. 222.
Barron, Lieut., his good service in western Bihár, M. iii 463.
Barrow, Capt. Lousada, chief civil officer at Sálon, K. iii. 471.
Barrow, Capt., drives off rebel turning force at A'lambágh M. ii. 355.
Barrow, Major, Mr. Forjett shows him secretly his own men conspiring, M. iii. 53.
Bartholomew, Capt., trains mounted infantry for service in Bihár (Oct. '58), M. ii. 487.
Barúch, dispute between Pársís and Muhammadans at, M. iii. 8; Lord Elphinstone represses riot at, M. iii. 8.
Bashíratganj, first battle at (July 29), M. i. 494; second

Bashíratganj—*cont.* battle at (Aug. 5), M. i. 503; third battle at (Aug. 12), M. i. 506.
Bates, Major, forces Shergátí pass in Chútiá Nágpúr (Jan. 7, '58), M. ii. 441a.
Batson, Dr., attempts to convey letter from Dehlí to Mírat (May 11), K. ii. 91; he is detected and stripped by villagers, K. ii. 92.
Batt, Lieut., distinguishes himself at Kálí Kankí (Aug.), M. iii. 462.
Battle of—
 Ágrá (Oct. 10), M. ii. 101.
 Ámorhá (Mar. 5, '58), M. ii. 452.
 A'on (July 15), K. ii. 369.
 Balandshahr (Sept. 28), M. ii. 90.
 Bashíratganj (July 29), M. i. 495; second battle (Aug. 5), M. i. 503; third battle (Aug. 12), M. i. 506.
 Bithúr (Aug. 16), M. i. 511.
 Chánda (Feb. 19, '58), M. ii. 330.
 Chánda (Oct. 30), M. ii. 320.
 Chattra (Oct. 2), M. ii. 141.
 Chilliánwálá (1849),K.i. 41.
 Chinhat (June 30), K. ii. 410, iii. 504, M. i. 425.
 Fathpúr (July 12), K. ii. 360.
 Gorakhpúr (Jan. 5, '58), M. ii. 323.
 Gujrát, (1849), K. i. 45.
 Hindan (May 31), M. i. 10.
 Káhnpúr (July 16), K. ii. 376-381.
 Kajwá (Nov. 2), M. ii. 145.
 Khásganj (Dec. 15), M. ii. 288.
 Kotá-kí-saráí (June 17, '58), M. iii. 221.
 Naghína (April 21, '58), M. ii. 517-519.

Battles—*cont.*
Najafgarh (Aug. 25), K. ii. 652–655.
Nárnúl (Nov. 16), M. ii. 116.
Nasratpúr (Jan. 23, '58), M. ii. 328.
Nawábganj (June 13), '58, M. iii. 268.
Pálí (Sept. 8), M. ii. 565.
Panná (Oct. 8, '58), M. iii. 287.
Pattiálí (Dec. 17), M. ii. 291.
Rámnagar (1848), K. i. 37.
Sháhganj (July 5), K. iii. 384.
Sivarájpúr (Dec. 9), M. ii. 278.
Sobanpúr (Dec. 26), M. ii. 322.
Sultánpúr (Feb. 23, '58), M. ii. 334.
Unáo (July 29), M. i. 492.
Battye, Quintin, his bravery and noble death, K. ii. 469.
Beadon, Mr. Cecil, Secretary in the Home Department, Calcutta, his theory of "a passing and groundless panic," M. i. 2; his line of six hundred miles of tranquillity, M. i. 1, 7, 36, 37; his line rudely snapped, M. i. 36; the four men who preserved his line of six hundred miles, M. i. 142, 143.
Beatson, Capt., noble death of, K. ii. 378.
Beawur, *see* Biáwar.
Becher, Col. Charles, attacks Tántiá Topí near Bagrod, M. iii. 342.
Becher, Major John, catches and executes mutineers escaping from Hot-Mardán, K. ii. 494, 495.
Beebeeghur, *see* Bíbíghar.
Begam Kothí, *see* Lakhnau.
Behar, *see* Bihár.
Behaudur Sháh, *see* Bahádur Sháh.

Behunáth Singh, rebel leader in Oudh, M. iii. 271.
Belgáon, the garrison of, M. iii. 26; the state of the fort, M. iii. 27; Major-Gen. Lester assumes command at, M. iii. 27. Effect of mutiny at Mírat on, M. iii. 26; a rebel emissary arrives at, M. iii. 27; Mr. Seton-Karr seizes the emissary and blows him from a gun, M. iii. 33; Mr. Seton-Karr disarms people at (Aug. 20), M. iii. 33; chief of Nargúnd executed at (June 12, '58), M. iii. 245 *n*.
Thákur Singh, the leader of disaffection at, M. iii. 32; he is sent to command at Badámí, M. iii. 32; reinforcements arrive at, M. iii. 33.
Bell, Major Evans, his statement about removal of treasure from Residency at Indor controverted, M. i. 218.
Bellew, Mr. Henry, takes medical charge of Mission to Kandahár, K. i. 442.
Belwá, in Gorakhpúr, rebel entrenched camp at, M. ii. 451.
Benares, *see* Banáras.
Beneí Singh, Rájá of Alwar, places a contingent at service of the English, M. i. 259.
Bengal, the Mutiny approaches, K. iii. 60.
Bengal provinces and people, K. iii. 61; mixed character of population, K. iii. 62; their method of resistance, K. iii. 62.
Bengal Army, its growth and constitution, K. i. 213; Sepoys mostly of high caste, K. i. 212; local and general service discussed, K. i. 333; influence of system of promotion in, K. i. 335; the policy of admixture of caste in, K. i. 331; the

THE HISTORY OF THE INDIAN MUTINY. 19

Bengal Army—*cont.*
policy of admixture of nationalities in, K. i. 332; the presence or absence of Sepoy's family with, discussed, K. i. 334; unsoundness of army denounced, K. i. 324.
Mutiny of (1764), K. i. 208; mutiny of European officers (1766), K. i. 209, 210 n.; increase of British officers in (1784), K. i. 211; marched to Chittagong (1824), K. i. 265; decline to construct their own barracks at Arakán (1825), K. i. 270.
Reforms in, tend to provoke mutiny, M. iii. 475; impracticability of disarming in May, K. ii. 124.
Bengal Artillery, the 5th troop, 1st brigade, the only part which remains loyal, M. iii. 502.
Bengal Yeomanry Cavalry, their organisation, M. ii. 434.
Bení Mádhava, chief of Shankarpúr, refuses to surrender, M. iii. 291; threatens road between Lakhnau and Káhupúr, M. iii. 266; chased from Atrauliá, M. ii. 319; defeated at Dhúndhiá Khere by Col. Evelegh (Nov. 10, '58), M. iii. 292; totally defeated at Dhúndhiá Khere (Nov. 24, '58), M. iii. 292.
Bentinck, Lord William, visits Oudh to warn the ruler, (1831), K. i. 121.
Berford, Mr., deserts his post at Mozaffarnagar on the first alarm, K. iii. 247 n., M. i. 301.
Beresford, Mr., and his wife, fight bravely for their lives, K. ii. 81.
Berhampore, *see* Brahmapúr.
Berkeley, Brig., his character and services at the A'lambágh,

Berkeley, Brig.—*cont.*
M. ii. 361; captures fort of Bairpúr, M. iii. 281; clears forts of Oudh, M. iii. 281; commands Soráon Field Force, M. iii. 280; attacks and cuts up the rebels at Daháin, M. iii. 280; drives the rebels from Tírul, M. iii. 281.
Bethune Female School, visits of Lady Canning to, cause alarm in native mind, K. i. 475.
Betwá, the, Tántiá Topí fails in attempt to cross at Kajúriá, M. iii. 341.
Bhágalpúr, Sepoy garrison of, M. ii. 130; Mr. G. Yule, Commissioner at, M. ii. 129; he tries to maintain order without British troops, M. ii. 130; mutiny at (Aug. 14), M. ii. 133.
Bhágpat, found on the point of rebellion by Mr. Dunlop, M. iii. 426.
Bhairpúr, *see* Bairpúr.
Bhandárá, garrison of, M. iii. 113.
Bharatpúr, one of Rájpút states, M. i. 245 n.; Major Nixon agent at, M. i. 259; applied to, by Mr. Colvin, for aid, M. i. 153; sends a regiment to assist Mr. Colvin, M. i. 154.
Bharatpúr Contingent, mutiny of (May 31), K. iii. 241, M. i. 164; force their officers to leave them, M. i. 165.
Bharatpúr, Rájá of, sends troops to protect Muthrá, K. iii. 209.
Bhaugáon, murder of Capt. Fletcher Hayes at, K. iii. 522 n.
Bhijalpúr rebels, defeated by Lieut. Sherriff, M. iii. 211 n.
Bhíls, free from caste prejudices, M. i. 208; summoned to Indor, by Col. Durand, M.

2 *

Bhils—*cont.*
i. 208; at Indor, commanded by Col. Stockley, M. i. 209.
Party of, surprise and disarm Burhánpúr mutineers, M. iii. 59.
Bhilwárá, Tántiá Topí takes up position near, M. iii. 321; he is driven from, by Gen. Roberts, M. iii. 322; he contemplates surrender at, M. iii. 356.
Bhím Ráo Bhonslá, courteously receives the returning plunderers of Bhúpáwar and Sirdúrpúr, M. iii. 69.
Bhím Ráo, chief of Kopáldurg, joined by Dhárwár insurgents, May '58, M. iii. 243; killed at Kopáldurg, M. iii. 244.
Bhogníwálá, Col. Coke defeats rebels at, M. ii. 515.
Bhonslá territory, annexed by Lord Dalhousie, M. iii. 481.
Bhopal, *see* Bhúpál.
Bhopawur, *see* Bhúpáwar.
Bhowan, rebels defeated at, by Mr. Dunlop, M. iii. 436.
Bhúmij, a tribe in Chútiá Nágpúr, M. ii. 134.
Bhúpál, Begam of, sends troops to reinforce Sir Hugh Rose, M. iii. 138.
Bhúpál Contingent, inactive at Indor, K. iii. 331.
Bhúpál Singh, rebel leader in Oudh, M. iii. 271.
Bhúpáwar, plundered by mercenaries of Dhár and Amjherá, M. iii. 69; Capt. Hutchinson and other Europeans escape from, K. iii. 342.
Bhurtpore, *see* Bharatpúr.
Biáwar, fugitives from Nasírábád escape to, K. iii. 322.
Bíbíghar, at Káhnpúr, description of, K. ii. 354 *n.*
Biddulph, Col., killed at Lakhnau, M. ii. 212.

Bihár, district of Patná Division, K. iii. 71 *n.*; Alláhábád the key of, M. ii. 447.
Alarm in, K. iii. 63; increasing excitement in, K. iii. 68; grounds of alarm in, K. iii. 77; summary of events in June and July, M. ii. 442; Europeans of, have full confidence in Mr. W. Tayler, M. i. 60; jeopardised by Gen. Lloyd and the Government, M. i. 117; saved by Mr. W. Tayler and Major Eyre, M. i. 116, 117; the administration which succeeded that of Mr. Tayler, M. ii. 443.
Receives influx of rebels from other parts, M. ii. 444; mutinous cavalry plunder unchecked, M. ii. 444; troops guarding, in Oct., M. ii. 445; Kunwar Singh reappears on the Son river, M. ii. 444; danger to, from mutinies at Dákhá and Chatgáon, M. ii. 426.
Bihár, Eastern, Sepoy garrison of, M. ii. 130; the disaffected of Eastern, severed from Western, by Mr. G. Yule, M. ii. 132.
Bíjerájugarh, captured by Lieut. W. Osborne, M. iii. 112.
Bignor, *see* Bíjnúr.
Bíjnúr, its situation and extent, M. iii. 400; civil officers at, M. iii. 401; Mr. Shakespear Collector and Magistrate at, M. iii. 400.
Invaded by mutineers from Rúrkí, M. iii. 402; Mr. Shakespear receives native assistance in suppressing disorder, M. iii. 402; prisoners break out of jail, M. iii. 403; Mr. Shakespear stops exit of prisoners from jail, M. iii. 403; Hindú zamíndárs and others

Bíjnúr—cont.
help in restoration of order, M. iii. 404; Mr. Shakespear secures all the money in a well, M. iii. 404.
The Nawáb of Najíbábád attempts to plunder, M. iii. 404; Mr. Shakespear induces him to retire, M. iii. 405; the Nawáb makes second attempt on, M. iii. 405; Mr. Shakespear gets rid of his native infantry, M. iii. 406; a third time threatened by the Nawáb, M. iii. 406; the treasure safely conveyed from, M. iii. 406; Mr. Shakespear renders the Nawáb of Najíbábád passive, M. iii. 407.
The district left for ten days to the care of Nawáb of Najíbábád, M. iii. 408; Mr. Shakespear, with officers and ladies, retires to Rúrkí (June 11), M. iii. 409; the Nawáb proclaims himself ruler, under the King of Dehlí, M. iii. 409; the chaudrís of, rise and chase the Nawáb from the place, Aug. 6, M. iii. 411; Mr. Shakespear directs two native officials to take charge of, M. iii. 411; the town seized and sacked by the Nawáb, Aug. 23, M. iii. 412.
Riotous condition of, during Sept., M. iii. 412; three princes of Dehlí family head the rebels at, M. iii. 413; Muhammadans of, gain the supremacy, M. iii. 413; chaudrís of, escape to Mírat, M. iii. 413.
Rebels from, attack and burn Miránpúr, Kankhal, and Haridwár, M. iii. 413; they are defeated by Capt. Boisragon, M. iii. 415; this victory makes rebel authority

Bíjnúr—cont.
totter at, M. iii. 416; reconquered by Mr. Shakespear with troops from Rúrkí (April '58), M. iii. 417.
Bikanír, one of Rájpút states, M. i. 245 n.
Bikanír, Rájá of, 600 of Tántiá Topí's troops surrender to him (Jan. 26, '59), M. iii. 367.
Biláspúr, garrison of, M. iii. 113.
Bína, Sir Hugh Rose defeats Rájá of Bánpúr there, M. iii. 143.
Birch, Col. Richard, Military Secretary to Government of India in 1857, K. i. 513.
Birch, Lieut.-Col., marches 41st N.I. against mutineers with success, M. i. 378; murder of, at Sítápúr, K. iii. 456, M. i. 380.
Birch, Fort Adjutant, killed in the revolt at Alláhábád (June 6), K. ii. 252.
Birch, Lieut., surprises and disarms Burhánpúr, M. iii. 59; attacked by Kols in Singhbhúm, M. ii. 439.
Bird, Mr., joint magistrate of Gorakhpúr, M. iii. 447; successfully resists attempt of prisoners to escape from Gorakhpúr jail, M. iii. 450; remains behind alone at Gorakhpúr, M. iii. 456; insulted and forced to fly, M. iii. 456; a price set on his head, but he escapes to Betiá, M. iii. 457.
Birmá, relations with (1826–49), K. i. 65; annexation of Pegu (1849), K. i. 66; difficulty in garrisoning, K. i. 459; difficulty of marching troops to, K. i. 463.
Bírwá, captured by Brig. Barker (Oct. '58), M. iii. 287.
Bithaulí, evacuated by the Begam of Lakhnau, M. ii. 497.

Bithoor, see Bithúr.
Bithor, see Bithúr.
Bithúr, near Káhnpúr, asylum of the Peshwás, K. i. 99; Gen. Neill sends three river parties to annoy, M. i. 499, 507, 508; he marches men past, for moral effect, M. i. 509; flight of Náná Sáhib from, July 18, K. ii. 390; destruction of the palace at, K. ii. 392; Náná Sáhib's force at, M. i. 510; their defeat (Aug. 16), M. i. 511; Náná Sáhib's palace and temple destroyed at, M. ii. 281.
Blowing from guns at Hot-Mardán, excellent moral effect of, K. ii. 491.
Blunt, Major, his brilliant act, at attack on Sikandar Bágh, M. ii. 181.
Board of Control, see Control, Board of.
Bogle, Lieut., rescues Sítápúr fugitives, at Lakhnau (Mar. 17, '58), M. ii. 403 n.
Boisragon, Capt. H., attacks and defeats Bíjnúr raiders at Kankhal, M. iii. 415; his victory causes rebel authority in Bíjnúr to totter, M. iii. 416.
Bombay, Sepoy and European garrison of, M. iii. 46; Gen. Shortt commands at, M. iii. 43; nature of Lord Elphinstone's defence of, M. iii. 54; he cheerfully responds to Lord Canning's application for aid, K. i. 611, 612.
Mr. Forjett, Soperintendent of Police at, K. iii. 408, M. iii. 43; he organises force of mounted Europeans, M. iii. 43; panic at (Aug.), K. iii. 408; Gen. Shortt and Mr. Forjett mutually distrust each others forces, M. iii. 47; disturbance at the Muharram, M. iii. 48;

Bombay—cont.
outbreak of Sepoys, M. iii. 49; Mr. Forjett hurries to Sepoy lines, M. iii. 49; he defies and quells Sepoy rising, M. iii. 50.
Gangá Parshád's house used for mutinous meetings, M. iii. 53; Sepoys resolve to break out at the Diwálí festival, M. iii. 52; detection and punishment of conspirators, M. iii. 53; substantial gratitude of inhabitants to Mr. Forjett, M. iii. 51 n., 52 n.; the Queen's proclamation read with ceremony at (Nov. 1, '58), M. iii. 395.
Bombay Army, its constitution, K. i. 213.
Bombay Presidency, description and extent of, M. iii. 1; native states subordinate to, M. iii. 2; Inam Commission, K. i. 175; critical condition of (Oct. '58), M. iii. 343.
Bone-dust, defilement of caste, by, feared, K. i. 569, 639.
Bonham, Lieut., his activity and skill, K. iii. 539; remains alone at Sikrorá, K. iii. 476, M. i. 393; forced to fly from Sikrorá, K. iii. 476, M. i. 393; his great bravery at battle of Chinhat, K. iii. 507 and n.; heroically strives to save howitzer, M. i. 427 n.
Bonus, Lieut., his gallantry at storming of Jhánsí, M. iii. 169.
Boulton, Lieut., escapes from mutiny of 48th N.I., M. i. 372.
Boyle, Mr. Vicars, his house at Árá, K. iii. 125; provisions his house, anticipating danger, K. iii. 126; fortifies his house at Árá, M. i. 80; he, Colvin, and Wake, noble associates of the four who saved

THE HISTORIES OF THE INDIAN MUTINY. 23

Boyle, Mr. Vicars—*cont*.
Mr. Beadon's line of six hundred miles, M. i. 143.
Bráhmans alarmed by spread of education, K. i. 183; irritated by great public works, K. i. 191.
Bráhmanism, K. i. 181; undermined by spread of education, K. i. 184; suppression of cruel rites by the English, K.'i. 184.
Braj Mohan Singh, the first man to use the greased cartridges, his house burnt, M. iii. 47.
Bramley, Lieut., killed at Rúiyá, M. ii. 506.
Brasyer, Capt., bravery of his Sikhs at Lakhnau, M. ii. 392; turns third rebel line of defence at Lakhnau, M. ii. 392.
Brigade Mess, a post at Lakhnau Residency, M. i. 443. *See also* Lakhnau.
Briggs, Capt., organises military transport train at Ludhíáná, K. ii. 511.
Brind, Major James, commands heavy artillery at Dehlí, K. iii. 560; commands right section of No. 1 battery at Dehlí, M. ii. 13; his dauntless courage, K. iii. 560 *n*.; given the task of securing possession of Dehlí, M. ii. 81; vigorously restores order in Dehlí, M. ii. 82.
British administration, some faults of, disclosed by the Mutiny, K. iii. 287 *n*.
British Army in India, before the Mutiny, its number and constitution, K. i. 341; effect of partial withdrawal of, for Crimean War, K. i. 343; impolicy of leaving large tracts of country unguarded by, K. i. 340, 343.

British officers at Madras Mutiny (1809), K. i. 252; why British officers are respected by Sepoys, K. i. 328; dangerous proselytisers among, K. i. 479.
British supremacy saved by mutiny at Mírat, opinion on, K. ii. 108.
British troops sympathise with the Sepoys in their mutiny at Firozpúr (1844), K. i. 279.
Broach, *see* Barúch.
Browne, Capt., his gallantry at Kúrsí, M. ii. 411.
Browne, Capt. Samuel, leads attack on Sirpúra, M. iii. 277; his daring gallantry in capturing a gun, M. iii. 277; severely wounded, M. iii. 278; completely defeats rebels, M. iii. 279.
Brownlow, Lieut., blown up, by accident, at Lakhnau, M. ii. 404.
Brownlow, Midshipman, his energy and bravery at Hetampúr, M. iii. 462.
Budháyan, manœuvring of Gen. Franks and Mahndí Husain to ,gain fort of, M. ii. 332; Gen. Franks enters fort of, M. ii. 332.
Bukht Khan, *see* Bakht Khán.
Búndí, one of Rájpút states, M. i. 245 *n*.; Tántiá Topí marches on, M. iii. 320; the Maháráo shuts his gates against Tántiá Topí, M. iii. 320; Tántiá Topí turns from, M. iii. 320.
Bundlekund, *see* Bundelkhand.
Burbank, Capt., his good service in Chutiá Nágpúr, M. ii. 432, iii. 463.
Burgess, Corporal, one of explosion party at Kashmír gate, Dehlí, M. ii. 32.
Burhánpúr, mutiny at (July), M. iii. 59.

Burmah, *see* Birmá.
Burney, Col., commands at Báosí, M. ii. 133; wins the confidence of his Sepoys, M. ii. 133; drives away approaching mutineers, M. ii. 134.
Burning of villages by Europeans, deprecated by Lord Canning, K. iii. 54.
Burton, Major, political agent at Kota, M. ii. 568; after heroic resistance, is murdered with his sons at Kotá, M. ii. 570.
Bushby, Mr., succeeds Col. Sleeman as political agent in Ságar, M. iii. 89.
Busher, Sergt.-Major, sole survivor of three boats escaping from Faizábád, K. iii. 468.
Butler, Lieut. Thomas, his daring deed at Lakhnau, M. ii. 376.
Byng, Major, finds the Chatgáon mutineers at Látú, M. ii. 423; his death in attacking them, M. ii. 424.
Byram Ghaut, *see* Bairám Ghát.

C.

CALCUTTA, condition of, in May 1857, K. ii. 112; alarm in, during May, K. ii. 113; just causes of alarm, K. ii. 114; Government had not fully realised danger up to end of May, M. i. 1; Government order 84th Regiment back to Rángún (May 3), M. i. 6; refuses aid of citizens (May 20), M. i. 6; anticipates speedy suppression of the Mutiny (May 25), M. i. 2; reason for false security of Government at, M. i. 7; Government relies

Calcutta—*cont.*
on possibilities, M. i. 5; the community distrusts Lord Canning, K. ii. 116.
Despatch of 84th Regiment for the North-West Provinces (May 20), M. i. 2; arrival of first reinforcements at (May 23), K. ii. 128, M. i. 2, 8.
Queen's birthday celebrated with usual honours at (May 25), K. ii. 118; special points of danger near, K. ii. 122; failure to aid in pushing troops to the front, K. ii. 131; deficiency in means of transport at, K. iii. 3.
Government confident as to speedy fall of Dehlí, M. i. 3; Government at, sent thanks to 6th Regiment at Alláhábád for loyalty, M. i. 9; receives alarming news from beyond Alláhábád, M. i. 3.
Unprotected state of (June 1), M. i. 5; Government deluded by loyal professions of Sepoys, M. i. 9; but guilty of fatuity in trusting Sepoys, M. i. 46; communication with North-West Provinces interrupted, K. iii. 5; reinforcements sent on with rapidity, M. i. 8.
Volunteer Corps formed at, (June 12), K. iii. 12, M. i. 15; Volunteer force formed in a few days, M. i. 15; useful services of Volunteers at, K. iii. 42.
Alarm at (June), K. iii. 25; European troops in vicinity of, M. i. 22; outburst of indignation against "Gagging Act," M. i. 20; state of (June 13), M. i. 22.
"Panic Sunday" at (June 14), K. iii. 29; discreditable

Calcutta—*cont.*
pusillanimity of higher officials at, M. i. 25; complete desertion of parts of city, K. iii. 32; Natives as much scared as Europeans, K. iii. 33; courage of mercantile and trading community during, M. i. 26 *n.*; description of "Panic Sunday," by "Friend of India," K. iii. 35 *n.*; probable exaggeration in account of, K. iii. 34.
Escape of prisoner from Fort William, K. iii. 35 *n.*, 665, 678; arrest of King of Oudh at (June 15), K. iii. 38, 41, M. i. 27.
Proposals for disarming Natives at, K. iii. 56; the merchants of, press upon Lord Canning the disarming of Dánápúr Sepoys, M. i. 63; deputation of merchants wait on Lord Canning (July 20), M. i. 63; they remonstrate with Lord Canning for not disarming Dánápúr Sepoys, M. i. 63; Lord Canning refuses request of merchants of, M. i. 64; Government at, mainly responsible for mutiny at Dánápúr, M. i. 71; the Grand Jury suggest the disarming of native pppulation of, M. i. 137; Lord Canning disarms both Eoropeans and natives (July 31), M. i. 138; intense unpopularity of this measure, M. i. 138.
Arrival of Sir P. Grant at (June 17), M. i. 29; false report of capture of Dehlí, M. i. 33; Sir H. Lawrence announces Káhnpúr massacre to, M. i. 34; Gen. Havelock starts from (June 24), M. i .35; gloomy prospects at, on arrival of Sir J. Outram, (Aug.

Calcutta—*cont.*
1), M. 133; Madras Sepoys land at (Aug. 5), M. ii. 138; arrival of Lord Elgin at (Aug. 8), M. i. 140; arrival of Capt. Peel and Capt. Sotheby, M. i. 141; the Naval Brigade starts (Aug. 18), M. ii. 126; Sir Colin Campbell arrives in (Aug. 13), M. i. 142; he has to force authorities to procure supplies, M. ii. 122.
Arrival of troops from Africa (Sept.), M. ii. 125; troops from China expedition arrive (Aug. 13–Oct. 26), M. ii. 125, 128; ceases to be the centre of real authority (Nov. 27), M. ii. 417.
Panic of Mar. 3, '58, M. ii. 418; Major Cavenagh's account of the cause of the panic, M. ii. 510; Mr. J. P. Grant returns to, as President of the Council, M. ii. 418; Queen's proclamation read with ceremony at (Nov. 1, '58), M. iii. 395.
Campbell, Capt. Rose, sent as envoy to Rájá of Shorápúr, M. iii. 127; returns unsuccessful, M. iii. 127; receives political charge of Shorápúr, M. iii. 129.
Campbell, Col., commands third column of assault at Dehlí, M. ii. 28.
Campbell, Brig., clears the district on left bank of the Ganges, M. ii. 449; ordered to cut off retreat from Músá Bágh, M. ii. 406; fails to do so, M. ii. 408; incalculable mischief caused by his neglect, M. ii. 408 *n.*; his failure justified by Sir Colin Campbell, M. ii. 414.
Campbell, Mrs., her romantic escape from Gwáliár, K. iii. 318 *n.*

Campbell, Sir Colin, overcomes the mutinous Sepoy regiments in the Panjáb (1849), K. i. 311.
His capacity as a commander, M. ii. 279; his capacity as a general, M. ii. 413; his extraordinary order to Gen. Outram, M. ii. 413; a general of the second rank, M. ii. 414; his appreciation of the services of Adrian Hope, M. ii. 510; his encomium on Capt. S. Browne's gallantry, M. iii. 278 *n*.
Arrives at Calcutta (Aug. 13), M. i. 142, ii. 119; position of affairs on his arrival, M. ii. 119; nothing done by Government before his arrival, M. ii. 121; has to force Calcutta departments to procure supplies, M. ii. 122; confirms and extols Gen. Outram's order of Sept. 16, M. i. 524; organises bullock-train to Alláhábád, M. ii. 123; sends patrolling columns along Grand Trunk Road, M. ii. 124; the civil authorities divert his patrolling parties, M. ii. 124; reinforcements reach him in October, M. ii. 128.
Starts, with his staff, for Alláhábád (Oct. 27), M. ii. 129, 142; he is nearly captured at Sherghátí (Oct. 29), M. ii. 142; reaches Alláhábád (Nov. 1), M. ii. 143; sends a force to clear A'zamgarh, M. ii. 146.
Resolves to relieve Lakhnau, M. ii. 146, 148; the troops with which he advanced to Lakhnau, M. ii. 165; strength of his final attacking force, M. ii. 170; his instructions to Gen. Windham for holding Káhnpúr, M.

Campbell, Sir Colin—*cont.*
ii. 149, 226; the careful forethought of his instructions, M. ii. 227; joins Brig. Hope Grant at Baní, M. ii. 150; meets Mr. Kavanagh from Lakhnau Residency, M. ii. 150; his plan of operations against Lakhnau, M. ii. 167; substantially adopts Gen. Outram's plan of attack on Lakhnau, M. ii. 168; encamps behind the A'lambágh, M. ii. 169.
His advance from the A'lambágh (Nov. 14), M. ii. 172; penetrates the Dilkhúsha Park, M. ii. 173; carries and occupies the Martinière, M. ii. 174; the rebels attack centre, but fail, M. ii. 175; rebels make second attempt on centre, but fail, M. ii. 176; leaves his baggage and invalids at Dilkhúsha, M. ii. 178; again advances (Nov. 16), M. ii. 179; signals his advance to Gen. Outram, M. ii. 179; rebels attack the right, but fail, M. ii. 179; resolves to silence the Kaisar Bágh, M. ii. 209; his movement on the Sikandar Bágh, M. ii. 180; resolves to capture Sháh Najíf, M. ii. 189; his address to Highlanders before assault on Sháh Najíf, M. ii. 191; leads assault in person, M. ii. 192; the band of heroes who fought with him on Nov. 16, M. ii. 197, 198; his plan of operations for Nov. 17, M. ii. 199; secures his left flank, M. ii. 200; attacks the Mess House, M. ii. 201; his rage at Capt. Wolseley for exceeding orders, M. ii. 203 *n.*; relieves Lakhnau (Nov. 17), M. ii. 204.

Campbell, Sir Colin—*cont.*
His communications with Káhnpúr severed by Tántiá Topí (Nov. 19), M. ii. 232; successfully withdraws garrison, &c. from Lakhnau (Nov. 22), M. ii. 216; his forces re-unite at the Dilkhúsha (Nov. 23), M. ii. 217; resolves to retire by road he advanced, M. ii. 214; reaches the A'lambágh (Nov. 25), M. ii. 221; leaves Gen. Outram in charge of A'lambágh, M. ii. 222.
Becomes the real Governor of India (Nov. 27–Jan. '58), M. ii. 417.
Leaves the A'lambágh for Káhnpúr (Nov. 27), M. ii. 222; receives urgent call for help, M. ii. 223; leads forced march back to Káhnpúr, M. ii. 224; crosses the bridge into Káhnpúr (Nov. 28), M. ii. 225; begins to drive Tántiá Topí from Káhnpúr (Nov. 29), M. ii. 259; the whole of his force crosses into Káhnpúr (Nov. 30), M. ii. 261; sends non-combatants to Alláhábád, M. ii. 263.
Tántiá Topí attacks his position at Káhnpúr (Dec. 2), M. ii. 263; Tántiá Topí renews attack (Dec. 4), M. ii. 265; his plan for driving Tántiá Topí from Káhnpúr, M. ii. 265; strength of his forces at Káhnpúr, M. ii. 267.
Begins attack on Tántiá Topí (Dec. 6), M. ii. 268; captures camp of Gwáliár Contingent, at Káhnpúr, M. ii. 271; defeats Tántiá Topí at Káhnpúr, M. ii. 271; pursues his troops from Káhnpúr, M. ii. 272; sends Gen. Mansfield to cut off Tántiá Topí's retreat, who fails, M.

Campbell, Sir Colin—*cont.*
ii. 273; sends Gen. Hope Grant in pursuit of Tántiá Topí, M. ii. 276.
In want of transport at Káhnpúr, M. ii. 283; sends Gen. Walpole to I'táwá and Mainpúrí, M. ii. 284; his plan for clearing the Doáb, M. ii. 284; receives carriages for transport, M. ii. 299.
Starts from Káhnpúr (Dec. 24), M. ii. 299; arrives at Míran-kí-saráí, M. ii. 299; meets Capt. Hodson, M. ii. 297, 299; reaches Gurusaháíganj, M. ii. 299; approaches Fathgarh, M. ii. 301; defeats the rebels at Fathgarh, M. ii. 303; ovation given him by soldiers, M. ii. 304; enters Fathgarh (Jan. 3, '58), M. ii. 305.
Joined by Brig. Seaton and Gen. Walpole, at Fathgarh, M. ii. 306; importance of his position at Fathgarh, M. ii. 309; directs Carthew to clear district east of Jamná, M. ii. 448; wishes to attack Rohilkhand, M. ii. 306; induced by Lord Canning to attack Oudh first, M. ii. 309; strength of his force for subduing Oudh, M. ii. 314; orders siege-train from A'grá, M. ii. 310; sends Gen. Walpole against Alláhganj, M. ii. 311; deceives the Rohilkhand rebels, M. ii. 311; leaves Fathgarh for Káhnpúr (Feb. 1, '58), M. ii. 314.
His force for capture of Lakhnau, M. ii. 364; decides to attack east side of Lakhnau, M. ii. 367; his plan for capture of the town, M. ii. 368; captures the Dilkhúsha, Lakhnau, M. ii. 369; throws

Campbell, Sir Colin—*cont.*
two pontoon bridges across Gúmtí, M. ii. 370; his position opposite Lakhnau, M. ii. 370; sends Gen. Outram across the Gúmtí, M. ii. 371; captures the Martinière, M. ii. 377; storms and captures Banks's House, M. ii. 379; capture of second rebel line of defence, M. ii. 391; capture of Qaisar Bágh, and third line of defence, M. ii. 394.

His extraordinary order to Gen. Outram (Mar. 14, '58), M. ii. 397; disastrous consequences of that order, M. ii. 398; sends Hope Grant along Sítápúr road, M. ii. 399; sends Brig. Campbell along Sandíla road, M. ii. 399; his instructions to Gen. Outram, M. ii. 399; sends him to capture Músá Bágh, M. ii. 405; sends Col. Maxwell against Kálpí, M. ii. 450; his work after the fall of Lakhnau, M. ii. 467.

Lord Canning insists on his immediate attack of Rohilkhand. M. ii. 498; Sir Colin organises three columns to attack Rohilkhand, M. ii. 498; allows the Maulaví to escape from Sháhjahánpúr, M. ii. 522; arrives at Farídpúr, M. ii. 522; his force for attack of Barailí, M. ii. 524; drives rebels across Natiá rivulet, M. ii. 525; pauses in his attack on Barailí, M. ii. 528; his pause allows Khán Bahádur Khán to escape, M. ii. 529.

Distributes his troops over the north-west, M. ii. 537; leaves Barailí for Fathgarh, M. ii. 538; turns aside to support Brig. Jones at Sháhja-

Campbell, Sir Colin—*cont.*
hánpúr, M. ii. 538; joins Brig. Jones there, M. ii. 537; repulses the Maulaví's troops at Panhat (May 18, '58), M. ii. 539; sends for, and is joined by Col. Coke, M. ii. 540; again out-manœuvred by the Maulaví, M. ii. 540.

Orders Sir Hugh Rose to march on Charkhárí, M. iii. 154; Sir R. Hamilton authorises Sir Hugh Rose to disobey this order, M. iii. 155; thinks campaign in Central India ended with capture of Kálpí, M. iii. 189; admitted to participate in Bándá and Kirwí booty, M. iii. 202; reprimands Sir H. Rose for reassuming command without authority, M. iii. 213 *n.*; places troops at service of Sir H. Rose, M. iii. 214.

Created Lord Clyde, M. iii. 288.

His plan for finally crushing the Mutiny (Oct. '58), M. iii. 288; orders Gen. Hope Grant to move up the Gúmtí, M. iii. 289; marches on Amíthí and receives submission of Rájá, M. iii. 291; offers terms to Bení Mádhava, which are rejected, M. iii. 291; totally defeats Bení Mádhava at Dhúndhiá Khere, M. iii. 292; drives the Begam and Náná Sáhib into Nipál, M. iii. 294; complete success of his plan for clearing Oudh, M. iii. 297.

Camp-followers, the want of, stops Neill's advance from Alláhábád, K. ii. 273.

Candahar, *see* Kandahár.

Canning, Lord.
Biographical details.—His birth, K. i. 362; memorials

Canning, Lord—*cont.*
of his early life, K. i. 627;
his school-days, K. i. 363; at
Eton, K. i. 364; at Oxford,
K. i. 366; takes his degree at
Oxford, K. i. 368; his marriage, K. i. 368; his excess of
conscientiousness, K. i. 584;
his serenity in danger, K. i.
598; enters Parliament (1836),
K. i. 368; his father named
Governor-General in 1822, K.
i. 361; Lord Ellenborough
offers him the Private Secretaryship, K. i. 369; takes
office in English Ministry, K.
i. 370; declines the seals of
the Foreign Office under Lord
Derby, K. i. 371; accepts the
Postmaster-Generalship under
Lord Aberdeen, K. i. 372; reappointed to Post Office by
Lord Palmerston, K. i. 373.

Appointed Governor-General, K. i. 360, 374; his appointment received with disapprobation, K. i. 374; banquet at London Tavern on his
appointment, K. i. 375; his
speech before starting to
India, K. i. 377–379.

His reception at Bombay,
on first landing in India, K.
i. 384; lands at Calcutta
(Feb. 29, '56), K. i. 385; first
days as Governor-General, K.
i. 385; guided at first by
Lord Dalhousie's policy and
advisers, M. iii. 491; becomes
really great when he stands
alone at Alláhábád, M. iii.
493; his low estimate of the
higher Indian officials, M. iii.
495; his personal vexations,
K. iii. 51; extraneous correspondence poured upon him,
K. iii. 6.

General Policy.—Dislikes
the idea of war with Persia,

Canning, Lord—*cont.*
K. i. 415; dislikes Central
Asian affairs, K. i. 415; averse
to interfering with Hirát, K.
i. 447; declines to send a
Mission to Hirát, K. i. 416;
driven into alliance with Afghanistan, K. i. 428; delighted
with alliance of Dost Muhammad, K. i. 444.

His reasons for doubting
the Panjáb, K. ii. 417–419;
forbids Sir J. Lawrence to
cede Peshawar, K. ii. 619.

Approves annexation of
Oudh, K. i. 381; endeavours
to reconcile disputes of officials in Oudh, K. i. 400; his
courteous rebukes to Mr. C.
Jackson, K. i. 400 *n.*, 406; resolves to remove Mr. C. Jackson from Oudh, K. i. 408.

On the position of the Dehlí
Emperor, K. ii. 29; endorses
Lord Dalhousie's policy with
respect to Dehlí sovereign, K.
ii. 29–31; his terms with respect to the Dehlí succession,
K. ii. 32.

His financial measures, K.
iii. 48–50; stops reproductive public works, K. iii. 50;
his instructions to executive
officers, K. iii. 52, 53; prudently endeavours to prevent
famine following Mutiny, K.
iii. 192; his views on regulating polygamy, K. i. 478 *n.*;
his defence of General Service
enlistment, K. i. 468; his
opinion of the greased cartridges, K. i. 559; fears undue concession, K. i. 559;
orders the amended cartridges
to be used, K. i. 560.

His views on the Bihár outbreak, K. iii. 170; his private
secretary exonerates Mr. Tayler from all blame, M. i.

Canning, Lord—*cont.*
121 *n.*; commends Mr. A. Money's retreat from Gayá, K. iii. 158; thanks De Kantzow for his noble deed at Mainpúrí, K. iii. 227; his letter of thanks to Do Kantzow, M. i. 160; commends Mr. Tucker's calm fortitude at Banáras, K. ii. 211; his record of Adrian Hope's ability, M. ii. 509; his testimony to the worth of Capt. W. Peel, M. ii. 547; his tribute to the memory of Mr. Venables, M. ii. 548 *n.*; thanks Mr. Wynward in autograph letter, M. iii. 453; his confidence in the Lawrences, K. i. 613.

Outbreak of the Mutiny.—Great anxiety of, in beginning of year, K. i. 532, 561; regains confidence in May, K. i. 583; confident bearing of, on outbreak of Mutiny, K. ii. 115; his immediate measure of defence on outbreak at Mírat, K. ii. 111, 127; perceives political motives in the Mutiny, K. i. 617; suspects ex-King of Oudh's ministers of spreading injurious rumours, K. i. 573; his reasons for arresting the King of Oudh, K. iii. 41 *n.*; refuses to change his native personal guard, K. ii. 119; refuses to disarm his body-guard, K. iii. 57; reluctantly changes his native body-guard, K. iii. 59.

Declines to organise Volunteer force at Calcutta, K. ii. 117; blamed for not accepting services of Volunteers, K. ii. 123 *n.*; accepts the services of Calcutta Volunteers, K. iii. 9, 11 *n.*; sanctions the enrol-

Canning, Lord—*cont.*
ment of a Volunteer corps, M. i. 15.

Charged with not realising gravity of the position, K. iii. 9; misapprehends temper of European society in India, K. iii. 24; lacks the moral support of many of the English, K. i. 610; the public have no confidence in, M. i. 137.

Objects to restrict the Press, M. i. 18; proposes restrictions on Press, K. iii. 17; places Press under restraint for one year, K. iii. 18; represses both European and Native press, M. i. 19; passes the "Gagging Act" (June 15), K. iii. 18; the charge of insulting European community by so doing, K. iii. 19; defends his action against Native Press, K. iii. 20; and against European Press, K. iii. 21; his unpopularity after "Gagging Act," K. iii. 24; increasing unpopularity of, K. iii. 25, 52, 180.

Passes the Arms Act (Sept. 11), K. iii. 177; disarms both Europeans and Natives in Calcutta, M. i. 138; intense unpopularity of measure, M. i. 138.

Increases power of military authorities, K. i. 609; General Order of (May 19), K. i. 610; gives powers of life and death to executive officers (June 6), K. iii. 9; fears the growth of a national hatred, K. iii. 8; directs moderation in punitive measures, K. iii. 7, M. i. 135; his order criticised, M. i. 136; his order a statesman-like measure, M. i. 137; his efforts to moderate fierceness of retribution, K.

Canning, Lord—*cont.*
iii. 54; denounced for his moderation, K. iii. 55; refuses to place Lower Bengal under martial law, K. iii. 179; his proclamation at A'grá, K. iii. 235.
The Oudh Proclamation.—
His impolitic proclamation in Oudh (Mar. 20, '58), M. ii. 409; its nature, M. iii. 247, 248; excludes from mercy those who had murdered Englishmen and women in Oudh, M. iii. 249; Dr. Russell's remark on his Oudh proclamation, M. ii. 410; proclamation condemned by Gen. Outram, M. iii. 250; Gen. Outram's reasons for objecting to, M. iii. 251; gets qualifying clause added to it, M. ii. 410; amends his proclamation to Oudh, M. iii. 252; apparent severity, but real leniency, of proclamation, M. iii. 253; sends home his proclamation to Oudh, with explanatory letter, M. iii. 254; proclamation condemned by Lord Ellenborough, M. iii. 255; Lord Ellenborough resigns office, after his hasty censure, M. iii. 257; Lord Canning solicited by Lord Derby to retain Governor-Generalship, M. iii. 258; his vindication of his Oudh policy, M. iii. 259–261; takes credit for its leniency, M. iii. 250; successful in his refutation of Lord Ellenborough's charges, M. iii. 262; his conduct under these strictures, M. iii. 494.
Reinforcements Collected.—
Hastily gathers up reinforcements, K. i. 600, 601; organises transport for reinforcements, K. i. 602; looks to

Canning, Lord—*cont.*
the Panjáb for English troops, K. i. 603; his appeal to Lord Elgin, K. i. 607; accepts the *Shannon* and *Pearl* from Lord Elgin, M. i. 141; diverts Chinese expedition to India, K. i. 600; assumes all the responsibility of so doing, K. i. 605; calls for an immediate addition to the Company's Army, K. i. 606; tries moral, as well as physical, force, K. i. 607; issues a tranquillising proclamation, K. i. 608.
Fears effect of disarming Sepoys, M. i. 46; orders disbandment of 34th Regiment in May, K. i. 585; on method of executing sentence on 3rd Cavalry mutineers, K. ii. 53; temporises with Sepoys, M. i. 47; doubts policy of disarming Sepoys at Bárákpúr, K. iii. 28 n.; permits disarmament of Sepoys at Bárákpúr, K. iii. 28; neglects opportunities for disarming Dánápúr Sepoys, M. i. 61; his reasons for not disarming Dánápúr Sepoys, K. iii. 65; refuses to disarm them, M. i. 64; summary of his decisions with respect to disarming Sepoys at Dánápúr, M. i. 65; his refusal to disarm Dánápúr Sepoys on July 20, followed on 25th by mutiny, M. i. 73.
Succours he demands from England (May), K. iii. 46; Lord Elphinstone suggests to him a special steamer to England for reinforcements, M. iii. 7; refuses to send one, M. iii. 7; additional succours demanded from England, K. iii. 47; calls for the 12th Lancers from Bombay (June 28), M. iii. 15.

Canning, Lord—*cont.*
Military Operations.—Resolves to strike for Dehlí first, K. ii. 120; urges Gen. Anson to immediate attack of Dehlí, K. ii. 121; his personal regard for Gen. Anson, K. i. 394 *n.*; disagrees with him, K. i. 394; rejoiced at his active preparations, K. ii. 150.
On impracticability of disarming Bengal Army, K. ii. 124; European troops within his reach for suppressing outbreak, K. ii. 127; directs a semblance of activity on part of European troops, K. ii. 127; authorises any degree of severity in dealing with Dehlí, K. ii. 159.
Underrates military difficulties in advance on Dehlí, K. ii. 159; directs Gen. Anson to divide his force, to relieve Káhnpúr, K. ii. 159; his letter urging him to detach troops for service in the field, M. i. 4, 12, 13 *n.*; his estimate of Gen. Anson's course of action, K. ii. 167; feels his inability to send adequate succours, K. iii. 3; his painful solicitation for Káhnpúr, K. iii. 4; misconceives English strength in North-West Provinces, K. iii. 5; directs Sir H. Barnard to detach a regiment to succour Káhnpúr, K. iii. 4.
Appoints Sir P. Grant Acting Commander-in-Chief (June 3), K. ii. 280; receives false report of fall of Dehlí (June 24), K. iii. 180; recommends Sir Patrick Grant for chief command, M. i. 142; but Lord Palmerston sends Sir Colin Campbell, M. i. 142.

Canning, Lord—*cont.*
Urges Sir Colin Campbell to attack Oudh, M. ii. 307; sound reasons for his wish to have Oudh subjected, M. ii. 308; accepts Jang Bahádur's offer of assistance, M. ii. 316; accepts further aid from Jang Bahádur, M. ii. 320.
Residence in the North-West.—Proceeds to Alláhábád (Jan. '58), M. ii. 417; abolishes Chief Commissionership of Ágrá (Feb. 9, '58), M. ii. 418; eager for the capture of Jhánsí, M. iii. 153; orders Sir R. Hamilton to relieve Rájá of Chárkhárí, M. iii. 154; Sir R. Hamilton disobeys his order, M. iii. 156; sends Lord Mark Kerr to relieve Ázamgarh, M. ii. 459; insists on immediate attack of Rohilkhand, M. ii. 498; sends field force to clear country around Soráon, M. iii. 279.
Created First Viceroy of India (Nov. 1, '58), M. iii. 392; assiduously explains the Queen's proclamation to India, M. iii. 396.
Carew, Lieut., his skill and energy at Hetampúr, M. iii. 462.
Carmichael, Brig., clears country south of Ghághrá, M. iii. 293.
Carmichael, Sergt., one of explosion party at Kashmír gate, Dehlí, M. ii. 32.
Carnatic, Nawábship of, extinguished (1854), K. i. 111.
Carnegy, Capt., Chief of Oudh Police, K. iii. 439; reports dangerous condition of 7th Regiment, K. i. 587; his daring entrance into the Qaddam Rasúl, Lakhnau, M. ii. 383.
Carnegy, Mr. Patrick, his character, M. ii. 339; ably assists

Carnegy, Mr. Patrick—*cont.*
Gen. Franks during his campaign, M. ii. 340.
Carnell, Lieut., his prompt march to Ajmír, M. i. 250.
Carpenter, Col., commands first brigade Jabalpúr column, M. iii. 191.
Carthew, Brig. M., his character, M. ii. 138; commands Madras Sepoys in Bengal, M. ii. 138; warns Gen. Windham of approach of Tántiá Topí, M. ii. 235; protects the Bithúr road to Káhnpúr, M. ii. 239; ordered to fall back on brick-kilns at Káhnpúr, M. ii. 242; beats off Tántiá Topí on the right, M. ii. 244; on Nov. 27 victorious in every encounter, M. ii. 244.
Protects right of Káhnpúr (Nov. 28), M. ii. 247; beats off Tántiá Topí's attack on his position, M. ii. 248; ordered to advance through parade-ground, M. ii. 250; Brig. Wilson ordered to cover his right, M. ii. 250; forced to fall back by failure of Brig. Wilson, M. ii. 252; sends for, but receives no supports, M. ii. 253; his brave and soldierly conduct on Nov. 28, M. ii. 253, 256; attempts the impossible, M. ii. 258.
Sir Colin Campbell induced to censure him, M. ii. 254; his reluctance to retire, M. ii. 254 n.; receives a trifling support to cover his retreat, M. ii. 255; forces Gen. Windham to acknowledge that he ordered him to retire, M. ii. 255; Sir Colin Campbell expresses regret for censure he was led to pass on him, M. ii. 255.
Left in command of Fath-

Carthew, Brig. M.—*cont.*
púr, M. ii. 446; marches to Bhognípúr, and clears district of rebels, M. ii. 448.
Cartridges, greased, *see* Greased cartridges.
Case, Col., heroic death of, at battle of Chinhat, K. iii. 507.
Caste, its hold on native society, K. i. 194; Native rumours of intended pollution of, K. ii. 118; desire to defile the general population believed, K. i. 568; origin of the reports concerning attempts to destroy, M. i. 351; sinister rumours in circulation long before outbreak of Mutiny, M. i. 353; reported interference of Government with, K. i. 248; feared destruction of, by overwhelming force of Europeans, K. i. 537.
Messing-system in gaols supposed to threaten, K. i. 305; how affected by prison discipline, K. i. 195; outbreaks in gaols on caste questions, K. i. 198; prisoners deprived of their *lotás*, K. i. 199; bone-dust a means of destroying, K. i. 639; desire to defile by means of bone-dust believed, K. i. 159; the destruction of, feared in all acts of the English, K. i. 350; additional excitement caused by circulation of chapátís, K. i. 572; riots from anticipated violation of, K. i. 199; Patná conspiracy (1846) caused by dread of interference with, K. i. 304; reassuring proclamation by Governor of Bengal, K. i. 308; opinions of a Brahman on attempts to tamper with, K. i. 592, 593.
In the Army, K. i. 212, 621-626; its advantages and

Caste—*cont.*
dangers in the Army, K. i. 330; the policy of a mixture of caste in the Army, K. i. 331; effect of General Service enlistment on, K. i. 471; hardships which it entails on sea voyages, K. i. 460 *n.*
The suggestion of lard on the cartridges turns the Muhammadans against the English, M. i. 354; Native officers at Ambálá state universal dread of interference with, K. i. 557.
Causes of discontent distinct from questions of, M. i. 351.
Caulfield, Capt., assumes command of Col. Gerrard's column, M. ii. 117.
Cavenagh, Major Orfeur, energetically prepares for expected reinforcements at Calcutta, M. iii. 503; appointed to organise Volunteer force at Calcutta, K. iii. 12; his two accounts of "Panic Sunday," K. iii. 31 *n.*; his account of the cause of the panic of Mar. 3, '58, at Calcutta, M. iii. 510.
Cawnpore, *see* Káhnpúr.
Central India, constituent states of, M. i. 204; military occupation of, M. i. 205; rising of Sepoys in, M. i. 12; plan of operations proposed by Sir R. Hamilton, M. iii. 133.
Central India Field Force, composition of, M. iii. 137; Sir Hugh Rose takes up command at Máu, M. iii. 134; broken up, and distributed, M. iii. 232, 233.
See also Rose, Sir Hugh, and Whitlock, Brig.
Centralisation, its bad effect illustrated, K. i. 319; humi-

Centralisation—*cont.*
liates Sepoy officer, K. i. 258; breaks down on emergencies, K. i. 609.
Central Provinces, popular feeling in favour of English, M. iii. 345.
Chaibásá, Sepoy garrison of, M. ii. 134; mutiny at (Aug. 5), M. ii. 136.
Chait Singh of Banáras, his descendants still recognised as rájás, M. iii. 483 *n.*
Chákar Kothí, key to rebel position at Lakhnau, M. ii. 374.
Chakkarnagar, rebels defeated at, by Mr. Lauce and Capt. Gordon, M. iii. 310.
Chamberlain, Brig. Neville, his character and services, K. ii. 456, M. ii. 55; summoned to Pesháwar (May 13), K. ii. 457; commands Panjáb Irregular Force, K. ii. 456; created Chief of the Staff, before Dehlí, K. ii. 512, M. ii. 56; reaches Dehlí (June 24), K. ii. 561; severely wounded, M. ii. 56; his pertinacity before Dehlí, K. iii. 546, witnesses storming of Dehlí from top of Hindú Ráo's house, M. ii. 56; urges Brig. Wilson to persevere in attack on Dehlí, M. ii. 57; his opinion of Gen. Barnard, K. ii. 569.
Chambers, Mrs., her murder at Mírat, K. ii. 69.
Champáran, district of Patná division, K. iii. 71 *n.*, M. i. 40; placed under martial law, by Major Holmes, K. iii. 103.
Chándá, garrison of, M. iii. 113; Nipálese troops beat the rebels at, M. ii. 319; Gen. Franks defeats the rebels at, M. ii. 330.

Chanda Bakhsh, rebel leader in Oudh, M. iii. 271.
Chandairí, part of Ságar territory, M. iii. 88; its position and description, M. iii. 151; stormed and captured by Brig. Stuart, M. iii. 153; Tántiá Topí attacks, but is repulsed, M. iii. 338.
Chandípúr, Capt. Sotheby attacks and captures fort of (Feb. '58), M. ii. 451.
Chapátís, as an incitement to revolt, M. iii. 471; the mysterious, circulated from the North-West, K. i. 570; particulars of their mysterious circulation, K. i. 632; brought to Capt. Ternan at Narsinghpúr, who divines their meaning, M. iii. 92; Major Erskine ridicules their importance, M. iii. 92; the mysterious circulation traced, K. i. 572 n.; known to have originated in Oudh, to unsettle men's minds, M. iii. 93; Native evidence concerning, K. i. 647.
Chaprá, out-station of Patná, K. iii. 71, M. i. 40; excited condition of people, K. iii. 73 and n.; treasure at, removed to Patná by Mr. W. Tayler, M. i. 49; placed under martial law, by Major J. Holmes (June 19), K. iii. 103; panic at (April '58), M. ii. 478, iii. 461.
Chárda, Rájá of, assists Mahmúdí Husain at Belwá, M. ii. 452.
Charkhárí, fidelity of Rájá of, to the English, M. iii. 154; Tántiá Topí besieges, M. iii. 155; Sir Hugh Rose ordered to march on, M. iii. 155; Sir R. Hamilton authorises Sir Hugh Rose to disobey order,

Charkhárí—cont.
M. iii. 156; captured by Tántiá Topí, M. iii. 161; Gen. Whitlock ordered to relieve, M. iii. 194.
Chárwá, Brig. Parke occupies (Nov. '58), M. iii. 347.
Chatarpúr, the Rání of, assists fugitives from Naogáon, M. i. 194.
Chatgáon, Mutiny at (Nov. 18), M. ii. 419; mutineers march on Manipúr, M. ii. 423; harassed march of mutineers from, M. ii. 422; the Commissioner calls on Rájá of Tiparah to cut off escaping mutineers, M. ii. 421; detachment sent to cut off mutineers from, M. ii. 421; mutineers, attacked and defeated at Látú, M. ii. 424; they escape into jungles at Manipúr, M. ii. 424; they are defeated by Capt. Stevens, M. ii. 425; the remnant perishes miserably in the hills, M. ii. 425.
Chattarbhuj pass, Brig. Somerset pursues RáoSáhib through (Feb. 15, '59), M. iii. 368.
Chattarpúr, the Rání of, succours fugitives from Náogáon, K. iii. 373; occupied by Gen. Whitlock, M. iii. 195.
Chatterbúj, see Chattarbhuj.
Chatterpore, see Chattarpúr.
Chattra, battle of (Oct. 2), M. ii. 141.
Chatur Singh, declares against the British in the Panjáb (1848), K. i. 34.
Check, Ensign Arthur, noble fortitude of, at Alláhábád, K. ii. 253.
Chester, Col., killed at Badlí-ká-Saráí (June 8), K. ii. 195.
Chester, Mr. C., Commissioner at Alláhábád (May), M. iii. 438.

3 *

Chhotá Udaipúr, Tántiá Topí overtaken at, by Brig. Parke, M. iii. 352; Tántiá Topí defeated at, M. iii. 354.
Chibramau, Capt. Hodson's escort destroyed at, M. ii. 297.
Chicken, Acting-Master George, his daring at Pirú, M. iii. 463.
Chikání, Rájá of, joins rebels on right bank of the Jamná, M. ii. 448.
Chilliánwálá, battle of 1849, K. i. 41.
Chillianwallah, see Chilliánwálá.
China expedition, its interception suggested by Gen. Hearsey, H. Lawrence, and Sir P. Grant, on the 15th, 16th, and 17th May respectively, K. i. 615 n.
Chinhat, battle of, K. ii. 410, iii. 504, M. i. 425; Mr. M. Gubbins' concern in the advance on, K. iii. 669; great bravery of Lieut. Bonham at, K. iii. 507 and n.; heroic death of Col. Case at, K. iii. 507, M. i. 425; noble charge of Volunteer cavalry at Kokárálí bridge, K. iii. 509, M. i. 426; defeat of the English, K. iii. 510, M. i. 427.
Chinhut, see Chinhat.
Chinsará, Highlanders ordered from, to disarm Bárákpúr Sepoys, M. i. 26.
Chírápúr, Capt. Ternan surprises and defeats rebels at, M. iii. 108.
Chirkárí, see Chárkhárí.
Chittagong to Akyab, nature of road between, in 1856, K. i. 463.
Chitty, Lieut., his excellent service on the Bombay coast, M. iii. 464.
Chotá Nágpúr, see Chutiá Nágpúr.

Christian, Mr. George Jackson, Commissioner at Sítápúr, K. iii. 452, M. i. 377; his dislike of the policy of weakening Oudh Talúqdárs, K. iii. 453. Anticipates mutiny at Sítápúr, M. i. 379; secures the women and children in his house at Sítapúr, K. iii. 454, M. i. 379; his murder, and that of his family, K. iii. 456, M. i. 380.
Christie, Lieut., his gallantry in the Málwá campaign, M. iii. 87.
Christie, Col., leads moveable column to left bank of Jamná to clear district, M. ii. 449; forces rebels to evacuate Siraulí, M. ii. 450.
Chumparun, see Champáran.
Chupattie, see Chapátí.
Chuprah, see Chaprá.
Churcher, Mr., his devotion to Major Robertson, M. i. 345 n.
Church garrison, a post at Lakhnau Residency, M. i. 444.
Chute, Col., his column disarms Frontier regiments, K. iii. 497.
Chutiá Nágpúr, its situation, M. ii. 134; Capt. Dalton, Acting-Commissioner of, M. ii. 134; left in charge of Rattray and his Sikhs, M. ii. 141; defeat of mutineers at Chattra by Major English, M. ii. 141, 436; nature of operations in, M. ii. 437; tranquillity gradually restored in, M. ii. 441 a.; not fully settled till end of 1858, M. ii. 441 b.
Chuttur Singh, see Chatur Singh.
Cis-Satlaj States, trusted and found worthy, K. ii. 162 and n.
Civil privileges of the Sepoys, K. i. 619.
Civil stations, typical examples of their condition during the Mutiny, M. iii. 400.

THE HISTORIES OF THE INDIAN MUTINY. 37

Civilians, their devotion, K. iii. 116; eager to accompany Árá relieving force, K. iii. 110; induce military not to abandon Banáras, K. ii. 202, 203.
Clarke, Lieut. Melville, his bravery on outbreak of mutiny at Mírat (May 10), K. ii. 64 and n.
Clarke, Lieut. Longueville, his murder at Bairám Ghát, K. iii. 478.
Clarke, Capt., blown up, by accident, at Lakhnau, M. ii. 404.
Clerk, Sir George, on the policy of "lapse," K. i. 72.
Clifford, Miss, her murder at Dehlí, K. ii. 80.
Clifton, Capt., greatly distinguishes himself at Bándá, M. iii. 197.
Clive, Lord, originates the Bengal Army, K. i. 205.
Clyde, Lord, see Campbell, Sir Colin.
Cockburn, Mr., appointed to superintendence of Sambalpúr, M. ii. 441 a; sends all his troops into Sambalpúr, M. ii. 441; raises two companies of Sepoys for service in Sambalpúr, M. ii. 441.
Cockburn, Lieut., commands part of Gwáliár Contingent at Hátrás, M. i. 293; one hundred of his troopers mutiny, M. i. 293; out-manœuvres and destroys mutinous troopers, M. i. 293.
Coke, Col., his character and antecedents, M. ii. 511; his splendid audacity at Dehlí, M. ii. 512 n.; named for command of Rúrkí column, M. ii. 511; organises transport for his column, M. ii. 513; superseded by Brig. Jones, M. ii. 513; retains the practical

Coke, Col.—cont. command of column, M. ii. 514; leads Rúrkí column to Bhogníwálá, M. ii. 515; defeats rebels at Bhogníwálá, M. ii. 515; captures ringleaders of rebellion in Murádábád, M. ii. 521; Hindús attempt to deceive him by false intelligence, M. ii. 530; forces entrance to Barailí, M. ii. 530; effects junction with Sir Colin Campbell, M. ii. 531; sent in pursuit of Khán Bahádur Khán, M. ii. 538; summoned to Sháhjahánpúr, M. ii. 540; joins Sir Colin Campbell, M. ii. 540.
Colbeck, Lieut., his gallantry and death at Bándá, M. iii. 197.
Collector of a disturbed district, his multifarious and contradictory duties, M. iii. 445; his thankless office, M. iii. 446.
Colter, Major, relieves Lieut. Graham from blockade at Palámau (Dec. 8), M. ii. 438.
Colvin, Wake, and Boyle, noble associates of the four, who saved Mr. Beadon's line of six hundred miles, M. i. 143.
Colvin, Mr. John Russell, Lieut.-Governor of the North-West Provinces, K. iii. 195, M. i. 146; his antecedents, M. i. 147; prime mover in first Afghan war, K. iii. 195; insists on Rání of Jhánsí paying her husband's debts out of her pension, M. i. 182; proposes great changes in Ságar and Narbadá territories, but is restrained by Capt. Ternan, M. iii. 90; degrades the Rája of Dilherí (1855), M. iii. 94; Capt. Ternan mitigates de-

Colvin, Mr.—*cont.*
gradation of Rájá of Dilherí, M. iii. 94; wanting in self-reliance, M. i. 146. Does not realise gravity of the first outbreak at Mírat, K. iii. 196; the Mírat mutiny a surprise to him, M. i. 148; when aroused, accurately gauges the peril, K. iii. 197; his activity at outbreak of the Mutiny, K. i. 603; urges Mírat garrison to do something, K. ii. 179; failing action of Gen. Hewitt, he applies direct to Brig. Wilson, K. ii. 179.
Calls a Council of War at Ágrá (May 14), K. iii. 199, M. i. 148; proposes to retire into Fort of Ágrá, M. i. 149; his proposal protested against, M. i. 149; the tendency of his policy to ignore the surrounding danger, K. iii. 202; perplexed by multitude of counsellors, K. iii. 201.
Addresses troops at Ágrá (May 15), K. iii. 205, M. i. 149; informs British troops of the murder of Miss Jennings, K. iii. 206; the Sepoys scowl upon him after his address, M. i. 150.
Urges Gen. Anson to march on Dehlí, K. iii. 206; sends Mr. G. Harvey with escort towards Dehlí, K. iii. 207; authorised to apply to Rájás of Patiálá and Jhínd for aid, K. i. 603; almost severed from Calcutta, K. iii. 181; flatters Native states by asking their assistance, K. iii. 209; applies to Sindhiá and Bharatpúr for aid, M. i. 153.
His proclamation of May 25, K. iii. 232, M. i. 163; his proclamation disapproved by

Colvin, Mr.—*cont.*
Government of India, M. i. 164; Lord Canning supersedes his proclamation, K. iii. 233; defends his proclamation, K. iii. 237. Advised by Col. Fraser to distrust Sepoys, M. i. 151; failure of his attempts to stop mutiny in his district, M. i. 296; resolves to remove treasure from Mathurá, K. iii. 240; the mutiny at Mathurá destroys his hopes, M. i. 165.
Disarms Sepoys at Ágra (May 31), M. i. 167; raises Volunteers in Ágrá, M. i. 167; despatches troops to Alígarh, M. i. 294; orders Col. Lawrence to abandon Rájpútáná and concentrate on Ágrá, K. iii. 352; Col. Lawrence refuses to abandon Rájpútáná, K. iii. 353; directs ladies to remain at Gwáliár until mutiny actually occurs, M. i. 172.
Authorises retirement into Fort of Ágrá, M. i. 264; forbids the removal of property into Fort, M. i. 264; insubordinate conduct of his officials, K. iii. 377; improperly treated by his subordinates, K. iii. 415; illness of (July 3), K. iii. 379; forced by ill health to resign his power to a commission, M. i. 266; resumes authority, and retires into Fort, K. iii. 381, M. i. 268; his excessive devotion to detail, K. iii. 414; sinks under over-work and unkindness, K. iii. 414, 415; his health broken by anxiety, M. i. 288; his death at Ágrá (Sept. 9), K. iii. 416, M. i. 290; notification of his death in Official Gazette, M. i. 291.

Commander-in-Chief and Governor-General are in official collision (1856), K. 394. Sir Patrick Grant succeeds Gen. Anson as (June 17), M. i. 29; his presence in the field wanted, M. i. 31; clings to routine work at Calcutta, instead of taking the field, M. i. 31; his reasons for not taking the field, M. i. 30; his reasons unsound, M. i. 31; his sound, but extraordinary reason, for not taking the field, M. i. 32; selects Gen. Havelock to command army in the field, M. i. 32.
See also Anson, Gen.; Grant, Sir Patrick; Campbell, Sir Colin.
Commissariat, the stumbling-block to immediate advance, K. ii. 154; danger of not maintaining establishment, K. ii. 168.
Compensation to Sepoys, for variable prices of commodities, K. i. 316 n.
Composition of Sepoy Army, in 1857, K. i. 621-626.
Concession or resistance, policy of, K. i. 322.
Condition of Northern India in July, K. ii. 411.
Confidence in English power revives in the Panjáb (June), K. ii. 291, 292.
Conflict of English authorities, their disastrous effects, K. i. 320.
Conolly, Lieut., attempts to stop mutiny at I'rinpúra (Aug. 22), M. ii. 558; refuses to escape without the two sergeants and their wives, M. ii. 560; the mutineers keep him, and send away the sergeants and their families, M. ii. 561; allowed to depart by mutineers, M. ii.

Conolly, Lieut.—*cont.*
562; account of his treatment by I'rinpúra mutineers, M. ii. 593.
Conspiracy for general rising of Native Army, evidence in support of, K. ii. 108, 109; not absolutely proved, K. ii. 110.
Conspiracy at Patná (1845), K. i. 304.
Contention between chief officials in Oudh (1856), K. i. 400.
Control, Board of, averse to maintenance of title of Dehlí sovereigns, K. ii. 19; conflict with Court of Directors, K. ii. 19.
Cookworthy, Capt., his feat at Nárnúl (Nov. 16), M. ii. 116.
Cooper, Capt. Joshua, his unrecognised deed of heroism at Sebastopol, M. ii. 591.
Cooper, Ensign Richard, his daring leap at assault of Sikandar Bágh, Lakhnau (Nov. 16), M. ii. 182; wounded at Sikandar Bágh, M. ii. 184; his daring gallantry never officially mentioned, K. ii. 186 n.
Cooper, Lieut., hand to hand with four Gházís, M. ii. 529.
Cooper, Mr., Deputy Commissioner at Amritsar, secures Goviudgarh, K. ii. 436.
Coopland, Mrs., her keen insight into character, M. i. 174; her description of the fearful suspense at Gwáliár, M. i. 171 n., 173 n.; spared by mutineers at massacre of Gwáliár, M. i. 175 n.; her practical experience of the feigning confidence policy, M. i. 172 n.
Corbett, Brig. Stuart, in command at Mián Mír, his character, K. ii. 428; resolves to disarm troops at Mián Mír,

Corbett, Brig.—*cont.*
K. ii. 429; successfully disarms Sepoys there (May 13), K. ii. 432; sends troops to Amritsar, K. ii. 434.
Corfield, Col., fights his way to Sahasrám (May 11, '58), M. ii. 480.
Cornwallis, Lord, his policy towards the Rájpúts, M. ii. 576.
Corporal punishment abolished in Sepoy Army (1832), K. i. 272; revived in Sepoy Army (1842), K. i. 273.
Cortlandt, Van, assists Edwardes to attack Múltán, K. i. 29.
Cosserat, Capt., killed in attack on Kúrsí (March 22, '58), M. ii. 412.
Cotgrave, Midshipman, his energy and bravery at Hetampúr (May 11, '58), M. iii. 462.
Cotter, Major, attacks Machhí Bháwan with his guns (March 16, '58), M. ii. 401.
Cotton, Brig. Sydney, commands at Peshúwar in May, K. ii. 453; his character, 453; resolves to disarm three Sepoy regiments at Peshúwar, K. ii. 478; disarms three regiments of Sepoys (May 22), K. ii. 479.
Cotton, Col., supersedes Brig. Polwhele at Ágrá (Aug. 5), K. iii. 410, M. i. 285.
Couper, Mr. George, his buoyant and active spirit, M. i. 484.
Court, Mr. M. H., Magistrate of Alláhábád, his character, M. iii. 438; uses his large powers with judgment, M. iii. 442; his extraordinary monetary duties, M. iii. 444.
Court of Inquiry into mutinous conduct of 3rd Cavalry at Mírat, K. ii. 46.

Court of Directors, *see* Directors, Court of.
Court-martial at Mírat, charge against the 3rd Cavalry mutineers, K. ii. 48.
Cox, Major, attacks and defeats rebels at Amorhá (June 9, '58), M. iii. 282.
Craigie, Capt., rides to the gaol at Mírat on first notice of outbreak (May 10), K. ii. 64.
Craigie, Lieut., sent to protect Núriá, M. iii. 275; repulses rebels at Núriá (Aug. 29, '58), M. iii. 276.
Craigie, Mrs., preserved at Mírat by faithful Sepoys (May 10), K. ii. 70.
Crawford, Brig., commands artillery at final attack on Lakhnau, M. ii. 171.
Crimean War, rumours concerning, in India, K. i. 342; its effect on Persia, K. i. 412.
Crommelin, Capt., commands mining parties at Phillips' garden, Lakhnau, M. ii. 159.
Cross, Lieut., commands Firozpúr Regiment advancing from Lakhnau Residency (Nov. 6), M. ii. 206.
Cumberlege, Col., outwitted by Kunwar Singh (April 20,'58), M. ii. 475; disarms 4th Light Cavalry at Nágpúr, M. iii. 114.
Cuppage, Mr., murdered at Jánpúr (June 8), K. ii. 238.
Cunliffe, Mr., his murder at Bairám Ghát, K. iii. 478.
Cureton, Capt., his gallantry at Naghína, M. ii. 517; routs an an enormous body of rebels (April 21, '58), M. ii. 518.
Currie, Sir Frederick, appointed Resident at Lahor (1847), K. i. 15; his minute on the Kiráolí question, K. i. 93 *n.*

THE HISTORIES OF THE INDIAN MUTINY. 41

Curtis, Capt., commands advance guard of Gen. Penny's column (Apr. '58), M. ii. 501.
Curzon, Capt., pursues Dákhá mutineers, but fails to catch them, M. ii. 432.
Cust, Mr., his description of the hasty sentences of amateur judges in disturbed districts, M. iii. 441.
Cuttack, *see* Katták.

D.

Da Costa, Capt., his death at the storming of the Imámbárá, Lakhnau (Mar. 14, '58), M. ii. 391.
Daháin, Brig. Berkeley cuts up the rebels at (July 14, '58), M. iii. 280.
Dájí Krishna Pandit, his administration at Kolhápúr, M. iii. 36.
Dákhá, attempt to disarm Sepoys at (Nov. 22), M. ii. 419; Sepoys resist disarmament, M. ii. 420; Midshipman Arthur Mayo, bravely captures a gun, M. ii. 420; Lieut. Lewis attacks and defeats Sepoys, M. ii. 420; Government of India sends detachment to cut off mutineers from, M. ii. 421.
Mutineers from, threaten Jalpaigorí, M. ii. 431; they seize Cháwa Ghát (Dec. 26), M. ii. 431; Mr. Yule marches against them, M. ii. 431; they elude his pursuit, M. ii. 432; and out-manœuvre him (Dec. 28). M. ii. 432.
Jang Bahádur orders his lieutenant to attack the mutineers from, M. ii. 434; the

Dákhá—*cont.*
mutineers escape from both Major Richardson and Mr. Yule, M. ii. 435; and succeed in reaching Oudh, M. ii. 436; and ultimately take refuge in Bhútán, M. ii. 340.
Dakhan, futility of only attempt to disturb, M. iii. 129.
Dalaur, village near Jagadíspúr, fortified by Kunwar Singh, M. i. 128; gallant charge of the 10th Foot at, K. iii. 143.
Dal Ganjan, captured and executed by Capt. Ternan, M. iii. 108.
Dalhousie, Lord, his character, K. i. 354; purity of his intentions, K. i. 359; his deficiency in imaginative power, K. i. 356.
Created Governor-General (1848), K. i. 16; character of his administration, K. i. 1; strength of his Government, K. i. 358; energetically promotes enlightenment of India, K. i. 185; encourages female education, K. i. 187; establishes railways and telegraphs in India, K. i. 192, 193.
His confidence in the Sepoy Army, K. i. 203; disinclined to change military system, K. i. 330; fails in attempt to send a Bengal regiment to to Birmá, M. iii. 477; favourable to local volunteer corps in India, K. iii. 10.
Not the originator of the annexation policy, K. i. 355; annexes the Panjáb (1849), K. i. 47, M. i. 152; frames schemes for the administration of the Panjáb, K. i. 48; condemns the Lahor Board, K. i. 60; condemns the action of Sir C. Napier in granting increased allowances to Sepoys

Dalhousie, Lord—*cont.*
in Panjáb (1850), K. i. 316–323.
Annexes Pegu, K. i. 66; settles administration of Pegu, K. i. 67.
His policy of lapsed succession, K. i. 69; policy of "lapse," K. i. 71, 73.
Annexes Sitárá, K. i. 74.
Annexes Nágpúr, K. i. 83, M. iii. 481; on the Nágpúr succession (1854), K. i. 85 *n*.
Declares Jhánsí lapsed to the British, K. i. 91, M. i. 182. iii. 481; his minute on the Jhánsí succession, K. i. 91; reasons for annexing Jhánsí, K. i. 92.
Shows no respect to the right of adoption, M. iii. 23; refuses to recognise right of adoption, M. iii. 481; refuses privilege of adoption to chief of Nargúnd, M. iii. 23; approves the succession of Madan Pál to the Kiráolí ráj, K. i. 96; extinguishes the Nawábship of the Carnatic (1854), K. i. 111; extinguishes the Ráj of Tanjor (1855), K. i. 111; refuses to-recognise Náná Sáhib as Bájí Ráo's heir, K. i. 103, M. iii. 482.
His scheme for administering without annexing Oudh, K. i. 144; his scheme tantamount to annexation, K. i. 145.
Resigns (1856), K. i. 353; consents to remain in India to superintend annexation of Oudh, K. i. 147; annexes Oudh (1856), K. i. 148.
His policy with respect to the Emperor of Dehli, K. ii. 15; seeks to suppress the kingly dignity of Dehli sovereigns, K. ii. 16; desires to

Dalhousie, Lord—*cont.*
garrison the residence of Dehli sovereigns, K. ii. 17; wishes to secure the magazine at Dehli, K. ii. 17; hopes to remove Dehli sovereigns to the Kutb, K. ii. 18; stays action against Dehli sovereigns, K. ii. 24.
His measures assist the outbreak of mutiny, M. iii. 388.
Dalílpúr, Col. Lugard defeats the rebels at (May 27, '58), M. ii. 480.
Dalton, Capt., Acting Commission of Chutiá Nágpúr, M. ii. 134; mutineers steal his elephants, M. ii. 135; forced to abandon Ránchí, M. ii. 135; restores order in Hazáríbágh, M. ii. 136.
Asks for a European regiment for Hazáríbágh, M. ii. 137; government promise to send him troops, M. ii. 138; he is forced to abandon Hazáríbágh (Aug. 13,) M. ii. 139; returns to Hazáríbágh with a few of Rattray's Sikhs, M. ii. 139.
His services in Western Bihár, M. ii. 436; and Lieut. Graham completely defeat rebels at Palámau (June 21, '58) M. ii. 441 *b*.
Daly, Capt. Henry, commands Guide Corps in May, K. ii. 465; his noble enthusiasm, K. ii. 467; his gallant charge (June 18), K. ii. 551; induced to burn a village on his way to Delhí, K. ii. 468.
Dalyell, Lieut.-Col., killed in attack of Niraulí (Sept. 15), M. iii. 107.
Dam-Dam, School of Musketry established at, K. i. 489; dangerous proximity to Calcutta of Sind Amírs in, M. i. 22;

Dam-Dam—cont.
excitement at, aggravated by official delay, K. i. 511; Sepoys at, disarmed (June 14), K. iii. 29.
Damoh, part of Ságar territory, M. iii. 88; plundered by mutinous 52nd N. I., M. iii. 107; recovered by Gen. Whitlock (March 4, '58), M. iii. 193.
Dánápúr, description of station, M. i. 65; its contiguity to Patná, M. i. 40; allegiance of troops at, tampered with (1845), K. i. 304, 308.
Sepoy regiments stationed at, K. iii. 63, M. i. 40; urgency for disarming Sepoys at, K. iii. 64; the only European regiment between Calcutta and Lakhnau stationed at, M. i. 41; but one European regiment between Dánápúr and Mírat (June 1), M. i. 6.
Lord Canning neglects to disarm Sepoys at (June 1), K. iii. 64, M. i. 5; Gen. Lloyd reports Sepoys as trustworthy (June 2), K. iii. 66, M. i. 45; Mr. W. Tayler presses for disarmament of Sepoys at, M. i. 50; merchants of Calcutta also press on Lord Canning their disarmament, M. i. 63; no difficulty in disarming them, M. i. 46; the opportunity for doing so, K. iii. 89; Lord Canning's reasons for not disarming these Sepoys, K. iii. 65.
Lord Canning temporises with Sepoys at, M. i. 47; Gen. Lloyd acts in the same manner, K. iii. 68; Lord Canning refuses to disarm Sepoys, M. i. 64; Gen. Lloyd also refuses to disarm them, M. i. 50; summary of Government de-

Dánápúr—cont.
cisions with respect to disarming Sepoys at, M. i. 64.
Preliminary excitement at, K. iii. 66; disturbed by rush of panic-struck Europeans (June 1), K. iii. 77.
Disarmament of Sepoys at, permitted by Sir P. Grant, K. iii. 90; Gen. Lloyd shrinks from responsibility, M. i. 64; he detains two companies of 37th Regiment, M. i. 65; and decides on depriving Sepoys of percussion-caps, K. iii. 91, M. i. 65; the method of doing this, K. iii. 92; the extreme injudiciousness of Gen. Lloyd's measure, M. i. 66; but he succeeds in moving percussion-caps from magazine, M. i. 67.
Gen. Lloyd resolves to take percussion-caps from persons of Sepoys, M. i. 68; Gen. Lloyd goes on board steamboat during disarmament of Sepoys (July 25), K. iii. 94, M. i. 67.
The mutiny breaks out (July 25), K. iii. 93, M. i. 68; the Government mainly responsible for mutiny at, M. i. 71.
Why the mutiny was not suppressed, M. i. 67; European troops burn Sepoys' huts and await orders, M. i. 70; escape of the mutineers, K. iii. 95; they start for Árá unmolested (July 25), K. iii. 96, M. i. 70; orders for their pursuit issued too late, M. i. 70.
Gen. Lloyd thinks of entrenching himself at (July 26), K. iii. 101, M. i. 76; Mr. W. Tayler begs him not to do so, K. iii. 101.
Gen. Lloyd at last resolves to pursue mutineers (July

Dánápúr—*cont.*
27), M. i. 78; he sends riflemen up the Son to stop them, M. i. 76; the riflemen are stopped by a sand-bank, M. i. 78; another party of troops sent after mutineers (July 29), M. i. 79; feeble efforts after escape of mutineers, K. iii. 107. Mutineers joined by Kunwar Singh, M. i. 76; mutineers assisted across Son by Kunwar Singh, M. i. 79; they besiege A'rá (July 27), M. i. 78.
The third attempt, under command of Capt. Dunbar, against mutineers, K. iii. 109, M. i. 79; Capt. Dunbar's expedition falls into ambuscade (July 29), K. iii. 112, M. i. 85; disastrous retreat of the expedition, K. iii. 113, M. i. 86; slaughter of A'rá relieving force at Son ferry, M. i. 87; return of the shattered fragment of Capt. Dunbar's expedition (July 30), K. iii. 115, M. i. 89; number of survivors of the ill-fated expedition, K. iii. 116 and *n*, M. i. 88.
Rage of inhabitants against Sepoys, K. iii. 115; British troops attempt to bayonet friendly Sepoys at, K. iii. 122.
Gen. Lloyd refuses to assist Major Eyre, M. i. 106 *n.*
Gen. Lloyd's actions at, disapproved by Lord Canning, K. iii. 170; he is ordered to be tried by court-martial, M. i. 115.
Effect of mutiny at, upon Bhágalpúr, M ii. 131; and upon Hazáríbágh, M. ii. 134.
Daniell, Mr., assistant magistrate at I'táwá, M. i. 160; goes to Hindú temple with Mr. Hume to capture troopers, M.

Daniell, Mr.—*cont.*
i. 161; shot through the face in attempting to assault the temple, M. i. 162.
Daraopúr, the fort of the noble-minded Rájá Hanmant Singh, M. i. 407.
Darby, Capt., storms the breach at Jhánsí (Apr. 3, '58), M. iii. 167.
Daríábád, Capt. W. H. Hawes commands at, K. iii. 479, M. i. 408; mutiny at (June 9), K. iii. 480, M. i. 409; Capt. Hawes endeavours to move treasure, but fails, M. i. 408; he again tries to move treasure, and produces mutiny, K. iii. 480, M. i. 409; miraculous escape of Capt. Hawes, K. iii. 481.
Davidson, Major Cuthburt, Resident with the Nizám, M. iii. 119; success of his policy in Haidarábád, M. iii. 125.
Attacked in Residency, Haidárábád (July 17), M. iii. 121; rebels attack, M. iii. 122; receives reinforcements (July), M. iii. 124.
Forms Haidarábád column, for service in Central India (Aug.), M. iii. 124; makes military demonstrations against Shorápúr, M. iii. 126; sends Capt. Campbell to Rájá of Shorápúr (Jan. '58), M. iii. 127.
Davies, Lieut., of the Enniskillens, holds Hot-Mardán against mutineers, K. ii. 483.
Davis, Private, his bravery at Rúiyá (Apr. 15,'58), M. ii. 507.
Dawson, Capt., and Mr. Kavanagh storm and capture Sandíla (July 30,'58), M. iii. 284.
Dawson, Capt., of the Military Train, killed at Dalílpúr (May 27, '58), M. ii. 480.

Debí Bakkas Ráí, seized by Lieut. Graham at Palámau, M. ii. 438.

Debidín Misr, conspicuously gallant havildár at Lakhnau, M. ii. 156 n.

Defenceless condition of Northern India, K. ii. 111.

Dehlí Field Force, siege-train reaches (June 4), K. ii. 188; enters Alípúr (June 5), K. ii. 188; gunners for siege-train, reach Ambálá from Firozpúr, K. ii. 189; Sepoys escort siege-train to the Satlaj, K. ii. 189; strength of siege-train, K. ii. 189 n; command of, assumed by Sir H. Barnard (May 27), M. i. 11.

Delhí and Alláhábád, imminent peril of road between (June 1), M. i. 5.

Dehlí, the story of, K. ii. 3.

Descriptive Details. — Description of, K. ii. 513; the fortifications of, M. ii. 7; defences of, K. ii. 521; description of defending walls, M. ii. 8; the gates of, K. ii. 522; the Palace, or Fort of, K. ii. 522; the Díwán-i-Khás at, K. iii. 701.

Description of the ridge at, K. ii. 516, M. ii. 9; Hindú Ráo's house at, K. ii. 517; Metcalfe House at, traditions concerning, K. ii. 543; Sabzí-Mandí, its position, K. ii. 518; Najafgarh Canal at, K. ii. 515; ancient observatory at, K. ii. 518; Flagstaff Tower at, K. ii. 517; condition of Flagstaff Tower (May 11), K. ii. 92 n; Sepoy cantonments at, their position, K. ii. 82.

Troops.—Sepoy garrison of, K. ii. 523; strength of Sepoy garrison, M. ii. 2 n; troops in cantonment (May 11), K. ii.

Dehlí—*cont.*
83; Main Guard, held by British officers and Sepoys (May 11), K. ii. 86.

The Mutiny. — Excitement in palace, during spring of 1857, K. ii. 41; troops in the town, ready for revolt, K. ii. 83; they fraternise with mutineers from Mírat (May 11), K. ii. 84, 85; murder of Douglas, Hutchinson, and the Jenningses (May 11), K. ii. 80; Royal family join the mutineers, K. ii. 93; the Dehlí Bank gutted, and occupants murdered, K. ii. 81; the compositors of Dehlí Press slaughtered, and the house destroyed, K. ii. 81, 82; troops of the Main Guard break into mutiny, K. ii. 94.

Flight of Europeans.—Officers and ladies escape from the Main Guard (May 11), K. ii. 95; ladies and children of cantoument, collect in the Flagstaff Tower, K. ii. 92; cantonment troops rise in revolt (May 11), K. ii. 95; officers and ladies at cantonments allowed to escape, K. ii. 96; the flight from cantonments, K. ii. 96; fearful dangers of flight from, K. ii. 97; compassionate acts of some Natives during flight, K. ii. 98.

Defence of the Magazine.—Imperial residence, commands the chief magazine of upper India, K. ii. 17; position of magazine, K. ii. 17 n; magazine attacked (May 11), K. ii. 89; preparations for its defence, K. ii. 89; the nine heroic defenders of the magazine, K. ii. 88, 90; explosion of great magazine (May 11), K. ii. 87, 90; four of the de-

Dehlí—*cont.*
fenders escape the explosion, K. ii. 90.

The Massacre. — Christian prisoners in, K. ii. 98, 99; the massacre of 50 Christians at, in cold blood (May 16), K. ii. 99.

The Advance against.—State of Sepoy garrison in July, K. ii. 606; political significance of seizure of, K. ii. 1; probabilities of saving (May 10), K. ii. 106; Gen. Anson fears to advance on, K. ii. 148; strength of the first force which advanced against (May 23), K. ii. 158; moral effect of first defeats of mutineers before, K. ii. 196.

Preliminary Operations against.—British position before, K. ii. 514; dangerous proximity to British position of suburbs, K. ii. 518, 519; defences of the Mound in rear of right, K. ii. 575 *n*; constitution of first investing force, K. ii. 524; state of Commissariat during July, K. ii. 598; cheerfulness in camp, K. ii. 597; sports of the men in camp, K. ii. 599; quinine served out as a ration, K. ii. 600.

Startling news in camp, K. ii. 601; passions aroused in camp by news of massacre of Káhnpúr, K. ii. 602.

Proportion of Native servants to European soldiers, K. ii. 604 *n*; fidelity of Native attendants, K. ii. 549; rough treatment of Native attendants by British, K. ii. 605; devotion of Native driver at, K. ii. 604 *n*.

British force the besieged not the besiegers, K. ii. 587;

Dehlí—*cont.*
the Force rests entirely on the Panjáb, K. ii. 600; belief in easy capture of the town, K. ii. 525; its speedy capture anticipated by Government, M. i. 3; the ease with which former captures had been effected, M. i. 3.

Reid's picquet, disposition of troops, K. ii. 545 *n*; Metcalfe House, occupied by British, June 12, K. ii. 545.

Sepoy attacks.—Sepoy artillery superior to that of the English (June), K. ii. 548; annoying fire from Morí bastion, K. ii. 549; sortie of Sepoys (June 12), K. ii. 544; Reid's picquet attacked, K. ii. 546; desertion of Native Irregular Cavalry (June 12), K. ii. 546.

Desperate sortie from (June 15), K. ii. 547 and *n*.

The centenary of Plassey (June 23), K. ii. 554; fierce sortie on that day, K. ii. 554; Sepoys attack bravely, K. ii. 555; but are repulsed at all points, K. ii. 556.

Sepoys try to cut off our rear communications (July 4), K. ii. 565; English protect rear of the Ridge, K. ii. 567.

Discussion of Assault. — Brig. Wilson counsels delay in assault of, K. ii. 533; Gen. Reed also advocates delay, K. ii. 534; plan of *coup-de-main* for capture of, K. ii. 526; *coup-de-main* delayed by act of Brig. Graves, K. ii. 528; revised scheme of assault, K. ii. 529, 530; council of war (June 14), K. ii. 531; Col. Greathed three times counsels immediate assault of (June 14, 16, 18), K. ii. 530, 532, 539

Dehlí—cont.
another council of war (June 16), K. ii. 532; idea of immediate assault abandoned, K. ii. 537; irritation in camp at delay in assault, K. ii. 541.
Further Operations. — Reinforcement received by Sepoys, K. ii. 539; Sepoys driven from Kishan-ganj and Trevelyan-ganj (June 17), K. ii. 547; repulse of sortie of June 17, K. ii. 539 *n*; Sepoy method of attack, K. ii. 540; English begin to act on offensive (June 17), K. ii. 547; Sepoys attack English rear (June 18), K. ii. 550.
British camp receives re-inforcements (June 23), K. ii. 555; Brig. N. Chamberlain arrives in camp (June 24), K. ii. 561; Gen. Barnard's view of his position at end of June, K. ii. 559; fresh re-inforcements reach the camp (between June 26 and July 3), K. ii. 564 *n*.
Assault again projected and postponed (July 3), K. ii. 563; reasons for again abandoning projected assault, K. ii. 564 *n*.
Death of Gen. Barnard, by cholera (July 5), K. ii. 567; result of the first month's fighting, K. ii. 570; English force miserably deficient in siege matériel, K. ii. 571.
Col. Baird Smith counsels assault (July 6), K. ii. 573; question of assault argued by him, K. ii. 572; Gen. Reed assumes command of force before Delhí (July 6), K. ii. 573.
Renewed activity of Sepoys. —Great sortie of July 9, K. ii. 574; splendid Cavalry charge of Sepoys, K. ii. 580; they

Dehlí—cont.
penetrate British camp, K. ii. 575; flight of English Artillery and Dragoons, K. ii. 580; perilous position of Major Tombs, K. ii. 578; courageous promptitude of Fagan of the Artillery, K. ii. 581 *n*; English counter-attack on Sabzí-Mandí, K. ii. 582.
Sortie against Hindú Ráo's House (July 14), K. ii. 583; English counter-attack against attackers of Hindú Ráo's House, K. ii. 584; heavy casualties on this day, K. ii. 585; Chamberlain badly wounded, K. ii. 584.
Gen. Wilson takes command. —Gen. Reed resigns command to Brig. Wilson (July 17), K. ii. 586; Gen. Wilson's irritability, K. iii. 587; he lacks confidence in his men, K. iii. 589; want of sympathy between Gen. Wilson and Baird Smith, K. iii. 548.
Retirement of British force discussed (July 17), K. ii. 588; Col. Baird Smith scouts the idea of withdrawal, K. ii. 589, 590; he demands a siege-train, K. ii. 591.
Sepoys make their last attack from Sabzí-Mandí (July 18), K. ii. 592; another sortie from the town (July 23), K. ii. 592; pursuit of defeated Sepoys forbidden, K. ii. 593; Sepoys restore bridge over Najafgarh Canal (Aug. 2), K. ii. 646.
Last re-inforcements from Panjáb.—Arrival of Gen. Nicholson (Aug. 7), K. ii. 646; his coming felt to be a great deliverance, K. ii. 648; he visits the picquets immediately, K. ii. 649.

Dehlí—cont.
English attack of Ludlow Castle (Aug. 12), K. ii. 650. Panjáb Movable Column arrives (Aug. 14), K. ii. 652. Neville Chamberlain's pertinacity, K. iii. 546; Baird Smith's wounds, and his exhaustless energy, K. iii. 547n; Gen. J. Nicholson's impetuosity, K. iii. 548; his victory at Najafgarh secures safety of siege train, M. ii. 1; arrival of last re-inforcements, K. iii. 549.

Preparations for the Siege.— Mutinous feeling in camp, through Gen. Wilson's delay in assaulting, K. iii. 550.

Gen. Wilson's letter to Major Baird Smith (Aug. 20), K. iii. 551, M. ii. 2 n; Major Baird Smith's reply, K. iii. 553, M. ii. 5; Brig. Wilson yields to the opinion of Major Baird Smith, M. ii. 6; and authorises him to press the siege, K. iii. 554; but throws responsibility of assault on the Major, M. ii. 6; who becomes solely responsible for success of the siege works, K. iii. 576.

Sepoys neglect to strengthen outer defences, M. ii. 9; impossibility of scientific approach, K. iii. 556; Major Baird Smith's plan of attack, K. iii. 545, 557, 702, M. ii. 10; arrival of siege-train and reinforcements (Sept. 6), M. ii. 10.

The Siege begins. — Gen. Wilson's order of the day (Sept. 7), K. iii. 555, M. ii. 11; construction of Reid's battery (Sept. 7), M. ii. 12; erection of battery No. 1, or Brind's battery, K. iii. 559, 560, M. ii. 12; Sepoys attempt to destroy

Dehlí—cont.
No. 1 battery before completion, M. ii. 14; Major Brind completes his battery under fire, K. iii. 561; Major Reid diverts fire from working parties, M. ii. 14; completion of No. 1 battery, M. ii. 15; destruction of Morí bastion by No. 1 battery, M. ii. 15; left section of No. 1 battery takes fire, M. ii 16; heroic conduct of Lieut. Lockhart, M. ii. 16; destruction of No. 1 battery, K. iii. 563.

Construction of No. 2 battery (Sept. 8), K. iii. 564, M. ii. 18; Khudsayah Bágh, and Ludlow Castle occupied by English, M. ii. 18; construction of No. 3 battery (Sept. 9-11), K. iii. 565, M. ii. 19; British Engineers induce Kashmír troops to work in battery, K. iii. 566; mortar battery in Khudsayah Bágh, K. iii. 567; construction of No. 4 battery (Sept. 10), M. ii. 20; calm courage of Native working parties, M. ii. 20 n; necessary delay in breaching, K. iii. 568.

Effect of fire from English batteries, M. ii. 21; Sepoys begin to arm curtain of walls, K. iii. 569; they attempt to silence English batteries, M. ii. 21; Kashmír bastion silenced and breach effected, K. iii. 570; Sepoys succeed in enfilading No. 1 and No. 2 batteries, M. ii. 22.

No 3 battery opens, with tremendous effect, K. iii. 571, M. ii. 23; the Water Bastion crushed into ruins, K. iii. 571; two breaches effected, M. ii. 24; midnight examination of breaches, K. iii. 584, M. ii.

Dehlí—cont.
24–26; they are reported practicable (Sept. 13), K. iii. 581. Capt. A. Tayler's fertility of resource, K. iii. 573; Baird Smith and Alex. Taylor complement each other, K. iii. 574.
Preparation for Assault.—Major Baird Smith advises assault (Sept. 14), M. ii. 26; fearful responsibity of delivering the assault, K. iii. 586; Gen. Wilson agrees to assault, M. ii. 27; his anxiety on morning of its delivery, M. ii. 33; Baird Smith's knowledge of the streets, K. iii. 588; general plan of the assault, K. iii. 589, M. ii. 32.
Meeting of officers preparatory to assault, K. iii. 581.
Constitution of assaulting columns, K. iii. 582, 583; the strength of each, M. ii. 27–29; John Nicholson chosen to lead the assault, K. iii. 580; he leads the first column, M. ii. 27; Brig. Jones commands second column of assault, M. ii. 27; Col. Campbell commands the third column, M. ii. 28; Major C. Reid commands the fourth column, M. ii. 28; Brig. Longfield commands the reserve, M. ii. 29; antecedents of leaders of assaulting colums, M. ii. 30; short delay in the assault, K. iii. 585.
The Assault.—The assault delivered (Sept. 14), K. iii. 591, M. ii. 33; first column enters the breach, M. ii. 34; escalade, of the first column, K. iii. 593; attack of the second column, K. iii. 592; success of second column, M. ii. 35; capture of Morí Bastion, K. iii. 594; first and second

Dehlí—cont.
columns penetrate to Kábul gate, M. ii. 44; capture of Kábul gate, K. iii. 595.
Nicholson resolves to capture Lahor gate, K. iii. 597, M. ii. 45; the rush to Láhor gate, M. ii. 46; fearful slaughter in lane leading to the gate, M. ii. 47; failure to capture Láhor gate, M. ii. 48; Gen. Nicholson falls mortally wounded, M. ii. 48; death of Gen. Nicholson (Sept. 22), K. iii. 599, M. ii. 83.
Attack of third assaulting column, K. iii. 599; M. ii. 38; third column penetrates to Begam Bágh, K. iii. 604, M. ii. 39.
Explosion party for Kashmír gate, M. ii. 32; explosion of the gate, K. iii. 600, 601, 673, M. ii. 37; survivors of exploding party, rewarded with Victoria Cross, K. iii. 602.
Attack of fourth column, K. iii. 604; the column advances with only one gun, K. iii. 607, M. ii. 40; noble devotion of Gorkhá troops, K. iii. 605; the fourth column hampered by Jammú troops, K. iii. 606; precipitancy of Jammú troops, M. ii. 40; Major Reid's plan of attack on Kishan-ganj, M. ii. 579; the attack commenced, M. ii. 41; Major Reid falls wounded, K. iii. 608, M. ii. 41; and makes over command to Capt. Lawrence, M. ii. 42; on fall of Major Reid, Captain Muter assumes command, M. ii. 43; Major Lawrence and Capt. Muter both exercise command, K. iii. 694–697; Capt. Muter withdraws fourth column from assault, K. iii. 695; repulse of fourth column, K.

Dehlí—*cont.*
iii. 608, M. ii. 43; conduct of troops of fourth column, K. iii. 609; opinion of Sir Herbert Edwardes on action of fourth column of assault, after the fall of Major Reid, M. ii. 581.
Cavalry support the assaulting columns, K. iii. 612, M. ii. 49; courageous calmness of Cavalry, K. iii. 613, 614, M. ii. 50.
The reserve column occupies part of city (Sept. 14), M. ii. 51; unsupported condition of third column, M. ii. 51; third column retires to the Church for the night, M. ii. 52.
Critical position of English camp during assault, K. iii. 611; gallantry of enemy during assault, K. iii. 610; result of first day's assault, M. ii. 53; the brave who fell in the first day's assault, M. ii. 54; casualties of first day's assault, K. iii. 616.
Capture of the City.—Gen. Wilson inclined to abandon city after first day's assault, K. iii. 617, M. ii. 55; Gen. N. Chamberlain urges that the positions gained should be held, M. ii. 56; Baird Smith insists on continuing the assault, K. iii. 618, M. ii. 57; Capt. Edwin Johnson sustains the feeble mind of Gen. Wilson, M. ii. 57 *n.*
Disorder after assault, M. ii. 58; the English troops given up to drunkenness, (Sept. 15), K. iii. 619; Gen. Wilson destroys the alcoholic liquors, K. iii. 620, M. ii. 58.
Evacuation of Kishan-ganj by Sepoys (Sept. 16), M. ii.

Dehlí—*cont.*
59; capture of magazine, K. iii. 621, M. ii. 59; great dejection of Gen. Wilson during assault, K. iii. 622; Gen. Wilson's desponding state, M. ii. 60 *n.*
Capt. Taylor's project for worming through the houses, K. iii. 626; the troops advance through the walls of the houses (Sept. 17, 18), M. ii. 61; and gradually capture the city, K. iii. 625.
Importance of Lahor Bastion, K. iii. 632; Greathed attacks the Láhor gate and fails (Sept. 18), K. iii. 628, M. ii. 62; capture of Láhor bastion (Sept. 19), K. iii. 627; despairing condition of Gen. Wilson, K. iii. 630, M. ii. 63; capture of Burn bastion, M. ii. 65; capture of Jamá Masjid by Major Brind, M. ii. 66; capture of the Palace, K. iii. 633, 676, M. ii. 67; Lieut. Aikman cuts off Sepoy retreat from King's Palace, M. ii. 68; and secures the Selimgarh, M. ii. 68; the town deserted by Natives (Sept. 19), K. iii. 635; complete possession of town gained (Sept. 20) K. iii. 631.
Capture of the King.—Bakht Khán urges the king to fly with him, M. ii. 71; the king resolves to fly (Sept. 19), M. ii. 71; and retires to tomb of Humáyun, M. ii. 73; Mirzá Iláhi Bakhsh induces the king to break with the Sepoys, M. ii. 73; and accomplishes his purpose (Sept. 20), M. ii. 74; the king surrenders to Hodson (Sept. 21), K. iii. 645-647, M. ii. 76; Mr. Saunders receives the king from Capt. Hodson, M. ii. 77.

Dehlí—*cont.*
Capture of the Princes.—
Hodson disarms the people at
Humáyun's Tomb, K. iii. 649;
he captures Princes, K. iii.
648-650, M. ii. 78; Hodson
shoots the Princes, K. iii. 650,
M. ii. 79.
Restoration of order.—Interior of city, after assault, M.
ii. 69; remarks on the siege,
M. ii. 84; reprisals at, after
capture, K. iii. 636, 637; task
of securing possession of city
given to Major Brind, M. ii.
81; who clears the city of
secret assassins, K. iii. 637,
638; Major Brind vigorously
restores order, M. ii. 82; systematic plunder of the city by
the Sikhs, K. iii. 640; English troops respect Native
women during attack, K. iii.
639.
Special acts of gallantry.—
Minor incidents of the siege,
K. ii. 596; the artillery materially assist in the street
fighting, M. iii. 501; splendid
exertions of Bengal Artillery,
M. ii. 23; noble services of
the heavy Artillery, K. ii. 595,
iii. 578, 579; improvised artillerymen, K. iii. 572.
Unrecorded heroism at, K.
ii. 594; many brave officers
neglected through official
punctilios, M. ii. 17 *n*; the
heroes of the siege, M. ii. 86;
splendid audacity of Col.
Coke (Aug. 21), M. ii. 512 *n*;
Capt. Renny's bravery at capture of magazine, K. iii. 700.
After the siege.—Gen. Penny
takes command after Gen Wilson, M. ii. 105; Brig. Wilson
proceeds to Himálayas on sick
certificate, M. ii. 105; effect
of fall of Dehlí on Gwáliár,

Dehlí—*cont.*
M. ii. 147; the Queen's proclamation read with ceremony
(Nov. 1, '58), M. iii. 395.
Dehlí, Emperor of, influence of
his name, K. ii. 2; state of the
Emperor, in 1804, K. ii. 6;
last *nazar* to him, K. ii. 661.
Dehlí, King of, agents tamper
with Sepoys in his name in
1845, K. i. 306, 308; ceremonial usages of his family,
K. ii. 685; profligacy of his
household, K. ii. 10; summary
of argument touching reduction of his dignities, K. ii.
22; his dignities diminished,
K. ii. 9; extinction of his titular dignity urged, K. ii. 14;
Board of Control oppose continuance of his title, K. ii. 19;
the titular dignity supported
by Court of Directors, K. ii.
19 *n*; amount of stipend of,
K. ii. 12, 13 *n*; increase of
stipend refused, K. ii. 12; his
palace intrigues, K. ii. 24;
Lord Canning's terms with
respect to his successor, K. ii.
32; the King joins the insurgents (May 11), K. i. 596, ii.
80; his trial in the Díwán-i-
Kháss (Jan. 27, '58), M. iii.
387; sentenced to transportation for life, M. iii. 387.
See also Bahádur Sháh.
Dehrá Dún, its situation, extent,
and garrison, M. iii. 419; Mr.
Keene chief civil officer at, M.
iii. 419; Major Reid commands Gorkhas at, M. iii.
420.
Major Reid marches from,
to Mírat (May), M. iii. 420;
Mr. Keene raises recruits to
maintain order, M. iii. 420;
Rájá Lál Singh, a political
prisoner, places his retainers
at the service of Mr. Keene

4 *

Dehrá Dún—*cont.*
(May), M. iii. 420 ; Mr. Keene organises patrols at irregular times at (June), M. iii. 421.
The Jálándhár brigade of rebels march upon (June 15), M. iii. 421; Mr. Keene marches against them, M. iii. 421 ; the Jálándhár brigade escapes, M. iii. 422.
Mr. Keene sends the treasure up to Masúrí (June 15), M. iii. 421 ; difficulty of procuring money and food, M. iii. 423 ; Mr. Keene issues paper money on his own responsibility, M. iii. 424 ; he carries the district through the Mutiny unharmed, M. iii. 424.
Dehrá Ismáíl Khán, Malwáí Sikhs at, plan a mutiny, M. iii. 305 ; leaders of threatened insurrection arrested (July 20, '58), M. iii. 306.
De Kantzow, nobly risks his life in quelling mutiny at Mainpúrí, K. iii. 225 ; his noble courage and presence of mind, M. i. 158; checks the torrent of mutiny, M. i. 159 ; and succeeds, K. iii. 227 ; for three hours keeps mutineers at bay, M. i. 159; Ráo Bhawání Singh bravely comes to his assistance, M. i. 159 ; the treasury saved, M. i. 160.
Lord Canning's letter of thanks to, K. iii. 227, M. i. 160; he receives command of police force, M. i. 160.
His gallantry at attack on Alígarh (Aug. 20), M. i. 287 ; greatly distinguishes himself at attack on Kankar (April 6, '58), M. ii. 500; at Sháhjahánpúr (April 30, '58), M. ii. 522 ; desires to charge the

De Kantzow—*cont.*
Maulaví's army (May 3, '58), M. ii. 533 ; protects Rájá of Powáin (Aug. '58), M. iii. 275.
Delafosse, Lieut., saves the magazine of the entrenchment at Káhnpúr, K. ii. 320.
Dempsey, Private Dennis, rescues Ensign Erskine and wins the Victoria Cross, K. iii. 122 and *n*, M. i. 88 *n*.
Deogarh, mutiny at (Oct. 9), M. ii. 139, 445.
Deogarh Bárí, Tántiá Topí collects his scattered force at (Dec. 10, '58), M. iii. 355.
Deo-Náráyan Singh, nobly assists the English at Banáras (June 5), K. ii. 231.
Deonaraiu Singh, *see* Deo-Náráyan Singh.
Departments of the Army, obstruction of, K. ii. 146.
Derby, Lord, begs Lord Canning to retain the Governor-Generalship, M. iii. 258 ; draws up Queen's proclamation to India, M. iii. 389.
Desáí of Jámbotí, discontented sufferer under Inám Commission, M. iii. 29.
Desáí of Kittúr, the discontented chief of Lingayat population, M. iii. 29.
Desáís of Nipaní, discontented sufferers under Inám Commission, M. iii. 28.
Desáí of Wantmúrí, a discontented chief, M. iii. 29.
Deserters, Punishment of, at Pesháwar, K. ii. 481.
Desmazures, an indigo-planter, assists in suppressing outbreak at Gorakhpúr jail, M. iii. 450.
Despatches, the stereotyped praises of, valueless, M. ii. 196.

THE HISTORIES OF THE INDIAN MUTINY. 53

Despondency of English in Calcutta a source of anxiety to Lord Canning, K. i. 611.
Dewássa, *see* Diwásá.
Dhanchuá, Capt. Rattray fights the rebels at (Nov. 6), M. ii. 446.
Dhaorára, *see* Dhaurára.
Dhár, governed by Ánand Ráo Púńr, a lad, M. iii. 68; description of fort of, M. iii. 71; Col. Durand recommends annexation of, K. iii. 347; Court of Directors refuse to annex, K. iii. 348.
    Mutiny at (July), K. iii. 347; Capt. Hutchinson suspects Darbár of complicity in rebellion at, M. iii. 69; mercenaries of, get possession of fort (Aug. 31), M. iii. 69; mercenary troops plunder Bhúpáwar and Sirdárpur, M. iii. 69; mercenaries advance to oppose Col. Durand (Oct.), M. iii. 70; Col. Durand arrives at (Oct. 22), M. iii. 70; mercenaries defeated and driven into fort, M. iii. 70; fort besieged by Col. Durand (Oct. 25). M. iii. 71; mercenaries evacuate fort unperceived (Oct. 31), M. iii. 72; Darbár escapes punishment, and the Rájá is pardoned, M. iii. 73 *n.*
Dharma Sabhá, society for the conservation of Hindúism, K. i. 493.
Dhárwár, insurrection at (May 28, '58), M. iii. 240; insurgents join Bhím Ráo, chief of Kopáldúrg, M. iii. 243; they are attacked by Col. Hughes, M. iii. 243; mutinous state of troops (July), M. iii. 31; reinforcements arrive (Aug.), M. iii. 33.
Dhaulána, inhabitants declare

Dhaulána—*cont.*
against English, and attack loyal village of Solána, M. iii. 435; Mr. Dunlop captures village and gives the land to inhabitants of Solána, M. iii. 436.
Dhaulpúr, Rájá of, generously assists fugitive women and children, K. iii. 318.
Dhaurírá, Rájá of, protects fugitives from Mallápúr, K. iii. 479; and those from Sítápúr and Sháhjáhánpúr, M. i. 382.
Dhaurára, Gen. Franks repulsed at (March 4, '58), M. ii. 337.
Dholpúr, one of Rájpút states, M. i. 245 *n*; Sepoys at, threaten Ágrá (Sept. 9–11), M. ii. 95.
Dholpúr, the Rájá of, generously assists English refugees, M. i. 176.
Dhúdu Pant (=Dhundu Pant), *see* Náná Sáhib.
Dhulíp Singh, the mother of, K. i. 3; she plots against the Resident, K. i. 15; and is banished to Shaikhpúr, K. i. 15; she is removed from Shaikhpúr to Benares, K. i. 30; and ultimately dies in England, K. i. 48.
Dhulíp Singh, Mahárájá, deposed by the British (1849), K. i. 47; punished for the crime of others, M. iii. 484 *n*.
Dhúndhiyá Khere, Bení Mádhava defeated at, by Col. Evelegh (Nov. 10, '58), M. iii. 292; Bení Mádhava totally defeated at (Nov. 24, '58), M. iii. 292.
Dhundu Pant, *see* Náná Sáhib.
Dick, Lieut., his gallantry and death at storming of Jhánsí (April 3, '58), M. iii. 169.

Dilherí, Rájá of, his difficulties, M. iii. 93; disgraced by Government, M. iii. 94; Capt. Ternan befriends him in his disgrace, M. iii. 94; he gratefully defends Capt. Ternan when Mutiny breaks out; M. iii. 95.
Dilkhusha, see Lakhnau.
Dinájpúr, Mr. Elphinstone-Dalrymple, Collector at, M. ii. 427; mutinous 11th Irreg. Cavalry march on (Dec.), M. ii. 427; Mr. Elphinstone-Dalrymple prepares to defend his post to the last, M. ii. 428; mutineers move off to Púrniá, and do not attack, M. ii. 428.
Dinapore, see Dánápúr.
Dinkar Ráo, the able Díwán of Sindhiá, K. iii. 311; has no love for the English, M. iii. 488; his loyalty, M. i. 176; probable reason for his loyalty, M. iii. 206.
Directors, Court of, advantages of their public dinners, K. i. 374; fear any act implying change of policy on the part of the British, K. ii. 21; support titular dignity of Dehlí sovereigns, K. ii. 19 n; disclaim responsibility of interfering with dignity of Dehlí sovereign, K. ii. 21; conflict with Board of Control, K. ii. 19; discourage extensions of territory, K. i. 123; refuse to annex petty state of Dhár, K. iii. 348; the Court abolished (Aug. 2, '58), M. iii. 389; no more blameworthy for the Mutiny than the English Ministry, M. iii. 389.
See also East India Company.
Dirg Bíje Singh, undertakes to protect refugees from Sikrorá, M. i. 391.

Disarmament only a temporary and local advantage, K. iii. 244.
Sepoys disarmed at Banáras (June 4), K. ii. 221; the disarmament mismanaged, K. ii. 224.
Beneficial effect of disarming Sepoys in the Panjáb, K. ii. 420, 480.
The 64th Regiment disarmed (June), K. ii. 497.
Sepoys at Bárákpúr disarmed (June 14), K. iii. 28, M. i. 27.
Suggestions for disarming Natives in Calcutta (July 20-22), K. iii. 56.
Disarmament of Patná, K. iii. 84.
Disbandment of mutinous regiments, the policy of, K. i. 297; 66th Regiment disbanded at Govindgarh (1850), K. i. 315.
Disbandment of the 19th Regiment (March '57), K. i. 545; peaceably carried out, K. i. 546.
Disbandment of the 7th Regiment at Lakhnau (May 4), K. i. 590.
The 34th Regiment disbanded in May, K. i. 585.
Discipline in the Army, undermined by the Government itself, M. iii. 476.
Ditryá, see Ditraiyá.
Ditraiyá, Rájá of, sides with the English, K. ii. 260.
Diwálí, nature of festival, M. iii. 52.
Diwásá, Tántiá Topí's troops scattered by Brig. Showers at (Jan. 16, '59), M. iii. 366.
Dixon, Col., his politic treatment of the Mairs, K. iii. 354; summons Mairwárá battalion to Ajmír (May), M. i.

Dixon, Col.—*cont.*
150; dies at Biáwar, K. iii. 355.
Doáb, the, anarchy rampant therein (June), M. iii. 440.
Dodgson, Capt., his character, and services at the A'lambágh, M. ii. 362; assists Gen. Havelock under a shower of bullets, M. ii. 205.
Dongarpúr, one of the Rájpút states, M. i. 245 *n.*
Doondoo Punt, *see* Náná Sáhib.
Doorma Soobha, *see* Dharma Sabhá.
Dorandá, *see* Dúranda.
Dorin, Mr., Member of Supreme Council (1856), K. i. 387; his character, K. i. 388; recants his adverse decision against Mr. Tayler, M. i. 121.
Dost Muhammad, of Kábul, desires to extend his dominion westwards, K. i. 413; annexes Kandahar, K. i. 414; he is distrusted (1856), K. i. 430; confers with English at Peshátwar (1856), K. i. 433; his friendship doubted, K. ii. 448; he offers to prove that Russia instigated Persia to seize Hirát, K. i. 448 *n.*
Douglas, Brig., sent in pursuit of Kunwar Singh (April 16, '58), M. ii. 473; pursues Kunwar Singh to Sikandarpúr, M. ii. 474; defeats Kunwar Singh at Sikandarpúr (April 20, '58), M. ii. 475; crosses the Ganges to attack Kunwar Singh, M. ii. 478.
   Succeeds Col. Lugard in command in Sháhábád (June '58), M. ii. 483; his method of rooting out the rebels, M. ii. 483; causes seven columns to converge on Jagadíspúr (Oct. '58), M. ii. 485; defeats

Douglas, Brig.—*cont.*
rebels at Kárísát (Oct. 14, '58), M. ii. 486; guided by Major Havelock, keeps close on the rebels' track, M. ii. 489; rebels escape by a mistake (Oct. 21, '58), M. ii. 490; surprises and defeats main body of Sháhábád rebels (Nov. 24, '58), M. ii. 492.
Douglas, Capt., Commandant of King of Dehlí's Palace Guard, K. ii. 76; escapes to Emperor's palace on outbreak of Mutiny (May 11), K. ii. 78; attempts to stop the mutineers at Dehlí, K. ii. 78; his murder, K. ii. 80.
Douglas, Lieut., killed at Rúiyá (April 15, '58), M. ii. 506.
Dowling, Private William, wins the Victoria Cross at Lakhnau (Sept. 27), M. ii. 154 *n.*
Downfall of the English ráj in 1857 prophecied, K. i. 485; Mr. E. A. Reade on the prophecy concerning, K. i. 486.
Doyle, Capt., killed in attempt to stop Firoz Sháh at I'táwá (Dec. '58), M. iii. 360.
D'Oyley, Capt., his splendid conduct at Sháhganj, M. i. 274; dies fighting his guns at Sháhganj (July 7), K. iii. 385, M. i. 275.
Drummond, Mr., Magistrate at A'grá, thinks the Mutiny transient, K. iii. 201; disbelieves in danger at A'grá, K. iii. 202; opposes Mr. Colvin's proposal to retire into A'grá Fort, M. i. 149; his opinion changed by mutiny at Mathurá, M. i. 166.
Duffy, Private, his daring and ingenuity in recovering a gun, M. i. 540.
Duleep Singh, *see* Dhulíp Singh.
Dum-Dum, *see* Dam-Dam.

Dunbar, Capt., commands first relieving party sent to Árá, K. iii. 109; charged with incompetency, K. iii. 110; a brave, but inexperienced, officer, K. iii. 111.

Starts from Dánápúr (July 29), M. i. 79; advances to relieve Árá, M. i. 84; mismanagement of his expedition, K. iii. 111; his expedition falls into an ambuscade (July 29); K. iii. 112, M. i. 85; he is shot dead (July 29), K. iii. 112, M. i. 85.

His expedition finds shelter in an empty tank, K. iii. 113, M. i. 86; disastrous retreat of his expedition, K. iii. 113, M. i. 86; complete rout of the remnant of his expedition (July 30), K. iii. 114.

Dúndia Khéra, *see* Dhúndhiyá Khere.

Dunley, Sergt., his daring leap into Sikandar Bágh (Nov. 16), M. ii. 183, 197.

Dunlop, Capt., commands troops at Jhánsí, M. i. 183.

Dunlop, Mr. R. H. W., Magistrate and Collector at Mírát (June), M. iii. 425.

Hastens to the camp at Dehlí, M. iii. 425; ordered to Mírat (June 13), M. iii. 425; rides through Bhágpat on the eve of rebellion, M. iii. 426; assumes charge of Mírat (June 15), M. iii. 426; enlists nine Sikhs as nucleus of a force (June 17), M. iii. 427; organises a Volunteer force at Mírat, M. iii. 428.

Captures and burns Basaud (July), M. iii. 431; force with which he marched on Barauth, M. iii. 431; collects revenue along the east Jamná Canal by the mere prestige of

Dunlop—*cont.*
his name, M. iii. 432; his fight with the rebel Bagdá at Barká, M. iii. 433; defeats Sáh Mall's army, and kills him, M. iii. 434; storms and captures village of Akalpúra, M. iii. 435; defeats the rebels at Galautí (July 21), M. iii. 436; defeats the rebels at Bhowan (Aug.), M. iii. 436.

Important services rendered by his little column of Volunteers, M. iii. 436; his description of the Khákí Rísála, and the cause of its success, M. iii. 437.

Dupuis, Col., commands Artillery at attack on Tántiá Topí (Dec. 5), M. ii. 267.

Dúranda, mutiny at (Aug.), M. ii. 135.

Durand, Col. Henry Marion, officiating agent at Indor, K. iii. 323, M. i. 199; description of the Residency at Indor, M. i. 215; districts under his superintendence, M. i. 204; his character, K. iii. 324, M. i. 199; his former services, M. i. 202; his great capacity, his foresight, and splendid achievements, M. iii. 84-86.

Applies to Lord Elphinstone for arms for Holkar's troops (June 5), K. iii. 327; anticipates outbreak at Máú (June 13), K. iii. 329; not deceived by outward loyalty of troops, M. i. 211; his policy for preserving order at Indor, M. i. 208; summons Bhíls to Indor, M. i. 208.

Receives guard of troops from Holkár (May 14), M. i. 209; his critical position at Indor, during June, M. i. 210; his account of Native allies

THE HISTORIES OF THE INDIAN MUTINY. 57

Durand, Col.—*cont.*
at Indor, K. iii. 332 *n*; his chance of safety lies in approach of Gen. Woodburn's column, M. i. 212; Gen. Woodburn's column diverted to Aurangábád, M. i. 212; and halts there, M. i. 213.

Hears false report of fall of Dehlí, M. i. 213; intention to remove treasure from Residency falsely imputed to him, M. i. 218 and *n*.

Mutiny at Indor, breaks out (July 1), M. i. 215; attacked by Holkar's troops, K. iii. 330; Holkár's troops the assailants of Residency, M. i. 217; the attack headed by Sa'adat Khán, M. i. 217; conflicting accounts of office of Sa'adat Khán, M. i. 217 *n*.; the Residency guard join in the revolt, M. i. 219; suddenness of attack on Residency, M. i. 217; position of troops defending Residency, M. i. 216; Col. Travers fights the rebel guns, M. i. 221; Capt. Hungerford ordered to Indor, K. iii. 345, M. i. 221; Residency reduced to 31 defenders, M. i. 223; imminent danger to occupants of Residency, M. i. 224; Cavalry resolve to abandon the place, M. i. 224; hopelessness of waiting for Hungerford's battery, M. i. 225; the Residency abandoned (July 1), M. i. 226.

Retreats from Indor, K. iii. 332; the skill and success of his retreat, M. i. 242; his reasons for retreat from Indor, K. iii. 333, 343; reasons against his quitting Residency, K. iii. 344; his abandonment of the Residency

Durand, Col.—*cont.*
criticised, M. i. 241; his rejoinder to reasons against, K. iii. 344; his retreat from Indor, disapproved of by Lord Elphinstone, K. iii. 345, 346.

Charges Holkár with treachery, K. iii. 346; believes in Holkár's loyalty up to July 1, M. i. 227; Holkár's conduct during attack of Residency reconcileable with loyalty, M. i. 230; Holkár's communication with mutineers after attack, M. i. 231; Holkár writes to all British authorities for help, M. i. 232; Holkár held free from complicity in mutiny, M. i. 233.

Finds it impossible to retreat to Maú, M. i. 236; cut off from Simrol pass by Holkár's troops, M. i. 239; his troops refuse to force Simrol pass, M. i. 239; resolves to retreat on Aurangábád, M. i. 239; his cavalry demand to retreat on Sihor, M. i. 238, 240; he reaches Sihor (July 4), M. i. 241; he urges Gen. Woodburn to secure the line of the Narbadá, M. i. 242; hurries on to Hoshangábád, M. i. 242; starts for Aurangábád, M. i. 243; effect of his letter to Mr. Plowden at Aurangábád, M. iii. 17 *n*.; Lord Elphinstone's letter to him (July 27), M. iii. 18 *n*.; he arrives at Asírgarh and joins Col. Stuart, M. iii. 60; review of his march from Indúr to Asírgarh, M. iii. 60.

Receives request for aid from Mahárájá Hokar (July 30), M. iii. 61; offer to march into Indúr (July 30), M. iii. 61; authorises officers to dis-

Durand, Col.—*cont.*
regard orders to abandon line of the Narbadá, M. i. 243; marches back with Brig. Stuart's column to Máú (Aug. 2), M. i. 243, iii. 61; is joined by some European infantry (Aug. 5), M. iii. 62; asks orders of Lord Canning with respect to Holkár, M. iii. 63. Resolves to attack Mandíswar rebels (Aug.), M. iii. 66; strength of his force to oppose Mandíswar rebels (Aug.), M. iii. 66 *n.*; receives concurrent news of advance of Mandíswar rebels (Oct.), M. iii. 67; marches on Dhár (Oct. 19), M. iii. 68, 69; defeats Dhár mercenaries (Oct. 22), M. iii. 70; besieges fort of Dhár (Oct. 25), M. iii. 71; storms the fort of Dhár and finds it empty, M. iii. 72; reaches Hiranza, on the Chambal (Nov. 19), M. iii. 76; crosses the Chambal unopposed, M. iii. 77; encamps near Mandíswar, M. iii. 78; arranges his troops to meet the rebels, M. iii. 78; drives off rebel attack (Nov. 20), M. iii. 79; interposes between Mandíswar and Nímach rebels (Nov. 22), M. iii. 79; meets Nímach rebels at Goráriá, and has a severe struggle with them (Nov. 24), M. iii. 80; crushes out rebellion in Málwá, M. iii. 81.
Disarms Holkár's Cavalry (Dec. 14), M. iii. 82; orders disarmament of Holkár's troops under threat of doing it himself, M. iii. 82; disarmament of Holkár's troops, M. iii. 83; marches into Indor (Dec. 14), M. iii. 82; visits Holkár, M. iii. 83.

Durand, Col.—*cont.*
Honours conferred on him since 1857, K. iii. 350; his services unrewarded, M. iii. 86.
Durnford, Col., defeats the rebels at Kámpságar (Oct. 16, '58), M. ii. 486.
Durriabad, *see* Daríábád.
Duval, Lieut., his good service in western Bihár, M. iii. 463.
Dúvím, Col. Corfield drives the rebels from (May 12, '58), M. ii. 480.

E.

Eagerness of British troops to attack Dehlí, K. ii. 190.
East India Company, authority failing in Oudh, K. ii. 407 *n.*, 408; abolished, as a scapegoat to public opinion (Aug. 2, '58), M. iii. 388.
Edmonstone, Mr. George, deputed to arrest the King of Oudh to Calcutta, K. iii. 37; arrests the King (June 15), M. i. 28.
Privately explains the purport of Lord Canning's proclamation (March '58), M. iii. 249; his further despatch on Lord Canning's Oudh proclamation (March 31, '58), M. iii. 252.
Edwardes, Mr. Herbert, Commissioner at Pesháwar (1856), K. i. 431; his character, K. i. 27; marches against Múltán (1848), K. i. 26; desires the alliance of Dost Muhammad (1856), K. i. 432; his confidence in Pesháwar, K. ii. 455;

Edwardes, Mr.—*cont.*
testifies to the reality of the Wahábí conspiracy at Patná, K. iii. 165 *n.*
His just appreciation of the nature of the rising at Mírát, K. ii. 456; counsels the immediate formation of a moveable column, K. ii. 455; his instructions to commander of Guide Corps (May 13), K. ii. 465; he and John Nicholson prudently exalt Gen. Reed into a useless position, K. ii. 458–460; he disarms 24th Regiment at Fort Mackeson (July 8), K. ii. 637 and *n.*; energetically opposes Sir J. Lawrence's suggestion to cede the Panjáb, K. ii. 614, 615; his opinion on action of the fourth column at storming of Dehlí, after the fall of Major Reid, M. ii. 581.

Edwards, Mr. Williams, Magistrate and Collector at Badáon, M. i. 323; the solitary European in charge of Badáon, K. iii. 281; his character, K. iii. 282; his views on settlements, K. i. 166.
He is joined by three Englishmen (June 1), K. iii. 285, M. i. 323; applies to Baraílí for help, M. i. 323; flies from Badáon, and is protected by a Muhammadan gentleman (June 1), K. iii. 286; reaches Dharampúr (June 10), M. i. 324; arrives at Káhnpúr in safety (Sept. 1), M. i. 325.

Eden, Major William, Political Agent at Jaipúr, K. iii. 353, M. i. 257.

Education, spread of, alarming to Bráhmans, K. i. 185; and Natives generally, K. i. 186; female education additional

Education—*cont.*
source of alarm to native mind, K. i. 187.

Elgin, Lord, receives Lord Canning's demand for assistance (June 3), K. iii. 183; at first scarcely realizes the gravity of affairs in India, K. iii. 183; again receives urgent appeals for help from Lord Canning, K. iii. 184; arrives in Calcutta (Aug. 8), K. iii. 185, M. i. 140; places the *Shannon* and *Pearl* at the disposal of Lord Canning, K. iii. 186, M. i. 141.

Ellenborough, Lord, on the fidelity of the Sepoy, K. i. 300; distributes *mitháis* (sweets) to the Sepoys, after the battle of Mahárájpúr, K. i. 300; conceals disunion among English authorities, K. i. 321; offers Private Secretaryship to Lord Canning, K. i. 369; abolishes *nazarána* to Emperor of Dehlí, K. ii. 12; his prudent course with respect to Sindhiá, 1843, M. i. 151; his generous treatment secures the loyalty of Sindhiá, M. i. 152, iii. 489.
Receives Lord Canning's proclamation to Oudh without explanation, M. iii. 251; sharply condemns it, M. iii. 255; his hasty condemnation repudiated by Lord Derby, M. iii. 258; resigns office, M. iii. 257.

Elliot, Lieut. Minto, his guns do much execution in street fighting in Dehlí, M. iii. 501.

Elphinstone, Lord, Governor of Bombay, his character and antecedents, K. i. 421, M. iii. 2, 3; his boldness and generosity of conduct, M. iii. ix.; his foresight and true mili-

Elphinstone, Lord—*cont.*
tary instincts, M. iii. 54; his generous trust in his subordinates, M. iii. 497; places complete trust in Mr. Forjett, M. iii. 46.
His clear perception of the nature of the outbreak of May, M. iii. 496; re-appointed Governor of Bombay (July), K. ii. 413; named by three Secretaries of State to succeed Lord Canning, M. iii. 498; sends immediate help to Calcutta and the Panjáb, M. iii. 5; cheerfully responds to Lord Canning's application for aid, K. i. 611; first suggests to Lord Ashburnham that he should offer the China expeditionary force to Lord Canning, M. iii. 4; sends Capt. Jenkins to the Mauritius and the Cape for troops, M. iii. 6; suggests a special steamer to England for reinforcements, M. iii. 7.
Strips Bombay of European troops (May), M. iii. 8; his policy of offensive defence, M. iii. 9; organises column under Gen. Woodburn, M. iii. 9; seeks to equip a special column for Central India, M. i. 213; orders Gen. Woodburn to march on Máú (June), M. iii. 10; again presses Gen. Woodburn to advance to Máú (June 22), M. iii. 13; Gen. Woodburn excuses himself from advancing (June 25), M. iii. 14; almost peremptorily orders Gen. Woodburn to advance to Máú (June 27), M. iii. 15; reluctantly yields to the opinion of Sir H. Somerset (July), M. iii. 17; his letter to Col. Durand (July 27), M. iii. 18 *n*.; sends a co-

Elphinstone, Lord—*cont.*
lumn of troops to Rájpútáná (July), M. iii. 19.
Grants plenary powers to Mr. Seton-Karr, M. iii. 30; his bold but prudent orders to Col. Le Grand Jacob, M. iii. 39 *n*.
Supports Capt. Hungerford's irregular acts, K. iii. 345; disapproves of Col. Durand's retreat from Indor, K. iii. 345, 346; fully persuaded of Holkar's innocence, K. iii. 349.
Assists Major Davidson to overawe Shorápúr (Jan. '58), M. iii. 126; eager for the capture of Jhánsí, M. iii. 154; his grave apprehensions at presence of Ráo Sáhib in Nagpúr territory (Oct. '58), M. iii. 343.
Elphinstone - Dalrymple, Mr. Francis Anstruther, Collector at Dinájpúr, his character and antecedents, M. ii. 427.
English authorities, disastrous effects of conflicts among, K. i. 320.
English considered helpless after Mírat mutiny, K. ii. 108 *n*.
English courage manifesting itself in divers ways, K. ii. 206.
English avoid alarming the natives, K. ii. 105.
English Government, equally responsible with the Court of Directors, for the Mutiny, M. iii. 388.
English in India, blind to danger, K. ii. 103.
English ladies compelled to grind corn for Náná Sáhib, K. ii. 354; leave Bárákpúr for Calcutta (March), K. i. 543; their noble endurance

English ladies—*cont.*
at Káhnpúr, K. ii. 322; and at Lakhnau, M. i. 487.
English officers, swift executions by, K. ii. 235.
English officers of Sepoy regiments, K. i. 213.
English policy, the defeat of, K. ii. 104.
English Press, its dangers, K. iii. 14.
English troops, their avenging spirit uproused, K. ii. 170; their rage at Káhnpúr, K. ii. 386; exact a fearful retribution there, K. ii. 387, 388.
English soldier and Indian Sepoy compared, K. i. 254.
English, unprepared for attack, K. ii. 104.
Englishmen, gratify vengeance at Alláhábád, K. ii. 270.
English, Major, strength of his party, M. ii. 141; sent by Col. Fischer towards Dúranda, M. ii. 140; sent against the Rámgarh mutineers, M. ii. 141; catches the mutineers at Chattra (Oct. 2), M. ii. 141; defeats them there, M. ii. 141, 436.
Enmity between Sikh and Sepoy, K. ii. 472.
Erskine, Major, created Commissioner of Jabalpúr (1855), M. iii. 90, 102; his mental calibre, M. iii. 92; his injudicious advice counteracted by Col. Durand, M. iii. 85; receives report about mysterious chapátís, but disregards it, M. iii. 92.
Etawah, *see* I'táwá.
European inhabitants of Calcutta demand martial law (Aug.), K. iii. 178; Lord Canning refuses request, K. iii. 179.
European troops available, at

European troops—*cont.*
commencement of Mutiny, K. i. 600, 601; paucity of, near Bárákpúr and Barhampúr (March), K. i. 527; only one regiment between Calcutta and Lakhnau (May), K. ii. 111, M. i. 41; the services of many lost by not disarming suspected Sepoys, M. i. 22; some detained at Barhámpúr to watch Sepoys, M. i. 39; others kept at Dánápúr for the same purpose, M. i. 42.
Evelegh, Col., hastens to assistance of Mohan on the Sáí, M. iii. 283; meets and cuts up rebels at Husainganj (Aug. 8, 58), M. iii. 283; defeats rebels at Miyánganj (Oct. 5, '58), M. iii. 287; captures fort of Simrí (Nov. 9, '58), M. iii. 291; defeats Bení Mádhava at Dhundhiyá Khere (Nov. 10, '58), M. iii. 292.
Ewart, Col., implores his regiment of Sepoys to stand to its duty, K. ii. 307; commands rear-guard of Sir Colin Campbell's army, M. ii. 177; succeeds in bringing in baggage with rear-guard (Nov. 15), M. ii. 178.
Bravely enters the Sikandar Bágh at assault, M. ii. 183; captures standard at Sikandar Bágh with his own hand, M. ii. 187; his gallant deed at the Sikandar Bágh never mentioned officially, M. ii. 186 *n*.
Ewart, Lieut., dies during retreat from Naogáon, M. i. 196.
Executions at Pesháwar (May), K. ii. 482.
Execution of mutineers at Hazára (June), K. ii. 495.

Extinction of titular dignity of Emperor of Dehlí, urged, K. ii. 14; but resisted by Court of Directors, K. ii. 19 n.

Eyre, Major Vincent, his character and antecedents, M. i. 93; his former services, K. iii. 134; his noble courage in Afghanistan, M. i. 93 n.

Offers his services to Gen. Lloyd, M. i. 94; hastens to protect Gházípúr (July 29), M. i. 95; stops at Baksar to concentrate, M. i. 95; returns to Baksar and finds some troops, M. i. 95.

Assumes entire responsibility of relief of A'rá, M. i. 96; shrinks from no responsibility, K. iii. 137; improvises a field force, K. iii. 135; picks up help at Baksar, K. iii. 136; number of his A'rá relieving force, K. iii. 137; his relieving force, M. i. 97 and n.; appoints Capt. Hastings his staff officer, M. i. 97; assisted to transport and commissariat by Mr. Bax Ironside, M. i. 97; hears of Capt. Dunbar's defeat, M. i. 98; reports what he is doing to Gen. Lloyd, K. iii. 137; Gen. Lloyd refuses to assist him, M. i. 106 n.

His march to A'rá, K. iii. 138, M. i. 96; meets the besiegers of A'rá (Aug. 2), K. iii. 138; his advance opposed in force, M. i. 99; enemy cut through bridge at Balautí, M. i. 98; he repulses first attack of mutineers, K. iii. 138; forces his way through a wood, M. i. 99; tries a flank movement along railway embankment, M. i. 100; he is stopped at Bíbíganj, M. i. 100; second attack of muti-

Eyre, Major—*cont.*
neers upon him, K. iii. 139; critical position of his force, M. i. 101; charges upon, and disperses Sepoys, K. iii. 140, M. i. 101; marches into A'rá (Aug. 2), K. iii. 141, M. i. 102.

Disarms the city of A'rá, M. i. 127; punishes criminals at A'rá, K. iii. 142; atones for the feebleness of Government, M. i. 103.

His great feat of arms at A'rá, M. i. 116; the importance of his victory, M. i. 125; he and Mr. Tayler save Bihár, M. i. 103; his troops have unbounded confidence in him, M. i. 126.

He resolves to follow up his victory, M. i. 126; his reinforcements, M. i. 127; encounters and defeats Kunwar Singh at Dálaor, K. iii. 143, M. i. 129; advances against Jagadíspúr (Aug. 11), K. iii. 143, M. i. 127; finally defeats Kunwar Singh, K. iii. 144; and captures Jagadíspúr, M. i. 130; blows up Kunwar Singh's stronghold (Aug. 16), K. iii. 145; destroys the palace and other buildings at Jagadíspúr, M. i. 130.

Immediate results of his brilliant exploit, K. iii. 146, M. i. 131 n.; he is one of the four who preserved Mr. Beadon's line of six hundred miles, M. i. 143.

Ordered to Alláhábád (Aug. 14), M. i. 130; leaves A'rá (Aug. 20), M. i. 131; sent to attack party at Kúdanpati (Sept. 10), M. i. 520; catches the insurgents there, M. i. 521; crushes and annihilates them (Sept. 11), M. i. 521.

Eyre, Major—*cont.*
Commands Artillery advancing from Lakhnau Residency (May 16), M. ii. 206; his services at the A'lambágh, M. ii. 361; beats off rebel attack at A'lambágh (March 16, '58), M. ii. 402.

F.

Faddy, Capt., surprises and disperses party of mutineers near Murádábád, M. i. 326.
Fagan, Adjt., murdered at Máu (July 1), M. i. 235.
Faizábád, Col. Goldney, Commissioner at, K. iii. 460, M. i. 396; troops stationed at, K. iii. 461, M. i. 396; excited state of troops in May, K. iii. 462 *n.*; officers at, store provisions in Capt. Thurburn's house, M. i. 396; but rely on pensioned Sepoys, M. i. 397; and on help from Talúqdárs, M. i. 397; pensioners and Talúqdárs alike fail to help, M. i. 398.
Capt. A. Orr induces Mán Singh to receive all the women and children, M. i. 399; the families of civil officers and subordinates take refuge with Mán Singh (June 7), M. i. 399; mutiny breaks out (June 8), K. iii. 464, M. i. 399; Sepoys give their officers boats and money, and order them to go, K. iii. 465, M. i. 400; but ask 17th N.I. to murder the officers they have helped to escape, K. iii. 466, M. i. 400; fugitives attacked at Begamganj, M. i. 400;

Faizábád—*cont.*
they quit boats and run for life, M. i. 401; fugitives from, murder of Col. Goldney and his party, K. iii. 467, M. i. 401; Col. O'Brien's boat escapes by a ruse, K. iii. 468, M. i. 402; fugitives reach Amorá in safety, M. i. 401; of three boats of fugitives only one man escapes, M. i. 401; Col. Lennox and family escape from town, after departure of boats, K. iii. 469, M. i. 403.
Narrative of Mrs. Mill's escape, K. iii. 687; Rájá Mán Singh finds and protects Mrs. Mills, M. i. 403; Mrs. Mills and children sent into Gorakhpúr by mutineers, M. i. 402; civil officers refused shelter by Mán Singh, M. i. 404; they take to boat, and are robbed of everything, M. i. 404; but succeed in reaching Dánápúr in safety (June 29), M. i. 405.
Fakeer, *see* Faqír.
Fakir-ood-Deen, *see* Fikru-d-Dín.
Fanaticism at Patná, K. iii. 78.
Faqír, excites soldiery at Mirát, K. i. 566.
Farrukhábád, story of leather rupees, circulated at, K. iii. 293; rebellion breaks out in May, K. iii. 292.
Farrukhábád, Tafazzul Husain Khán, Nawáb of, his character, K. iii. 303, 304; becomes bitterly antagonistic to the English, K. iii. 297; he becomes supreme at Farrukhábád, M. i. 346; murders forty Europeans at, M. i. 346; he threatens Powáin (Aug. '58), M. iii. 274; his unauthorised pardon, M. i.

Furrakhábád—*cont.*
347; his Hakím slain at Patiálí (Dec. 17), M. ii. 292.
Farídpúr, Sir Colin Campbell arrives at (May 4, '58), M. ii. 522; again there (May 16, '58), M. ii. 538.
Fathgarh, its population and garrison, K. iii. 296, M. i. 335; Col. G. A. Smith commauds at, K. iii. 294, M. i. 335.
Col. G. A. Smith sends women and children by boat to Káhnpúr (June 3), K. iii. 294; some of the fugitives return (June 13), M. i. 336; several stop at Dharampúr, M. i. 336.
Sepoys obey Col. Smith's order to destroy bridge of boats on approach of Sítápúr mutineers, K. iii. 295, M. i. 336; but they refuse to allow treasure to go into Fort, M. i. 336; Col. Smith and his followers retire into the Fort, K. iii. 295, M. i. 337; Col. Smith's appeal for help, K. iii. 669; arrival of mutinous 41st N.I. at, M. i. 337; Sepoys repulse traitorous overtures (June 17), M. i. 337; but break into mutiny (June 18), M. i. 337.
Col. Smith prepares fort for defence, M. i. 338; he provisions the fort, through delay in Sepoy attack, M. i. 339; the Sepoys place themselves under a Pathán Nawáb, M. i. 338.
Contention between the 10th and 41st Regiments on account of stolen treasure, K. iii. 296, 297; fight between the Sepoys of 10th and 41st Regiments N.I., M. i. 339; Sepoys attack the fort (June

Fathgarh—*cont.*
25), M. i. 339; they fail in direct attack, and take to mining, M. i. 340; they assault, but fail, K. iii. 299; Mr. Jones defeats first attempt to storm fort, M. i. 341; Sepoys establish effective fire against fort, M. i. 341; gallant resistance of garrison of fort, K. iii. 298.
Europeans evacuate fort, K. iii. 300; and attempt to escape in boats, M. i. 342; the boats are fired upon and pursued, K. iii. 300; villagers attack the boats, M. i. 343; fugitive boats from, reach Sangrámpúr, M. i. 343.
Major Robertson's boat takes the ground, M. i. 344; and is then attacked by two boats of Sepoys, M. i. 344; the boats are again attacked, K. iii. 301; gallant charge of five officers against three hundred villagers, M. i. 344; noble conduct of Mr. David Churcher, after destruction of second boat, K. iii. 302; Col. Smith's boat reaches Kúsúmkhor, M. i. 345; Mr. Jones remains at Kúsúmkhor and escapes death by doing so, M. i. 346; last remaining boat reaches Káhnpúr, where all on board are murdered by Náná Sáhib, K. ii. 353, iii. 303, M. i. 336, 346.
Concentration of rebels upon (Dec. 30, 31), M. ii. 300; rebels attempt to destoy suspension-bridge, M. ii. 300; British capture and repair the bridge at (Jan. 1, '58), M. ii. 300; Sir Colin Campbell arrives there, M. ii. 301; Col. Adrian Hope holds the bridge (Jan. 2, '58), M.

THE HISTORIES OF THE INDIAN MUTINY. 65

Fathgarh—*cont.*
ii. 302; spontaneous charge of 53rd Regiment, M. ii. 303; complete defeat of the rebels at (Jan. 2, '58), M. ii. 303; rebels fly to Rohilkhand, M. ii. 304; Sir Colin Campbell enters fort (Jan. 3, '58), M. ii. 305; importance of Sir Colin Cambpell's position at, M. ii. 309.
    Sir Colin Campbell leaves for Káhnpúr (Feb. 1, '58), M. ii. 314; Col. Seaton given command of troops at, M. ii. 311; the place strengthened and prepared by Colonel Seaton, M. ii. 499; Col. M'Causland succeeds Brig. Seaton in command of (May '58), M. ii. 541.
Fathpúr liable to attack on all sides, M. ii. 446; Mr. R. T. Tucker, Judge at, K. ii. 363; the Judge of, beloved by the Natives, K. ii. 364; and openly endeavours to convert the Natives, K. ii. 364; he refuses to leave his post, K. ii. 365; outbreak at (June 9), K. ii. 364; European residents flee, K. ii. 365; fugitives reach Bándá in safety, K. ii. 365.
    Battle of (July 12), K. ii. 360; and defeat of Náná Sáhib's troops, K. ii. 362; the town given up to plunder by the English, K. ii. 363; Brig. Carthew left in command of, M. ii. 446; Col. Barker clears the villages around (Dec. 11), M. ii. 447.
Fawcett, Lieut., killed in fight with Ajít Singh (Sept. 4, '58), M. iii. 336.
Fayrer's house, a post at Lakhnau Residency, M. i. 442.
Fazl Azím, lieutenant of Mahndí

Fazl Azím—*cont.*
Husain, M. ii. 326; falls back on Nasratpúr to oppose Gen. Franks (Jan. '58), M. ii. 328.
Feigning confidence policy of Government, M. i. 21; its fruits show themselves, M. i. 23, 26; Mrs. Coopland's practical experience of, M. i. 172 *n*; its frightful result at Gwáliár, M. i. 176.
Fenwick, Col., retires in disgust from command of Árá relieving force, K. iii. 109 *n.*; charged with knowingly selecting an incompetent officer to command Árá relieving force, K. iii. 110.
Ferozepore, *see* Firozpúr.
Fifty-fifth Regiment, escaped mutineers of, miserably perish in Kohistán, K. ii. 493-495.
Fikru-d-Dín, next in succession to Bahádur Sháh, K. ii. 14, 15; circumcision of, K. ii. 24 and *n.*; agrees to terms of the British with respect to his succession, K. ii. 26; suddenly dies (July '56), K. ii. 27.
Financial Garrison, a post at Lakhnau Residency, M. i. 442.
Finnis, Col., killed while remonstrating with his troops (May 10), K. ii. 59.
Firozpúr, mutiny of 34th Regiment at (1844), K. i. 278.
    State of troops at, K. ii. 438; Mutiny at (May 13), K. ii. 437, M. i. 3; importance of its magazine, K. ii. 442 *n.*; magazine saved, K. ii. 442; Brig. Innes blows up magazines of mutinous regiments, K. ii. 441; flight and pursuit of mutineers from, K. ii. 441.
Firoz Sháh, rebel leader in Oudh, M. iii. 271; commands rebels at Mandíswar (Aug.), M. iii. 66; joins Central

5

Firoz Shah—*cont.*
Indian mutineers (Sept. 26), M. ii. 96; advances his troops from Amjhera to the Bombay road (Oct.), M. iii. 67; retreats from Mandíswar to Mángarh (Nov. 24), M. iii. 81; enters Rohilkhand (Nov. '57), M. iii. 359; forced to retreat from Murádábád (April 21, '58), M. ii. 520; escapes from Murádábád (April 26, '58), M. ii. 521; joins the Maulaví at Sháhjahánpúr (May 12, '58), M. ii. 536; attacks Mohan on the Sáí (Aug. 7, '58), M. iii. 282; operates in Oudh during 1858, M. iii. 359; marches from Sítápúr (Dec. 7, '58), M. iii. 360; attempts to sack Ránod (Dec. 17, '58), M. iii. 362; completely defeated at Ránod (Dec. 17, '58), M. iii. 363; seizes part of Lieut. Stack's convoy, near Rámpúr, M. iii. 364; marches to assist Tántiá Topí in Bánswárá, M. iii. 356; defeated by Capt. Rice, at Sarpúr (Dec. 22, '58), M. iii. 364; hurries to Aruní, M. iii. 364; joins Tántiá Topí at Indragarh (Jan. 13, '59), M. iii. 359, 365; positions of British columns around, M. iii. 365; leaves Tántiá Topí (Jan. 21, '59), M. iii. 367; hidden in the Sironj jungle (April '59), M. iii. 378; disappears into obscurity (Feb. '59), M. iii. 369.

Fischer, Col., commands Madras Sepoys marching from Katák, M. ii. 138; sends Major English towards Dúranda, M. ii. 140; marches on Hazáríbágh (Sept. 13), M. ii. 140; directed to protect the trunk road, M. ii. 141; enters

Fischer, Col.—*cont.*
Bihár with Madras troops (Oct.), M. ii. 445.

Fisher, Col. Sam., commands at Sultánpúr, K. iii. 469; his murder at Sultánpúr (June 9), K. iii. 470, M. i. 406.

Fitzgerald, Brig.-Gen., receives command of combined British and Portuguese troops (Nov. '58), M. iii. 246.

FitzGerald, Lieut. M. M., his guns do much execution in street-fighting in Dehlí, M. iii. 501.

Flagstaff Tower at Dehlí, *see* Dehlí.

Fleming, Mrs., interview with Jawán Bakht, K. ii. 34 n.

Follett, Major, assumes temporary command of Central Indian Column (June), M. iii. 16; is averse to moving from Aurangábád, M. iii. 16; stultifies himself by offering to advance on Máú (July 7), M. iii. 17.

Forjett, Mr., Superintendent of Police, Bombay, K. iii. 408, M. iii. 43; his character, and great acquirements, M. iii. 44; his extraordinary test of the Bombay police, M. iii. 45. Organises force of mounted Europeans (Aug.), M. iii. 43; distrusts the Sepoys of Bombay (Sept.), M. iii. 47; intimates his necessity for disobeying orders, M. iii. 47; hurries to Sepoy lines on outbreak (Sept.), M. iii. 49; defies and quells Sepoy outbreak, M. iii. 50; preserves tranquillity during the Muharram, M. iii. 51; discovers conspiracy at Gangá Parshád's house (Oct.), M. iii. 53; secretly shows Major Barrow his own men conspiring, M. iii. 53.

Forjett, Mr.—*cont.*
His eminent services unrecognised by Government, M. iii. 51 *n.*; substantial gratitude of inhabitants of Bombay to him, M. iii. 51 *n.*, 52 *n.*
Forrest, Lieut., one of the brave Artillerymen who defended the magazine at Dehlí (May 11), K. ii. 88.
Forster, Col., his services in Western Bihár, M. ii. 436; assists in relieving Lieut. Graham from blockade at Palámau (Dec. 8), M. ii. 438; restores order in Singhbhúm (Jan. '58), M. ii. 441 *b*.
Forsyth, Mr. Douglas, energetically collects transport for Gen. Anson's army, K. ii. 160; wins the active support of the Protected Sikh States, K. ii. 162.
Fort William, escape of prisoner from, K. iii. 35 *n.*, 665, 678.
Fox, Lieut., killed at the storming of Jhánsí (April 3, '58), M. iii. 169.
Francis, Capt., skilfully abandons Machhí Bháwan, M. i.429.
Franklyn, Brig., commands at the A'lambágh (Mar. 16, '58), M. ii. 401; defeats rebel attack on the A'lambágh (Mar. 16, '58), M. ii. 402.
Franks, Gen., appointed to command Jánpúr force (Nov.), M. ii. 321; strength of his force there (Nov. 29), M. ii. 325; Capt. H. Havelock volunteers to serve with him, M. ii. 325; he is directed to cover Banáras (Nov.), M. ii. 325; advances to Nasratpúr against Fazl Azím, M. ii. 328; defeats the rebels at Nasratpúr (Jan. 23, '58), M. ii. 328; receives re-inforcement of Cavalry, M.

Franks, Gen.—*cont.*
ii. 327; re-establishes order around Alláhábád (Feb. '58), M. ii. 329.
Marches to Singramáu (Feb. '58), M. ii. 329; enters Oudh, M. ii. 329; defeats the rebels at Chánda (Feb. 19, '58), M. ii. 330; and also at Hamírpúr, M. ii. 331; outmanœuvres Mahndí Husain and enters fort Budháyan (Feb. 21, '58), M. ii. 332; defeats the rebels at Sultánpúr (Feb. 23,'58), M.ii.335; attacks Dhaurára, and is repulsed (March 4, '58), M. ii. 337; results of his successful campaign in Oudh, M. ii. 338.
Marches on Lakhnau (Mar. 4, '58), M. ii. 337; arrives there (March 5, '58), M. ii. 370; storms the Imámbárá (March 14, '58), M. ii. 390; advances to and captures Chíní Bázár, M. ii. 393.
Fraser, Col. Hugh, Chief Engineer at A'grá, his character, K. iii. 203; his personal courage, K. iii. 203 *n.*; builds iron bridge at Lakhnau (1842), K. iii. 435 *n.*
Advises Mr. J. Colvin to distrust Sepoys, M. i. 151; recommends prompt measure of precaution at A'grá, K. iii. 204.
Created Chief Commissioner of A'grá (Sept. 30), M. ii. 96; ceases to be Chief Commissioner of A'grá (Feb. 9, '58), M. ii. 418.
Fraser, Major, of Native Sappers, murdered at Mírat (May 15), K. ii. 178.
Fraser, Mr., Political Agent in Ságar and Narbadá territories, M. iii. 89.
Fraser, Mr. Simon, Commissioner at Dehlí, K. ii. 79; en-

Fraser, Mr. Simon—*cont.*
deavours to secure loyalty of Sepoy Guard at Dehlí, K. ii. 77; murder at Dehlí, K. ii. 79, 665.
French residents at Calcutta, Government declines their offer to raise Volunteers, M. i. 2.
French, Capt., killed in cavalry charge at Ágrá (Oct. 10), M. ii. 101.
French, Capt., destroys rebel boats on the Son (Sept. 20), '58), M. ii. 484.
Ffrench, Lieut., his conspicuous daring at the Sikandar Bágh, M. ii. 197.
Frontier of Panjáb, intrigues along, K. ii. 495.
Fulton, Capt., his skill and daring, at Lakhnau, M. i. 483; his death at Lakhnau (Sept. 14), K. iii. 540, M. i. 483.
Furruckabad, *see* Farrukhábád.
Futtehpore, *see* Fathpúr.

G.

"Gagging Act," passed by Legislative Council (June 13), K. iii. 18, M. i. 19; passed the day before "panic Sunday" at Calcutta, M. i. 23; the Act a mistake, M. i. 21; Lord Canning's unpopularity on account of, K. iii. 24.
Galautí, rebels defeated at, by Mr. Dunlop, M. iii. 436.
Gall, Major, his gallantry in the Málwá campaign, M. iii. 87; leads west attack at storming of Jhánsí (April 3, '58), M. iii. 166; sent to watch garrison of Kotá (April 22,

Gall, Major—*cont.*
'58), M. iii. 173; captures fort of Lohárí (May '58), M. iii. 175.
Galway, Capt., his gallantry at Lakhnau (Sept. 27), M. ii. 154.
Galwey, Col., gallantly carries two villages near Sultánpúr (Aug. 25, '58), M. iii. 273.
Gambhír Singh, Lieut., his conspicuous gallantry at battle of Chánda (Oct. 30), M. ii. 320.
Gangádhar Ráo, becomes Rájá of Jhánsí (1843), K. i. 90; he dies childless (1853), K. i. 90.
Gangá Parshád, his house at Bombay the meeting-place of mutinous Sepoys, M. iii. 53.
Gangá Rám, conspires against the English at Lahor (1848), K. i. 29.
Ganges, anarchy rampant in districts on left bank of, M. iii. 441.
Ganjan Singh, a rebel leader, defeated and slain by Capt. Woolley (Nov.), M. iii. 108.
Garden Reach, abode of King of Oudh at Calcutta, full of disaffected people, M. i. 14, 22, 27; the dangerous occupants of, rendered powerless by arrest of King of Oudh, M. i. 28.
Gardiner, Major, arrests mutinous Sikhs, at Derá Ismáíl Khán (July 20, '58), M. iii. 306.
Gardner, Colour-Sergeant, saves Cameron's life from the Gházís (May 5, '58), M. ii. 527.
Garhákot, description of, M. iii. 144; its garrison (Feb. '58), M. iii. 145; captured and held by Jabalpúr mutineers, M. iii. 107; Sir Hugh Rose arrives

Garhákot—cont.
before (Feb. 11, '58), M. iii.
145; Sir Hugh Rose begins
his attack, M. iii. 145; the
rebels evacuate (Feb. 12, '58),
M. iii. 146.
Gaussen, Major, leads detachment from Ságar towards Lallatpúr, M. iii. 98; captures
fort of Bálábet, M. iii. 99;
his Sepoys compel him to release his prisoners, M. iii. 99.
Gayá, out-station of Patná, K.
iii. 71, M. i. 40; officers at,
K. iii. 151; Mr. Alonzo Money, Magistrate at, M. i. 109.
Disaffection in (June 11),
K. iii. 73; execution for treason at (July 22), K. iii. 152;
effect of Dánápúr mutiny
upon (July 28), K. iii. 153;
ordered to be abandoned by
Mr. Tayler (July 31), M. i.
108.
Mr. A. Money resolves to
abandon treasure at, M. i.
110; inexplicable character of
Mr. Money's first abandonment of treasure at, M. i.
110; Mr. Money urged to return to, for treasure, by Mr.
Hollings, M. i. 111; he repents and returns, with Mr.
Hollings, M. i. 112; Mr. A.
Money condemns himself, M.
i. 112.
The town remains tranquil
after first abandonment, K.
iii. 155; Mr. Money on his
return summons detachment
of 64th Regiment, M. i. 112;
and burns Governmentstamped paper, M. i. 113; he
despatches treasure from
(Aug. 4), M. i. 113; outbreak
at (Aug. 4), K. iii. 157; Mr.
Money flies from town, M. i.
113; and resolves to retire on
Calcutta, M. i. 113; where he

Gayá—cont.
arrived without molestation,
M. i. 114; fortune converts
Mr. A. Money's disobedience
into a triumph, M. i. 115.
Threatened by mutinous
Cavalry after Mr. Money's
return there (Sept. 8), M. ii.
444; Mr. Money induces
Capt. Rattray to march out
and attack Cavalry, M. ii.
444; the Cavalry sweep
round Capt. Rattray and enter the town, M. ii. 445;
saved from plunder by
bravery of Mr. Skipwith Tayler, son of late Commissioner, M. ii. 445.
English forced into intrenchment by revolt in city
(June '58), M. ii. 483.
General condition of Northern
India in July, K. ii. 411.
General conspiracy, evidence in
support of, K. ii. 108, 109.
General Service enlistment, Lord
Canning's opinion of, K. i.
468; native opinion of, K. i.
469; effect of, K. i. 471.
Gerrard, Col., leads expedition
against mutineers in Jodhpúr, M. ii. 109; marches on
Nárnúl, M. ii. 110-113; defeats the mutineers at Nárnúl (Nov. 16), M. ii. 116,
118; his death during pursuit
of mutineers (Nov. 16), M.
ii. 117; Capt. Caulfield assumes command of column
after death of, M. ii. 117;
Col. Seaton sent from Dehlí
to command his column (Nov.
23), M. ii. 118.
Ghághrá, fugitives from Bahráich murdered on banks of,
M. iii. 478.
Ghátampúr, rebels plunder and
burn (Mar. 26), M. ii. 450.
Ghazís, their desperate courage

Gházís—*cont.*
at Alígarh, M. i. 287; desperate conflict with, at Kakraulí (April 30, '58), M. ii. 502; fierce attack of, at Barailí (May 5, '58), M. ii. 526.
Gházípúr, revolt in district of (June), M. iii. 451; Mr. Venables forced to retreat to (July 30), M. ii. 316.
Ghází-ud-Dín Nagar, British victory near (May 31), M. i. 10.
Gholáb Singh, *see* Guláb Singh.
Ghussa Khán, styles himself Súbahdár of Alígarh (Aug.), K. iii. 411.
Gibbings Capt., murder of, at Sultánpúr (June 8), M. i. 406.
Gibbins, Lieut., killed at Káhnpúr (Nov. 28), M. ii. 252.
Gilbert, Sir Walter, drives the Afgháns from the Panjáb (1849), K. i. 45.
Goa, Portuguese Viceroy places his troops under British command (Nov. 58), M. iii. 246.
Gogra, *see* Ghághrá.
Gokool Chund, *see* Gokul Chand.
Gokul Chand, Pandit, staunch in assistance of the English at Banáras (June 5), K. ii. 231.
Goldney, Col. Philip, Commissioner at Faizábád, K. iii. 460; realises from the first the gravity of the Mírat outbreak, K. iii. 461 *n.*; chivalrous bearing, and death of, K. iii. 467.
Golundauze = Gol-andází = Artilleryman.
Gond clans, Rájá of Dilherí feudal lord over, M. iii. 93.
Gondá, Mr. C. Wingfield retires to, from Sikrorá (May), K. iii. 475; Mr. C. Wingfield abandons (June 10), K. iii.

Gondá—*cont.*
476; Mr. C. Wingfield starts for Balrámpúr, M. i. 393; mutiny at (June 10), M. i. 393; rebels retreat to (July '58), M. iii. 271.
Gondá, Rájá of, assists Mahndí Husain at Belwá (March '58), M. ii. 452; chased from the Ghághrá, by Gen. Hope Grant (Nov. 24, '58), M. iii. 292.
Goojrat, *see* Gujrát.
Goojur = Gújar = a predatory Rájpút caste, *hence* a thief.
Gopálpúr, Ráo Sáhib, the Rání of Jhánsí, and Tántiá Topí, meet at (May '58), M. iii. 203; desperate condition of rebel cause at (May '58), M. iii. 203, 204; Sir Hugh Rose sends column to, in pursuit of rebels (May 25, '58), M. iii. 211.
Gopálpúr, Rájá of, releases prisoners at Gorakhpúr (Sept.), M. iii. 456.
Gorakhpúr, its situation and extent, M. iii. 447; its garrison, M. iii. 448; Capt. Steel commands Sepoys at, M. iii. 449; Mr. Wynward receives unlimited power in, M. iii. 449.
Mr. Wynward raises Volunteers in, M. iii. 449; attempt of prisoners to break out of jail (June 7), M. iii. 450; the Sepoys refuse to obey orders (June 6), M. iii. 450; second attempt of Sepoys to mutiny prevented (June 7), M. iii. 450; placed under martial law by Major J. Holmes (June 19), K. iii. 103; Mr. Wynward proclaims martial-law in, M. iii. 451.
Arrival and despatch of fugitives from Oudh (June 17–20), M. iii. 452; Mr. Tucker endeavours to prevent the

THE HISTORIES OF THE INDIAN MUTINY. 71

Gorakhpúr—cont.
Gorkhas from giving assistance, M. iii. 452; Major Ramsay brings Gorkhas from Pálpa (June 28), M. iii. 452; Mr. Wynward disarms his detachment of 17th N. I. (Aug. 1), M. iii. 455; mutiny of the 12th Irregulars at (Aug. 1), M. iii. 455.
Mr. Wynward and officials forced to abandon, M. iii. 455; Mr. Wynward leaves district in charge of loyal landowners (Aug. 31), M. iii. 456; Mr. Bird alone remains behind, M. iii. 456; prisoners released from jail by Rájá of Gopálpúr, M. iii. 456; Mr. Bird insulted and forced to fly, M. iii. 456.
Seized by Muhammad Husain, M. iii. 456; Jang Bahádur enters (Dec. 23), M. ii. 323.
Mr. Wynward receives the thanks of Lord Canning June 28), M. iii. 453.
Goráriá, battle of (Nov. 24), M. iii. 80; desperate resistance of Rohillas at (Nov. 24), M. iii. 81.
Gordon, Brig., clears country south of Ghághrá (Nov. '58), M. iii. 293.
Gordon, Capt., advances against Rúp Singh at Barhí (Aug. '58), M. iii. 309; captures Barhí, M. iii. 310; captures Chakkarnagar (Aug. '58), M. iii. 310.
Gordon, Capt. John, destroys and captures Náná Sáhib's boats at Jájaman (July 31), M. i. 499; his second expedition to Bithúr (Aug. 5), M. i. 507; leads third river party to Bithúr (Aug. 8), M. i. 508; succeeds in recovering the

Gordon, Capt. John—cont.
wife and daughters of Náráyan Ráo, M. i. 508; steams down Ganges to Rájghát, and destroys enemy's boats (Aug. 20), M. i. 517.
Gordon, Lieut. D., his death at the Álambágh (Jan.), M. ii. 346.
Gordon, Lieut. John, Fort Adjutant of Asírgarh, M. iii. 58; raises body of Volunteers at Asírgarh (June), M. iii. 58; sends one company of garrison to Burhánpúr (June 19), M. iii. 58; saves Asírgarh from threatened attack of mutineers (July), M. iii. 59.
Gordon, Lieut., Deputy Commissioner of Chandairí, escapes from Lallatpúr mutiny, M. iii. 98 n.
Gordon, Major, defeats rebel attack at Álambágh (Jan. 16, '58), M. ii. 352.
Gorkhás, trusted to escort artillery (May 14), K. ii. 140; revolt of, at Nasirí (May), K. ii. 143; subsidence of mutiny among, K. ii. 145; attempt to seduce into mutiny, K. ii. 190.
Goruckpore, see Gorakhpúr.
Gosling, Lieut., fights bravely at Bhogníwálá (April '58), M. ii. 515; killed at Naghína (April 21, '58), M. ii. 519.
Gough, Lord, his character, K. i. 36.
Government of India, its mental range, M. i. 11; betrays utter ignorance of the condition of India, M. iii. 492; judges its servants' conduct by results, M. i. 102; success the sole standard of its servants' worth, M. i. 513; supersedes the victorious Havelock, M. i. 512; its treatment of Have-

Government of India—*cont.*
lock contrasted with Rome's treatment of Varro, M. i. 513; list of unjust supersessions by, M. i. 513–515; the public have no confidence in (July 31), M. i. 137; justified in instituting Inám Commission, M. iii. 22 *n.*; invests private people with powers of life and death, M. iii. 441; inconsistency in respecting the honour of Sepoys, but disregarding the lives of villagers, M. iii. 442.

Confident attitude of (June 1), M. i. 5; neglects present resources for immediate suppression of Mutiny, M. i. 5; its blindness in refusing aid of citizens of Calcutta (May 20), M. i. 6; risks everything in order to appear strong, M. i. 7; the danger and weakness of its trusting policy, M. i. 9; causelessly detains 84th Regiment at Bárákpúr, M. i. 6; by first delays, causes the loss of Káhnpúr, M. i. 6, 7.

Aroused to a sense of insecurity by Mr. J. P. Grant (June 12), M. i. 8, 13; pushes forward all reinforcements in June, M. i. 8; fears rupture of central line of communication (June 10), M. i. 13; efforts to strengthen central line of communication, M. i. 29; accepts aid from Jang Bahádur (June), M. ii. 316; sanctions enrolment of Volunteer corps at Calcutta (June 12), M. i. 15.

Continues to feign confidence (June 13), M. i. 21; regards the outbreak as partial and temporary (June 22), M. i. 30; fears effect of disarming Sepoys, M. i. 46;

Government of India—*cont.*
guilty of fatuity in trusting Sepoys, M. i. 46.

Neglects opportunities for disarming Dánápúr Sepoys, M. i. 61; fatuity of, in not disarming Sepoys at Dánápúr, M. i. 513; its decisions respecting disarming Sepoys at Dánápúr, M. i. 64; transfers its responsibility to Gen. Lloyd, M. i. 61; mainly responsible for mutiny at Dánápúr, M. i. 71; orders Gen. Lloyd to be tried by court-martial, M. i. 115.

Neutralises greatly Mr. Tayler's good work, M. i. 103; unjustly dismisses Mr. Tayler from his post, M. i. 117; in despite of incontestable evidence, still denies justice to Mr. W. Tayler, M. i. 122.

Does nothing to prepare for Sir Colin Campbell's advance, M. ii. 121; issues order on the treatment of mutineers (July 31), M. i. 135; the order on the treatment of mutineers criticised, M. i. 136; the order a statesman-like measure, M. i. 137; the order forbidding the making of terms with armed rebels, unfortunate to the British cause, M. ii. 562, 564; disarms both Europeans and Natives in Calcutta (July 31), M. i. 138; intense unpopularity of measure, M. i. 138; employs Madrays Sepoys in Bengal, M. ii. 137; causes the rupture in Mr. Beadon's line of six hundred miles, M. i. 143.

Disapproves Mr. Colvin's proclamation at A'grá, M. i. 164; its vacillation in N.W.P., compared with Col.

THE HISTORIES OF THE INDIAN MUTINY. 73

Government of India—*cont.*
G. Lawrence's decision in Rájpútáná, M. i. 260; accepts further aid from Jang Bahádur (Nov.), M. ii. 320; sends detachment to cut off mutineers from Chatgáon and Dákhá, M. ii. 421.
Governor - General of India, amount of work of, K. i. 385; intricacy of duties of, K. i. 386; Supreme Council of, in 1856, K. i. 387; he and Commander-in-Chief are in official collision (1856), K. i. 394.
See also Dalhousie (Lord), and Canning (Lord).
Govindgarh, the stronghold of Amritsar, K. ii. 434.
Govindghur, *see* Govindgarh.
Graham, Lieut., his party mutiny on road to Hazáríbágh (July 31), M. ii. 135; his services in Western Bihár, M. ii. 436; blockaded in Palámau, M. ii. 437; relieved from blockade at Palámau (Dec. 8), M. ii. 438; seizes Debí Bakkas Ráí, and the rebellion at Palámau collapses, M. ii. 438; he and Capt. Dalton completely defeat rebels at Palámau (Jan 21, '58), M. ii. 441 *b*.
Grant, Assist.-Surg., murderously attacked at Rohiní (June 12), K. iii. 171, M. i. 37.
Grant, Brig. Hope, takes part in the battle of Badlí-kí-Saráí (June 8), K. ii. 192; ordered to take the field by Secretary Muir of A'grá, M. ii. 105; advances towards Lakhnau, M. ii. 106; reaches Káhnpúr (Oct. 26), M. ii. 106; assumes command of Col. Greathed's troops (Oct. 19), M. ii. 106; halts at Banthíra for Sir

Grant, Brig. Hope—*cont.*
Colin Campbell (Oct. 30), M. ii. 107; his column at Baní the *point d'appui* of relieving force, M. ii. 149.
Commands general attack of Tántiá Topí (Dec. 5), M. ii. 267; sent in pursuit of Tántiá Topí from Káhnpúr (Dec. 8), M. ii. 276; catches Tántiá Topí at Shivarájpúr, M. ii. 277; defeats him there (Dec. 9), M. ii. 278; attacks Bithúr and destroys Náná Sáhib's palace (Dec. 11), M. ii. 281.
Commands Cavalry on the Gúmtí (March '58), M. ii. 379; moves along Sítápúr road (March 15, '58), M. iii. 399; co-operates in attack on Músá Bágh (March 19, '58), M. ii. 405; defeats the rebels at Kúrsí (March 22, '58), M. ii. 411.
Left in command of Lakhnau (March '58), M. ii. 468; marches against the Maulaví (April '58), M. ii. 493; composition of his force, M. ii. 494; his description of Nipálese on the march, M. ii. 497.
The Maulaví's skilful attempt to overthrow him (April '58), M. ii. 495; marches unopposed to Bithaulí, M. ii. 497; arrives at Jallálábád (May 16, '58), M. ii. 498.
Marches against Bení Mádhava, M. iii. 267; joined by Rájá of Kappartolá (June 4, '58), M. iii. 267; strength of his Oudh column (1858), M. iii. 267 *n.*; marches on Nawábganj, on Faizábád road, M. iii. 267; defeats rebels at Nawábganj (June 13, '58), M. iii. 269; marches to relieve

Grant, Brig. Hope—*cont.*
Mán Singh, M. iii. 270; raises the siege of Sháhganj, and releases Mán Singh (July '58), M. iii. 271; destroys rebel boats at Ayodhya (July '58), M. iii. 271.
Sends Brig. Horsford to Sultánpúr (Aug. '58), M. iii. 271; follows Brig. Horsford to Sultánpúr, M. iii. 272; repulses rebels at Sultánpúr (Aug. 28, '58), M. iii. 273.
Orders Brig. Wetherall to join him in attack on Rámpúr Kussiá, M. iii. 289; marches on Amíthí (Nov. 7, '58), M. iii. 290; marches on Shankarpúr, M. iii. 291; occupies Shankarpúr (Nov. 9, '58), M. iii. 292; again defeats rebels at Machhlígáon (Dec. 4, '58), M. iii. 292; arrives at Balrámpúr (Dec. 16, '58), M. iii. 292; pursues Bálá Ráo, from Tulsípúr, M. iii. 293; drives Bálá Ráo and his army into Nipál, M. iii. 294; scatters the last remnant of rebels at Serwa pass (Jan. '59), M. iii. 297.
Nominated K.C.B., M. iii. 266.
Grant, Charles, Brig.-Gen. at Bárákpúr (1857), K. i. 495.
Grant, Gen. Sir Patrick, his antecedents, M. i. 29; suggests intercepting the China expedition (May 17), K. i. 615 n.; summoned to Calcutta as acting Commander-in-Chief (June 3), K. ii. 280; starts from Madras for Calcutta (June 17), K. ii. 281; arrives at Calcutta (June 17), K. iii. 44, M. i. 29; the task before him on landing at Calcutta, M. i. 30; unpopular with Bengal Army, M. i. 29.

Grant, Gen. Sir Patrick—*cont.*
His reasons for not taking the field, M. i. 30; unsound reasons, M. i. 31; clings to routine work at Calcutta instead of taking the field, M. i. 31; his sound, but extraordinary reason, for not taking the field, M. i. 32; selects Gen. Havelock to command army in the field, M. i. 32; counsels Neill to be cautious in advance from Alláhábád, K. ii. 285 n.; urges Gen. Neill to Káhnpúr to assist Gen. Havelock, M. i. 489.
Throws responsibility of disarming Dánápúr Sepoys on Gen. Lloyd, M. i. 62; permits disarmament of Dánápúr Sepoys, K. iii. 90; collects transport and supplies at Calcutta, K. iii. 45.
Grant, Lieut., murdered at Lakhnau (May 30), M. i. 374.
Grant, Mr., presses on Lord Canning the acceptance of Calcutta Volunteers, K. iii. 9; his letter to Lord Canning concerning the emergency, K. iii. 11 n.
Grant, Sir John Peter, Member of Supreme Council, K. i. 387; his character, K. i. 388, M. i. 134; awakens the Government to the danger of the confiding policy (June 12), M. i. 13, 14; embarks for Dánápúr with Sir J. Outram (Aug. 6), K. iii. 190; created temporary Lieut.-Gov. of Central Provinces, K. iii. 191, M. i. 134; informs Gen. Franks of the state of the rebel forces in Gorakhpúr, M. ii. 326; returns to Calcutta as President of the Council (March '58), M. ii. 418.

Grant, Private, daring leap into Sikandar Bágh (Nov. 16), M. ii. 183, 197.
Granville, Lord, writes letter of sympathy to Lord Canning (March '58), M. iii. 257.
Graves, Brig., commands at Dehlí, K. ii. 91; endeavours energetically to keep Sepoys to their allegiance (May 11), K. ii. 91; causes postponement of *coup de main* on Dehlí, K. ii. 528.
Graves, Lieut., murdered at Sítápúr (June 3), M. i. 380.
Graydon, Lieut., his death at Lakhnau, M. ii. 161.
Greased cartridges, the story of the, K. i. 489, 516; as a cause of the Mutiny argued, M. iii. 470; the looked-for pretext for revolt, M. iii. 486; only in lesser sense the cause of Mutiny, M. iii. 487; story of, spreads with lightning rapidity, K. i. 392; nature of grease employed, K. i. 519; mutton fat used at Mírat before 1857, K. i. 515; those made with mutton fat and wax allowed to be issued, K. i. 516; manufactured but not issued, K. i. 514, 515; alarm caused by, K. i. 488, 490; the paper of, greatly dreaded, K. i. 558 n.; tearing substituted for biting, in drill, K. i. 521; feeling against, apparently subsiding, in May, K. i. 582.
Greathed, Capt., examines breach at Dehlí, M. ii. 26.
Greathed, Col. Edward, starts in pursuit of Sepoys (Sept. 24), M. ii. 87, 88; the force with which he advanced into the Doáb, M. ii. 88; destroys Dádrí (Sept. 26), M. ii. 89; defeats the Sepoys at Balandshahr (Sept. 28), M. ii. 90;

Greathed, Col. Edward—*cont.* captures Málagarh, M. ii. 91; discovers skeleton of European female at Kúrjah (Oct. 3), M. ii. 92; captures Alígarh, M. ii. 93; executes the rebels Mangal Singh and Maitáb Singh at Akbarábád, M. ii. 93.
Marches on to Ágrá (Oct. 9), M. ii. 93; reason for urgent appeals to help Ágrá, M. ii. 97; emaciated condition of his troops, M. ii. 98; reaches Ágrá, but finds enemy retreated, M. ii. 98; dispute about encamping his force there (Oct. 10), M. ii. 99; his force encamps on the parade-ground, M. ii. 100; his force surprised, M. ii. 101; he drives off Sepoys from Ágrá (Oct. 10), M. ii. 103; his great victory, M. ii. 104.
Superseded by Brig. Hope Grant (Oct. 19), M. ii. 106; commands third brigade at final attack on Lakhnau, M. ii. 172; commands third brigade at attack on Tántiá Topí (Dec. 5), M. ii. 267.
Greathed, Hervey, Commissioner of Mírat, and his wife, saved by a native servant, K. ii. 68; advises immediate assault of Dehlí (June 14), K. ii. 531; his opinion of Gen. Barnard, K. ii. 569; dies of cholera, at Dehlí (Sept. 19), K. iii. 642.
Greathed, Wilberforce, urges immediate attack on Dehlí (June 14, 16, 18), K. ii. 530, 532, 539.
Green, Lieut., his gallantry at Pannú (Oct. 8, '58), M. iii. 287.
Grey, Sir George, sends to Calcutta and Bombay both troops

Gray, Sir George—*cont.*
and horses from the Cape, M. iii. 6; orders all ships of China expedition to call at Singapor for instructions, M. iii. 7.

Griffith, Artillery subaltern at Phillaur, manfully holds the Fort there (May 12), K. ii. 445; prepares siege-train for Dehlí Field Force, K. ii. 146.

Gubbins, Mr. Frederick, inspires confidence in Native population at Banáras, K. ii. 234; begs military officers not to quit Banáras in May, K. ii. 203; suppresses mutiny at Banáras (June), M. i. 12; executes stern justice at Banáras, K. ii. 237; Lord Canning's letter of thanks to, K. ii. 212; one of the four who preserved Mr. Beadon's line of six hundred miles, M. i. 143.

Gubbins, Mr. Martin, Financial Commissioner in Oudh, K. i. 399; his character, K. i. 399, iii. 494, M. i. 415; hasty in temper, K. i. 399; he and Mr. C. Jackson in violent antagonism, K. i. 399; his administration makes the Oudh people desire return of Native rulers, M. iii. 479.

His description of Oudh at end of June, K. iii. 408-410; urges that help should be sent to Káhnpúr, K. iii. 500; the only malcontent at Lakhnau, K. iii. 500; bravely heads an attack (May 31), K. iii. 447, M. i. 376; distinguishes himself in pursuit of mutineers, M. i. 376; in temporary command, attempts to disarm Sepoy troops, K. iii. 498, M. i. 416; his concern in the advance on Chinhat, K. iii. 669-671; his account

Gubbins, Mr. Martin—*cont.*
of Sítápúr mutiny, K. iii. 455 n.

Gubbins's post, a post at Lakhnau Residency, M. i. 443.

Guide Corps, ordered to Naushíra (May 13), K. ii. 465; ordered to Aták (May 13), K. ii. 466; moves from Aták, (May 16), K. ii. 466; reaches Ráwal Pindi (May 18), K. ii. 466; reaches Ambálá (June 4), K. ii. 467; diverted from advance on Dehlí by request to burn a village, K. ii. 468; joins the Dehlí Field Force (June 9), K. ii. 468; their extraordinary march, K. ii. 468 n.

Guise, Capt., storms the Mess House, Lakhnau (Nov. 17), M. ii. 201.

Gújádar Singh, returns from Nipál, and makes raid on Sikrora (April '59), M. iii. 296.

Gújars, begin a course of plundering, M. iii. 401; around Mírat, attacked and defeated by Mr. Dunlop, M. iii. 430.

Gujrát, battle of (1849), K. i. 45.

Gújrí, Col. Durand intercepts rebels at (Oct. 12), M. iii. 68.

Guláb Singh, receives Káshmír from the English, K. i. 5; sends contingent to English before Dehlí, K. iii. 549.

Guláb Singh, rebel leader in Oudh, M. iii. 271.

Gunga Rám, *see* Gangá Rám.

Gungadhur Rao, *see* Gangádhar Ráo.

Gurgáon, Hákim Abdu-l Haqq, chief of, hanged at Dehlí (Oct.), M. ii. 109.

Gúrsahaiganj, *see* Gurusaháíganj.

Gurusaháíganj, reported headquarters of Sir Colin Campbell (Dec.), M. ii. 295.
Gwáliár, military strength of, K. iii. 309 n.; Major C. Macpherson, Resident at, K. iii. 311; Dinkar Ráo, Díwán at, K. iii. 311.
Lord Ellenborough's prudent generosity towards (1843), M. i. 152; excellent results of Lord Ellenborough's treatment, M. i. 152; supports the English cause, M. i. 153; Resident warned by Sindhiá of the general character of the revolt, M. i. 153; Sindhiá suggests the removal of women and children to Residency, M. i. 171; Brig. Ramsey objects to families of Contingent officers removing to Residency, K. iii. 314; Native officers resent the removal of women and children, M. i. 170; Mr. Colvin directs ladies to remain, until actual occurrence of mutiny, M. i. 172.
First panic in cantonments (May 28), K. iii. 314; Mrs. Coopland's description of fearful suspense at, M. i. 171 n., 173 n.; premonitory disrespect of Sepoys, M. i. 174; mutiny at (June 14), K. iii. 316, M. i. 173, 174; every commanding officer killed, K. iii. 317; mutineers murder the officers, but spare the ladies, M. i. 175; murder of Capt. Stewart and family, K. iii. 317; murder of Dr. Kirk, K. iii. 318; number of Europeans murdered, K. iii. 318, M. i. 175 n.; the massacre at, one result of the feigning confidence policy, M. i. 176; some women and

Gwáliár—cont.
children escape to Ágrá, K. iii. 319, M. i. 176.
Mutineers at, ready to sever British line of communications, M. ii. 125; Rání of Jhánsí proposes the seizure of, M. iii. 205; Tántiá Topí appears before (May 30, '58), M. iii. 205, 208; captured by Tántiá Topí (June l. '58), M. iii. 209; Ráo Sáhib made governor of, M. iii. 209; grave political and military incidence of capture of, M. iii. 213; captured by Sir H. Rose (June 19, '58), M. iii. 226; rock-fortress of, captured by Lieut. Rose and Lieut. Waller (June 18, '58), M. iii. 228; Tántiá Topí's account of his defeat at, M. iii. 518; apparent tranquillity of, M. iii. 331; Brig. R. Napier moves from to assist Brig. Smith at Paurí (Aug. 11, '58), M. iii. 334.
Gwáliár Contingent, its constitution, M. i. 169; restores order in Ítáwá (May 24), M. i. 162; part mutinies at Hátrás (May 26), M. i. 293; mutiny of (June 15), M. i. 34; Artillery of, mutiny (July 2), M. i. 294; others mutiny at Burhánpúr (July), M. iii. 59; troops of, disarmed at Asírgarh (July), M. iii. 59; effect of fall of Dehlí upon, M. ii. 147; places itself under Tántiá Topí, M. ii. 148.
Gwalior, see Gwáliár.
Gya, see Gayá.

H.

Hagart, Col. James, his gallantry at capture of Músá

Hagart, Col. James—*cont.*
Bágh (March 19, '58), M. ii. 407; recommended for Victoria Cross by Gen. Hope Grant, M. ii. 407 *n.*; Sir Colin Campbell's curious reason for not forwarding recommendation, M. ii. 408 *n.*
Haidarábád, description of, M. iii. 117; garrison of, M. iii. 120 *n.*; disaffected classes in, M. iii. 123; mercenary troops of, M. iii. 123; Sepoys at, ripe for revolt (1806), K. i. 234; programme of the mutineers of 1806, K. i. 235 *n.*; the Nizám of, abstains from encouraging mutinous spirit, K. i. 236; threatened mutiny suppressed (1806), K. i. 237. Major C. Davidson, Resident at, M. iii. 119; plot to murder the Europeans in (June 12), M. iii. 119; Major Davidson meets the conspiracy with vigour, M. iii. 119; Sálar Jang represses incipient rising in (June 15), M. iii. 120; insurrection in (July 17), M. iii. 121; insurgents attack Residency, M. iii. 121; insurgents repulsed, M. iii. 122; ringleaders of insurrection captured, M. iii. 122; suppression of attempt to disturb (Feb. '58), M. iii. 129.
Major Davidson forms Haidarábád column, for service in Central India, M. iii. 124; he receives reinforcements, M. iii. 124; success of his policy, M. iii. 125.
Hakím, the, killed by Capt. Hodson at battle of Pattiálí (Dec. 17), M. ii. 292.
Hákim Abdu-l Haqq, chief of Gurgáon, hanged at Dehlí (Oct.), M. ii. 109.

Haldúr, defeat of Hindús at, by Muhammadan rebels (Aug. 23), M. iii. 412.
Hale, Capt., attacked by Kols in Singhbhúm (Dec.), M. ii. 439; suppresses insurrection at Singhbhúm with party of Rattray's Sikhs, M. ii. 439.
Hale, Col., covers retirement of Sir Colin Campbell, M. ii. 216; left in command of Sháhjahánpúr (April 30, '58), M. ii. 522; makes Sháhjahánpúr defensible (May '58), M. ii. 532; hears of advance of the Maulaví, and prepares for him, M. ii. 533; besieged by the Maulaví (May 3, '58), M. ii. 533.
Half-batta Order (1830), K. i. 271.
Halgalli, captured by help of Col. G. Malcolm (Nov. 29), M. iii. 237.
Haliburton, Major, killed at Lakhnau (Oct. 4), M. ii. 158.
Hall, Capt., commands at Mount Abú, M. ii. 555; attacked while asleep, by Jodhpúr troops (Aug. 21), M. ii. 556; drives off attackers, M. ii. 557.
Halliday, Mr. F., Lieut.-Gov. of Bengal, his personal appearance and character, K. iii. 58; want of judgment and incapacity of, M. i. 553; proved, by subsequent events, to have been totally in the wrong, M. i. 554; induces Lord Canning to change his Native bodyguard, K. iii. 58, '59.
His personal dislike of Mr. W. Tayler, M. i. 116; revenges himself accordingly, M. i. 116; resolves to remove Mr. Tayler from Patná before outbreak of Mutiny, K. iii. 71; marks his disapproba-

THE HISTORIES OF THE INDIAN MUTINY. 79

Halliday, Mr. F.—*cont.*
tion of arrest of Wahábís at Patná, M. i. 549; his grave neglect of duty with respect to the Wahábís, M. i. 550; he denounces two loyal natives, for the purpose of screening the Wahábís, M. i. ˙551; fully aware of existence of Wahábí fanatics at Patná, M. i. 549; holds that a mutiny at Dánápúr is inconceivable, M. i. 550; charges trumped up by him against Mr. Tayler, M. i. 118 *n.*; his comments on Mr. W. Tayler's order to abandon out-stations, K. iii. 159; charges Mr. Tayler with panic, M. i. 117; his charge of panic against Mr. Tayler confuted by Sir John Kaye, M. i. 118 *n.*, his charge everywhere recognised as untrue, M. i. 121; he dismisses Mr. Tayler from his post, K. iii. 160.
His policy compared with that of Mr. W. Tayler, M. i. 59; his services less valuable than those of Mr. W. Tayler, M. i. 120; commits a much graver error than Mr. W. Tayler, while punishing him, K. iii. 190.
Hamilton, Col., gallantly carries the Martinière, Lakhnau, M. ii. 174.
Hamilton, Sir Henry, Agent at Indúr, his character, K. iii. 324; his excellent local knowledge, M. iii. 132.
Returns to India, M. iii. 131; arrives at Indúr (Dec. 16), M. iii. 133; relieves Col. Durand, M. iii. 84; his plan of operations for Central India, M. iii. 133; his plan of campaign completely carried out by Sir H. Rose, M.

Hamilton, Sir Henry—*cont.*
iii. 188; proposes measures for tranquillisation of Central India, M. iii. 132.
Hamírpúr, Gen. Franks defeats rebels at (Feb.), M. ii. 331.
Hampton, Major, commands at Nagod, M. iii. 109.
Handscomb, Brig., murdered at Lakhnau (May 30), M. i. 375.
Hanmant Singh, Rájá, nobility and generosity of his conduct to fugitive English, M. i. 407 *n.*; his estates restored to him, M. i. 408 *n.*
Hanna, Mr., his desperate gallantry at battle of Naghina (April 21, '58), M. ii. 519.
Hansborough, Mr., Superintendent of Barailí Gaol, defies Khán Bahádur Khán, K. iii. 276; murder of (June 1), K. iii. 276.
Hanumant Singh, rebel leader in Oudh (Oct. '58), M. iii. 286.
Haqqdád Khán, Risáldár, repulses desperate cavalry charge at Núriá (Aug. 29, '58), M. iii. 276.
Hardinge, Lieut., brilliant services of, at outbreak of Lakhnau mutiny, K. iii. 446; leads sortie at Lakhnau (Sept. 29), M. ii. 155; leads another sortie (Nov. 2), M. ii. 156.
Hardinge, Lord, his character, K. i. 16; his policy with respect to the Panjáb, K. i. 2; annexes part of Jálandhar (1847), M. i. 152; returns to England (1848), K. i. 15.
Hare, Capt., pursues rebels from Garhákot (Feb. '58), M. iii. 146.
Harichand, rebel leader in Oudh, M. iii. 286; attacks Sandíla (Oct. 3, '58), M. iii. 286.

Haridatta Singh, rebel leader in Oudh (Oct. '58), M. iii. 286.
Harideo Bakkas, protects fugitives from Fathgarh, M. i. 336.
Haridwár, attacked and burned by rebels from Bíjnúr (Jan. 7, '58), M. iii. 413.
Harington, Lieut., killed at Rúiyá (April 15, '58), M. ii. 507 n.
Harington, Mr., opposes Mr. Colvin's proposal to retire in Ágrá Fort (May 18), M. i. 149.
Hariyá, Col. Rowcroft attacks and defeats Muhammad Husain at (June 18, '58), M. iii. 282.
Harness, Col., commands Engineers at attack on Tántiá Topí (Dec. 5), M. ii. 267.
Harriah, see Hariyá.
Harrington, Lieut., his brave deed at Lakhnau, M. ii. 213 n.
Harris, Lord, Governor of Madras, M. iii. 130; cheerfully responds to Lord Canning's application for aid, K. i. 611; the able manner in which he assisted to suppress the Mutiny, M. iii. 499; his grave anxiety for Madras through Tántiá Topí's invasion of Nágpúr (Oct. '58), M. iii. 344.
Harris, Major, commands Cavalry at Máú, M. i. 206; murdered at Máú (July 1), M. i. 235.
Hartigan, Sergt., energetically drills Meade's Horse (Jan.-March, '58), M. iii. 314.
Hashmat Alí Chaudrí, of Sandíla, capture of his camp at Lakhnau (March 11, '58), M. ii. 380.
Hassan Askarí, actively intrigues in the King's palace, at Dehlí, K. ii. 37.

Hastings, Capt., appointed staff officer by Major Eyre, M. i. 97.
Hastings, Lord, asserts the supremacy of the British in India, K. ii. 8.
Hátrás, mutiny at (July 1), M. i. 294; officers of mutinous troops escape to Ágrá, M. i. 295.
Havelock, Capt. H., joins Gen. Franks' force at Jánpúr, M. ii. 325; the able adviser of Gen. Franks, M. ii. 339.
Havelock, Gen. Henry, his character, K. ii. 277.
Havelock, Gen. Sir Henry, his character, M. ii. 218–220; his antecedents, M. i. 35; accompanies Outram to Persia, K. ii. 279; returns to Bombay (May 29), K. ii. 280; sails for Madras, K. ii. 280; starts from Madras for Calcutta (June 17), K. ii. 281.

Appointed by Lord Canning to command movable column at Alláhábád, K. ii. 282, M. i. 32; leaves Calcutta (June 24), M. i. 35; his directions on leaving Calcutta, K. ii. 282; arrives at Alláhábád (June 30), K. ii. 276; approves of all Col. Neill's preparations at Alláhábád, K. ii. 283; receives news of fall of Káhnpúr (July 3), K. ii. 284; differs from Col. Neill as to prudent course after fall of Káhnpúr, K. ii. 286.

Resolves to capture Káhnpúr, K. ii. 357; advances from Alláhábád (July 7), K. ii. 388; the force with which he left Alláhábád, K. ii. 358; hurries on to overtake Renaud, K. ii. 359; joins Renaud (July 12), K. ii. 359;

Havelock, Gen.—*cont.*
defeats Náná Sáhib's forces at Fathpúr (July 12), K. ii. 362; defeats them again at Áon (July 15), K. ii. 369; crosses the Pándu-nadí, K. ii. 370; approaches Káhnpúr, K. ii. 371; finds Náná Sáhib strongly posted before Káhnpúr, K. ii. 375; his great victory at Káhnpúr (July 16), K. ii. 376-381; his order of the day to the victorious army, K. ii. 382; stops the plunder of his troops at Káhnpúr, K. ii. 388; combats drunkenness of troops after capture of Káhnpúr, K. ii. 384; conscious of his dangerous position at Káhnpúr, K. ii. 389; is joined by Gen. Neill (July 20), K. ii. 397; occupies the Nawábganj at Káhnpúr, K. ii. 391; constructs entrenchment at Kánhpúr, K. ii. 404-406, M. i. 490. Hears report of Sir H. Lawrence's death (July), K. ii. 410; receives plan of Lakhnau Residency from Gen. Inglis, M. i. 455; he crosses the Ganges (July 25), K. ii. 414, M. i. 490; his force, on entering Oudh, K. ii. 414, M. i. 491; he halts at Mangalwár (July 28), K. ii. 415, M. i. 491; advances from Mangalwár (July 29), M. i. 491; meets the Sepoys posted at Unáo, M. i. 491; wins the battle of Unáo, M. i. 493; attacks and carries Bashíratganj, M. i. 494; his losses during first day's advance, M. i. 495; perceives the difficulties in his path to Lakhnau, K. ii. 416; finds it profitless to proceed, M. i. 496; falls back on Mangalwár

Havelock, Gen.—*cont.*
(July 30), M. i. 497; fury of Gen. Neill at retrograde movement of, M. i. 500; Gen. Neill's letter to him (July 31), M. i. 501 *n.*; his reply to Gen. Neill's letter, M. i. 502 *n.* Necessity of watching Sepoys at Dánápúr prevents reinforcements reaching, M. i. 502; renews his advance on Lakhnau (Aug. 4), M. i. 503; again captures Bashíratganj (Aug. 5), M. i. 504; cholera appears in his camp (Aug. 5), M. i. 504; dangerous state of the country in his rear, M. i. 505; fights a third battle at Bashíratganj (Aug. 12), M. i. 506; again forced to fall back on Mangalwár, M. i. 506.
Falls back on Káhnpúr (Aug. 13), M. i. 507; reassumes command there, M. i. 509; by advice of Gen. Neill, advances against Bithúr (Aug. 19), M. i. 510; force opposed to him at Bithúr, M. i. 510; attacks and defeats Sepoys at Bithúr (Aug. 16), M. i. 511; his losses at action of Bithúr, M. i. 512.
Stengthens Káhnpúr and prepares for final advance to Lakhnau, M. i. 515; sends Capt. Gordon to destroy enemy's boats at Rájghát (Aug. 20), M. i. 517; superseded by Gen. Outram, M. i. 572; Gen. Outram resigns command of Lakhnau relieving force to him, M. i. 524; reassumes command of Lakhnau relieving force, M. i. 525; the force with which he made final advance to Lakhnau, M. i. 526; crosses the Ganges (Sept. 18,

6

Havelock, Gen.—*cont.*
19), M. i. 527; constructs bridge across Ganges, M. i. 527; drives the enemy from Mangalwár (Sept. 21), M. i. 529; advances with all his force on Lakhnau, M. i. 529; chases the enemy through Unáo to Bashíratganj (Sept. 21), M. i. 530; the enemy fly panic-stricken across the Sáí, beyond Baní, M. i. 532.

Finds the enemy at the A'lambágh (Sept. 23), M. i. 532; drives the Sepoys thence, M. i. 534; halts and refits (Sept. 24), M. i. 534, 535; attack on the Chárbágh bridge, M. i. 537; carries the Chárbágh, M. i. 536; and the Chárbágh bridge, M. i. 537†; encounters severe opposition at the Qaisarhágh, M. i. 537‡; reaches the Baillie Guard, M. i. 539; his losses during relief of Lakhnau, M. i. 541.

Shut up in Lakhnau with garrison, M. i. 542; Sir J. Outram assumes command of garrison (Sept. 27), M. i. 542; occupies the palaces along Gúmtí at Lakhnau, M. ii. 152.

Composition of column for effecting junction with Sir Colin Campbell, M. ii. 206; his plan for co-operating with Sir Colin Campbell, M. ii. 207; occupies Farid Bakhsh Palace (Nov. 16), M. ii. 206; explodes mines under Harnkhána, M. ii. 208; captures the Harn-khána, M. ii. 208; his death (Nov. 24), M. ii. 218.

Havelock, Henry (the younger), deludes Gen. Neill into ordering a charge on Chárbágh bridge, M. i. 537; his daring

Havelock, Henry—*cont.*
in leading the charge on Chárbágh bridge, M. i. 537*; charges to the muzzle of a 24-pounder, K. ii. 381; captures second rebel line of defence at Lakhnau (March 14, '58), M. ii. 391; captures Tárá Kothí and Mess House at Lakhnau, M. ii. 392.

Havelock, Lieut. Charles, killed at Tigra (April '58), M. ii. 470.

Havelock, Major Henry, his plan for rooting out Amar Singh's adherents, M. ii. 487; proposes Mounted Infantry for service in Bihár, M. ii. 487; leads Mounted Infantry against Amar Singh, M. ii. 487; heads the rebels on the Son (Oct. 19, '58), M. ii. 488; cuts off rear-guard of rebels (Oct. 20, '58), M. ii. 489; rebel main-body escapes by a mistake (Oct. 21, '58), M. ii. 490; drives the rebels to the Kaimúr Hills, M. ii. 491.

Hawes, Capt. W. H., essays to move treasure from Daríábád, K. iii. 480; his miraculous escape from Daríábád, K. iii. 481.

Hawes, Quartermaster, killed in the revolt at Alláhábád (June 6), K. ii. 252.

Hawthorne, Bugler, one of explosion party at Kashmír gate, Dehlí, M. ii. 32.

Hayes, Capt. Fletcher, his character, K. ii. 296; his administrative character, K. iii. 421 n.; his murder at Bhaugáon (May 31), K. iii. 522 n.

Hayes, Dr., attacked by Kols in Singhbhúm (Dec.), M. ii. 439.

Hazára, execution of escaping

Hazára—cont.
mutineers at (June), K. ii. 495; Muhammadans of, plan a revolt (Sept.), M. iii. 303.
Hazáríbágh, Sepoy garrison of, M. ii. 134; mutiny at (July 30), M. ii. 134; Capt. Dalton restores order in (Aug.), M. ii. 136; Capt. Dalton asks for a European Regiment, M. ii. 137; Col. Fischer marches on, M. ii. 140.
Hearsey, John, General of Division at Bárákpúr, K. i. 495; reports uneasy feeling at Bárákpúr in (Jan. 1857), K. i. 496; feels the storm rising at Bárákpúr, K. i. 522; counsels disbandment of 34th Regiment (May), K. i. 585; suggests intercepting the China expedition, K. i. 615 n.; his judicious treatment of his Sepoys, K. i. 524; addresses his Sepoys with good effect, K. i. 525; again addresses his Sepoys, K. i. 533; he and his two sons, proceed to arrest Mangal Pándí, K. i. 542; prepares to disarm Sepoys at Bárákpúr, K. iii. 27.
Heathcote, Lieut., military adviser of Anár Singh, M. ii. 563; escapes from defeat of Anár Singh's army (Sept. 8), M. ii. 565.
Heberden, Mr., railway engineer, his heroic fortitude and death at Káhnpúr, K. ii. 321.
Hembájí, chief of, killed at Kopáldurg (May '58), M. iii. 244.
Henderson, Lieut., induces Kiraulí troops to surrender their two guns, M. i. 267.
Herat, see Hirát.
Herbert, Brig., pursues Firoz Sháh towards Jhánsí (Dec. '58), M. iii. 360.

Herbert, Mr. Sydney, writes letter of sympathy to Lord Canning (March '58), M. iii. 257.
Hernia, see Hiranya.
Heroes, undecorated, M. ii. 197.
Heroism in the ranks, K. iii. 121.
Hetampúr, Col. Lugard defeats rebels at (May 11, '58), M. ii. 480.
Hewitt, Gen., commands Mírat Division of the Army, K. ii. 44; his character, K. ii. 44, 463; resents interference with his authority, K. ii. 179. Orders Native Court of Inquiry on 3rd Cavalry mutineers, K. ii. 45; confirms sentence on 3rd Cavalry mutineers, K. ii. 49; what he did on outbreak of mutiny at Mírat (May 10), K. ii. 66; he delays moving from Mírat, K. ii. 179; sacrifices Dehlí to save Mírat cantonments, K. ii. 102; shifts blame of inaction at Mírat on to Brig. Wilson, K. ii. 101.
Higginson, Sir James, sends both troops and money from the Mauritius to Calcutta, M. iii. 6.
Hill, Brig. William, commands at Haidarábád, M. iii. 120 n; stops Tántiá Topí's southern progress to Nágpúr (Oct. '58), M. iii. 346.
Hills, Lieut., his desperate personal encounter with Sepoy troopers (July 9), K. ii. 576, 577; he and Major Tombs win the Victoria Cross, K. ii. 577-579.
Hindan, a river near Ghází-ud-Dín Nagar, scene of first fight with mutineers (May 30), K. ii. 183; defeat of mutineers, K. ii. 184, M. i. 10; sacrificial courage of a mutineer at, K. ii. 184; mu-

Hindan—*cont.*
tineers fly to Dehlí, K. ii. 185; mutineers stimulated by promise of reward to return to (May 31), K. ii. 185; mutineers again defeated, K. ii. 186.
Hindu Ráo's House at Dehlí, key to position on the Ridge, K. iii. 672.
See also Dehlí.
Hindú widows, act to remove obstacles to re-marriage of, K. i. 476.
Hindús, persecuted by Muhammadans whenever opportunity served, M. iii. 410; their number in Sepoy Army (1857), K. i. 621–626.
Hír, in Gorakhpúr, occupied by Col. Rowcroft (June '58), M. iii. 282.
Hiranya, Col. Durand crosses the Chambal at (Nov. 19), M. iii. 76.
Hírá Lál Misr, conspicuously gallant Sepoy at Lakhnau, M. ii. 156 *n*.
Híra Singh, a rebel leader in Central India, M. ii. 96.
Hírá Singh, a gallant Sikh at Lakhnau, M. ii. 157 *n*.
Hirát, its independence desired, K. i. 410; Persians march against (1852), K. i. 411; Yár Muhammad sides with Persia, K. i. 410; annexed by Persia, K. i. 411; rebellion in (1855), K. i. 413; Saiad Muhammad becomes ruler of, K. i. 411; Saiad Muhammad killed (1855), K. i. 413; Yúsuf Khán becomes ruler of, K. i. 413; revolution in (1856), K. i. 414; again attacked by Persia, K. i. 414; D'Arcy Todd and his Sepoys there, M. iii. 473.
Hodal, mutiny of Bharatpúr

Hodal—*cont.*
Contingent at (May 31), K. iii. 241, M. i. 164; Sepoys force their officers to leave them, M. i. 165.
Hodson, Capt., circumstances of his removal from Guide Corps, K. ii. 667; his character, M. ii. 75; his bravery and skill, M. ii. 295; his position on the capture of Dehlí, K. iii. 643; captures the King of Dehlí, K. iii. 645–647, M. ii. 75; disarms the people at Humáyun's Tomb, K. iii. 649; his capture of the Princes, K. iii. 648–650, M. ii. 78; shoots the three Princes himself, K. iii. 650, M. ii. 79; reflections on his shooting the Princes, K. iii. 651, M. ii. 80; his belief in the righteousness of his act, K. iii. 652; warmly congratulated by the Army on his shooting the Princes, K. iii. 653; Gen. Wilson commends his shooting the Princes, K. iii. 655.
Disposes of Jawáhir Singh and son (Dec. 22), M. ii. 293; bravely undertakes to communicate with Sir Colin Campbell, M. ii. 294; starts on his perilous journey to Sir Colin Campbell, M. ii. 296; finds Sir Colin Campbell at Míran-kí-saráí, M. ii. 297; led by a native in safety through rebels at Chibramau, M. ii. 297; returns in safety to Bewar (Dec. 31), M. ii. 298.
His death at the storming of the Begam Kothí, Lakhnau (March 10, '58), M. ii. 387.
Hodson, Lieut. William, of the Guides, his antecedents, K. ii. 181, 182 *n*.

THE HISTORIES OF THE INDIAN MUTINY. 85

Hofer, parallel between his acts and those of Tántiá Topí, M. iii. 381.

Holkár, the Mahárájá, his territory, M. i. 205; his education, K. iii. 325; his probable sentiments, K. iii. 327.
Supplies Col. Durand with guard of troops (May 14), M. i. 209; sends away mutinous troops (June 30), M. i. 228; loses command of his troops (July 1), M. i. 229; his troops mutiny (July 1), K. iii. 330; the attack on, and abandonment of Residency, M. i. 219–226; his surprise at the outbreak, K. iii. 338.
The question of his loyalty, M. i. 226; declares his unswerving loyalty to the British, K. iii. 337 and n.; temporises in hopes of return of Sir. R. Hamilton, M. iii. 63; free from charge of complicity in Mutiny, K. iii. 348, M. i. 233; Col. Durand believes in his loyalty up to July 1, M. i. 227; his defence for first inaction, K. iii. 339n.; his communication with mutineers after attack, M. i. 231; his conduct during attack of Residency reconcileable with loyalty, M. i. 230.
Writes to all British authorities for help, M. i. 232; refuses to give up fugitive Christians, M. i. 232; risks his own life to save concealed Europeans, K. iii. 340; sends a detachment to release Capt. and Mrs. Hutchinson, K. iii. 341; sends his own and the English treasure to Capt. Hungerford at Máú, K. iii. 341; urges the advance of Gen. Woodburn, K. iii. 341; sends to Col. Durand at the

Holkar, the Mahárájá—cont. Simrol pass for aid (July 30), M. iii. 61; evades Col. Durand's offer to march into Indor (July 30), M. iii. 61.
His Cavalry disarmed by Col. Durand (Dec. 14), M. iii. 82; his infantry disarmed by Darbár, M. iii. 83; visited by Col. Durand (Dec. 14), M. iii. 83; sacrificed to justify Durand, K. iii. 346; treated with suspicion since 1857, K. iii. 350.

Hollings, Mr., urges Mr. A. Money to return to Gayá for the treasure, M. i. 111; he and Mr. A. Money return to Gayá, after its first abandonment, K. iii. 155, M. i. 112.

Holmes, Col., marches against Áwah, M. ii. 572; captures Áwah, and destroys fort (Jan. 24, '58), M. ii. 573; chases Tántiá Topí to the Chambal, M. iii. 320; surprises and defeats Tántiá Topí, at Sikar (Jan. 21, '59), M. iii. 367.

Holmes, Major James, his character, K. iii. 102; his confidence in his Irregulars, K. iii. 105; counsels vigorous measures, K. iii. 103; the crimes which he proposed to deem capital, K. iii. 104; instance of his prompt executions, K. iii. 105; prevents an outbreak at Suggaulí, M. i. 58; proclaims martial law at Suggaulí (June 19), K. iii. 103, M. i. 72; he is supported by Mr. W. Tayler in his active measures, M. i. 72; his publication of martial law repudiated by Government, K. iii. 104; his murder at Suggaulí (July 25), K. iii. 106, M. i. 73.

Home, Lieut., examines breach at Dehlí, M. ii. 26; one of explosion party at Kashmír gate, Dehlí, M. ii. 32; killed by accident at Málagarh (Oct. 2), M. ii. 92.

Home, Major, his death at passage of the Ráptí (Dec. '58), M. iii. 295.

Honner, Brig., defeats Ráo Sáhib at Koshání (Feb. 10, '59), M. iii. 368.

Hope, Col. Adrian, his character, M. ii. 385; advances to the A'lambágh (Nov. 10), M. ii. 150; destroys fort at Jalálábád, near Lakhnau, M. ii. 170; commands fourth brigade at final attack on Lakhnau, M. ii. 172; leads his Highlanders at assault of Sháh Najíf, M. ii. 192; enters Sháh Najíf by a crevise, M. ii. 194.

Commands 4th Brigade at attack on Tántiá Topí (Dec. 5), M. ii. 267; holds the bridge at Fathgarh (Jan. 2, '58), M. ii. 302; advances against rebels at Shamsábád (Jan. 26, '58), M. ii. 312; storms and carries the Martinière (March 9, '58), M. ii. 377; occupies rebel first line of defence at Lakhnau (March 9, '58), M. ii. 378; leads storming party against Begam Kothí (March 10, '58), M. ii. 385.

Accompanies Gen. Walpole's column from Lakhnau, M. ii. 502; his rage at the useless slaughter at Rúiyá M. ii. 508; killed at Rúiyá (April 15, '58), M. ii. 508; grief and rage of the troops at his untimely death, M. ii. 509; account of his death at Rúiyá, M. iii. 513.

Lord Canning's apprecia-

Hope, Col. Adrian—*cont.*
tion of his ability, M. ii. 509; Sir Colin Campbell's tribute in his praise, M. ii. 510.

Hope Grant, Brig., *see* Grant, Brig. Hope.

Hope, Col., joins Col. Lockhart at Nálkhere (Aug. '58), M. iii. 328.

Hopkins, Capt., his bravery in carrying the Mess House at Lakhnau (Nov. 17), M. ii. 201, iii. 505.

Horsford, Brig., leads force against Sultánpúr (Aug. 12, '58), M. iii. 272; clears country south of the Ghághrá (Nov. '58), M. iii. 293; crosses Ráptí and defeats rebels in Nipál (Jan. '59), M. iii. 296.

Hoshangábád, part of Ságar territory, M. iii. 88; garrison of, M. iii. 96; Col. Durand arrives there (July 6), M. i. 242.

Hote-Murdán, *see* Hot-Mardán.

Hot-Mardán, in the Panjáb, troops at, in May, K. ii. 483; mutiny at, K. ii. 483; destruction of 55th Regiment at (May 25), K. ii. 485.

Hughes, Capt., his death at Lakhnau, M. ii. 161.

Hughes, Col., attacks Dhárwár insurgents at Kopáldurg, M. iii. 243; storms and captures Kopáldurg (May '58), M. iii. 244.

Hughes, Major, employed to watch eastern frontier of Shorápúr (Jan. '58), M. iii. 126; marches on Shorápúr (Feb. 8, '58), M. iii. 128.

Hume, Mr. Allan, magistrate and collector at I'táwá, K. iii. 217, M. i. 160; intercepts a small party of mutineers, K. iii. 218; intercepted mutineers try to escape and are killed, K. iii. 218; proceeds

Hume, Mr. Allen—*cont.*
to capture party of mutineers at Jaswantnagar (May 19), K. iii. 219; mutineers escape by aid of populace, K. iii. 220; goes to Hindú temple with Mr. Daniell to capture troopers, M. i. 161; attempts to assault Hindú temple, but fails, M. i. 162; great bravery of his act, K. iii. 221.
Orders 9th Regiment to Barpúrá (May 20), K. iii. 221; the 9th Regiment mutiny, but spare his house, K. iii. 222; secures Government records, and half the treasure, K. iii. 222; recovers authority at I'táwá (May 25), K. iii. 223.
Makes gallant attempt to stop Firoz Sháh at I'táwá (Dec. '58), M. iii. 360.
Hungerford, Capt. Townsend, commands artillery at Máú, M. i. 206; urges precautionary measures at Máú, K. iii. 330; summoned to Indor with his guns (July 1), K. iii. 334, 345; turned back to Máú, K. iii. 334, M. i. 234.
Reiterates his demand for precautionary measures at Máú, K. iii. 334; assumes command at Máú (July 2), K. iii. 336; clears the lines at Máú, with his guns, K. iii. 336, M. i. 235; boldly assumes authority, but is afterwards rebuked, K. iii. 338, M. i. 235; his assumption of authority supported by Lord Elphinstone, K. iii. 345.
Firmly believes in Holkar's innocence on July 1, M. iii. 62.
Hunter, Mr., his evidence as to Wahábís at Patná, M. i. 547.
Hunter, Gen. George, his cha-

Hunter, Gen. George—*cont.*
racter, K. i. 284; subdues the mutiny of the 64th Regiment at Firozpúr (1844), K. i. 285-288.
Hunter, Mr. William, quoted, on the Wahábí conspiracy, K. iii. 166 *n.*, 167 *n.*
Husainganj, Col. Evelegh, meets and scatters rebels near (Aug. 8, '58), M. iii. 283.
Hutchinson, Capt., sent with party of Sepoys to Sandílá, M. 1. 371; detects mutinous temper of his escort, M. i. 371; refuses to cross Ganges with his escort, M. i. 371; his escort mutiny and murder their officers (June 7), M. i. 371; returns in safety to Lakhnau, M. i. 372.
Hutchinson, Capt., and others, escape from Bhúpáwar to Jabúá, K. iii. 342; escorted from Jabúá by Holkár's troops, K. iii. 342; assumes charge of Residency at Indor, K. iii. 342.
Hutchinson, Capt., reports that Darbár instigate rebellion of Dhár troops, M. iii. 69.
Hutchinson, Lieut., captures fort of Amjherá (Nov.), M. iii. 74.
Hutchinson, Mr., Collector of Dehlí, murder of (May 11), K. ii. 80.
Hyderabad, *see* Haidarábád.

I.

Ignorance, a grave source of danger, K. i. 509.
Iláhi Bakhsh, Mirzá, the wily counseller of King of Dehlí, M. ii. 79; moulds the King of Dehli to his purpose, M.

Iláhi Bakhsh—*cont.*
ii. 73; betrays the King of Dehlí, M. ii. 74.
Imám Alí, rebel leader in the Sironj jungle (April '59), M. iii. 378.
Imám Bakhsh Khán, Jamádár, his daring capture of fort Khot (April 18, '58), M. ii. 516.
Imámbárá, *see* Lakhnau.
Inaction of European troops at Mírat (May 10), K. ii. 62.
Inam Commission of Bombay, K. i. 175; constitution of, K. i. 176; its operation, K. i. 177; proceedings of, M. iii. 21; number of confiscations under, M. iii. 22; the Desáís of Nipaní, discontented sufferers under, M. iii. 28; also the Desáí of Jámbotí, M. iii. 29; the Government justified in instituting, M. iii. 22 *n.*
Incendiarism, a symptom of discontent, K. i. 497; at Ambálá (April '57), K. i. 562; at Lakhnau (May 7), K. i. 591; shows itself at Mírat, K. ii. 46; on night of May 10 at Mírat, K. ii. 67.
Indar Singh, gallant Sepoy at Lakhnau, M. ii. 157 *n.*
India, general condition of northern, K. ii. 411.
Indian Civil Servants, their devotion, K. iii. 116.
Indian Government taken by surprise, K. iii. 3.
See East India Government.
Indian Army, introduction of British system, tends to provoke mutiny, M. iii. 475.
Indian Navy, the gallant deeds of, unrewarded, and the service abolished, M. iii. 465.
Indigo districts of Bihár, alarm in, K. iii. 63.
Indor, description of country

Indor—*cont.*
around, M. iii. 138; situation and troops at, K. iii. 323; scattered disposition of Holkár's garrisons, K. iii. 327; description of Residency, M. i. 215; impossible of defence, M. i. 215 *n.*; Col. H. M. Durand, Agent at, K. iii. 323, M. i. 199; his character, M. i. 199; opposing sentiments of Sir R. Hamilton and Col. H. M. Durand, K. iii. 326.
Arrest of treasonable messenger to Darbár of Ríwá (April 25), M. i. 204; Col. Durand's policy for maintaining order, M. i. 208; Bhíls summoned to, by Col. Durand, M. i. 208; Bhíls commanded by Col. Stockley, M. i. 209; Holkár supplies Col. Durand with guard of troops (May 14), M. i. 209; Col. Travers arrives at, with Cavalry (June), M. i. 210; and receives command of troops at Residency, M. i. 210; critical position of town during June, M. i. 210; troops at Máú openly loyal, M. i. 211; Col. Durand not deceived by outward loyalty of Máú troops, M. i. 211; the chance of safety lies in approach of Gen. Woodburn's column, M. i. 212; Gen. Woodburn's column diverted to Aurangábád, M. i. 212; and halts there, M. i. 213; Holkár sends away a body of mutinous troops (June 30), M. i. 228.
Holkár loses command of his troops, M. i. 229; mutiny at (July 1), K. iii. 330, M. i. 215; attack on Residency headed by Sa'adat Khán, M. i. 217; conflicting accounts of office of Sa'adat Khán, M.

Indor—cont.
i. 217 n.; Holkár's troops the assailants of Residency, M. i. 217; suddenness of the attack, M. i. 217; position of troops defending Residency, M. i. 216; the Residency guard joins in the revolt, M. i. 219; Col. Travers, with five men, charges rebel guns, M. i. 220; he fights the rebel guns, and disables one, M. i. 221; Col. Durand sends to Máú for Hungerford's battery, M. i. 221; Capt. Hungerford stopped, and turned back to Máú, K. iii. 334; inactivity of Bhúpál Contingent at, K. iii. 331; Mahídpúr Contingent refuse to fight, M. i. 222; only twelve of Bhúpál Contingent obey orders, M. i. 223; Col. Travers again endeavours to form men for a charge, M. i. 222; Bhíls too cowed to act, M. i. 223; Residency reduced to 31 defenders, M. i. 223; imminent danger to occupants of Residency, M. i. 224; cowardice and disunion among the cavalry, M. i. 222; Cavalry resolve to abandon Residency, M. i. 224; hopelessness of waiting for Hungerford's battery, M. i. 225; the Residency abandoned, M. i. 226; evacuated in less than two hours from first attack, K. iii. 340.

Retreat of Col. Durand from, K. iii. 332; reasons for Col. Durand's quitting Residency, K. iii. 343; reasons against Col. Durand's quitting Residency, K. iii. 344, M. i. 241; Col. Durand's rejoinder to reasons against, K. iii. 344.

Account of massacre (July 1), K. iii. 330 n.; slaughter

Indor—cont.
of thirty-nine British subjects around Residency, M. i. 218 and n.
Holkár's conduct during attack on Residency reconcilable with loyalty, M. i. 230; he refuses to give up fugitive Christians, M. i. 232; he is free from charge of complicity in mutiny, M. i. 233.
The skill and success of Col. Durand's retreat, M. i. 242; line of retreat from, by Máú, impossible, M. i. 236–238; the fugitives cut off from Simrol pass by Holkár's troops, M. i. 239; Col. Durand's Cavalry demand to retreat on Sihor, M. i. 238, 240; reception of fugitives at Áshtá, M. i. 240 n.; Col. Durand offers to march into Indor (July 30), M. iii. 61.
Influence of position of affairs in India on mutinous Contingent (Aug.), M. iii. 64; both Holkár and Col. Durand disposed to temporise from opposite reasons, M. iii. 63; Col. Durand returns to Máú with Brig. Stuart's column (Aug. 2), M. i. 243; Holkár's troops invited to join Mandíswar rebels (Oct.), M. iii. 67.
Col. Durand marches towards Indor, M. iii. 82; Col. Durand disarms Holkár's Cavalry (Dec. 14), M. iii. 82; Col. Durand orders disarmament of Holkár's troops under threat of doing it himself, M. iii. 82; disarmament of Holkár's troops, M. iii. 83.
Indragarh, Firoz Sháh joins Tántiá Topí at (Jan. 13, '59), M. iii. 359.
Indúr, *see* Indor.

"Inexplicable inconsistency" of the Sepoys, K. ii. 189 n.
Ingelby, Lieut., his heroic bravery, M. i. 88; sad death of, K. iii. 115.
Inglis, Brig., his character, M. i. 414; his military ability, M. i. 481; sends Gen. Havelock a plan of his position at Lakhnau, M. i. 454; text of his despatch on the defence of Lakhnau, M. i. 556-575; commands 5th Brigade at attack on Tántiá Topí (Dec. 5), M. ii. 267; remarks on his proceedings at Firozpúr, K. ii. 442.
Innes, Lieut., storms mutineers' stronghold at Kolhapúr (Aug. 10), M. iii. 41.
Innes, Macleod, his splendid gallantry at Sultánpúr (Feb. 23, '58), M. ii. 334; severely wounded at Dhaurára (March 4, '58), M. ii. 338.
Innes house, a post at Lakhnau Residency, M. i. 442.
Insubordinate conduct of English officers at Pesháwur, K. ii. 480 n.
Irádat Khán, rebel leader, captured and hung (Sept. 27), M. ii. 319.
Irby, Capt., leads supports to stormers of Mess House, Lakhnau, M. ii. 202.
I'rinpúra, the few English in, in great straits, M. ii. 559; mutiny at (Aug. 22), M. ii. 558; devoted gallantry of a few Natives at, M. ii. 560; mutineers defeat Rájá of Jodhpúr's army at Pálí (Sept. 8), M. ii. 565; mutineers, after victory, fall back on A'wah, M. ii. 566; mutineers separate from the Thákur of A'wah, ii. 567; mutineers, defeated and cut up by Capt. Gerrard,

I'rinpúra—cont.
at Narnúl (Oct. 16), M. ii. 568.
Ironside, Mr. Bax, assists Major Eyre to transport and commissariat, M. i. 97.
Irregular Cavalry, constitution of regiments, K. ii. 220 n.
Irregular and Regular military systems, discussed, K. i. 337.
Irresolution, danger of, on part of the English, K. ii. 151.
Irwin, Lieut., escapes from Lallatpúr mutiny, M. iii. 98 n.
Irwin, Private, his conspicuous daring at the Sikandar Bágh, M. ii. 197.
I'sáogarh, plundered by Tántiá Topí (Sept. '58), M. iii. 337.
I'swarí Pándí, the Bárákpúr Jamádár, hanged (April 22), K. ii. 83 n.
I'tá, Mr. Phillipps, magistrate of, rides to Badáon for help, M. i. 322; mutiny at (May 27), K. iii. 283.
I'táwá, singularly prosperous condition of, K. iii. 217; Mr. Allan Hume, Magistrate and Collector at, K. iii. 217, M. i. 160; Mr. Hume organises patrolling parties, M. i. 160; attempted arrest of a cart containing troopers, M. i. 161; fight with seven captured troopers, five of whom are killed, K. iii. 218, M. i. 161.
Second party of mutineers escape by aid of neighbouring populace, K. iii. 220, M. i. 162; they escape to Hindú temple (May 19), K. iii. 218, M. i. 161; Mr. Hume and Mr. Daniell go to the Hindú temple to capture the troopers, K. iii. 219, M. i. 161; the troopers escape from the temple, M. i. 162.

THE HISTORIES OF THE INDIAN MUTINY. 91

I'táwá—*cont.*
Mr. A. Hume orders 9th Regiment to Barpúrá (May 20), K. iii. 221; mutiny of 9th Regiment and its return to I'táwá, K. iii. 222; mutiny at (May 23), M. i. 3, 162; Government records and half treasure at, saved by Mr. A. Hume, K. iii. 222; Gwáliár Contingent restores order in (May 24), M. i. 162; fugitives from, escorted back by Major Henessy, K. iii. 222; Mr. A. Hume again recovers authority at (May 25), K. iii. 223.
A few fanatics at, attempt to stop Walpole's column (Dec. 29), M. ii. 285; Walpole forced to blow up house occupied by them, M. ii. 286; settled condition of (Jan. '58), M. iii. 308.
Itáwah, *see* I'táwá.

J.

Jabalpúr, part of Ságar territory, M. iii. 88; garrison of, M. iii. 96, 102; Major Erskine, chief political officer at, M. iii. 90, 102; Col. Jamieson commands at, M. iii. 102. Attempt to murder Adjutant (June 16), M. iii. 102; arrival of Kámptí column at (Aug. 2), M. iii. 103; mutiny at (Sept. 18), M. iii. 104; Rájá Shankar Sháh and son blown from guns at (Sept. 18), M. iii. 103; mutineers from, seize Lieut. MacGregor at Patan, M. iii. 104; mutineers capture Garhákot, M. iii. 107; and they plunder Damoh, M. iii. 107; fight with rebels near (Nov.), M.

Jabalpúr—*cont.*
iii. 107; Gen. Whitlock arrives at (Feb. 6, '58), M. iii. 192.
Jabalpúr column, constitution of, M. iii. 191, 192.
Jackson, Col., stops incipient mutiny at Nímach (Aug. 12), M. ii. 554.
Jackson, Mr. Coverley, appointed Outram's successor in Oudh (1856), K. i. 398; unconciliating in deportment, K. i. 399; he and Mr. Mr. Gubbins in violent antagonism, K. i. 399; pursues his private quarrels to the detriment of the service, K. i. 407; his sense of profound tranquillity in Oudh, K. iii. 430 n.; fails to aid Lord Canning in rebutting charges of British cruelty in Oudh, K. i. 406; his administration makes the Oudh people desire return of native rulers, M. iii. 479; Lord Canning resolves to remove him from Oudh, K. i. 408; he is removed from Chief Commissionership of Oudh (1857), K. i. 450.
Jackson, Mr. Mountstuart, narrative of flight of his party from Sítápúr, K. iii. 482.
Jackson, Miss, her rescue at Lakhnau (March 17, '58), M. ii. 403 n.
Jacob, Col. Le Grand, made Commissioner of Southern Marátha country, M. iii. 236; suppresses mutiny at Kolhápúr (Dec. 6), M. iii. 236; receives military command of southern Marátha country (June '58), M. iii. 246; forces Chief of Miraj to give up his ammunition (June '58), M. iii. 245; receives supreme command of disturbed Bombay district, K. iii. 409.

Jacob, John, denounces the Bengal military system, K. i. 324; in favour of promotion by selection, K. i. 336.

Jagadíspúr, residence of Kunwar Singh, K. iii. 99; Kunwar Singh's treasonable preparations at, K. iii. 142; Sepoys from A'rá fly to (Aug. 2), M. i. 102; Major V. Eyre advances against, M. i. 127; captured by Major Eyre (Aug. 12), M. i. 130; palace and other buildings destroyed by Major Eyre, M. i. 130.

Kunwar Singh returns to (April 22, '58), M. ii. 476; reoccupied by Amar Singh (July '58), M. ii. 484; rebels cleared from the jungle of (Oct. '58), M. ii. 492.

Jagannáth Singh, closes the gates of Powáín on the Maulaví (June 5, '58), M. ii. 543; shoots the Maulaví and cuts off his head (June 5, '58), M. ii. 544; receives £5,000 for killing the Maulaví, M. ii. 544 n.

Jagathir, Jamádár, completely defeats detachment of Chatgáon mutineers (Jan. 30, '58), M. ii. 425.

Jaipúr, one of Rájpút states, M. i. 245 n.; Major W. Eden, Political Agent at, K. iii. 353, M. i. 257; Sepoys of the Rájá found untrustworthy, M. i. 258.

Jaipúr, Rám Singh, Rájá of, thoroughly devoted to the English, M. i. 257; cordially faithful to the British, K. iii. 357.

Jaipúr troops, ordered to protect Mathurá, K. iii. 357; prove doubtful and are brought back to Jaipúr, K. iii. 358.

Jaisalmír, one of Rájpút states, M. i. 245 n.

Jájamau, Náná Sáhib's boats destroyed and captured at (July 31), M. i. 499.

Jakes, Private, his great gallantry on Chárbágh bridge, Lakhnau, M. i. 537*.

Jakhání, captured by Lieut. W. Osborne (Dec. 31), M. iii. 112.

Jáklon, Tántiá Topí tries to escape through jungle of (Oct. '58), M. iii. 341.

Jálandhar, partly annexed by Lord Hardinge (1847), M. i. 152.

Col. Hartley commands there, K. ii. 444; preparations for defence of (May), K. ii. 444; plan of the mutiny at, K. ii. 500 n.; the mutiny breaks out (June 7), K. ii. 499; rebels from, march on Dehrá Dún (June 15), M. iii. 421.

Jalpáígorí, near Bhután, its isolated position, K. iii. 173; head-quarters of 73rd N.I., M. ii. 426; Col. Sherer commands there, K. iii. 173, M. i. 138; Col. Sherer's antecedents, and character, M. i. 138, 139.

Intense excitement there (June 25), K. iii. 175; Col. Sherer boldly allows the troops to parade with loaded arms, K. iii. 175; Col. Sherer seizes and condemns to death four conspirators in his regiment, M. i. 139; Col. Sherer blows the four conspirators from guns, M. i. 140; Col. Sherer a second time prevents an outbreak, K. iii. 176; mutiny at (Dec. 5), M. ii. 427; Col. Sherer blows two troopers from guns, M. ii. 430; mutineers driven into Nipál, M. ii. 429, 430; and

Jalpáígorí—*cont.*
arrested by Nipálese, M. ii. 430; Col. Sherer maintains order in (Jan. '58), M. ii. 425; Col. Sherer brings his regiment safely through the crisis, K. iii. 177, M. i. 140.

Jamádár of 34th Regiment and guard fail in their duty (March), K. i. 539; sentenced to be hanged (April), K. i. 549.

Jamá Masjid, Persian proclamation on walls of (March '57), K. ii. 40.

Jamná, crossed by Brig. Wilson (June 4), K. ii. 188; order preserved along right bank of, by Native landowners, M. iii. 440; mutineers assemble on right bank (Dec.), M. ii. 448.

Jámbotí, the Desáí of, a discontented sufferer under Inám Commission, M. iii. 29.

James, Lieut., Chief Commissariat Officer, Lakhnau, K. iii. 439.

Jamieson, Lieut.-Col., commands at Jabalpúr, M. iii. 102.

Jámkhandí, Native state of southern Marátha country, M. iii. 20; emissary from, seized at Belgáon (July), M. iii. 32; the emissary from, blown from a gun (Aug.), M. iii. 33; chief of, arrested by Mr. Manson (April '58), M. iii. 239.

Jammu Contingent, its conduct, on assault of Dehlí, K. iii. 693.

Jang Bahádur, offers his whole army to Government of India, M. ii. 315; his reason for helping England, M. ii. 316; marches his troops into Gorakhpúr (July), M. ii. 316; himself proceeds to Gorakhpúr (Nov.), M. ii. 321; enters Gorakhpúr (Dec. 23), M. ii.

Jang Bahádur—*cont.*
323; defeats the rebels at town of Gorakhpúr (Jan. 5, '58), M. ii. 323; reaches Barárí, and is joined by Col. Rowcroft's force (Jan. 19, '58), M. ii. 323; enters Oudh (Feb. 25, '58), M. ii. 324; reaches Lakhnau (March 10, '58), M. ii. 324, 388; clears the front of A'lambágh from rebels (March 16-18), M. ii. 403; his troops return to Nipál (June '58), M. ii. 498 *n.*; permits English to pursue rebels in Nipál, M. iii. 295.

Jánpúr, mutiny at (June 5), K. ii. 237, M. i. 33; general anarchy reigns there, K. ii. 238; fugitives from, saved, K. ii. 239; Nipálese troops occupy (Aug. 15), M. ii. 317; Col. Longden arrives at (Oct. 4), M. ii. 320; Gen. Franks commands force at, M. ii. 321; strength of Gen. Franks' force at (Nov. 29), M. ii. 325.

Jathin, Col. Lugard defeats the rebels at (May 12, '58), M. ii. 480.

Jatogh, reported murder of officers at, K. ii. 144.

Játs from Rohtak, offer their services at A'grá (Jan. '58), M. iii. 313.

Jaunpore, *see* Jánpúr.

Jawáhir Singh, blown from a gun at Khásganj (Dec. 22), M. ii. 293.

Jawán Bakht, desired as successor by Bahádur Sháh, K. ii. 28; his hatred of the English, K. ii. 34.

Jenkins, Capt., gallantly holds outposts beyond trenches at Káhnpúr, K. ii. 319.

Jenkins, Capt. Griffith, sent to the Mauritius and the Cape for troops (May), M. iii. 6;

Jenkins, Capt.—*cont.*
specially thanked by the Queen for his able services, M. iii. 465.
Jenkins, Major, cuts his way through surrounding Sepoys, at Katanjí, M. iii. 105.
Jenkinson, Mr., heroically interposes his own body to save his companions (June 4), K. ii. 232 *n.*
Jennings, Rev. Mr. and Miss, murder of, at Dehlí (May 11), K. ii. 80.
Jervis of the Engineers proudly dies at Káhnpúr, K. ii. 320.
Jewan Bakht, *see* Jawán Bakht.
Jhánsí, part of Ságar territory, M. iii. 88; description of ground near, M. iii. 157; great strength of fort, M. iii. 157, 172 *n.*; its early history, M. i. 179; various kings of, M. i. 180; declared our hereditary possession (1822), K. i. 89; created a kingdom by the British (1832), M. i. 180; Rájá of, dies childless (1853), K. i. 90; declared lapsed to the British (1854), M. i. 182; the British assume administration, K. i. 91, iii. 360, M. i. 181, iii. 481.

Numerous aggravating acts committed by British, M. i. 182; garrison of, in 1857, K. iii. 362, M. i. 183; Capt. A. Skene, Commissioner at, K. iii. 362, M. i. 183, iii. 90.

The Rání of, excites sedition among the Sepoys, M. i. 183; the Sepoys seize the Star Fort (June 5), M. i. 185; European families retire to Fort (June 5), K. iii. 364; the Rání visits the cantonments in military array (June 6), K. iii. 365, M. i. 185; Mutiny at (June 7), K. iii.

Jhánsí—*cont.*
315, 364, M. i. 33, 186; slaughter of British officers at cantonments, K. iii. 365; the surviving Europeans retire to large fort, M. i. 186; the Rání and the Sepoys differ, K. iii. 366; mutineers invite Sadáshir Ráo to occupy throne, K. iii. 366, 370; the Rání buys the support of mutineers, K. iii. 370; M. i. 191.

Sepoys attack large fort, but are repulsed, M. i. 187; desperate attempts of Sepoys to carry the Fort (June 7, 8), K. iii. 367, M. i. 188; treachery within Fort detected, K. iii. 367, M. i. 188; the European garrison treat for surrender, M. i. 187; the three envoys murdered, M. i. 188; the Rání offers terms to garrison, M. i. 189; surrender of the Fort, K. iii. 368; the garrison evacuate the Fort (June 8), M. i. 189; the massacre of the garrison (June 8), K. iii. 369, M. i. 190; the Rání proves herself a capable ruler, M. i. 191.

Sir Hugh Rose marches on, M. iii. 153; Sir Hugh Rose appears before, and reconnoitres (March 21, '58), M. iii. 156; rebel garrison of, M. iii. 158; batteries open against (March 24, '58), M. iii. 159; determined exertions of the defenders, M. iii. 160; breach in walls effected (March 29, '58), M. iii. 160; Tántiá Topí advances to the relief of (March 31, '58), M. iii. 161; dejection of rebel garrison at defeat of Tántiá Topí (April 1, '58), M. iii. 166; Tántiá Topí's account

THE HISTORIES OF THE INDIAN MUTINY. 95

Jhánsí—cont.
of his attempt to relieve, M.
iii. 518; fierce struggle of
right attack at storming of
(April 3, '58), M. iii. 168;
Major Boileau brings reinforcements to right attack at
storming of (April 3, '58),
M. iii. 168; Lieuts. Dick,
Meiklejohn, and Bonus, successfully lead escalade of, M.
iii. 169; Col. Lowth leads
attack on the palace, M. iii.
169; desperate resistance at
Ráni's palace, M. iii. 170; rebels driven from town, occupy a hill outside, M. iii.
170; Major Gall storms hill
outside town, and kills every
defender, M. iii. 171; the
Rání evacuates fort, and flies
to Kálpí (April 4, '58), M.
iii. 171; loss suffered in the
capture of, M. iii. 171; Col.
Liddell left in command of
(April 25, '58), M. iii. 173.
Jhánsí, Rání of, her character,
K. iii. 361; pleads against
annexation, K. i. 91; her pension of £6,000 a year, K. iii.
360, M. i. 182; her hatred of
the English, K. iii. 360; she
resolves on revenge, M. i.
183; Capt. Skene deceived by
her cunning, M. i. 184; gains
permission to raise a body of
armed men, K. iii. 364, M. i.
184; incites the Sepoys to
mutiny, K. iii. 365; buys the
support of the Sepoys, K. iii.
370; the English garrison of
fort treat for surrender, M. i.
187; the Rání sends the
English negotiators to be
murdered, K. iii. 367; her
complicity in the massacre of.
English garrison (June 8),
M. i. 190; she proves herself
a capable ruler, M. i. 191; and

Jhánsí, Rání of—cont.
receives adhesion of Gwáliár
Contingent (Nov. 3), M. ii.
148; she communicates with
Náná Sáhib, K. iii. 370; evacuates her fort and flies to
Kálpí (April 4, '58), M. iii.
171; she is defeated at
Kúnch, M. iii. 174; and flies
from Kúnch to Kálpí (May
'58), M. iii. 180; she revives
her expiring cause at Kálpí
(May 15, '58), M. iii. 182;
flies from Kálpí (May 22,
'58), M. iii. 186; flies from
Gulaulí to Gopálpúr, M. iii.
203; conceives the design of
seizing Gwáliár, M. iii. 205;
her bold plan succeeds in part
(June 1, '58), M. iii. 209; she
is killed at the battle near
Kotá-kí-saráí (June 17, '58),
M. iii. 221.
Jhájar, captured by Brig.
Showers (Oct. 18), M. ii.
108.
Jháláwar, one of Rájpút states,
M. i. 245 n.
Jhálrá Pátan, treacherously
yielded to Tántiá Topí (Aug.
'58), M. iii. 326; amount of
contribution exacted from, by
Ráo Sáhib, M. iii. 327 n.
Jhálrá Pátan, Ráná of, his
loyalty to the English, M. iii.
326; flies from Tántiá Topí
to Máu (Aug. '58), M. iii.
326.
Jhárá, Thákur of, raises body of
horse for the English (Jan.
'58), M. iii. 313.
Jheend, see Jhínd.
Jhelam, mutiny at (July 7), K.
ii. 624; sharp resistance of
Sepoys at, K. ii. 625, 626.
Jhigan, Gen. Whitlock catches
rebels evacuating (April 9,
'58), M. iii. 195.
Jhínd, Rájá of, his loyalty and

Jhínd, Rájá of—*cont.*
services, M. iii. 307; supports the English, K. ii. 162.
Jigní, Rájá of, gives supplies and carriage to the rebels (May '58), M. iii. 174.
Jilwáná, Major Sutherland occupies (Nov. 23), M. iii. 348.
Jíran near Nímach, seized by rebels from Mandíswar (Oct.), M. ii. 571; attacked by Capt. Tucker, who is repulsed (Oct. 23), M. ii. 571; Mandíswar rebels evacuate (Oct. 23), M. ii. 571.
Jodhpúr, one of Rájpút states, M. i. 245 *n.*; Capt. Monck-Mason, Political Agent at, K. iii. 354, M. i. 258; expedition against mutineers in, led by Col. Gerrard (Oct.), M. ii. 109; mutineers take up a strong position at Nárnúl (Nov. 16), M. ii. 110; mutineers abandon their position at Nárnúl for refreshment, M. ii. 111; in absence of mutineers Col. Gerrard occupies their position (Nov. 16), M. ii. 111; mutineers attempt to return to their position at Nárnúl, M. ii. 113; splendid charge and countercharge of cavalry at Nárnúl, M. ii. 114; defeat of mutineers at Nárnúl (Nov. 16), M. ii. 116, 118; constitution of legion of, M. ii. 555; the Contingent stealthily attacks Mount Abú, M. ii. 556.
Jodhpúr, Mahárájá of, anticipates request for assistance, K. iii. 352; places a contingent at service of the English, M. i. 257; not friendly to the English, M. i. 259; tries to intercept his mutinous troops at Pálí, M. ii. 563; his troops totally defeated (Sept. 8), M. ii. 109, 565.

Johnson, Capt. Edwin, commands left section No. 2 battery at Dehlí, M. ii. 19.
Johnstone, Brig., his indecision at Jálandhar, K. ii. 499; his apologies for delay in pursuit of mutineers, K. ii. 501 *n.*; hesitates to send help to Ludhíáná, K. ii. 507.
Jones, Brig. William, commands second column of assault at Dehlí. M. ii. 27; commands the Rúrkí column (April '58), M. ii. 511; leaves all practical command of Rúrkí to Col. Coke, M. ii. 514; defeats rebels at Naghína (April 21, '58), M. ii. 517; defeats the rebels at Núrganj, M. ii. 529; effects junction with Sir Colin Campbell (May 7, '58), M. ii. 531; sent against the Maulaví at Sháhjahánpúr, M. ii. 534; drives the Maulaví across the Kánárat Naddí (May 11, '58), M. ii. 535; enters Sháhjahánpúr, but cannot drive out the Maulaví's troops, M. ii. 536; severely attacked by the Maulaví (May 15, '58), M. ii. 537; joined by Sir Colin Campbell, M. ii. 537.
Jones, Col., assumes command of Gen Penny's column (April '58), M. ii. 502; joins Sir Colin Campbell (May 3, '58), M. ii. 502.
Jordan, Mr., his murder at Bairám Ghát, K. iii. 478.
Jootee Persaud, *see* Jotí Parsád.
Jotí Parsád, victuals Fort at A'grá, K. iii. 399.
Jouhdpore, *see* Jodhpúr.
Journalism, its dangers in times of excitement, K. iii. 15, 16.

THE HISTORIES OF THE INDIAN MUTINY. 97

Jubán Singh, joins Kunwár Singh on the Son, M. ii. 444.
Jugdispore, *see* Jagadíspúr.
Julápúr, near Kálpí, headquarters of the rebels, M. ii. 448.
Julpigooree, *see* Jalpáígorí.
Jumna, *see* Jamná.
Junction of Mírat and Dehlí Field forces, K. ii. 190.
Jutogh, *see* Jatogh.

K.

Kachh, Native state in Bombay Presidency, M. iii. 2.
Kachiání, fugitives from Sítápúr lodged in fort of, K. iii. 482; fugitives from Mohamdí sent to, M. i. 385; arrival of Sítápúr fugitives at, M. i. 388; story of the fugitives residing in, M. i. 389 n.
Kachrú, Brig. Showers catches rebel ringleaders at (March '58), M. iii. 311.
Káhnpúr, its situation and description, K. ii. 286; routes from, to Kálpí, M. ii. 228; the cantonment at, K. ii. 287; European soldiers at, in May, K. ii. 289; overfilled with non-combatants, K. ii. 291.
Agitation at, on first inkling of annexation of Oudh, M. iii. 480; perilous condition of, in May, K. ii. 292; magazine at, not occupied, K. ii. 294; Col. Neill's description of the Magazine at, K. ii. 295 n.
Small re-inforcement from Lakhnau arrives at (May), K. ii. 296; the Treasury at, resigned to the care of Náná

Káhnpúr—*cont.*
Sáhib, K. ii. 299; ridiculous character of entrenchment at, K. ii. 293; disorganised condition of barracks at, K. ii. 300; dangerous panic at (May 22), K. ii. 301; mutinous disposition of 2nd Cavalry at, K. ii. 302; non-combatants retire to entrenchment (May 22), K. ii. 300; believed to be safe (June 1), K. ii. 303.
Effect of half measures at, K. ii. 303; help sent to Lakhnau (June 3), K. ii. 304; hesitation of Sepoys to rise, K. ii. 305 and n.; worn-out condition of entrenched troops before outbreak, K. ii. 305 n.
Plot between Sepoys and Náná Sáhib, K. ii. 306; outbreak of Sepoys (June 4), K. ii. 307, M. i. 34; mutiny precipated by a casual incident, K. ii. 307 n.; at first outbreak of Mutiny, officers unmolested, K. ii. 307.
Magazine and Treasury fall into mutineers' hands, K. ii. 308; contents of Magazine said to have been unknown, K. ii. 308 n.; wavering regiments fired upon and driven into mutiny (June 5), K. ii. 309; mutineers propose march to Dehlí (June 5), K. ii. 309; return of mutineers a heavy blow to the English, K. ii. 313; all the Europeans concentrate at entrenchments (June 6), K. ii. 313; mutineers, on their return, pillage indiscriminately, K. ii. 314.
The mutineers attack entrenchment (June 6), K. ii. 315; siege of entrenchment (June 6-27), K. ii. 316; fearful condition of besieged, K.

7

Káhnpúr—cont.
ii. 316; contrast between besiegers and besieged, K. ii. 317; the heroes who defended the entrenchment, K. ii. 318-323; burning of the Barracks during siege (June 10), K. ii. 323; faithful natives obliged to be sent from entrenchment, K. ii. 325; destruction of all hospital stores and surgical appliances, K. ii. 324; fearful catalogue of casualties among garrison of, K. ii. 326, 327; the work done by entrenchment outposts, K. ii. 328; centenary of Plassey at, K. ii. 329; famine afflicts the garrison (June 23), K. ii. 331; number of garrison killed during siege, K. ii. 356 n.

Náná Sáhib offers terms of capitulation, K. ii. 332; opinions of officers concerning capitulation, K. ii. 333; terms agreed upon, K. ii. 334; treaty of capitulation signed (June 26), K. ii. 335; Lord Canning's efforts to relieve garrison, K. iii. 4; its loss caused by first delays of Government of India, M. i. 6, 7.

The garrison issue from the entrenchment (June 27), K. ii. 336; conducted to Satí Chaurá Ghát, K. ii. 337; murder of Col. and Mrs. Ewart, K. ii. 338; embarkation of the garrison, K. ii. 339; the massacre (June 27), K. ii. 341, M. i. 34; the officers of Nánà Sáhib present at massacre of, K. ii. 340; escape of a single boat, K. ii. 343; occupants of the escaping boat destroy a pursuing party (June 28), K. ii. 344; they land a party to beat off as-

Káhnpúr—cont.
sailants (June 29), K. ii. 345; last stand of fugitives from, K. ii. 346; four of the garrison fight their way to safety, K. ii. 347; capture of the last escaping boat, K. ii. 348; Nánà Sáhib slaughters men who escaped the massacre (June 30), K. ii. 348; Tántiá Topí's account of the massacre at, M. iii. 515.

Muhammadan influence reviving there (July), K. ii. 350; Nánà Sáhib murders Col. Smith's party escaping from Fathpúr (July), K. iii. 303; two hundred captive women and children penned in Bíbíghar, K. ii. 353; women captives made to grind corn for Nánà Sáhib, K. ii. 354; massacre of women and children (July 15), K. ii. 372, 373; number of women and children slaughtered by Nánà Sáhib, K. ii. 356 n.

The battle (July 16), K. ii. 376-381; re-occupied by British (July 17), K. ii. 381; fearful retribution exacted at, K. ii. 387, 388; joy of the inhabitants at return of the English, K. ii. 391; Gen. Havelock constructs entrenchment, K. ii. 404-406; the dispersed boatmen of, recovered, K. ii. 406; Gen. Neill arrives there (July 20), M. i. 489; who agrees to hold the place with a few sick and wounded men, M. i. 490; Gen. Havelock starts for relief of Lakhnau (July 21), M. i. 490; state of discipline at (July 22), K. ii. 406 n.; Gen. Neill restores order (July 25), M. i. 498; he sends party to

Káhnpúr—cont.
Jájaman, who destroy and capture Nána Sáhib's boats, M. i. 499; critical position of town (July 31), M. i. 501; Gen. Neill's letter to Gen. Havelock (July 31), M. i. 501 n.; Gen. Havelock's reply, M. i. 502 n.; Gen. Neill sends party, which recovers wife and daughters of Náráyan Ráo (Aug. 5), M. i. 507, 508; he sends third river party against Bithúr (Aug. 8), M. i. 508; he marches men along Bithúr road for moral effect, M. i. 509. Gen. Havelock returns and reassumes command at, M. i. 509; Gen. Neill advises Gen. Havelock to attack Bithúr, M. i. 510; Gen. Havelock moves against Bithúr (Aug. 16), M. i. 510; dangers surrounding (Aug. 17), M. i. 516; Capt. Gordon starts on fourth river trip, and destroys enemy's boats at Rájghát (Aug. 20), M. i. 517; arrival of fugitives there, M. i. 518; Gen. Outram arrives (Sept. 15), M. i. 518.
Tántiá Topí advances against (Nov. 4), M. ii. 148; strength of garrison at (Nov. 9), M. ii. 149; Gen. C. Windham left in command of, M. ii. 149; his instructions for holding, M. ii. 149; Gen. Windham secures the entrenchment at, M. ii. 227.
Tántiá Topí severs communication with W. and N.W., M. ii. 229; Gen. Windham guesses Tántiá.Topí's design on, M. ii. 230; Gen. Windham obtains permission to detain troops in, M. ii. 230; increase in Gen. Windham's

Káhnpúr—cont.
force, M. ii. 231; he advances beyond town to the west (Nov. 17), M. ii. 231; he advances six miles nearer to Tántiá Topí (Nov. 24), M. ii. 234; Tántiá Topí gradually closes round, M. ii. 234; Gen. Windham's dispositions for meeting advance of Tántiá Topí (Nov. 26), M. ii. 235; Gen. Windham marches back towards town, M. ii. 236; Gen. Windham attacks and defeats Tántiá Topí's troops at Pándu rivulet (Nov. 26), M. ii. 236; Tántiá Topí presses on Gen. Windham's retiring troops, M. ii. 237.
Tántiá Topí attacks Gen. Windham (Nov. 27), M. ii. 238; Brig. Carthew protects Bithúr road, M. ii. 239; Tántiá Topí's great superiority in artillery, M. ii. 240; Gen. Windham retires on brickkilns, M. ii. 241; Gen. Windham orders Brig. Carthew to fall back on brick-kilns (Nov. 27), M. ii. 242; Gen. Windham abandons tents and kits, M. ii. 243; Tántiá Topí occupies lower part of city, M. ii. 242; Gen. Windham drives Tántiá Topí's troops out of city, M. ii. 243; Brig. Carthew beats off enemy on the right, M. ii. 244; reason for Gen. Windham's defeat (Nov. 27), M. ii. 245.
Sir Colin Campbell's hurried march to (Nov. 28), M. ii. 224; Gen. Windham's dispositions for resisting Tántiá Topí (Nov. 28), M. ii. 246; Brig. Carthew beats off Tántiá Topí's attack on his position, M. ii. 248; Col. Walpole beats off Tántiá Topí's attack

Káhnpúr—*cont.*
on his position, M. ii. 249; Brig. Carthew ordered to advance again, M. ii. 250; Brig. Wilson ordered to cover Carthew's advance, M. ii. 250; failure of Brig. Wilson's attack, M. ii. 251; Brig. Carthew forced to fall back through failure of Brig. Wilson, M. ii. 252; criticisms on Gen. Windham's generalship (Nov. 28), M. ii. 249.
Sir Colin Campbell arrives (Nov. 28), M. ii. 257; Tántiá Topí destroys stores (Nov. 29), M. ii. 260; the whole of Sir Colin Campbell's force enters (Nov. 30), M. ii. 261.
Tántiá Topí attacks British position (Dec. 2), M. ii. 263; non-combatants sent to Alláhábád (Dec. 3), M. ii. 263; Sir Colin Campbell's plan for driving Tántiá Topí away (Dec. 5), M. ii. 265; Tántiá Topí renews attack on British position (Dec. 4), M. ii. 265; Tántiá Topí defeated, but allowed to escape by Gen. Mansfield (Dec. 6), M. ii. 275; Gen. Hope Grant sent to follow up Tántiá Topí (Dec. 8), M. ii. 276.
Sir Colin Campbell remains inactive till Dec. 23, for want of transport, M. ii. 284; Brig. Carthew marches from, to Bhognípúr, and clears district of rebels (Jan. '58), M. ii. 448; Sir Colin Campbell returns to (Feb. 4, '58), M. ii. 314; road to Lakhnau threatened by Bení Mádhava (May '58), M. iii. 266.
Káhnpúr battery, a post at Lakhnau battery, M. i. 443.
Kaisar Bágh, *see* Lakhnau.
Kajwá, its position and history,

Kajwá—*cont.*
M. ii. 144; Bihár mutineers found at, by Col. Powell (Oct. 31), M. ii. 143; battle of (Nov. 2), M. ii. 145; Col. Powell killed during battle, M. ii. 145; Capt. W. Peel assumes command of troops on Col. Powell's death, M. ii. 145; and completes defeat of mutineers, M. ii. 146.
Kakraulí, Gen. Penny attacked and killed at (April 30, '58), M. ii. 501.
Kálá Kankar, Rájá of Hanmant Singh of, his noble generosity to fugitive English, M. i. 407 *n.*
Kálpí, its situation and importance, M. iii. 172; routes from, to Káhnpúr, M. ii. 228; strength of the position, M. iii. 182; Dr. Lowe's description of rebel arsenal at, M. iii. 187 *n.*; Dr. Lowe's account of the capture of, M. iii. 186.
Nawáb of Bándá marches into, and garrisons (May 15, '58), M. iii. 181; Rání of Jhánsí revives her expiring cause at, M. iii. 182; Tántiá Topí's troops retreat to, M. iii. 178; the defeat at Kúnch causes rebels to evacuate (May '58), M. iii. 180; Sir Hugh Rose opens attack on (May 19, '58), M. iii. 183; skilful plan of rebel attack (May 22, '58), M. iii. 183; complete defeat of rebel attack, M. iii. 185.
Tántiá Topí reaches (Nov. 9), M. ii. 228.
Kambhayat, Native state in Bombay Presidency, M. iii. 2.
Kámpságar, Col. Durnford defeats rebels at (Oct. 16, '58), M. ii. 486.
Kámptí, garrison of, M. iii.

Kámptí—*cont.*
113; occupied by Gen. Whitlock (Jan. 10, '58), M. iii. 192.
Kánárat Naddí, Brig. Jones drives the Maulaví across (May 11, '58), M. ii. 535.
Kanaund, captured by Brig. Showers (Oct.), M. ii. 108.
Kanchanpúr, Lieut. W. Osborne defeats rebels at, M. iii. 112.
Kandahár, annexed by Dost Muhammad, K. i. 414.
Kánhpúr, *see* Káhnpúr.
Kankar, strong force of rebels at (April '58), M. ii. 500; Lieut. de Kantzow greatly distinguishes himself at attack on (April 6, '58), M. ii. 500.
Kankhal, attacked and burned by rebels from Bíjnúr (Jan. 7, '58), M. iii. 413; Capt. Boisragon attacks and defeats Bíjnúr raiders at (Jan. 9, 58), M. iii. 415.
Kan Singh, *see* Khán Singh.
Kantzow, De, *see* De Kantzow.
Kappartolá, Rájá of, joins Gen. Hope Grant's force (June 4, '58), M. iii. 267.
Karáchí, the Queen's Proclamation read with ceremony at (Nov. 1, '58), M. iii. 396.
Karaulí, one of Rájpút states, M. i. 245 *n*.
Kargun, Tántiá Topí forces Holkár's troops at, to join him (Nov. 19, '58), M. iii. 346.
Kárísát, Brig. Douglas defeats rebels at (Oct. 14, '58), M. ii. 486.
Karnál, Nawáb of, supports the English, K. ii. 162.
Kashmír Gate at Dehlí, the explosion of, K. iii. 673.
Kashmír Contingent, its conduct on assault of Dehlí, K. iii. 693; hampers fourth attacking column at Dehlí, K. iii. 606.

Kashmír Contingent—*cont.*
ing column at Dehlí, K. iii. 606.
Katák, Col. Fischer commands Madras Sepoys at, M. ii. 138; he marches from, into eastern Bihár, M. ii. 138; incipient sedition at, K. iii. 173.
Katanjí, a village on the river Hiran, M. iii. 105; 52nd N.I. attacked and defeated at, M. iii. 105.
Katchiání, *see* Kachiání.
Káthiyáwár, Native state in Bombay Presidency, M. iii. 2.
Káthwár, *see* Káthiyáwár.
Kavanagh, Thomas Henry, his personal description and disguise, M. ii. 164; offers to convey letter to Sir Colin Campbell (Nov. 9), M. ii. 163; he succeeds in his enterprise (Nov. 10), M. ii. 150, 165; Assistant-Commissioner at Malhiábád (July '58), M. iii. 284; proposes the capture of Sandíla, M. iii. 284; he and Capt. Dawson capture Sandíla (July 30, '58), M. iii. 284.
Kaye, Major, commands left section of No. 1 battery at Dehlí, M. ii. 13; transferred to right section of No. 2 battery at Dehlí, M. ii. 19.
Kaye, Sir John, his criticism of the arrest of Patná Wahábís contested, M. i. 53; his manly vindication of Mr. Tayler, M. i. 118 *n*.
Keatinge, Capt., fortifies a post fourteen miles from Asírgarh (July), M. iii. 59; his gallantry at Khúkwásás (March 5, '58), M. iii. 152; severely wounded while storming Chandairí (March 17, '58), M. iii. 153.
Keene, Mr. H. G., chief civil officer at Dehrá Dún, M. iii.

Keene, Mr. H. G.—*cont.*
419; raises recruits to preserve order at Dehrá Dún (May), M. iii. 420; organises patrols at irregular times in Dehrá Dún (June), M. iii. 421; sends the treasure up to Masúrí (June 15), M. iii. 421; marches against the Jálándhár brigade (June 16), M. iii. 421; the Jálándhár brigade escapes, M. iii. 422; issues paper money on his own responsibility, M. iii. 424; carries Dehrá Dún through the Mutiny unharmed, M. iii. 424.

Kelly, Col., chases rebels into Nipál, M. iii. 296.

Kennedy, Col. J. D., commands 43rd Regiment at Barákpúr, K. i. 495.

Kenny, Private, his conspicuous daring at the Sikandar Bágh, M. ii. 197.

Kerowlee, *see* Kiráolí.

Kerr, Lieut., storms and captures mutineers' stronghold at Kolhápúr (Aug. 10), M. iii. 41.

Kerr, Lord Mark, sent to relieve Ázamgarh (March 31, '58), M. ii. 459; attacks the rebels near Sarsána (April 6, '58), M. ii. 460; penetrates the rebel centre and relieves Ázamgarh (April 6, '58), M. ii. 462; the skill and daring of his relief of Ázamgarh, M. ii. 464.

Khairpúr, Native state in Bombay Presidency, M. iii. 2.

Khákí Risála, or Dust-coloured Regiment, raised at Mírat, M. iii. 428.

Khalsa, name of the old Sikh army, K. ii. 473.

Khán Bahádur Khán, pensioner of the Government, instigates mutiny at Barailí (May), M.

Khán Bahádur Khán—*cont.*
i. 307; elected ruler at Barailí (May 31), K. iii. 275; proclaimed Viceroy at Barailí, M. i. 316; destroys Mr. Thomason's tomb, M. i. 317; slaughters in cold blood the English men, women, and children, found in Barailí (June 1), K. iii. 276, M. i. 317; defied by Mr. Hansborough, K. iii. 276; persuades Bakht Khán to lead the Sepoys to Dehlí, M. i. 317.

Becomes supreme in Rohilkhand, M. i. 332; the nature of his rule in Rohilkhand, M. i. 333; unable to restore order in Barailí, K. iii. 277; his fights with the Thákurs, M. i. 333; his proclamation for extermination of Christians, K. iii. 288; his proclamation of British deceitfulness, K. iii. 289; rehearses legislative acts bearing on caste, K. iii. 290; he is in want of money, K. iii. 291; holds his position for months, K. iii. 291; the people sicken of his rule, and long for return of the English, M. i. 334.

His force at Barailí (May '58), M. ii. 522; resolves to meet the English in the plain (May 4, '58), M. ii. 523; evacuates Barailí (May 5, '58), M. ii. 529; pursued to Pílíbhít by Col. Coke, M. ii. 538; threatens Powáin (Aug. '58), M. iii. 274.

Khan Behadur Khan, *see* Khán Bahádur Khán.

Khán Singh, Sirdár, appointed Díwán of Múltán, K. i. 19 ; conspires against the English at Lahor (1848), K. i. 29.

Khorai, Tántiá Topí defeated at, with loss of half his army (Oct. '58), M. iii. 342.
Khásganj, battle of (Dec. 15), M. ii. 288.
Khot, daring capture of fort of, by Jamádár Imám Bakhsh Khán (April 18, '58), M. ii. 516.
Kiráolí, chief of, dies childless (1852), K. i. 92; claimants for the ráj, K. i. 94, 95; annexation of, forbidden by Court of Directors, K. i. 94; doubts as to the legitimacy of the adoption of Bharat Pál, K. i. 95; Madan Pál succeeds to the ráj of (1853), K. i. 96.
Kirchoff, Sergeant, his miraculous escape from Náogáon, M. i. 196.
Kirk, Dr., murdered at Gwáliár (June 14), K. iii. 318, M. i. 175.
Kirke, Major, extraordinary conduct of, during escape from Náogáon, K. iii. 373, 374; dies of sunstroke during retreat from Náogáon, M. i. 195.
Kirwí, historical sketch of, M. iii. 199; Rádhava Govind, Díwán of (May '58), M. iii. 199; the Ráos of, join heartily with Náná Sáhib, M. iii. 200; they profess loyalty and offer to surrender, M. iii. 200; they surrender to Gen. Whitlock (June 2, '58), M. iii. 200; Gen. Whitlock enters (June 6, '58), M. iii. 201; enormous treasure found there, M. iii. 201.
Kishngarh, one of Rájpút states, M. i. 245 n.
Kittúr, the Desáí of, discontented chief of the Lingayat population, M. iii. 29.
Knocker, Capt., storms and car-

Knocker, Capt.—cont.
ries the Shergátí pass, Sambalpúr (Nov. 5), M. ii. 440.
Knox, Capt., death of, at Dehlí (June 12), K. ii. 544 n.
Kóls, a tribe in Chutiá Nágpúr, M. ii. 134; attack party of English in Singhbhúm (Dec.), M. ii. 439.
Kolhápúr, Native state in Bombay Presidency, M. iii. 2; modern history of, M. iii. 36; mutiny at (July 31), K. iii. 408, M. iii. 31, 37; reason for mutiny at, K. iii. 407; the British disarm forts of, to the annoyance of the people, M. iii. 36; riot and murder at, M. iii. 38; some mutineers return to duty, and some retire to the jungles, M. iii. 40; Lieut. Kerr arrives with some Maráthá Horse, M. iii. 41; Lieut. Kerr attacks and cuts up rebels, M. iii. 41; desperate resistance of Sepoys at (Aug. 10), M. iii. 41; the prompt action of Bombay officers saves the district, M. iii. 42; Col. Le Grand Jacob arrives there (Aug. 14), M. iii. 40; Col. Le Grand Jacob disarms Sepoys at (Aug. 18), M. iii. 42; effect of mutiny at Mírat on, M. iii. 36.
Kootab, see Kutb.
Kopáldurg, chief of, joined by Dhárwár insurgents (May '58), M. iii. 243.
Kopaldrúg, see Kopáldurg.
Kórwá, a tribe in Chutiá Nágpúr, M. ii. 134.
Koshání, Brig. Honner defeats Ráo Sáhib at (Feb. 10, '59), M. iii. 368.
Kotá, one of Rájpút states, M. i. 245 n.; situation and population of, M. ii. 568; its great

Kotá—*cont.*
natural defences, M. ii. 574; the mutiny at (Oct. 15), M. ii. 569; Major Burton's heroic resistance at, M. ii. 570; Gen. Roberts marches against, M. ii. 574; Gen. Roberts captures (March 30, '58), M. ii. 575; garrison of, watched by Major Gall (April 22,'58), M. iii. 173.

Kotá Contingent, mutiny of, at A´grá (July 4), K. iii. 380, M. i. 268; a loyal gunner spikes their guns, M. i. 268; Dr. Mathias destroys their gun-ammunition, M. i. 268.

Kotah, *see* Kotá.

Kotá-kí-saráí, fierce battle near (June 17, '58), M. iii. 221.

Kotí, feudatory in Ságar territory, M. iii. 88.

Kotra, Major Orr defeats rebels at (April 30, '58), M. iii. 174.

Kúári, *see* Kuwárí.

Kudúa, Nipálese troops beat the rebels at (Oct. 19), M. ii. 319.

Kúnch, the rebels concentrate at (May '58), M. iii. 175; Tántiá Topí entrenches himself at, M. iii. 174; Sir Hugh Rose completely defeats rebels at, M. iii. 177; the defeat at, greatly discourages rebels, M. iii. 179.

Kunwar Singh, the Rájpút of Sháhábád, K. iii. 97.

Kunwar Singh, the remarkable landowner, M. ii. 442; his real generalship, M. ii. 453; his excellent strategy, M. ii. 465; his bad tactics, M. ii. 466; his history, M. i. 76; the true story of his implication in the Mutiny, K. iii. 98; his grievance, M. i. 77 and *n.*; particulars of his law case, K. iii. 100 *n.*; incited to

Kunwar Singh—*cont.*
rebellion by injudicious treatment, K. iii. 100; loses the support of Government in his great law case, K. iii. 99; excuses himself from leaving Jagadíspúr, K. iii. 99; Government warned by Mr. Wake of the effect of proposed treatment of, K. iii. 100 *n.*

His treasonable preparations at Jagadíspúr, K. iii. 142, M. i. 49; his enormous stores at Jagadíspúr, K. iii. 145 *n.*; assists Dánápúr mutineers across the Son, M. i. 79; joins the Dánápúr mutineers, M. i. 76; effect of his rising at Bhágalpúr, M. ii. 131; and at Hazáríbágh, M. ii. 134.

Reconnoitres in direction of Baksar, M. i. 128; re-organises his Sepoys, M. i. 128; fortifies the village of Dalaur, M. i. 128; makes a tactical blunder, M. i. 129; his defeat, and loss of Jagadíspúr, M. i. 129; defeated by Major V. Eyre at Dálaor (Aug. 12), K. iii. 143; flies from his stronghold at Jagadíspúr, K. iii. 144; his stronghold blown up by Major V. Eyre (Aug. 16), K. iii. 145.

Resolves to attack A´zamgarh (March '58), M. ii. 454; collects his force at Atrauliá, M. ii. 455; forces Col. Milman back on A´zamgarh (March 22, '58), M. ii. 457; assumes a threatening position at A´zamgarh (March 27, '58), M. ii. 458; defeated by Lord Mark Kerr (April 6, '58), M. ii. 462; divisions in his camp, M. ii. 466; opposes Sir E. Lugard at the river

THE HISTORIES OF THE INDIAN MUTINY. 105

Kunwar Singh—*cont.*
Tons, M. ii. 470; dexterously withdraws his force in face of Gen. Douglas (April 17, '58), M. ii. 473; crosses the Ghághrá at Sikandarpúr, M. ii. 474; defeated at Sikandarpúr (April 20, '58), M. ii. 475; succeeds in crossing the Ganges (April 20, '58), M. ii. 475; reappears in Bihár on the Son river, M. ii. 436 *n.*, 444; retires to Jagadíspúr (April 22, '58), M. ii. 471, 476; defeats Capt. Le Grand (April 23, '58), M. iii. 461; his death (April 26, '58), M. ii. 478.
Kurándwár, Native state of Southern Maráthá country, M. iii. 20.
Kurnaul, *see* Karnál.
Kúrsí, Gen. Hope Grant defeats rebels at (March 22, '58), M. ii. 411.
Kutb, the, suggested residence for Emperors of Dehlí, K. ii. 18.
Kutchianee, *see* Kachiání.
Kuwárí, Rúp Singh appears at, M. iii. 310; Rúp Singh completely defeated at (Oct. '58), M. iii. 310.

L.

Ladies in Fort of A'grá, their kindly ministrations, K. iii. 400–403.
Láhor, the cantonment of Mían Mír at, K. ii. 425; Board of Administration at, K. i. 50; Board of Administration condemned, K. i. 60; Henry Lawrence appointed resident at, K. i. 7.
Reported conspiracy to

Láhor—*cont.*
seize fort of (May 12), K. ii. 429; the station ball at, K. ii. 430; the fort seized by the English (May 13), K. ii. 433; disarming parade at Mían Mír (May 13), K. ii. 431; insurrection in (Sept. 14), M. iii. 304; the Queen's proclamation read with ceremony at (Nov. 1, '58), M. iii. 395.
Lake, Edward, assists Edwardes to attack Múltán, K. i. 29.
Lake, Lord, his interview with Sháh A'lam, K. ii. 3 *n.*
Lakhnao, *see* Lakhnau.
Lakhnau, description of its position, M. ii. 365; description of city, M. i. 367; strong positions within city, M. ii. 365; description of Begam Kothí, M. ii. 386; military hold of, K. iii. 434; the city devoted to the native king, the provinces, only tolerate him, M. iii. 263; garrison of, M. i. 356; disposition of troops (April), M. i. 360.
The Residency, M. i. 360; nature of Residency defences, K. iii. 522; the Residency made thoroughly defensible, M. i. 419; particular description of the Residency posts, M. i. 441; the Redan battery, M. i. 442; Innes' house, M. i. 442; the Banqueting hall, M. i. 442; the Water Gate, M. i. 442; Sago's house, M. i. 442; the Bailey Guard, M. i. 442; the Treasury buildings, M. i. 442; Dr. Fayrer's house, M. i. 442; the Financial garrison, M. i. 442; the Sikh Squares, M. i. 443; the Brigade Mess, M. i. 443; the Thag jail, M. i. 443; the Káhnpúr battery, M. i. 443;

Lakhnau—*cont.*
Anderson's post, M. i. 443;
the Judicial post, M. i. 443;
the Post Office, M. i. 443;
Gubbins' post, M. i. 443; the
Church garrison, M. i. 444;
Ommaney's post, M. i. 444;
the Residency the Plevna of
India, M. i. 440.
The Machhí Bháwan at, K.
iii. 437, M. i. 361; its indefensibility, K. ii. 409 the
Machhí Bháwan strengthened
and provisioned, M. i. 420.
Preparations for Defence.—
Redisposition of English
troops in, by Sir H. Lawrence,
K. iii. 436; Sepoys of the
48th N.I. burn their surgeon's house, M. i. 357; Sir
H. Lawrence prepares Residency for defence, K. iii. 437,
438 n., M. i. 361; holy places
at, spared by Sir H. Lawrence,
K. iii. 440; proposition to
disarm Sepoys at, K. iii. 441;
insubordination of 7th Irreg.
Inf. (April 30), M. i. 362; Sir
H. Lawrence disarms that regiment (May 3), M. i. 363.
The Outbreak.—Mutiny at
(May 3), M. i. 6, 362; Sir
H. Lawrence holds grand
darbár (May 12), M. i. 364;
he occupies Machhí Bháwan,
M. i. 366; and strengthens
it, M. i. 368; Sir H. Lawrence
moves European troops to
Residency, M. i. 366; Sir H.
Lawrence receives plenary military power (May 19), M. i.
367; women and children removed to Residency (May
27), M. i. 369; Sir H. Lawrence sends Capt. Hutchinson
out with a party of dangerous
Sepoys, M. i. 371; Capt.
Hutchinson returns, after mutiny of his escort, M. i. 372.

Lakhnau—*cont.*
Sir H. Lawrence is informed of intended rising, M.
i. 372; mutiny of 71st N.I.
(May 30), K. iii. 442, M. i.
372; critical position of Sir
H. Lawrence and staff, M. i.
373; Sir H. Lawrence cuts off
mutinous 71st N.I. from
city, M. i. 374; brilliant services of Lieut. Hardinge at,
K. iii. 446; division of feeling
in Sepoy camp, K. iii. 444;
some Sepoys join the English
on night of May 30, M. i.
375; murders and escapes on
outbreak of mutiny, K. iii.
445; mutinous 71st N.I. retire to Múdkípúr (May 31),
M. i. 375; Mr. Gubbins distinguishes himself in pursuit of
mutineers, M. i. 376; stronger
after, than before outbreak
of mutiny, K. iii. 448; the
mutiny clears the air, M. i.
376.
Mutiny of 7th Cavalry (May
31), M. i. 376; Sir H. Lawrence shut up in the town, M.
i. 34; condition of place in
June, described by Sir H.
Lawrence, M. i. 410; Sir H.
Lawrence's health breaks
down, M. i. 412; he resigns
his duties to a council of five,
M. i. 415; provisional council
acts for Sir H. Lawrence
(June 9–12), K. iii. 498; Mr.
M. Gubbins President of
council of five, M. i. 415; and
while in temporary command
disarms Sepoy troops, K. iii.
498; and dismisses them, M.
i. 416; Sir H. Lawrence resumes his duties and recalls
dismissed Sepoys, K. iii. 499,
M. i. 416; Sir H. Lawrence
collects Sikhs and Oudh men
into separate battalions, M. i.

Lakhnau—cont.
416; Sir H. Lawrence invites and receives the assistance of pensioners, M. i. 417.

Mutiny of 3rd Infantry of Military Police (June 12), M. i. 417; Capt. Weston gallops after police to bring them back to duty, M. i. 418; mutinous police pursued and attacked, M. i. 419.

Káhnpúr entreats help, M. i. 421; Sir H. Lawrence's reasons for not helping Káhnpúr, M. i. 421; soundness of his reasons for not helping Káhnpúr, M. i. 422.

The Battle of Chinhat.—Sir H. Lawrence brings troops into Residency from cantonments, M. i. 423; mutinous Sepoys collect at Nawábganj Bárá Bánkí, M. i. 422; Sir H. Lawrence resolves to go out to meet the mutineers, K. iii. 502; troops which marched to Chinhat, K. iii. 503, M. i. 423; Sepoys also advance on Chinhat, M. i. 422; battle of Chinhat (June 30), K. iii. 504, M. i. 425; treachery of Native gunners there, K. iii. 506; the British forced to retreat, K. iii. 510, M. i. 426; great bravery of Lieut. Bonham at Chinhat, K. iii. 507; the iron bridge gallantly held against advancing Sepoys, M. i. 427; Sir H. Lawrence saves his retreating troops by a ruse, M. i. 426; the shattered army returns to Residency, M. i. 427; fearful confusion in Residency after defeat of Chinhat, M. i. 444.

The Siege Begins.—Sepoys occupy the city and Residency (June 30), K. iii. 511, M. i. 428;

Lakhnau—cont.
Mr. Capper buried by falling verandah, M. i. 428*; daring courage of Capt. Anderson and Corpl. Oxenham in saving Mr. Capper, M. i. 428*; English abandon the Machhí Báwan, K. iii. 513, M. i. 429; nature of defences of Residency, M. i. 432; the Residency, in a military sense, not defensible, M. i. 430; strength of garrison of Residency (July 1), M. i. 429; Sepoys fear to assault Residency, M. i. 431, 445; method of Sepoy attack of Residency, M. i. 433; Sepoys pour into Residency continuous fire, M. i. 446; a shell bursts in Sir H. Lawrence's room (July 1), M. i. 433; a second shell bursts in his room, and wounds him mortally, M. i. 434; death of Sir H. Lawrence (July 4), K. iii. 515, M. i. 441.

Losses to garrison from fire from "holy places," K. iii. 521; list of early victims to Sepoys' fire, M. i. 446; death of Mr. Ommaney at, K. iii. 523; order restored in Residency, M. i. 447; sanitary duties in, K. iii. 525; night-work of the garrison of Residency, M. i. 448; noble services of the women, K. iii. 526, M. i. 487; food-supply during siege, K. iii. 527, M. i. 474 n.; supplies run short (Aug. 23), M. i. 471; further reduction in rations (Aug. 28), M. i. 472; hardships and diseases of garrison, M. i. 453; incessant nature of cannonade against, M. i. 474; ceaseless labour of the garrison, M. i. 457.

Causes of success of garri-

Lakhnau—*cont.*
son against assaults, M. i. 462; peculiar character of garrison, M. i. 463; paucity of numbers one. cause of success of garrison, M. i. 463; the reserve in garrison, and its duties, M. i. 464; precautions of garrison to save life, M. i. 465; the science of loopholing, M. i. 465; stillness of garrison at night daunts the enemy, M. i. 466; the "lookout" system organised during siege, M. i. 466; the British flag kept flying during siege, M. i. 467; mining operations and counter-mining, K. iii. 531, 535, M. i. 467, 468; Capt. Fulton countermines against Sepoys, K. iii. 532; Sepoys blow up part of defences, K. iii. 532; the hospital under fire, M. i. 469; scurvy attacks garrison, K. iii. 536; fearful ravages of death in the garrison, K. iii. 538; accumulating work of diminishing garrison (Aug. 23), M. i. 471.

Talúqdárs aid in attack on Residency, K. iii. 529; garrison of Residency make successful sortie (July 7), M. i. 448; Sepoys do everything but assault for three weeks, M. i. 447; Sepoys deliver their first assault on Residency (July 21), M. i. 449, 450; first general assault repulsed, M. i. 451; moral effects of repulse of first general assault, M. i. 451; death of Major Banks (July 21), K. iii. 524, M. i. 452; Mr. Gubbins wishes to assume chief civil functions, M. i. 452; office of Chief Commissioner held in abeyance, M. i. 453.

Lakhnau—*cont.*
Angad brings news (July 22), M. i. 454; the garrison receive intelligence of speedy relief, K. ii. 415 *n.*; Brig. Inglis sends Gen. Havelock a plan of his position, M. i. 454; Angad brings a letter from Col. Tytler (July 25), M. i. 455.

Sepoy Attacks. — Second general assault (Aug. 10), K. iii. 533, M. i. 455; failure of second general assault, M. i. 457; efforts of Sepoys to destroy Káhnpúr battery, M. i. 459; persistent efforts of garrison to hold Káhnpúr battery, M. i. 459; the garrison make a sortie of twelve men at Sago's house (Aug. 12), M. i. 460; third general assault of Sepoys (Aug. 18), M. i. 460; failure of third assault, M. i. 460; garrison capture and blow up house outside defences, M. i. 460; Sepoys breach defences with a mine (Aug. 18), K. iii. 534; the garrison destroy several houses outside defences (Aug. 18), M. i. 469; the garrison blow up Johannes' house, M. i. 470; Angad brings letter from Gen. Havelock (Aug. 28), M. i. 472; fourth general assault (Sept. 5), M. i. 472; repulse of fourth general assault, M. i. 473; excellent service of battery worked by natives, M. i. 473; Sepoys thoroughly dispirited by failure of fourth assault, M. i. 473; death of Capt. Fulton (Sept. 14), K. iii. 540; Angad brings news of approach of Havelock (Sept. 16), K. iii. 541, M. i. 475; Angad refuses to go out again, M. i. 476.

Lakhnau—*cont.*
The First Relief.—Approach of relieving force, M. i. 476; Gen. Havelock attacks (Sept. 25), M. i. 536; citizens and Sepoys begin to flee, M. i. 477; garrison fire on retreating foe, M. i. 477; Gen. Havelock carries the Chárbágh, M. i. 536; conspicuous gallantry of young Havelock and Private Jakes, M. i. 537*; the British gain the Chattar Manzil, M. i. 537‡; Gen. Havelock forces the Khás Bázár, M. i. 537§; young Hen. Havelock forces the Chárbágh bridge, M. i. 538; death of Gen. Neill, M. i. 538; the relieving force reaches the Baillie Guard, M. i. 539; Private Duffy recovers a gun, M. i. 540; relief of garrison (Sept. 25), K. iii. 542, M. i. 478; properly a reinforcement, not a relief, M. i. 479; death of Capt. Radcliffe, K. iii. 542; the rear-guard of relievers reaches Residency (Sept. 26), M. i. 540; the guns and waggons of relieving force brought into Residency (Oct. 1), M. i. 541; the brave men who brought the rear-guard into the Residency, M. ii. 151.

Brig. Inglis's despatch to Government, M. i. 480; nature of Brig. Inglis's despatch to Government, M. i. 445; services of Brig. Inglis, M. i. 480; military character of Brig. Inglis, M. i. 481; skill and daring of Capt. Wilson, M. i. 481; Capt. Fulton's fertility of resource, M. i. 483; death of Capt. Fulton (Sept. 14), M. i. 483; activity and buoyancy of Mr. G. Couper, M. i, 484; fidelity

Lakhnau—*cont.*
of Natives in garrison, M. i. 485; faithful Natives risk caste in helping English comrades, M. i. 486; noble endurance and courage of old pensioners in, M. i. 486.

Losses of the garrison up to first relief, M. i. 488; difficulties in forcing a way through streets, M. i. 542; losses of first relieving force, M. i. 541; list of the chiefs who fell during siege, M. i. 484; remarks on the relief, M. i. 543; the bravery of England's heroes emulated at, M. i. 543; the surviving heroes of the relief, M. i. 545.

Gen. Outram assumes command of troops (Sept. 26), M. i. 542; he extends the position occupied, M. ii. 151; he extends his position towards the Álambágh, M. ii. 158; capture of Captain Bázár (Sept. 26), M. ii. 152; capture of Faríd Bakhsh palace (Sept. 26), M. ii. 152; Gen. Havelock receives command of palaces along Gúmtí, M. ii. 152; Gen. Outram tries to send his Cavalry away at night, but fails, M. ii. 153.

Defence changed to attack, M. ii. 154; sortie of Sept. 27, M. ii. 154; three sorties on Sept. 29, M. ii. 155; mining and counter-mining at, during October, M. ii. 158; extent of ground undermined, M. ii. 159.

Garrison hear of the fall of Dehlí (Oct. 9), M. ii. 160; Gen. Outram commands the road to the iron bridge, M. ii. 159; change of rebel tactics against garrison, M. ii. 160; garrison hears of ar-

Lakhnau—cont.
rival of Gen. Hope Grant, M. ii. 162; Gen. Outram sends plan of city to A'lambágh, M. ii. 162; and establishes semaphore telegraph with A'lambágh, M. ii. 162; Col. Napier captures Phillips' Garden battery (Nov. 2), M. ii. 157; the Maulaví commands rebels, M. ii. 344.
The Second Relief. — Sir Colin Campbell's plan for relieving, M. ii. 167; Brig. Hope Grant's column the *point d'appui* of relieving force, M. ii. 149; strength of Sir Colin Campbell's final attacking force, M. ii. 170; he occupies the Martinière, M. ii. 174; the rebels attack English centre, and fail (Nov. 14), M. ii. 175; rebels make second attempt on English centre, and fail, M. ii. 176; rebels make repeated attacks on rear-guard, but fail, M. ii. 178; command of Dilkhúsha given to Brig. Little (Nov. 15), M. ii. 178; rebels attack the English right, but fail (Nov. 15), M. ii. 178; attack on Sikandar Bágh, M. ii. 180; capture of the Sikandar Bágh (Nov. 16), M. ii. 186, 187; slaughter of entire rebel garrison of the Sikandar Bágh, M. ii. 187; capture of the Barracks (Nov. 16), M. ii. 188; critical moment of relief, M. ii. 191; capture of Sháh Najíf (Nov. 16), M. ii. 194; Gen. Outram effects diversion during fight of Nov. 16, M. ii. 198; the heroes who fought in this attack, M. ii. 198; rebels attack the Martinière and Dilkhúsha (Nov. 16), M. ii. 199; capture of

Lakhnau—cont.
Motí Mahal by Capt. Wolseley, M. ii. 203; Capt. Hopkins carries the Mess House on one side, and Garnet Wolseley on the other, M. iii. 505; Gen. Havelock leads advance from Residency (Nov. 16), M. ii. 205; he occupies Faríd Bakhsh Palace, M. ii. 206; and captures the Harnkhána, M. ii. 208; relief of garrison (Nov. 17), M. ii. 204.
Brig. Russell captures Banks's house, M. ii. 210; rebels attack Banks's house (Nov. 18), M. ii. 210; Sir Colin Campbell sends Artillery to strengthen Banks's house, M. ii. 211; Col. Hale assumes command at Banks's house (Nov. 18), M. ii. 212; Brig. Russell wounded there, M. ii. 212; Col. Biddulph killed there (Nov. 18), M. ii. 212; the attack and retirement from Hospital (Nov. 18), M. ii. 213; successful evacuation of city by Sir Colin Campbell, M. ii. 215.
Gen. Outram left in charge of the A'lambágh (Nov. 26), M. ii. 222; strength of rebel forces (Jan. '58), M. ii. 360 n.; rebel lines of works within city (Feb. '58), M. ii. 366; unprotected on the north, M. ii. 367; rebels attack Gen. Outram in A'lambágh (Jan. 12, '58), M. ii. 347; their attack repulsed, M. ii. 348; they are exceedingly dejected by failure, M. ii. 350; contention among the rebels, (Jan. 22, '58), M. ii. 353; they make despairing attack on A'lambágh (Feb. 25, '58), M. ii. 356.

Lakhnau—*cont.*
The Final Advance.—Sir Colin Campbell's force for capture of city, M. ii. 364; British position opposite (Mar. 4, '58), M. ii. 370; Sir Colin Campbell throws two pontoon bridges across Gúmtí (Mar. 4, '58), M. ii. 370; Gen. Outram crosses the Gúmtí to attack (Mar. 6, '58), M. ii. 371; Gen. Outram's task on the Gúmtí, M. ii. 372; first line of rebel works at, enfiladed by him, M. ii. 375; rebels abandon first line of defence (Mar. 6, '58), M. ii. 273; Lieut. Butler's daring deed, M. ii. 376; British troops occupy first rebel line of defence, M. ii. 376; Sir Colin Campbell captures the Martinière (Mar. 9, '58), M. ii. 377; capture of Chákar Kothí, the key to rebel position (Mar. 9, '58), M. ii. 374; brave resistance of nine rebels, M. ii. 374.
Position of contending forces (Mar. 10, '58), M. ii. 379; Jang Bahádur arrives, M. ii. 324, 388; Sir Colin Campbell captures Banks's house (Mar. 10, '58), M. ii. 379; the Sikandar Bágh occupied by Col. Lugard, M. ii. 382; the audacity of three Engineers captures Sháh Najíf and Qaddam Rasúl (Mar. 10, '58), M. ii. 383; capture of the Begam Kothí, M. ii. 386; death of Capt. Hodson at storming of Begam Kothí (Mar. 10, '58), M. ii. 387; capture of Hashmat A'lí Chaudrí's camp (Mar. 11, '58), M. ii. 380; Brig. Napier proceeds by sap against second rebel line of defence (Mar. 13, '58),

Lakhnau—*cont.*
M. ii. 389; Gen. Outram enfilades second line of defence, M. ii. 382; Gen. Franks storms and captures the Imámbárá (Mar. 14, '58), M. ii. 390; capture of second rebel line of defence, M. ii. 391; capture of Tárá Kothí and Mess House, M. ii. 392; third rebel line of defence turned by young Havelock, M. ii. 393; capture of Qaisar Bágh (Mar. 14, '58), M. ii. 394; plunder of the Qaisar Bágh, M. ii. 394, 395; the successful leaders of Mar. 14, '58, M. ii. 396.
Sir Colin Campbell's extraordinary order to Gen. Outram, M. ii. 397; Sir Colin Campbell sends columns along Sítápúr and Sandíla roads, M. ii. 399; rebels escape by Faizábád road (Mar. 15, '58), M. ii. 399; Gen. Outram storms and carries the Residency (Mar. 16, '58), M. ii. 400; capture of Machhí Bháwan, M. ii. 401; rebels make counter-attack on Walpole's pickets (Mar. 16, '58), M. ii. 401; Jang Bahádur clears front of A'lambágh of rebels, M. ii. 403; rescue of Miss Jackson and Mrs. Orr from (March 17, '58), M. ii. 403 *n*.; Gen. Outram captures remaining positions in, M. ii. 404; accidental explosion, M. ii. 404.
Remarks on the capture of, M. ii. 412; its fall produces no change in resistance of Oudh Talúqdárs, M. iii. 264.
Road to Káhnpúr threatened by Bení Mádhava, M. iii. 266.
The Queen's proclamation

Lakhnau—*cont.*
read with ceremony at (Nov. 1, '58), M. iii. 396.
See also Campbell, Sir Colin; Havelock, Gen. Henry; Lawrence, Sir Henry, *and* Oudh.
Lálá Jotí Parshád, provisions Fort of A'grá, M. i. 286.
Lallatpúr, garrison of, M. iii. 97; mutiny at (June 12), M. iii. 97; European officers at, fly to Rájá of Bánpúr, M. iii. 98; Ráo Sáhib occupies (Sept. '58), M. iii. 338; he advances from, to Sindhwáo, and is fully defeated (Oct. '58), M. iii. 340; he returns to, after his defeat, M. iii. 340; Túntiá Topí retreats to (Oct. '58), M. iii. 340.
Lál Bahat, Túntiá Topí rests his men at (Oct. '58), M. iii. 341.
Lál Mádhava Singh, determined opponent to the English in Oudh, M. iii. 273.
Lál Singh, minister for Duleep Singh, his character, K. i. 4; plots against the English, K. i. 5; political prisoner on parole at Dehrá Dún in May, M. iii. 420; places his retainers at the service of Mr. Keene, M. iii. 420.
Lance, Mr., Magistrate of I'táwá, M. iii. 309; defeats the rebels at Chakkarnagar (Aug. '58), M. iii. 310.
Land Revenue, K. i. 156.
Lang, Lieut., examines breach at Dehlí, M. ii. 25; his daring entrance into the Qaddam Rásúl, Lakhnau (March 10, '58), M. ii. 383.
Larkins, Capt. Robert, commands at Pílíbhít (Aug. 58), M. iii. 275.
Látú, defeat of Chatgáon muti-

Látú—*cont.*
neers at (Dec. 18), M. ii. 424.
Laughnan, Private, plants British flag on Kábul Gate, M. ii. 36.
Lawrence, Col. A. W., commands Cavalry of Jabalpúr column (Nov.), M. iii. 191.
Lawrence, Col. George St. Patrick, Agent in Rájpútáná, K. iii. 351, M. i. 245; his character, M. i. 245, ii. 577; his former services, M. i. 246; his alleged dispute with the Mahárání of Udaipúr, K. iii. 683.
Ordered to abandon Rájpútáná, by Mr. J. Colvin, K. iii. 352; refuses to do so, K. iii. 353; arranges for defence of Rájpútáná, K. iii. 352.
Goes to Abú (April), M. i. 246; comprehends the full significance of Mírat outbreak, M. i. 247; dangerous guardianship of arsenal of A'jmír, M. i. 248; has no trustworthy troops in Rájpútáná, M. i. 248; summons British troops from Dísá (May), M. i. 249; his confidence in the Mairs, M. ii. 550; raises second battalion of Mairs, M. i. 250; sends regular garrison of A'jmír back to Nasírábád, M. i. 250; issues proclamation to Native states of Rájpútáná, M. i. 251; asks that troops from Bombay to A'grá should pass through Rájpútáná, M. i. 251.
Goes to Bíñor (June 1), M. i. 254; repairs and provisions fort of A'jmír, M. i. 255; created Brig.-Gen. without troops, M. i. 255; receives troops from Dísá (June 12), M. i. 255; occupies Nasír-

Lawrence, Col.—cont.
ábád and Nímach with British troops, M. i. 256; makes Ájmír his head-quarters (June), M. i. 256; strictly preserves routine of civil duties in Rájpútáná, M. i. 256 n., ii. 552; admirable results of his far-seeing policy, M. i. 261.
Outbreak at Ájmír (Aug. 9), M. ii. 553; pursues and cuts up rioters, M. ii. 553; advances with small force against Áwah (Sept. 18), M. ii. 566; falls back on Ájmír (Sept. 21), M. ii. 567; applies to Bombay for reinforcements (Nov.), M. ii. 572.
Lawrence, Sir Henry, his character, K. i. 9, K. iii. 519, M. i. 350, 436; on the desirability of increased number of Native officers, K. i. 338; on the want of a military pay-code, K. i. 322 n.; in favour of promotion by selection, K. i. 336; strongly opposes annexation of Native states, K. i. 454 n.; on injury done by newspaper articles, K. iii. 19; on the condition of the old and the new Oudh armies, K. iii. 424; opposed to revolutionary reforms, K. iii. 428; his description of Mr. Jackson's revolutionary reforms in Oudh, K. iii. 429; his opinion as to reason for spread of mutiny, K. iii. 7.
Biographical Details.—Appointed Resident at Lahor, K. i. 7; his administration as Resident in the Panjab, K. i. 12, 13; returns to England in 1848, K. i. 15; returns to India (Dec. 1848), K. i. 39; joins Gen. Whish before Múl-

Lawrence, Sir H.—cont.
tán (Dec. '48), K. i. 39; created President of the Board of Administration in the Panjáb (1849), K. i. 50; conciliates the Sikh Sirdárs after annexation of Panjáb, K. i. 59; transferred to Rájpútáná (1853), K. i. 61; supports the claim of Madan Pál to the Kiráolí ráj, K. i. 95; in favour of assuming the government of Oudh, K. i. 137 n.; offers to serve temporarily for Outram in Oudh, K. i. 398.
Oudh Administration.—Appointed Chief Commissioner of Oudh (March 20), K. i. 450, M. i. 349; sees the errors in Oudh administration, M. i. 350; anticipates outburst of Sepoy army, K. i. 453; warns Lord Canning of dangerous coalition in Oudh (April), K. i. 577; his views on dangerous condition of the army, K. i. 592, 593; attempts to restore confidence of people, M. i. 354; conciliates the trading class at Lakhnau, M. i. 355; pays the pensions of the retainers of former court, M. i. 355.
Suspects the 48th Regiment at Oudh, K. i. 586; reasons with the Sepoy officers, M. i. 358; prepares Residency for defence, M. i. 361; resolves to disarm the 7th Regiment, K. i. 589; disarms 7th Irreg. Inf. (May 3), M. i. 363; holds Darbár at Lakhnau (May 12), K. iii. 431, M. i. 365; rewards faithful officers and Sepoys, M i. 365.
Prepares for defence of Lakhnau, K. iii. 434; his dis-

Lawrence, Sir H.—*cont.*
position of European troops in Lakhnau (May), K. iii. 436; occupies Machhí Bháwan, M. i. 366; moves European troops to Residency (May 16, 17), M. i. 366; counsels the immediate employment of Gorkhás (May), K. i. 615, M. i. 367; receives authority to apply to Jang Bahádur for Gorkhá troops (May 22), M. i. 367; suggests intercepting the China expedition (May 16), K. i. 615 *n*.
Heroically sends help to Káhnpúr (May), K. ii. 296.
Preparations for the Siege.—Demands plenary military power, K. i. 613, iii. 433; invested with plenary military power (May 19), M. i. 367; strengthens the Machhí Bháwan, M. i. 368; removes women and children to Residency (May 27), M. i. 369; sends Capt. Weston and Mecham to pacify Malhíábád district, M. i. 370; plays off Irregulars against the Line at Lakhnau, K. ii. 407; is informed of intended rising at Lakhnau, M. i. 372; his conversation with the perverse Jamádár, M. i. 369; epitome of his measures for protection of Residency at Lakhnau, K. iii. 438 *n*.; spares the holy places, K. iii. 440.
The Mutiny.—Outbreak of Lakhnau mutiny (May 30), K. iii. 442; critical position of himself and staff, K. iii. 442, M. i. 373; cuts off mutineers from city of Lakhnau, K. iii. 443, M. i. 374; tries to warn Commissioner of Sítápúr, K. iii. 448; refuses to disarm remnant of Sepoys after mu-

Lawrence, Sir H.—*cont.*
tiny, K. iii. 449; resolves to hold Residency as the final point, M. i. 411.
His health gradually sinking, K. iii. 494, M. i. 412; recommends Major Banks as his successor, K. iii. 495, M. i. 413; recommends Col. Inglis to command troops after himself, M. i. 413; resigns his duties to a council of five (June 9), K. iii. 498, M. i. 415; during temporary illness Mr. Gubbins disarms Sepoy troops, K. iii. 499; resumes his duties and dissolves council (June 11), M. i. 416; recalls Sepoys disarmed by Mr. Gubbins, K. iii. 499; increases and consolidates Native troops in Residency, M. i. 416.
His description of Lakhnau (June 12), M. i. 410; Káhnpúr entreats help from him, M. i. 421; declines sending troops to Káhnpúr, K. iii. 501; his reasons for not assisting Káhnpúr, M. i. 421; soundness of his reasons for not helping Káhnpúr, M. i. 422.
The Battle of Chinhat.—Resolves to go out to meet the mutineers, K. iii. 502; his force for advancing on Chinhat, M. i. 423; fights the battle of Chinhat (June 30), M. i. 425; retreats from Chinhat, M. i. 426; saves his retreating troops by a ruse, M. i. 426; sends troops to hold the iron bridge, M. i. 427; his personal bravery at Chinhat, K. iii. 508; his calmness and courage during battle and retreat from Chinhat, M. i. 428; the policy of his attack at Chinhat, M. i. 423; aban-

Lawrence, Sir H.—*cont.*
dons Machhí Bháwan (July 1), M. i. 429.
The Siege begins.—Shut up in Lakhnau, M. i. 34; a shell bursts in his room (July 1), M. i. 433; a second shell bursts in his room, wounding him mortally (July 2), M. i. 434; his death (July 4), K. ii. 410, iii. 515, M. i. 441; what he did to secure successful defence of Residency, M. i. 439.

Lawrence, Sir John, appointed to office in the Panjáb (1849), K. i. 51; his character, K. i. 51, 63; his grasp of mind, K. ii. 463.
Created Chief Commissioner of the Panjáb (1853), K. i. 61; advises on the Persian expedition of 1856, K. i. 419, 420; recommends his brother as commander of the Persian expedition, K. i. 419; disbelieves in alliance of Dost Muhammad, K. i. 446; his policy in the Panjáb, K. ii. 472; abstains from superseding local authorities in the Panjáb, K. ii. 461; resides at Ráwal-Pindí, K. ii. 423.
After Mírat outbreak, counsels the raising of Sikh Irregulars, K. i. 614; resolves to wrench Dehlí from the Sepoys, K. ii. 464; sends Guide Corps to Dehlí (May 13), K. ii. 465; orders Jálandhar garrison to occupy Phillaur (May 16), K. ii. 140 *n.*; severs communication with disaffected district, K. ii. 474; everywhere secures Government treasure, K. ii. 474; sanctions stern measures of suppression, K. ii. 474; removes non-military Hindústánís from the

Lawrence, Sir J.—*cont.*
Panjáb, K. ii. 475; directs discrimination in punishment of captured mutineers, K. ii. 488.
Counsels immediate movement on Mírat (May), K. ii. 152; remonstrates with Gen. Anson on delay, K. ii. 151; writes urgently to Gen. Anson, K. ii. 154, 155; despises caution of Commissariat Department, K. ii. 156; sends in supplies of money to Debrá Dún (June), M. iii. 423; disarms 58th Regiment at Ráwal-Pindí (July 7), K. ii. 636; particulars of reinforcements sent to Dehlí on July 22, K. ii. 644.
Difficulties of his position in Sept., M. iii. 301; proposed cession of Pesháwar to Dost Muhammad, K. ii. 608; presses on Lord Canning the necessity for abandoning Pesháwar, K. ii. 618.
Garrison left in Panjáb after Nicholson's departure, M. iii. 302; congratulates Nicholson on battle of Najafgarh, K. ii. 657; forms a small movable column, M. iii. 303; moves against Lahor and Múltán insurgents, M. iii. 304; suppresses insurrection there (Sept. 14), M. iii. 305.
Ascribes the Mutiny to the greased cartridges, and to that only, M. iii. 470; his opinion of Gen. Barnard, K. ii. 568.

Lawrence, Lady John, discovers conspiracy in Hazárá country (Sept.), M. iii. 303.

Lawrence, Lieut. S., his distinguished gallantry at Lakhnau, on July 7, M. i. 449.

Lawrence, Major R., the question of his assuming command

8 *

Lawrence, Major R.—*cont.*
of fourth column at assault of Dehlí, K. iii. 693.
Leather rupees, story of, circulated at Farrukhábád, K. iii. 293.
Legislative Council, at the time of "Gagging Act," K. iii. 17; pass the "Gagging Act" (June 13), M. i. 19; unanimity of, in passing the Press Act, K. iii. 18; repressive measures passed by, K. ii. 275 *n.*; special legislation after outbreak of Mutiny, K. ii. 133; power over life and liberty given to executive officers of Government (June 8), K. ii. 134; senior military officer of whatsoever rank, to have power to execute sentence of court-martial, K. ii. 135; text of Act XIV. of 1857, K. iii. 661.
Le Grand, Capt., attacks Kunwar Singh, at Jagadíspúr (April 23, '58), M. ii. 476; his defeat, M. ii. 477, iii. 461; killed in attack, M. ii. 477.
Le Grand Jacob, Col. G., his character, M. iii. 38; ordered to Kolhápúr (Aug.), M. iii. 39; pushes on to Kolhápúr, with two guns and such troops as he can pick up, M. iii. 39; reaches Kolhápúr (Aug. 14), M. iii. 40; finds mutiny already quelled, M. iii. 41; disarms Sepoys at Kolhápúr (Aug. 18), M. iii. 42.
Leigh, Capt., calls in troops to preserve order in Sambalpúr (Oct.), M. ii. 440; scours the district of Sambalpúr (Nov.), M. ii. 440.
Le Mesurier, Col., commands at Asírgarh, M. iii. 58.
Lennox, Col., his romantic escape from Faizábád, K. iii. 469.

Lennox, Lieut., commands Engineers at final attack on Lakhnau, M. ii. 171.
Leslie, Sir Norman, Adjutant of 5th Irregular Cavalry, murdered at Rohiní (June 12), K. iii. 171, M. i. 37.
Lester, Lieut., leads party of fugitives from Sítápúr to Lakhnau, M. i. 381.
Lester, Major-Gen., assumes command at Belgáon (May), M. iii. 27, 240; receives reinforcements at Belgáon (Aug. 10), M. iii. 33; arrests and condemns five turbulent soldiers, M. iii. 33; his death (June '58), M. iii. 246.
L'Estrange, Capt., agrees to assist Major Eyre to relieve A'rá, M. i. 96.
Lewis, Lieut., attempts to disarm Sepoys at Dákhá (Nov. 22), M. ii. 419; attacks and defeats Sepoys, M. ii. 420; his gallantry at Dháká, M. iii. 460; his gallantry at Khúkwásás (March 5, '58), M. iii. 152.
Liddell, Lieut.-Col., leads the right attack at storming of Jhánsí (April 3, '58), M. iii. 166; left in command of Jhánsí, M. iii. 173; turns Tántiá Topí back from Betwá at Kajúriá (Oct. '58), M. iii. 341; leads force from Lalatpúr to Chandairí (Dec. '58), M. iii. 364.
Lightfoot, Capt., his dash at Jaurá-Alípúr (June 22, '58), M. iii. 230.
Lingayat population, the Desáí of Kittúr, their discontented chief, M. iii. 29.
Linsúgúr, occupied by Capt. Wyndham (Jan. '58), M. iii. 127.
Lip-loyalty of Sepoys, K. ii. 246.

THE HISTORIES OF THE INDIAN MUTINY. 117

Little, Brig., commands Cavalry at final attack on Lakhnau, M. ii. 171; given command of Dilkhúsha, Lakhnau (Nov. 15), M. ii. 178; commands Cavalry at attack on Tántiá Topí (Dec. 5), M. ii. 267.

Liyákat Alí, *see* Maulaví, the.

Lloyd, Major-Gen., suppresses Sánthál insurrection (1853), M. i. 40; commands at Dánápúr, M. i. 40; extent of his command at Dánápúr, M. i. 41; his measure to keep open the Grand Trunk Road, K. iii. 68.

Reports trustworthiness of Sepoys, M. i. 45; has faith in Dánápúr regiments, K. ii. 124, M. i. 45; his opinion of the Dánápúr Sepoys, K. iii. 66.

Personally opposed to disarming Sepoys, M. i. 62; refuses to disarm Sepoys, M. i. 50; Government of India transfers its responsibility to him, M. i. 61; shrinks from responsibility, K. iii. 90, M. i. 64.

Detains two companies of the 37th Regiment at Dánápúr, M. i. 65; decides on depriving the Sepoys at Dánápúr of percussion-caps, K. iii. 91, M. i. 65; his method of doing this (July 25), K. iii. 92; the extreme injudiciousness of his measure, M. i. 66; succeeds in removing percussion-caps from magazine at Dánápúr, M. i. 67; resolves to take percussion-caps from persons of Sepoys, M. i. 68; goes on board a steamboat during disarmament of Sepoys, K. iii. 94, M. i. 67; occasions mutiny (July 25), K. iii. 93; M. i. 68; absent from parade ground on occurrence of mutiny at Dánápúr, M. i. 69.

Lloyd, Major-Gen.—*cont.*
Fails to suppress the mutiny, M. i. 69; issues orders too late for pursuit of mutineers (July 25), M. i. 70; his mutineers start for Árá unmolested; M. i. 70; thinks pursuit of Dánápúr mutineers of little use, M. i. 75 *n.*; sends some riflemen up Son to stop escaping mutineers, M. i. 76; blameworthy for not having horse in readiness, M. i. 72 *n.*; he is responsible for mutiny at Dánápúr, M. i. 71.

Thinks of entrenching himself in Dánápúr (July 26), K. iii. 101, M. i. 76; Mr. W. Tayler begs him not to do so, K. iii. 101; he is urged by Mr. W. Tayler to pursue mutineers, M. i. 77; at last resolves to pursue mutineers, M. i. 78; sends a steamer up the Son (July 26), K. iii. 107; which is stopped by a sandbank, M. i. 78; again persuaded by Mr. Tayler to send troops after mutineers, M. i. 79; and again sends a steamer after mutineers (July 27), K. iii. 108; a third time sends a steamer up the Son (July 30), K. iii. 109.

Neutralises greatly Mr. Tayler's good work, M. i. 103; his exculpatory letter, K. iii. 666; Lord Canning disapproves of his acts, K. iii. 170; ordered to be tried by court-martial, M. i. 115.

Loans negotiated by Lord Canning, K. iii. 49, 50.

Lockhart, Capt., commands 78th Highlanders advancing from Lakhnau Residency (Nov. 16), M. ii. 206.

Lockhart, Col., covers Indor on the north (Aug. '58), M. iii.

Lockhart, Col.—*cont.*
328; joined by Col. Hope from Máu, at Nálkhere, M. iii. 328.
Logásí, Chief of, acts kindly to Major Kirke, K. iii. 373.
Logassee, *see* Logásí.
Lohárí, Major Gall captures fort of (May '58), M. iii. 175.
Longden, Col., moves to support Nipálese in Gorakhpúr (Sept.), M. ii. 319; enters Jánpúr (Oct. 4), M. ii. 320; recaptures Atrauliá (Oct. 9), M. ii. 320.
Longfield, Brig., commands reserve column at assault of Dehlí, M. ii. 29.
Loodhianah, *see* Ludhíáná.
Loonee Singh, *see* Lúní Singh.
Lootf Ali Khan, *see* Lutf Alí Khán.
Loudon, Marshal, anecdote of his early life, M. ii. 219.
Loughnan, Ensign, his gallantry at Lakhnau (July 21), M. i. 450.
Low, Gen. John, Member of Supreme Council (1856), K. i. 387; his character, K. i. 78, 387; opposes the annexation of Nágpúr, K. i. 80; supports adopted heir of Chief of Kiráolí, K. i. 92; his reasons for interfering in Oudh affairs, K. i. 142 *n.*; in favour of assuming the government of Oudh, K. i. 142; his remarks on Oudh affairs (1834), K. i. 125; counsels immediate move on Dehlí on outbreak of Mutiny, K. ii. 120; recants his adverse decision against Mr. Tayler, M. i. 121.
Low, Mr. Malcolm, procures guides to lead attack on Sirpúra (Aug. 29, '58), M. iii. 276.

Lowe, Capt., seizes possession of the Captain Bazar, Lakhnau (Sept. 26), M. ii. 152.
Lowe, Dr., his description of passage of the Chambal (Nov. 19), M. iii. 77; his account of the capture of Kálpí, M. iii. 186; his description of effect of the sun on the soldiers, M. iii. 188 *n.*
Lower Bengal, European troops in, M. i. 23.
Lowis, Mr., Magistrate of Patná, M. i. 54; his amusing attempt to arrest Alí Karím (June 23), M. i. 55; pursues, but fails to capture Alí Karím, K. iii. 80.
Lowth, Lieut.-Col., leads left attack at storming of Jhánsí (April 3, '58), M. iii. 167; enters Jhánsí, and leads attack on palace, M. iii. 169; leads attack on rebel left at Kotá-kí-saráí (June 19, '58), M. iii. 224.
Ludhíáná, strategic advantages of its retention, K. ii. 508; dangerous population at, their ravages, K. ii. 506; disarmament of town by Mr. Ricketts, K. ii. 509; executions at, K. ii. 509; mutiny at (June 9), K. ii. 505; mutineers escape from, K. ii. 508.
Lugard, Sir Edward, occupies the Sikandar Bágh (March 10, '58), M. ii. 382; storms the Begam Kothí, Lakhnau (March 10, '58), M. ii. 385; sent from Lakhnau to relieve A'zamgarh (March '58), M. ii. 468; drives the Maulaví from the Shádatganj, Lakhnau (March 21, '58), M. ii. 411; defeats a body of rebels at Tigrá, near Jánpúr (April 6, '58), M. ii. 469; reaches A'zamgarh (April 15, '58), M

THE HISTORIES OF THE INDIAN MUTINY. 119

Lugard, Sir E.—*cont.*
ii. 470; forces the passage of the Tons (April 15, '58), M. ii. 471; advances to A´rá, M. ii. 479; his plan for relieving A´rá, M. ii. 479; defeats Amar Singh and occupies Jagadíspúr (May 8, '58), M. ii. 480; defeats the rebels at Hetampúr (May 11, '58), M. ii. 480; defeats the rebels at Dalílpúr (May 27, '58), M. ii. 480; attacks and defeats rebels in jungle (June 4, '58), M. ii. 482; returns to England broken in health, M. ii. 482.
Lumsden, Major Henry, appointed head of Mission to Kandahár (1856), K. i. 442.
Lúní Singh, gives some assistance to English fugitives, K. iii. 483.
Lushington Mr., attacked by Kols in Singhbhúm (Dec.), M. ii. 439.
Lutf Alí Khán, his complicity with Pír Alí at Patná, K. iii. 86; his arrest and release at Patná (July 5), K. iii. 87, M. i. 57; Mr. Lowis's report of it, K. iii. 87 *n.*; his trial and acquittal, K. iii. 87 and *n.*; extravagantly felicitated on his acquittal, K. iii. 88.
Lyakut Ali=Liyákat Alí, *see* Maulaví, the.
Lyall, Dr., murdered by rioters of Patná (July 3), K. iii. 84; M. i. 56.
Lyall, Mr. A. C., distinguishes himself in the attack on Sáh Mall, M. iii. 434.

M.

Macan, Brig. Henry, 12th N. I. fail to obey his orders at Nasírábád (Aug. 10), M. ii.

Macan, Brig. H.—*cont.*
553; restores 12th N. I. to discipline, M. ii. 554.
McBean, Lieut. W., his bravery in the breach of the Begam Kothí, Lakhnau, M. ii. 386.
McCabe, Capt., his death in leading sortie at Lakhnau (Sept. 29), M. ii. 155.
M'Causland, Col., takes command at Fathgarh (May '58), M. ii. 541.
M'Crea, Capt., killed at Káhnpúr (Nov. 28), M. ii. 251.
Macdonald, Lieut., killed in attack on Kúrsí (March 22, '58), M. ii. 411.
Macdonald, Major, his determined courage in Sánthália, M. ii. 130; murderously attacked at Rohní (June 12), K. iii. 171, M. i. 37; the murderers are his own Sepoys, M. i. 38; seizes and hangs the murderers in face of the regiment, M. i. 38; his description of the hanging scene at Rohní, M. i. 39 *n.*
Macdonald, Mr., Collector of Rángpúr, saves Government treasure (Dec.), M. ii. 427.
M'Donell, Mr., acts as guide to Capt. Dunbar's expedition, K. iii. 119; his calm courage, M. i. 88 *n.*; heroically saves a boat-load of soldiers, K. iii. 120; wins the Victoria Cross, K. iii. 120, 121 *n.*
McDuff, Col., commands second brigade Jabalpúr column (Nov.), M. iii. 191.
MacGregor, Col., sent to command Jang Bahádur's column (Nov.), M. ii. 321.
MacGregor, Lieut., distinguishes himself at capture of Machhí Bháwan (March 16, '58), M. ii. 401.

MacGregor, Lieut., seized by Jabalpúr mutineers at Patan, M. iii. 104; shot by mutineers at Patan, M. iii. 104; his body found at Katanjí, M. iii. 106.
McKenna, Lieut., killed at Káhnpúr (Nov. 28), M. ii. 251.
McNeill, Capt., rescues Sítápúr fugitives at Lakhnau (March 17, '58), M. ii. 403 n.
McNeill, Sir John, desires Afghan possession of Kandahár and Hirát, K. i. 429 n.
McIntyre, Major, commands at A'lambágh, Lakhnau (Sept.), M. ii. 153; his able defence of the A'lambágh, M. ii. 169.
Machhí Bháwan at Lakhnau, K. iii. 437; its indefensibility, K. ii. 409; abandoned by the English, K. iii. 513.
See also Lakhnau.
Machhlígáon, defeat of rebels at by Gen. Hope Grant (Dec. 4, '58), M. iii. 292.
Macintire, Capt., greatly distinguishes himself at Bándá (April 19, '58), M. iii. 197.
Mackay, Private, his daring leap into Sikandar Bágh (Nov. 16), M. ii. 183, 197.
Mackenzie, Capt. A. M., Acting Commandant of 8th Irreg. Cavalry, M. i. 306; being warned is ready for outbreak at Barailí, M. i. 311; his gallant attempt to lead his men at Barailí (May 31), M. i. 313–315; attempts to lead Irregular Cavalry against mutineers at Barailí, K. iii. 272.
Mackillop, John, procures water for garrison of Káhnpúr until shot, K. ii. 332.
Macleod, Major, a commissioner during temporary illness of Mr. Colvin at A'grá, M. i. 266.

Macleod, Mr. Donald, assists Dehrá Dún to money (June), M. iii. 423.
Macnaghten, Mr., Assistant Commissioner, raises body of villagers to protect Govindgarh, K. ii. 436.
Macnaughten, Sir W., his murder by Muhammad Akbar, K. iii. 84, M. i. 53.
Macpherson, Major Charters, the able Resident at Gwáliár, K. iii. 311; his character, K. iii. 312; his influence with Mahárájá Sindhiá, M. iii. 207; induces Sindhiá to send his body-guard into A'grá, K. iii. 313; stops Gen. Napier at A'ntrí, and allows Firoz Sháh to escape (Dec. '58), M. iii. 361.
Madanpúr pass, description of, M. iii. 148; Capt. Ternan defeats rebels at (Jan. '58), M. iii. 109; the pass bravely defended by rebels (March 4, '58), M. iii. 149; rebels driven from pass by bayonet charge, M. iii. 150.
Madáríganj, mutiny at (Dec. 4), M. ii. 427.
Maddan Mán Singh, Col., Nipálese leader, killed at battle of Chánda (Oct. 30), M. ii. 320.
Mádhava Ráo, ruler of Kirwí, M. iii. 199.
Madho Ráo, see Mádhava Ráo.
Madras Presidency, critical condition of (Oct. '58), M. iii. 344.
Madras Government objects to employment of its army beyond seas, K. i. 465.
Madras, Governor of, cheerfully responds to Lord Canning's application for aid, K. i. 611.
Madras, the Queen's proclamation read with ceremony at (Nov. 1, '58), M. iii. 395.

THE HISTORIES OF THE INDIAN MUTINY. 121

Madras Army, its constitution, K. i. 213; available for transport beyond sea, K. i. 464; in motion, accompanied by families of Sepoys, K. i. 291; wives which accompany, act as hostages, K. iii. 173.
Dangerous changes in dress (1805), K. i. 218; *topí* (hat) imposed upon Sepoys, K. i. 218; *topí* hated as mark of Christianity, K. i. 218, 226; mutiny of (1806), K. i. 217–243; Lord Bentinck issues proclamation after Mutiny, K. i. 243; Governor of Madras, and others, dismissed from office in consequence of, K. i. 245; the Madras army trusts in its commanders, K. i. 465 n.; the officers mutiny (1809), K. i. 252; send list of grievances to Governor by post (1822), K. i. 263; 6th Madras Cavalry ordered to Jabbalpúr (1843), K. i. 291; mutiny of the 47th at Bombay (1844), K. i. 294.
Fusiliers embark for Calcutta (May 18), K. i. 612; and arrive there with Col. Neill (May 23), K. ii. 129, M. i. 2; the Sepoys employed in Bengal (Aug.), M. ii. 137.
Mahárájpúr, effect of battle of, in 1843, M. iii. 89.
Mahídpúr, attacked successfully by Mandíswar rebels (Nov. 8), M. iii. 73; plunderers of, pursued by Major Orr, M. iii. 75; they occupy strong position at Ráwal, M. iii. 75; rebels from, do not oppose passage of the Chambal (Nov. 19), M. iii. 77; plunderers of, defeated at Ráwal, with heavy loss, M. iii. 76.

Mahikántá, Native state in Bombay Presidency, M. iii. 2.
Mahmúd Husain Khán, shelters and protects Col. Lennox and family, K. iii. 469.
Mahmúd Khán, his negotiations with the rebels (May), M. iii. 402; attempts to plunder Bíjnúr (May 21), M. iii. 404; makes second attempt on Bíjnúr (May 23), M. iii. 405; returns a third time to Bíjnúr (June), M. iii. 406; he is rendered passive by Mr. Shakespear (June), M. iii. 407; he receives charge of Bíjnúr for ten days (June 7), M. iii. 408; but proclaims himself ruler of Bíjnúr, under King of Dehlí (June 11), M. iii. 409.
Begins to persecute the Hindús (July), M. iii. 410; chased from Bíjnúr by chaudrís of (Aug. 6), M. iii. 411; seizes Bíjnúr (Aug. 23), M. iii. 412, 413; transported for life, M. iii. 418 n.
Mahndí, Col. Colin Troup defeats rebels at (Nov. 18, '58), M. iii. 293.
Mahndí Husain, declares himself Názim of Sultánpúr, M. ii. 326; advances against Gen. Franks (Feb. 19, '58), M. ii. 330; concentrates on Bádsháhganj to oppose Gen. Franks (Feb. 22, '58), M. ii. 332; but is defeated by Gen. Franks at Hamírpúr (Feb.), M. ii. 331; completely defeated at Sultánpúr (Feb. 23, '58), M. ii. 335; displays real generalship, M. ii. 331; makes incursions into Bihár, M. ii. 444; establishes entrenched camp at Belwá (March '58), M. ii. 452; attacks Rowcroft at Ámorhá, and is totally de-

Mahndí Husain—*cont.*
feated (March 5, '58), M. ii.
452; chased from the Ghághrá by Gen. Hope Grant
(Nov. 24, '58), M. iii. 292.
Mahobá, occupied by Gen.
Whitlock (April '58), M. iii.
195.
Mahomedan, *see* Muhammadan.
Mahomed Nazím Khán, *see* Muhammad Nazím Khán.
Mahomed Shaffí, *see* Muhammad Sháfí.
Maihír, feudatory in Ságar territory, M. iii. 88; stormed
and captured by Lieut. W.
Osborne (Dec. 29), M. iii.
112.
Múilghát, held by Brig. Hill
against Tántiá Topí (Oct. '58),
M. iii. 346.
Mainpúrí, officers residing at,
K. iii. 224; the Christian families sent to A'grá (May 23),
K. iii. 223; women and children sent from, into A'grá,
M. i. 157; the Commissioner
goes to A'grá for help, K. iii.
224; mutiny at (May 23),
K. iii. 224, M. i. 3, 157;
Lieut. Crawford and Mr.
Cocks abandon the place, M.
i. 157, 158; the brothers
Power and Dr. Watson remain at their posts, K. iii.
225; a few brave Europeans
remain, M. i. 158; De Kantzow alone nobly stems the
tide of mutiny, K. iii. 225,
226; sublime courage of De
Kantzow, M. i. 158; he checks
the torrent of mutiny, M. i.
159; and keeps mutineers at
bay for three hours, M. i.
159; Ráo Bhawání Singh
bravely comes to De Kantzow's assistance, K. iii. 226,
M. i. 159; the treasury saved,
and mutineers depart, M. i.

Mainpúrí—*cont.*
160; the mutiny quelled, K.
iii. 226; Lord Canning thanks
De Kantzow, K. iii. 227.
Brig. Seaton marches
against (Dec. 23), M. ii. 293;
Tez Singh, the rebel Rájá of,
M. ii. 499; defeat of Tez
Singh at (Dec. 24), M. ii.
294.
Mainpúrí, Rájá of, his estate,
K. i. 161; Edmonstone's settlement of estate of, K. i. 162
and *n.*; R. Bird upholds this
settlement, K. i. 163; Lieut.-
Gov. Robertson objects to the
settlement, K. i. 163; R.
Hamilton also objects to the
settlement, K. i. 163; deprived of three-fourths of his
Talúqdárí, K. i. 165.
Mairs, confidence of Gen. G.
Lawrence in, M. ii. 550.
Mairwárá, civilised by Col.
Dixon, K. iii. 354; staunch
fidelity of the battalion, K. iii.
355.
Maisúr, the Queen's proclamation read with ceremony at
(Nov. 1, '58), M. iii. 396.
Maitáb Singh, a rebel chief,
executed at Akbarábád, M. ii.
93.
Maithaulí, Rájá of, receives fugitives from Sítápúr, K. iii.
482; sends Mrs. Orr to Kachiání, M. i. 385; preserves
Sítápúr fugitives for five
months, K. iii. 484, M. i.
381; orders the removal of
Sítápúr fugitives (Oct. 25),
K. iii. 485; betrays hiding-
place of Sítápúr fugitives, K.
iii. 485.
Maithaulí, captured by Col.
Troup (Oct. 8, '58), M. iii.
293.
Makdún Bakhsh, a brave orderly strives to save the Eng-

Makdún Bakhsh—*cont.*
lish at Irinpúra (Aug. 22),
M. ii. 560.
Makkaganj, fugitives from, cut
off by Capt. Gould Weston
(March 11, '58), M. ii. 381.
Maláon, Mr. Capper, Deputy
Commissioner at, M. i. 382;
mutiny at (June), M. i. 383;
Mr. Capper escapes to Lakhnau, K. iii. 459.
Malápúr, outbreak at, M. i.
395; officers forced to leave,
M. i. 395; fugitives from,
received by Rájá of Dhaurírá,
K. iii. 479; fugitives perish
with one exception, M. i. 396.
Malcolm, Ensign John, commands a detachment of Native troops when fifteen years
old, K. i. 214 *n.*
Malcolm, Col. George, storms
Halgalli with dismounted
troopers (Nov. 29), M. iii.
237; leads a force against
Shorápúr (Jan. '58), M. iii.
126; occupies Shorápúr (Feb.
9, '58), M. iii. 129; assists
Mr. Seton-Karr in disarming
Maráthá country (May '58),
M. iii. 237; marches on
Dhárwár to punish insurrection (May '58), M. iii. 242;
marches on Nargúnd (May
'58), M. iii. 244; attacks and
drives in Nargúnd troops
(June 1, '58), M. iii. 244.
Malcolm, Sir John, on the government of newly acquired
country, K. i. 55 *n.*; on the
title of Rájá conferred on the
Nawáb of Oudh, K. i. 119 *n.*;
his agreement with Bájí Ráo
(1818), M. iii. 482.
Malhíábád, rebellious condition
of, in May, M. i. 370; Mr.
T. H. Kavanagh, Assistant
Commissioner at (July '58),
M. iii. 284.

Malláon, cleared of rebels (July
'58), M. iii. 284 *n.*
Máltún, Sir Hugh Rose turns
flank of pass (March 4, '58),
M. iii. 148.
Máltún pass, evacuated by rebels, M. iii. 150.
Málwá, disaffected condition of
(June), M. iii. 11; Col. Durand crushes out rebellion in
(Nov.), M. iii. 81; Major-
Gen. Michel commands at
(Aug. '58), M. iii. 327.
Malwáí Sikhs, plan a mutiny at
Derá Ismáíl Khán (July '58),
M. iii. 305.
Mammu Khán, reputed paramour of the Begam of Oudh,
M. iii. 270.
Mán Singh, Talúqdár of Sháhganj, K. iii. 462 and *n.*; arrest
of (June), K. iii. 463 and *n.*, M.
i. 398; Capt. Alex. Orr, procures his release from arrest,
M. i. 398; while under arrest undertakes to protect
women and children, K. iii.
464; offers to protect the
wife and children of Capt. A.
Orr, M. i. 398; the story of
his visit to the King of Oudh
at Calcutta, K. iii. 36; besieged by rebels (July '58),
M. iii. 270; rebels leave his
fort on approach of Gen.
Hope Grant (July '58), M.
iii. 271.
Mán Singh, Rájá of Narwár,
seizes fort of Paurí (Aug. 2,
'58), M. iii 332; pleads his
excuse to Brig. Smith, which
cannot be accepted (Aug. 7,
'58), M. iii. 333; his uncle
Ajít Singh comes to his assistance, M. iii. 334; he and
Ajít Singh evacuate Paurí
(Aug. 23, '58), M. iii. 335;
cleverly eludes pursuit in retreat from Paurí (Sept. '58),

Mán Singh—*cont.*
M. iii. 336; enters Bánswárá to join Tántiá Topí (Dec. '58), M. iii. 356; joins with and speedily parts from Tántiá Topí (Jan. '59), M. iii. 358; rejoined by Tántiá Topí alone at Paron (Feb. '59), M. iii. 368; his surrender negotiated by his Díwán and Náráyan Singh (March 8, '59), M. iii. 372; surrender of his family (March 25, '59), M. iii. 373; terms on which he surrendered, M. iii. 374; surrenders to Capt. Meade (April 2, '59), M. iii. 374; joins English in attempt to capture his uncle (April 4, '59), M. iii. 375; agrees to betray Tántiá Topí (April 7, '59), M. iii. 377; and betrays him (April 8, '59), M. iii. 379.
Manda, Rájá of, sides with the English, K. ii. 260.
Mandalá, part of Ságar territory, M. iii. 88; Gen. Whitlock occupies (April 3, '58), M. iii. 195.
Mandalíswar, Col. Durand resolves to retreat through, M. i. 239; the place is protected by Col. Durand (Oct. 12), M. iii. 68.
Mandisúr, *see* Mandíswar.
Mandíswar, becomes a centre of insurrection (Aug.), M. iii. 65; composition of rebel force at, M. iii. 66; rebels fix Dasahará festival for opening of campaign (Oct.), M. iii. 67; rebels threaten Bombay road (Oct.), M. iii. 67; rebels from, seize Jíran near Nímach, M. ii. 571; they evacuate Jíran (Oct. 23), M. ii. 571; rebels stopped at Mandalíswar and Gújrí by Col. Durand (Oct.), M. iii. 68;

Mandíswar—*cont.*
they advance into Nímach (Nov. 8), M. ii. 572; and attack Mahídpúr successfully (Nov. 8), M. iii. 73; Col. Durand encamps near (Nov. 20), M. iii. 78; rebels come out to fight the British (Nov. 20), M. iii. 78; Col. Durand drives off rebel attack, M. iii. 79; extraordinary instance of rebel daring, M. iii. 79 *n.*; the gallantry of the Rohillas allows Firoz Sháh to escape, M. iii. 81; rebels fall back on Nángarh (Nov. 24), M. iii. 81; party of rebels from, attacked and put to flight by Thákur of Partábgarh, M. iii. 81; Tántiá Topí marches on (Dec. '58), M. iii. 357.
Mandlah, *see* Mandalá.
Mandlesar, *see* Mandalíswar.
Mandorí, Nipálese troops defeat the rebels at (Sept. 19), M. ii. 318; Mr. Venables' gallantry at, M. ii. 318.
Mangal Pándí, the first mutineer, K. i. 538; tries to destroy himself, K. i. 542; sentenced to be hanged, K. i. 549.
Mangal Singh, a rebel chief, executed at Akbárábád, M. ii. 93.
Manghír, Mr. Yule sends detachment to garrison (July), M. ii. 131; disturbed state of (Nov.–Dec.), M. ii. 426.
Mangles, Mr. Ross, the first civilian to receive the Victoria Cross, K. iii. 119 *n.*; his calm courage, M. i. 88 *n.*; his conspicuous gallantry in the retreat from A'rá, K. iii. 117; saves the life of a soldier with heroic devotion, K. iii. 118.
Mangraulí, Tántiá Topí marches

Mangraulí—cont.
on (Sept. '58), M. iii. 338;
Gen. Michel defeats Tántiá
Topí at (Oct. 9, '58), M. iii.
339.
Mansab Alí, the able assistant
of Capt. Evans at Púrwá, M.
i. 409; defeated by Lieut.
Aikman near the Gúmtí (Mar.
1, '58), M. ii, 336.
Mansel, Mr. Charles Grenville,
his character, K. i. 52; his
views on settlements, K. i.
174; retires from the Service
(1854), K. i. 85.
Mansfield, Gen. William, his
character, M. ii. 273; his defect in vision, M. ii. 274; sent
to cut off Tántiá Topí's retreat (Dec. 6), M. ii. 273;
marches his troops where
they could cut off the retreat,
M. ii. 275; allows Tántiá
Topí to escape, M. ii. 275;
Sir Colin Campbell's disastrous order to Gen. Outram,
attributed to him (Mar. 14,
'58), M. ii. 398; thinks the
rebellion crushed out (Dec.
'58), M. iii. 294; his encomium on Capt. S. Browne's
gallantry, M. iii. 278 n.
Manson, Mr. Charles, his character, M. iii. 235; succeeds
Mr. Seton-Karr in political
agency of Maráthá country,
M. iii. 235; his appointment
injudicious, M. iii. 235, 236;
does not understand his own
unpopularity, M. iii. 241; arrests the Chief of Jámkhandí
(April. '58), M. iii. 239.
Assumes political control
(May 16, '58), M. iii. 240; at
Rámdurg ascertains defection of Chief of Nargúnd, M.
iii. 242; rides on to Nargúnd,
to pacify Chief, M. iii. 241;
halts in a temple near Nar-

Manson, Mr. C.—cont.
gúnd, M. iii. 242; attacked
and murdered (May '58), M.
iii. 243.
Mansúb Alí, hovers about Gen.
Outram's line of communications (June '58), M. ii. 347.
Map of Northern India, to illustrate Sepoy War, K. iii.
193.
Map of Panjáb and North-West
Provinces, K. ii. 1.
Mara, Lieut., commands 5th
Fusiliers advancing from
Lakhnau Residency (Nov.
16), M. ii. 206; murdered at
Jánpúr (June 5), K. ii. 238.
Mára Khán, assists Náwáb of
Najíbábád in misgovernment
of Bíjnúr (Sept.), M. iii. 413.
Marátha character, K. iii. 348;
Native states in, M. iii. 20;
situation and extent of the
southern, M. iii. 19; Mr.
Seton-Karr has political
charge of, M. iii. 20.
Plan of uprising in, M. iii.
37; tranquillity restored
(Nov. 20, '58), M. iii. 246.
Maráthás, their antagonism to
the English, M. iii. 207, 208;
faithful to the rebel leaders,
M. iii. 385; their feelings
with respect to the Peshwás and the English, M. iii.
379.
Marátha Princes, inclined to
disaffection, K. i. 578.
Maraurá, rebels evacuate the
fort of, M. iii. 150.
Marches, extraordinary, in pursuit of Tántiá Topí, M. iii.
383.
Marching of Native troops assists in spreading sedition, K.
i. 499.
Mardán, destruction of 55th
Regiment at (May 25), K. ii.
485.

Martin, Mr. Simon Nicolson, Deputy Commissioner of Lakhnau, K. iii. 439.

Martineau, Lieut., discovers dangerous condition of Sepoys at Ambálá (March), K. i. 553; fully recognises the danger threatened, K. i. 557 n.

Martinière, see Lakhnau.

Martial Law, solicited by Europeans in Calcutta (Aug.), K. iii. 178; Lord Canning refuses to place Lower Bengal under, K. iii. 179.

Márwá Ghát, Gen. Whitlock arrives at (April 3, '58), M. iii. 195.

Márwár, one of Rájpút states, M. i. 245 n.; Tántiá Topí escapes into, from British cordon of troops (Jan. 18, '59), M. iii. 367.

Massacres—
Dehlí, see Dehlí.
Jhánsí, see Jhánsí.
Káhnpúr, see Káhnpúr.
Sháhjahánpúr, see Sháhjahánpúr.

Masonic Fraternity, Calcutta, Government declines their offer to raise Volunteers (May), M. i. 2.

Mathias, Dr., destroys gun ammunition of Kotá Contingent (July 4), M. i. 268.

Mathurá, to be protected by Jaipúr troops, K. iii. 357; occupied by troops of Rájá of Bharatpúr (May 15), K. iii. 209, 240; mutiny at (May 30), K. iii. 241, M. i. 164; a loyal gunner, spikes guns of Kotá Contingent (July 4), M. i. 268.

Maú, its position, M. i. 204 n.; its garrison, K. iii. 323, M. i. 206; Col. Platt commands at, M. i. 206.
Mutinous spirit of troops

Maú—cont.
at (May 14), M. i. 209; excited state of (June 13), K. iii. 329; outward loyalty of troops at, M. i. 211; Capt. Hungerford recommends precautionary measures, K. iii. 330; Col. Platt refuses to suspect Sepoys, K. iii. 333.
Hungerford summoned to Indor with his guns (July 1), K. iii. 334, M. i. 233; Capt. Hungerford's battery starts at noon, M. i. 234; Capt. Hungerford's battery advances a few miles and then returns, K. iii. 334, M. i. 234.
Hungerford's battery moved into fort, K. iii. 334; mutiny at (July 1), K. iii. 335, M. i. 235; Capt. Hungerford clears the lines of Sepoys, K. iii. 336, M. i. 235; Capt. Hungerford garrisons the fort, and prepares for a siege, K. iii. 338.

Maude, Capt., his splendid use of Artillery at Fathpúr (July 12), K. ii. 361.

Maughan, Col., political officer at Kolhápúr (May), M. iii. 37; holds Kolhápúr against the mutineers (Aug.), M. iii. 40.

Maulaví, the, known as Ahmad Sháh, M. ii. 344; his character and antecedents, K. ii. 261 n., M. ii. 541; his personal appearance, M. ii. 542; one of the conspirators who planned the rebellion, M. iii. 485; towns at which he resided, and which became centres of rebellion, M. iii. 485; establishes provisional Government, K. ii. 261; his tactical skill, M. ii. 495; his tactics spoilt by his own troops, M. ii. 496; his skilful strategy, M. ii. 531.

Maulaví—*cont.*
His first head-quarters at Khusrú Bágh, Alláhábád (June 7), K. ii. 261; escapes from Alláhábád to Káhnpúr (June 17), K. ii. 267; commands rebels at Lakhnau (Nov.), M. ii. 344; his plan for driving Gen. Outram from the Álambágh, M. ii. 344; attacks Gen. Outram (Dec. 22), M. ii. 345; defeated by Gen. Outram, M. ii. 346; his oath to defeat Gen. Outram (Jan. 13, '58), M. ii. 350; defeated and wounded in attack on Major Olpherts (Jan. 14, '58), M. ii. 351; imprisoned by rebels at Lakhnau (Jan. 23, '58), M. ii. 353; holds the Shádatganj in Lakhnau (Mar. 21, '58), M. ii. 410; escapes from Lakhnau (Mar. 21, '58), M. ii. 411.
Sir Hope Grant marches against (April '58), M. ii. 493; escapes with his army from Sháhjahánpúr, M. ii. 522; joined by reinforcements at Mohamdí (May 2, '58), M. ii. 532; marches on Sháhjahánpúr, M. ii. 532; reinforcements flock in to him at Sháhjahánpúr (May 11–14, '58), M. ii. 536; commands the entire road from Sháhjahánpúr to Mohamdí, M. ii. 538; forced across the Kánárat Naddí by Brig. Jones (May 11, '58), M. ii. 535; makes a severe attack on Brig. Jones (May 15, '58), M. ii. 537; again outmanœuvres Sir Colin Campbell (May 24, '58), M. ii. 540.
Refused admittance into Powáín (June 5, '58), M. ii. 543; attempts to force an entrance into Powáín, M. ii.

Maulaví—*cont.*
543; and is killed in the attempt (June 5, '58), M. ii. 544; his head exposed at Sháhjahánpúr, M. ii. 544; tribute to his patriotism and manliness, M. ii. 544.
Maulaví Mahdí, patrolling magistrate of Patná, arrested by Mr. W. Tayler, M. i. 54.
Maulavis, arrest of the three at Patná, K. iii. 82.
Maun Singh, *see* Mán Singh.
Mawe, Dr., dies during retreat from Naogáon, M. i. 196.
Maxwell, Col. G. V., advances against Kálpí, M. ii. 450; marches to Gulaulí to join Sir H. Rose (May 15, '58), M. iii. 181.
Maynard, Major, relieves Capt. Dawson at Sandíla (Oct. 6, '58), M. iii. 286; drives the rebels to Pannú, M. iii. 287; his gallantry at Pannú (Oct. 8, '58), M. iii. 287.
Mayne, Capt., leads party of Cavalry from Ságar, M. iii. 108; his death in attack on Lakhnau (Nov. 14), M. ii. 177 *n*.
Mayo, Mr. Arthur, midshipman, bravely captures a gun at Dákhá (Nov. 22), M. ii. 420; his gallantry at Dháká, M. iii. 460.
Meade, Capt. R. J., his character, M. iii. 313; raises a regiment of horse at Ágrá (Dec.), M. iii. 313; adds Játs and Gwáliár natives to his regiment, M. iii. 313; gains the confidence of Náráyan Singh (March 8, '59), M. iii. 371; induces Náráyan Singh to negotiate surrender of Mán Singh, M. iii. 372; Mán Singh's family surrender to him (March 25, '59), M. iii.

Meade, Capt. R. J.—*cont.*
373; Mán Singh surrenders to him (April 2, '59), M. iii. 374; pursues Ajít Singh, but fails to capture him (April 4, '59), M. iii. 376; refuses specific guarantee for betrayal of Tántiá Topí (April 7, '59), M. iii. 377; persuades Mán Singh to betray Tántiá Topí, M. iii. 376; captures and tries Tántiá Topí (April 8, '59), M. iii. 379; hangs Tántiá Topí at Siprí (April 18, '59), M. iii. 380.
Meade's Horse, raised by Capt. R. J. Meade, at A'grá, M. iii. 312; excellent service rendered by, M. iii. 314.
Mecham, Lieut., his presence of mind saves his life, M. i. 362 n.; sent to pacify Malhíábád district, M. i. 370.
Medley, Capt., traces batteries before Dehlí, M. ii. 12, 18, 19; examines breach at Dehlí, M. ii. 25; his daring entrance into the Qaddam Rasúl, Lakhnau (March 10, '58), M. ii. 383; occupies Sháh Najíf, M. ii. 384.
Meerut, *see* Mírut.
Meerza Korash, *see* Mírzá Muhammad Kúrash.
Meetings, nightly, to discuss the greased-cartridge fable, K. i. 497.
Méhndí Húsén, *see* Mahndí Husain.
Meiklejohn, Lieut., his gallantry and death at the storming of Jhánsí (April 3, '58), M. iii. 169.
Mess House, *see* Lakhnau.
Messing system in gaols, misunderstood by Sepoys, K. i. 305; system in gaols, affecting caste, K. i. 195.
Metcalfe, Charles, in 1806 sees

Metcalfe, Charles—*cont.*
the danger of subservience to Mughál Emperor, K. ii. 7.
Metcalfe, Sir Charles, on limitation of succession to grants, K. i. 91 n.
Metcalfe, Sir Thomas, British Agent with Dehlí sovereign, K. ii. 26.
Mewár, one of Rájpút states, M. i. 245 n.; head of the Rájpút Confederacy, K. iii. 355.
Mewár troops, aid Capt. Showers in rescuing English fugitives, K. iii. 356.
Meywar, *see* Mewár.
Mhow, *see* Máú.
Miánganj, *see* Miyánganj.
Mián Mír, its situation and importance, K. ii. 425; the disarming parade (May 13), K. ii. 431.
Michel, Gen., succeeds Gen. Roberts in command of Rájpútáná (Aug. '58), M. iii. 328; commands in Málwá, M. iii. 327; joins Col. Lockhart at Nálkhere, M. iii. 328; sends troops to cover Ujjain, north of Indúr, M. iii. 328; meets Tántiá Topí at Rájgarh (Sept. '58), M. iii. 329; completely defeats Tántiá Topí, near Rájgarh, M. iii. 330; marches upon Mangraulí, and defeats Tántiá Topí (Oct. 9, '58), M. iii. 339; catches Tántiá Topí at Khorai, and destroys half his army (Oct. 25, '58), M. iii. 342; moves upon Chárwá (Nov. '58), M. iii. 347; bars the Narbadá against Tántiá Topí, M. iii. 347; crosses the Narbadá and sends Parke after Tántiá Topí, M. iii. 352; equips light columns for pursuit of Tántiá Topí,

Michel, Gen.—*cont.*
M. iii. 384; himself marches 1,700 miles in pursuit of Tántiá Topí, M. iii. 384.
Middleton, Lieut., his gallantry at Nathupúr, M. iii. 511.
Miles, Lieut., killed in rising at Múltán (Aug. 31, '58), M. iii. 307.
Military Train, converted into Cavalry regiment, M. ii. 126.
Mill, Mrs., her miraculous escape from Faizábád, K. iii. 469 and *n*.
Millar, Col., commands Kámptí movable column, M. iii. 103.
Miller, Lieut.-Col. W. H., commands Artillery of Jabalpúr column (Nov.), M. iii. 191; distinguishes himself at Bándá (April 19, '58), M. iii. 197.
Mills, Capt., killed in charge at Mahídpúr (Nov. 8), M. iii. 73.
Mills, Lieut., killed in attack on Gwáliár (June 18, '58), M. iii. 226.
Milman, Col., advances against rebels at Atrauliá (March 21, '58), M. ii. 455; is forced back on Ázamgarh (March 22, '58), M. ii. 457.
Ministry, the English, just as responsible for the Mutiny as the Court of Directors, M. iii. 389.
Miránpúr, burnt by rebels from Bíjnúr (Jan. 5, '58), M. iii. 413.
Miranpúr Katra, Gen. Penny's column joins Sir Colin Campbell at (May 3, '58), M. ii. 502; Gen. Walpole's column arrives at, M. ii. 510; Sir Colin Campbell arrives there, M. ii. 522.
Míraj, Native state of Southern Marátha country, M. iii. 20.

Míraj, Chief of, forced to give up his ammunition (June '58), M. iii. 245.
Míran-kí-saráí, Capt. Hodson communicates with Sir Colin Campbell at (Dec. 30), M. ii. 297.
Mírat, an important station, K. i. 565; description of the cantonment, K. ii. 53; disbandment of mutinous 34th Regiment at (1844), K. i. 298.
Mutton fat used with cartridges at, K. i. 515; greased cartridges in process of manufacture at, K. i. 515; excitement at, in April, K. i. 566; 3rd Cavalry at, refuse ammunition, K. i. 567; Court of Inquiry as to conduct of 3rd Cavalry at (May), K. ii. 45; court-martial ordered, K. ii. 48; mutineers sentenced, K. ii. 49; sentence executed on the Cavalry troopers, K. ii. 51.
Revolt at (May 10), K. i. 595, ii. 56, M. i. 43; release of the Cavalry troopers (May 10), K. ii. 58.
Revolt of the Infantry (May 10), K. ii. 59; massacre at, K. ii. 60; horrors of the night of May 10, K. ii. 67; slaughter of Europeans on that night, K. i. 595, ii. 68; wanton destruction of life and property, K. ii. 71; Mrs. Craigie saved by fidelity of her husband's troopers, K. ii. 70; instances of fidelity of Natives during outbreak, K. ii. 74 *n*.
Mutineers unchecked in their revolt, K. ii. 62; no attempt made to punish rioters after outbreak of Mutiny, K. ii. 72; instances of bravery of

Mírat—cont.
Europeans during outbreak, K. ii. 74 n.
Strength of Europeans at (May 10), K. ii. 61; conduct of principal European officers during the revolt, K. ii. 63; Capt. Craigie and Lieut. Clarke boldly try to control mutiny, K. ii. 64; prompt conduct of Col. A. Wilson on outbreak, K. ii. 65; reported delay in turning out Carabineers, K. ii. 687; deliberate action of Gen. Hewitt, K. ii. 66; astounding inactivity of European troops during and after mutiny, K. ii. 72; concentration of Europeans and property at Cantonments (May 12), K. ii. 172; British authority comes to an end, K. ii. 173.
Mutineers communicate with Dehlí troops before outbreak, K. ii. 83; they hurry on to Dehlí during night of May 10, K. i. 596, ii. 75; probabilities of overtaking them, K. ii. 106; moral and political results of a pursuit, K. ii. 107; the mutineers reach the Emperor's palace at Dehlí, K. ii. 76; on entering Dehlí they recommence their work of slaughter (May 11), K. ii. 77; they seize the palace of the Emperor, K. ii. 80.
Native Sappers mutiny (May 15), K. ii. 176.
Timidity and selfishness of authorities at, M. i. 298; remain inactive for a fortnight after outbreak of mutiny, K. ii. 181; the garrison moves out (May 27), K. ii. 183; and defeats Dehlí mutineers, near Ghází-ud-Dín Nagar (May 31), M. i. 10.

Mírat—cont.
Mr. Dunlop becomes Magistrate and Collector at (June), M. iii. 425; he assumes civil charge (June 15), M. iii. 426; and finds the treasury empty, M. iii. 427; he organises a Volunteer force called Khákí Risála (June), M. iii. 428; first enterprise of the Khákí Risála (July), M. iii. 428.
But one European regiment between Mírat and Dánápúr (June 1), M. i. 6.
Míratb, see Mírat.
Mirzá Alláhí Bakhsh, a relative of the Emperor of Dehlí, but favourable to the English, K. iii. 644; detains the Emperor of Dehlí and his sons, K. iii. 644.
Mirzá Gaffúr Beg, sent to defeat Gen. Franks (Feb. '58), M. ii. 332; his position at Bádsháhganj, M. ii. 332; completely defeated at Sultánpúr (Feb. 23, '58), M. ii. 335.
Mirzá Haidar, nephew of King of Dehlí, converts him to Shi'ah faith, K. ii. 39.
Mirzá Iláhí Bakhsh, see Iláhi Bakhsh, Mirzá.
Mirzá Muhammad Kúrash, opposes succession of Jawán Bakht to Dehlí sovereignty, K. ii. 28.
Missionary devotion at Ágrá, K. iii. 228 n.
Missionary military officers, their plain duty, K. i. 481.
Missionary zeal among British officers, indiscretion of, K. i. 480.
Missionaries specially contribute to alarm native religious susceptibilities, K. i. 472.
Mitchell, Col., by injudicious

THE HISTORIES OF THE INDIAN MUTINY. 131

Mitchell, Col.—*cont.*
anger, confirms suspicions of Sepoys at Brahmapúr, K. i. 502; his measures to overawe troops at Brahmapúr increase their excitement, K. i. 504, 505; ordered to march his regiment to Barákpúr for disbandment (March), K. i. 527.

Mítholí, *see* Maithaulí.

Miyánganj, Brig. Evelegh defeats rebels at (Oct. 5, '58), M. iii. 287.

Miyán Sáhib, a Lakhnau chief, joins the Maulaví (May 2, '58), M. ii. 532.

Mobarik Shah, *see* Mubárik Sháh.

Mohan on the Sáí, Mr. Pat. Carnegy civil officer at, M. iii. 282; attacked by Firoz Sháh (Aug. 7, '58), M. iii. 282; Col. Evelegh hastens to assistance of, M. iii. 283; rebels retreat from, and are defeated by Col. Evelegh (Aug. 8, '58), M. iii. 283.

Mohamdí, Mr. Thomason, Deputy Commissioner at, M. i. 383; garrison of (May), M. i. 384; Mr. Thomason sends conveyances for fugitives from Sháhjahánpúr, M. i. 384; he moves treasure into fort, M. i. 385; Mrs. Orr and child sent to Maithaulí, M. i. 385; they ultimately reach British camp at Lakhnau (March 19, '58), M. i. 389 *n.*
English retire to fort (June 1), M. i. 386; fugitives from Sháhjahánpúr arrive, K. iii. 459, M. i. 386; escort sent from Sítápúr to convey Europeans thither, M. i. 386; the Sítápúr escort disposed to be mutinous, M. i. 386; Capt. Orr reasons with escort, and they swear to protect Euro-

Mohamdí—*cont.*
peans as far as Sítápúr, M. i. 386.
Mutiny at (June 4), K. iii. 459; Europeans permitted to escape, K. iii. 459; the fugitives from, murdered by Sítápúr escort (June 4), K. iii. 460, M. i. 387.

Mohamdí, the Rájá of, joins the Maulaví (May 2, '58), M. ii. 532.

Möller, Lieut., arrests the murderer of Mrs. Chambers (May 14), K. ii. 73.

Momín Khán, gallant trooper who stood by Lieut. Conolly at Írinpúra, M. ii. 594.

Monck-Mason, Capt., Political Agent at Jodhpúr, K. iii. 354, M. i. 258; reluctantly refuses pardon to Abbás Alí (Aug. 24), M. ii. 562; reluctantly obliged to refuse terms of the Thákur of A'wah, M. ii. 564; killed at A'wah (Sept. 18), M. ii. 567.

Moncrieff, Capt., operates in Chútiá Nágpúr (Jan.), M. ii. 441 *b.*

Moncrieff, Mr., chaplain, his devotion at Káhnpúr, K. ii. 321.

Money, Mr. Alonzo, Magistrate at Gayá, K. iii. 151, M. i. 109; reports disaffection at Gayá (July 24), K. iii. 152; his opinion as to the safety of Gayá, M. i. 110 *n.*; his plan for defence of Gayá (July 28), K. iii. 153.
Quits Gayá on receipt of Mr. W. Tayler's order, K. iii. 154; resolves to abandon the treasure, M. i. 110; inexplicable character of his abandonment of treasure, M. i. 110; urged to return for treasure by Mr. Hollings, M.

9 *

Money, Mr.—*cont.*
i. 111; he repents and returns with Mr. Hollings to Gayá, K. iii. 155, M. i. 112; condemns his own actions, M. i. 112.
On return to Gayá summons detachment of 64th Regiment, K. iii. 156, M. i. 112; burns the Government paper at Gayá, K. iii. 156, M. i. 113; despatches treasure from Gayá (Aug. 4), M. i. 113; flies from Gayá himself, K. iii. 157, M. i. 113; resolves to take treasure to Calcutta, M. i. 113; brings treasure safely into Calcutta, K. iii. 158.
His entire conduct inexplicable, M. i. 114; his act in no way meritorious, M. i. 114; converts his duty into a sensational drama, M. i. 116; Fortune converts his disobedience into a triumph, M. i. 115.
Leads Capt. Rattray into a false position (Sept. 8), M. ii. 444.
Monghír, district of Bhágalpúr, M. ii. 129.
Moore, Capt., his noble chivalry at Káhnpúr, K. ii. 318.
Moore, Dr., murdered by rebels in Sambalpúr (Dec.), M. ii. 441.
Moolraj, *see* Múlráj.
Mooltan, *see* Múltán.
Moorsom, Lieut., his services at Lakhnau and the A'lambágh, M. ii. 362; death of, at Lakhnau (March 11, '58), M. ii. 381.
Montgomery, Mr. Robert, his character, K. ii. 423; and antecedents, M. iii. 262; averse to betraying suspicion, K. ii. 426.

Montgomery, Mr.—*cont.*
Ascertains the unfaithfulness of Sepoys at Míán Mír, K. ii. 427; holds the council at Anárkalí, K. ii. 427; proposes to deprive Sepoys at Míán Mír of their ammunition, K. ii. 428; successfully disarms the troops (May 13), K. ii. 432; prepares for security of Amritsar, K. ii. 435; counsels his subordinates to preserve exterior calmness, K. ii. 437.
Succeeds Gen. J. Outram as Commissioner in Oudh (May '58), M. iii. 262; his difficulties in pacifying Oudh, M. iii. 265; persuades Mán Singh to return to his allegiance (July '58), M. iii. 270.
Morádábád, *see* Murádábád.
Morár, the rebels desperately defend, but are driven out (June 16, '58), M. iii. 217.
Morphy, Capt., killed at Káhnpúr (Nov. 28), M. ii. 251.
Moteharee, *see* Motíhárí.
Motíhárí, out-station of Patná, K. iii. 71, M. i. 40.
Motí Mahal, *see* Lakhnau.
Mouat, Dr., his description of "Panic Sunday," K. iii. 31 *n.*, 32 *n.*
Moulavee, *see* Maulaví.
Mount Abú, garrison of, M. ii. 555; English in, stealthily attacked by Jodhpúr troops (Aug. 21), M. ii. 556; Jodhpúr troops driven away, M. ii. 557.
Mounted Infantry tried in Bihár (Oct. '58), M. ii. 487; their great success, M. ii. 491.
Mowbray-Thomson, Lieut., his reckless bravery at Káhnpúr, K. ii. 319.
Mozaffarnagar, its situation and

Mozaffarnagar—cont.
garrison, M. i. 301; ignominious flight of Mr. Berford, K. iii. 247; who hides himself on news of Mírat outbreak, M. i. 301; disastrous effects of Mr. Berford's pusillanimity, K. iii. 248; mutiny and insurrection at (May 14), K. iii. 247, M. i. 301. Oudh rebels appear at (Aug. '58), M. iii. 273; Mr. Dunlop clears the country of rebels near, M. iii. 436.

Mozaffarpúr, out-station of Patná, K. iii. 71, M. i. 40; officials desire to withdraw from (July 29), K. iii. 149; ordered to be abandoned by Mr. Tayler, M. i. 108; withdrawal of Europeans and mutiny of Irregulars (July 31), K. iii. 150, M. i, 108; treasury saved by native officials and police, K. iii. 150, M. i. 109.

Mozufferpore, see Mozaffarpúr.

Mubárakpúr, captured and occupied (Sept. 27), M. ii. 319.

Mubárik Sháh, pretender to power in Barailí, K. iii. 275; his claims favoured by Bakht Khán, K. iii. 277.

Muchee Bhowan, see Machhí Bháwan.

Mudhol, Native state of Southern Marátha country, M. iii. 20.

Mughál sovereigns, their removal from Dehlí, proposed, K. ii. 14–23.

Mughál empire, restoration of, proclaimed, K. i. 597.

Muhammadan eastern capital at Patná, M. i. 39.

Muhammadan fanaticism feared at Pesháwar, K. ii. 492.

Muhammadan feeling with re-

Muhammadan—cont.
spect to English ideas, K. i. 196.

Muhammadan grievances(1822), K. i. 262.

Muhammadan population, effect of removal of Dehlí sovereign upon, feared, K. ii. 21.

Muhammadan revolutionary plot at Belgáon (Aug.), M. iii. 33.

Muhammadans, their number in 'Sepoy Army, K. i. 621–626; where they gain temporary supremacy begin to persecute Hindús, M. iii. 410; dispute between them and the Pársís at Barúch (May), M. iii. 8; excitement among those at Dehlí in spring of 1857, K. ii. 35; those of the Hazárá country plan a revolt (Sept.), M. iii. 303.

Muhammad Akbar, his murder of Sir W. Macnaughten, K. iii. 84, M. i. 53.

Muhammad Bakhsh, Risáldár, his good service during the Mutiny, M. iii. 455 n.

Muhammad Husain, defeated at Amorhá by Major Cox (June 9, '58), M. iii. 282; attacked and defeated at Hariyá (June 18, '58), M. iii. 282; takes possession of Gorakhpúr, M. iii. 456; sets a price on Mr. Bird's head, but is baffled, M. iii. 456.

Muhammad Nazím Khán, loyal rissaldár of 8th Irreg. Cavalry, M. i. 315 n.

Muhammad Rahmat Khán and Sáyad Ahmad Khán, directed by Mr. Shakespear to take charge of Bíjnúr (Aug. 6), M. iii. 411.

Muhammad Sháfí, traitor in 8th Irreg. Cavalry, M. i. 313.

Muir, Mr. William, made chief

Muir, Mr.—*cont.*
of Intelligence Department at A'grá Fort, K. iii. 406.
Múlráj, Díwán of Múltán, K. i. 18; threatened by the Sikh Darbár, K. i. 18; appeals to the English, K. i. 18; resigns the Díwánship of Múltán, K. i. 19; declares against the English, K. i. 21; Sir F. Currie hesitates to act against, K. i. 25; surrenders to the British (1849), K. i. 40.
Múltán, the British besiege (1848), K. i. 33; but are compelled to raise the siege, K. i. 33; murder of Mr. Vans Agnew and Lieut. Anderson in, K. i. 21; capture of (1849), K. i. 39.
Rising of disarmed Sepoys at (Aug. 31, '58), M. iii. 307; terrible retaliation on revolted Sepoys, M. iii. 307; insurrection around (Sept. 14), M. iii. 304.
Múltání horse, splendid services of, at Naghína (April 21, '58), M. ii. 517, 518.
Múlví Mehdí, *see* Maulaví Mahdí.
Mundá, a tribe in Chutiá Nágpúr, M. ii. 134.
Munro, Sergeant, his heroism at the Sikandar Bágh (Nov. 16), M. ii. 197.
Munro, Sir Thomas, receives a letter by post stating grievances of Madras Army (1822), K. i. 263; his views on the Indian Press, K. iii. 664.
Mungul Pandy, *see* Mangal Pándí.
Munshí Rajab Alí, *see* Rajab Alí, Munshí.
Murád Alí, Kotwál of A'grá, proclaims King of Dehlí, M. i. 277.

Murádábád, its garrison, M. i. 325; Mr. Cracroft Wilson, Judge of, K. iii. 252; who receives enlarged powers, K. iii. 252.
Treason of Nawáb Ní'amatulláh Khán at, K. iii. 253 *n.*; party of Mírat mutineers encamp near, M. i. 325; Capt. Faddy surprises and disperses the Mírat mutineers (May 18), M. i. 326; loyalty of 29th N. I. tested by attack on Mírat mutineers, M. i. 326; incompleteness of defeat of mutineers ascribed to lukewarmness of 29th N.I., M. i. 326; escaped Sepoys enter the lines of the 29th N.I., and are shot at and captured, K. iii. 255, M. i. 327; some men of the 29th N.I. riot and release prisoners from jail (May 19), K. iii. 255, M. i. 327, iii. 402; remainder of 29th N.I. pursue and capture 150 rioters and prisoners, M. i. 328.
Detachment of Sepoys from assist in attack of mutineers from Muzaffarnagar, K. iii. 254; Mr. C. Wilson restores confidence, K. iii. 257; Muhammadans from Rámpúr encamp near, and incite to mutiny (May 21), M. i. 328; Mr. C. Wilson defeats rebellious party advancing from Rámpúr, K. iii. 258, M. i. 328.
Two companies of armed mutineers approach (May 23), M. i. 329; Mr. C. Wilson and Capt. Whish disarm mutinous Sappers moving against them, K. iii. 259; Capt. Whish pursues and forces mutineers to surrender (May 23), M. i. 329; evidences of

Murádábád—*cont.*
rebellion at, K. iii. 261;
news of Barailí mutiny causes
outbreak of 29th N. I., M. i.
330; Sepoys ridicule Mr.
Wilson for proposing to lead
them to Mírat, M. i. 330.
Mutiny at (June 2), M. i.
330; civil officers confide
treasure to Sepoys, M. i.
331; Sepoys prepare to shoot
Europeans, but are induced
to desist, M. i. 331; Mr.
Saunders destroys Government paper, K. iii. 263, M.
i. 331; massacre at, K. iii.
264; escape of Europeans
from (June 3), K. iii.
264, M. i. 332; murder of
Christians who remain after
mutiny, M. i. 332; Mr.
Powell and others become
Mussalmans to save their
lives, M. i. 332.
Inhabitants refuse supplies
to the King of Dehlí (April
21, 58), M. ii. 520; Firoz
Sháh escapes from (April
26, '58), M. ii. 521; Col. Coke
captures many ring-leaders of
rebellion at (April 26, '58),
M. ii. 521.
Murdán, *see* Mardán.
Murder, punishment for, Ccl. J.
Nicholson's views on, K. ii. 401.
Murphy, Farrier, his gallantry
at Nathupúr, M. iii. 511.
Músá Bágh, near Lakhnau,
Gen. Outram sent to reduce
(March 19, '58), M. ii. 405;
Gen. Hope Grant co-operates
in attack on, M. ii. 405;
Gen. Outram captures it, M.
ii. 406; gallantry of Col. J.
Hagart at, M. ii. 407; Capt.
Wilkin's distinguished bravery at, M. iii. 509; Gen. Outram pursues rebels from, M.
ii. 408; Brig. Campbell or-

Mísá Bágh—*cont.*
dered to cut off retreat from,
M. ii. 406; Brig. Campbell
neglects to do so, M. ii. 408;
incalculable mischief caused
by Brig. Campbell's neglect,
M. ii. 408 *n.*
Musketry Schools, final orders
of, K. i. 630.
Mutiny of Sepoy Army, the first,
in Bengal (1764), K. i. 206;
the second, in Bengal (1764),
K. i. 206.
Mutiny—
At Haidarábád suppressed
(1806), K. i. 237.
At Nandídurg threatened
(1806), K. i. 238.
At Pallamcotta threatened
(1806), K. i. 239.
Of Vellore, first outburst
(May 7, 1806), K. i. 224;
its causes, K. i. 245; in part
caused by injudicious changes
in Sepoys' dress, K. i. 218,
226; neglect of premonitory
symptoms, K. i. 224; precipitated by an excited Jamádár, K. i. 228; the Mysore
Princes encourage the revolt,
K. i. 229; second outburst
(July 10, 1806), K. i. 227;
mutiny suppressed, K. i. 232.
At Wallajáhábád suspected
(1806), K. i. 242.
Of Madras officers (1809),
K. i. 252.
At Bárákpúr (1824), K. i.
266, 268, 269.
Of the 6th Madras Cavalry
(1843), K. i. 290.
At Jabbalpúr (1843), K. i.
292.
Of the Madras 47th at
Bombay (1844), K. i. 294.
Of 7th Bengal Cavalry at
Firozpúr (1844), K. i. 278.
Of the 34th Regiment at
Firozpúr (1844), K. i. 278

Mutiny—*cont.*
the Regiment disbanded at Mírut (1844), K. i. 298.
At Firozpúr, the 64th Regiment first refuse, and then agree to march into Sindh (1844), K. i. 282; a second time mutiny, and again resume the march to Sindh, K. i. 283; the 64th Regiment break into open mutiny, K. i. 285, 287; pardon of 64th Regiment, K. i. 289; disaffection spreads to 69th and 4th Regiments, K. i. 280; caused by reduction of pay, K. i. 278.
The great mutiny threatened in 1846, K. i. 309 *n*.
Of 22nd Regiment at Ráwalpindí (1849), K. i. 310; caused by reduction of pay, K. i. 310.
At Wazírábád, stopped by John Hearsey (1849), K. i. 313.
Of 66th Regiment at Govindgarh (1850), K. i. 315.
Mutiny, great outburst at Mírat (May 10), K. i. 595; is it mutiny or rebellion? K. i. 617; the English Government is responsible for, as the Court of Directors, M. iii. 388; its cause, K. i. xii.; resulted from an attempt to govern an Eastern nation on Western ideas, M. iii. 490; only a manifestation of political discontent, M. iii. 399; caused by general discontent and annexation of Oudh, M. iii. vii; bad faith the prime cause, M. iii. 472; supposed to have originated among Hindús, K. i. 564; a faqír the emissary of, at Mírat, K. i. 566; union of Hindús and Muhammadans apparent, K.

Mutiny—*cont.*
i. 565; said to have been planned for 10th of March, 1857, K. i. 529.
Native version of its beginning, K. i. 651; first symptoms of, K. i. 487; outbreak at Brahmapúr (Feb. 27, '57), K. i. 500, 503; its second manifestation is at Bárákpúr in March, K. i. 538; 3rd Cavalry at Mírat refuse to take ammunition (April), K. i. 567; 7th Regiment at Lakhnau refuse to use cartridges (May 3), K. i. 588.
The mutiny a surprise, K. iii. 3; Government anticipates its speedy suppression (May 25), M. i. 2; deemed by Mr. Secretary Beadon " a passing and groundless panic," M. i. 2.
Pause after first outbreak of, K. ii. 198; its distribution over Hindústán, M. iii. 487; its final suppression in Oudh (Jan. '59), M. iii. 297; its final suppression in Central India (Feb. '59), M. iii. 369; tries and proves the character of the English race, M. iii. 500.
Mutiny, chronological list of its spread:—
Mírat (May 10), K. ii. 56, M. i. 43.
Dehlí (May 11), K. ii. 77.
Firozpúr (May 13), K. ii. 439.
Muzaffarnagar (May 14), K. iii. 247, M. i. 301.
Alígarh (May 20), K. iii. 211, 213, M. i. 154.
Naushíra (May 21), K. ii. 476.
Hot-Mardán, in the Panjáb (May), K. ii. 483.
Ítáwá (May 23), M. i. 162.

THE HISTORIES OF THE INDIAN MUTINY. 137

Mutiny—*cont.*
Mainpúrí (May 23), K. iii. 224.
Rúrkí (May 25), K. iii. 258.
Ítá (May 27), K. iii. 283.
Nasírábád (May 28), K. iii. 321, M. i. 252.
Hodal, near Mathurá (May 30), K. iii. 241, M. i. 164.
Lakhnau (May 30), K. iii. 442, M. i. 372.
Mathurá (May 30), K. iii. 241, M. i. 164.
Barailí (May 31), K. iii. 270, M. i. 310.
Sháhjahánpúr (May 31), K. iii. 279, M. i. 318.
Murádábád (June 1), K. iii. 261-263.
Badáon (June 1), K. iii. 286, M. i. 323.
Murádábád (June 2), M. i. 330.
Ázamgarh (June 3), K. ii. 213, M. iii. 449.
Sítápúr (June 3), K. iii. 455, M. i. 379.
Nímach (June 4), K. iii. 315, 322, M. i. 33, 254.
Maláon (June 4), K. iii. 459, M. i. 383.
Banáras (June 4), K. ii. 222, M. i. 12.
Káhnpúr (June 4), K. ii. 307, M. i. 34.
Mohamdí, in Oudh (June 4), K. iii. 459.
Jánpúr (June 5), K. ii. 238, M. i. 33.
Jhánsí (June 5), K. iii. 364, M. i. 186.
Alláhábád (June 6), K. ii. 250, M. i. 12, iii. 438.
Faizábád (June 7), K. iii. 464, M. i. 399.
Jálandhar (June 7), K. ii. 499.
Jhánsí, K. iii. 315,,M. i. 33.

Mutiny—*cont.*
Daríábád (June 9), K. iii. 480, M. i. 409.
Fathpúr (June 9), K. ii. 364.
Ludhíáná (June 9), K. ii. 505.
Naogáon (June 9), M. i. 33, 193.
Saloní (June 9), K. iii. 472, M. i. 407.
Sikrorá (June 9), M. i. 392.
Gondá (June 10), M. i. 393.
Náogáon (June 10), K. iii. 372.
Lallatpúr (June 12), M. iii. 97.
Rohtak (June), K. ii. 546.
Bándá (June 14), M. i. 197.
Gwáliár (June 14), K. iii. 316, M. i. 173, 174, 262.
Fathgarh (June 18), M. i. 337.
Aurangábád (June 23), M. iii. 13.
Indor (July 1), K. iii. 330, M. i. 215.
Hátrás (July 1), M. i. 294.
Máú (July 1), K. iii. 335, M. i. 235.
Ságar (July 1), M. iii. 100.
Sánsí (July 2), M. i. 294.
Jhelam (July 7), K. ii. 624.
Syálkot (July 9), K. ii. 627.
Burhánpúr (July), M. iii. 59.
Dánápúr (July 25), K. iii. 93, M. i. 68.
Suggaulí (July 25), K. iii. 106, M. i. 72, 73.
Hazáríbágh (July 30), M. ii. 134.
Kolhápúr (July 31), K. iii. 408, M. iii. 31, 37.

Mutiny—*cont.*
Muzaffarpúr (July 31), K. iii. 150.
Chaibásá (Aug. 5), M. ii. 136.
Parúliá (Aug. 5), M. ii. 136.
Nasírábád (Aug. 10), M. ii. 553.
Nímach (Aug. 12), M. ii. 554.
Deogarh (Aug.), M. ii. 139.
Bhágalpúr (Aug. 14), M. ii. 133.
Anádra (Aug. 21), M. ii. 556.
Trinpúra (Aug. 22), M. ii. 558.
Jabalpúr (Sept. 18), M. iii. 104.
Nagod (Sept.), M. iii. 109.
Deogarh (Oct. 9), M. ii. 445.
Kotá (Oct. 15), M. ii. 569.
Chatgáon (Nov. 18), M. ii. 419.
Madáríganj (Dec. 4), M. ii. 427.
Jalpaigorí (Dec. 5), M. ii. 427.
Mutineers, first battle with (May 30), K. ii. 184; Lord Canning's efforts to discriminate in punishment of, K. iii. 53; those at Syálkot, offer commands in rebel army to two British officers, K. ii. 630; Gen. Neill's punishment of those at Káhnpúr, K. ii. 399; escape of the mutineers from Júlandhar (June 7), K. ii. 501; mutineers escape from Ludhíáná, K. ii. 508; and from Phillaur (June 8), K. ii. 502.
Mutinous Sepoys blown from guns in 1764, K. i. 207; first attempt to organise their rebellion, K. ii. 315.

Muter, Capt., withdraws fourth column from assault of Dehlí, K. iii. 695; his account of attack of that column at assault of Dehlí, K. iii. 698.
Mutchee-Bhawun, *see* Machhí Bháwan.
Muttrá, *see* Mathurá.
Mynpooree, *see* Mainpúrí.
Mysore (Maisúr) Princes, encourage revolt at Vellore, K. i. 229.

N.

Nabhá, Rájá of, his loyalty and services, K. ii. 162, M. iii. 308.
Naghína, plundered by Rúrkí mutineers (May), M. iii. 402; seizure and sack of (Aug. 23), M. iii. 412; Brig. Jones defeats the rebels at (April 21, '58), M. ii. 517; splendid Cavalry charge at, M. ii. 518; Lieut. Gosling killed at, M. ii. 519.
Nagod, part of Ságar territory, M. iii. 88; garrison of, M. iii. 109; Major Hampton commands at, M. iii. 109; mutiny at (Sept.), M. iii. 109; mutineers from, escort their officers to Mirzapúr, M. iii. 110.
Nágpúr, description of town, M. iii. 113; good cotton-growing district, K. i. 86 n.; garrison of, M. iii. 113; subsidiary force, commanded by Brig. H. Prior, M. iii. 114; annexation of, K. i. 83; its justice discussed, K. i. 87; Rájá of, dies (1853), K. i. 75; sale of Rájá's effects, K. i. 83, 84 n.; Bánká Báí threatens to burn the palace (1854), K. i. 84.

THE HISTORIES OF THE INDIAN MUTINY. 139

Nágpúr—*cont.*
  Mr. Plowden, Commissioner of, M. iii. 113; he strengthens Sítábaldí, as a place of refuge, M. iii. 114; Col. Cumberlege disarms 4th Light Cavalry at (June 17), M. iii. 114; [Mr. Plowden prevents mutiny at, M. iii. 115.
  Tántiá Topí invades (Oct. '58), M. iii. 342; grave importance of Tántiá Topí's invasion of, M. iii. 343; the Queen's proclamation read with ceremony at (Nov. 1, '58), M. iii. 396.
  See also Chutiá Nágpúr.
Najafgarh Canal at Dehlí, K. ii. 515 and *n.*; battle of (Aug. 25), K. ii. 652–655; Gen. Nicholson's victory at secures safety of Dehlí siege train, M. ii. 1.
Najíbábád, destroyed by Mr. Shakespear (April '58), M. iii. 418.
Najíbábád, Nawáb of, his negotiations with the rebels (May), M. iii. 402; attempts to plunder Bíjnúr (May 21), M. iii. 404; makes second attempt on Bíjnúr (May 23), M. iii. 405; returns a third time to Bíjnúr (June), M. iii. 406; rendered passive by Mr. Shakespear, M. iii. 407; receives charge of Bíjnúr for ten days (June 7), M. iii. 408; proclaims himself ruler of Bíjnúr, under King of Dehlí (June 11), M. iii. 409; he begins to persecute the Hindús (July), M. iii. 410; chased from Bíjnúr by chaudrís (Aug. 6), M. iii. 411; again seizes Bíjnúr (Aug. 23), M. iii. 412; gains supremacy at Bíjnúr (Sept.), M.

Najíbábád—*cont.*
  iii. 413; transported for life, M. iii. 418 *n.*
Náná Náráyan Ráo tenders his allegiance to the British (July 19), K. ii. 393.
Náná Sáhib, adopted heir of Bájí Ráo, K. i. 101; the undoubted heir of the last Peshwá, M. iii. 482; his friends in the Maráthá country, M. iii. 28; his claimed inheritance south of the Táptí, M. iii. 346.
  His claim to the *gaddí* of ex-Peshwá, not recognised by the Company, K. i. 101; but supported by Commissioner at Bithúr, K. i. 102; and opposed by Mr. Thomason and Lord Dalhousie, K. i. 103; he appeals to the Court of Directors, K. i. 103; his memorial, K. i. 104–108; his memorial rejected by the Court of Directors (1853), K. i. 109; he sends Azim-ullah Khán as his agent to England, K. i. 109.
  He visits Kálpí, Dehlí, and Lakhnau, early in 1857, K. i. 574, 576; his schemes assisted by annexation of Oudh, K. i. 579 *n.*; his visit to Lakhnau, K. i. 644.
  Gen. Wheeler solicits aid from (May), K. ii. 297; receives charge of the Káhnpúr Treasury from Gen. Wheeler, K. ii. 299; he induces mutineers to return to Káhnpúr (June 5), K. ii. 310; his reasons for counselling return of mutineers, K. ii. 311; joins in mutiny, M. i. 34; begins regular organisation of mutineers, K. ii. 315; informs Gen. Wheeler that he is about to attack the entrenchment

Nâná Sáhíb—cont.
at Káhnpúr, K. ii. 313; attacks the entrenchment on centenary of Plassey, and is defeated, K. ii. 330, 331.
Signs treaty of capitulation of Káhnpúr, K. ii. 335; stops the slaughter of women and children at Káhnpúr, K. ii. 342; orders execution of men who escaped the Massacre at Káhnpúr, K. ii. 348; proclaims the defeat of the English, K. ii. 352; compels English ladies to grind corn, K. ii. 354.
His letter to Hulás Singh (June 24), K. ii. 672; his letter to Raghunáth Singh (June 27), K. ii. 672; another letter to Hulás Singh (July 1), K. ii. 673; goes to Bithúr to be proclaimed, K. ii. 349; proclaimed Peshwá (July 1), K. ii. 349; his letter to Rámbakkas, Taluqdár (July 3), K. ii. 673; third letter to Hulás Singh (July 5), K. ii. 674.
Returns to Káhnpúr (July 6), K. ii. 351; his proclamation of that date, K. ii. 670; his address to the officers of his army (July 7), K. ii. 674; his letter to Kalkaprasháḍ (July 9), K. ii. 675; his letter to the Thánádár of Sirsál (July 13), K. ii. 675; his letter to the mutineers at Lakhnau (July 16), K. ii. 676.
Murders fugitives from Fathgarh, M. i. 336, 346; orders the massacre of the women and children at Káhnpúr (July 15), K. ii. 372; advances to meet Gen. Havelock (July 16), K. ii. 374; makes energetic stand at Káhnpúr, K. ii. 379; his

Náná Sáhib—cont.
flight to Bithúr (July 16), K. ii. 389; pretends self-immolation, but escapes from Bithúr, K. ii. 390; before flight from Bithúr, murders the last woman in his hands, K. ii. 390 n.
Commands the left of Tántiá Topí's position at Káhnpúr (Dec. 5), M. ii. 266; his palace and temple destroyed at Bithúr (Dec. 11), M. ii. 281; he exercises sovereignty west of the Jamná (Jan. '58), M. ii. 448; destroys all official buildings in Sháhjahánpúr (April '58), M. ii. 522 n.; sends troops to the Maulaví at Sháhjahánpúr (May 13, '58), M. ii. 536.
Proclaimed Peshwá at Gwáliár (June 1, '58), M. iii. 209; creates Rám Ráo Govind his minister, M. iii. 210.
Occupies north-east corner of Oudh (Oct. '58), M. iii. 286; he is driven into Nipál (Dec. '58), M. iii. 294.
See also Dhundu Pant.
Nandídurg, threatened mutiny suppressed (1806), K. i. 239.
Nanní Nawáb, assists Náná Sáhib at Káhnpúr, K. ii. 350; his good artillery practice, K. ii. 350.
Nánpárá, Oudh rebels driven from (Dec. '58), M. iii. 294.
Nánpárá, Rájá of, refuses to protect English fugitives, M. i. 394.
Naogáon, Major Kirke commands at, M. i. 191; extravagant demonstrations of loyalty there (June 5), K. iii. 371; mutiny at (June 10), K. iii. 372, M. i. 33, 193; flight of Europeans with 87 faithful

Naogáon—*cont.*
Sepoys, K. iii. 372, M. i. 193; the fugitives by a series of fortunate mistakes reach Chatarpúr in safety, M. i. 194; and are assisted by the Rání, K. iii. 373; Sepoys escort fugitives in guise of prisoners, K. iii. 376; the fugitives reach Kalrai, M. i. 195; they are deserted by Sepoys, K. iii. 377, M. i. 195; and are attacked by *dakáits*, K. iii. 374, M. i. 195; the fugitives are nobly led by Capt. Scot, after death of Major Kirke, K. iii. 375; fugitives reach Nágod, and are saved, K. iii. 377.

A few of the fugitives reach Bándá, M. i. 196; the Nawáb of Bándá acts generously towards them, M. i. 196.

A remnant of the fugitives reach Mahobá, M. i. 196.

Naogáng and Naogong, *see* Naogáon.

Napier, Sir Charles, in favour of seniority system, K. i. 336; sees the unsound state of the Sepoy Army (1849), K. i. 312; anticipates a general rising of Sepoys in the Panjáb, K. i. 314; staggers mutiny by employing the Gorkhas (1850), K. i. 315; grants increased allowances to Sepoys in the Panjáb, K. i. 316; conflict between him and Lord Dalhousie, K. i. 316–323; resigns command of the Indian Army (1850), K. i. 318.

Napier, Brig. Robert, captures Phillips' Garden battery at Lakhnau (Oct. 2), M. ii. 157.

Recommends attack of Lakhnau on east side (March '58), M. ii. 366; his plan of

Napier, Brig.—*cont.*
attack on Lakhnau, M. iii. 507; occupies Banks's House (March 10, '58), M. ii. 382.

Joins Sir Hugh Rose at Bahádurpúr (June 16, '58), M. iii. 215; succeeds Sir Hugh Rose in command of Central India Forces (June 20, '58), M. iii. 318; distributes his force in Gwáliár, Jhánsí, Sipú, and Gúná, M. iii. 318; he is ordered to pursue rebels from Gwáliár (June 18, '58), M. iii. 227; catches retreating rebels at Jaurá-Alípúr (June 22, '58), M. iii. 229; defeats rebels and captures entire matériel, M. iii. 230; moves from Gwáliár to assist Brig. Smith at Paurí (Aug. 11, '58), M. iii. 334; attacks and captures Paurí (Aug. 23, '58), M. iii. 335; endeavours to intercept Firoz Sháh (Dec. '58), M. iii. 360; he is stopped at Antrí, which allows Firoz Sháh to escape, M. iii. 361; gets to Ránod (Dec. 17, '58), M. iii. 362; and completely defeats Firoz Sháh there, M. iii. 363.

Conceives the idea of gaining over Mán Singh (Feb. '59), M. iii. 370; accelerates the decision of Mán Singh (March 14, '59), M. iii. 373; opens communication with him through Capt. Meade (March 8, '59), M. iii. 372; effects surrender of Mán Singh (April 2, '59), M. iii. 374.

Napier, Sir William, his eulogy of the British soldier, M. i. 458.

Náráyan Ráo, relative of Náná Sáhib, a staunch friend of English, M. i. 507; the Eng-

Náráyan Rao—*cont.*
lish recover his wife and daughters, M. i. 508.
Náráyan Ráo, ruler of Kirwí (May '58), M. iii. 199.
Náráyan Singh, opens negotiation for Mán Singh's surrender (March 8, '59), M. iii. 372.
Náráin Ráo, *see* Náráyan Ráo.
Narbadá, the line of communication by, of grave importance to Central India, M. i. 207; weak points in the line, M. i. 207; the line jeopardised by mutiny at Indor, M. i. 242; but saved by Col. Durand, M. i. 243.
Tántiá Topí operates in the vicinity of (Oct.-Nov. '58), M. iii. 345-347; Tántiá Topí crosses northward to march on Barodá (Nov. 26, '58), M. iii. 351.
Nargúnd, Native state of Southern Marátha country, M. iii. 20; the chief of, refused right of adoption, M. iii. 23, 240; the chief becomes a thoroughly discontented chief, M. iii. 29; his doubtful loyalty (May '58), M. iii. 238; he begins to send his guns to Dhárwár, M. iii. 238; he resents the appointment of Mr. Manson, M. iii. 238; and is urged to resist the English, M. iii. 239; he fears personal arrest, M. iii. 239; he attacks and murders Mr. C. Manson, M. iii. 243; and declares war against the British Government (May 27, '58), M. iii. 240; he advances against Col. Malcolm, but is driven back (June 1), M. iii. 244; and escapes in disguise from his fort (June 2, '58), M. iii. 245; he is

Nargúnd—*cont.*
tracked and captured by Mr. F. Souter (June 3, '58), M. iii. 245; and tried and executed at Belgáon (June 12, '58), M. iii. 245 *n.*
Nárnúl, l'rinpúra mutineers defeated at (Oct. 16), M. ii. 568; splendid Cavalry charge and countercharge at (Nov. 16), M. ii. 114; defeat of mutineers at (Nov. 16), M. ii. 116, 118.
Nárpat Singh, his character, M. ii. 504; his intentions, M. ii. 505; he is attacked by Gen. Walpole (April 15, '58), M. ii. 506; beats off Gen. Walpole from Rúiyá, M. ii. 507; but evacuates the fort, M. ii. 508.
Narpat Singh, rebel leader in Oudh, M. iii. 271; slain at the capture of Akalpúra by Mr. Dunlop (July), M. iii. 435.
Narsangpúr *and* Narsingpúr, *see* Narsinghpúr.
Narsinghpúr, part of Ságar territory, M. iii. 88; garrison of, M. iii. 108; Capt. Woolley commands at, M. iii. 91, 108; Capt. Ternan, Deputy Commissioner of, M. iii. 90; Kotwál of, distributes mysterious *chapátís* (Jan.), M. iii. 91.
Nárút, rebels evacuate fort of, M. iii. 150.
Narwár, Mán Singh, Rájá of, seizes fort of Paurí (Aug. 2, '58), M. iii. 332.
Nasírábád, garrisoned entirely by Sepoys, M. i. 251; strength of garrison of, M. i. 252; mutiny at (May 28), K. iii. 321, M. i. 252; British officers forced to abandon, M. i. 253; treacherous conduct of Bombay troops at (May 28), K.

Nasírábád—*cont.*
iii. 321, M. i. 253; Europeans escape to Biáwar (May 28), K. iii. 322.
12th N.I. fail to obey orders (Aug. 10), M. ii. 553; attempt to cause mutiny at, M. ii. 553; discipline restored at (Aug. 10), M. ii. 554.
Gen. Roberts occupies (June '58), M. iii. 319.
Nasír-ud-Daula, the Nizám, M. iii. 118.
Nasír-ud-Dín, gallant trooper who stood by Lieut. Conolly at Trinpúra, M. ii. 594.
Nasratpúr, Gen. Franks defeats the rebels at (Jan. 23, '58), M. ii. 328.
Nathupúr, Lieut. Middleton's gallantry at, M. iii. 511.
Native Army, its extent, K. i. 201; re-organization of (1824), K. i. 264; mutiny of, in Madras (1806), K. i. 217–243; its fidelity, K. i. 202; troops commanded by boy-officers, K. i. 214 *n.*; attachment between men and officers weakened, K. i. 260.
Native aristocracy, British policy antagonistic to, K. i. 57, 154, 158; lose their position in the army (1784), K. i. 211; no profitable employment for, under British rule, K. i. 180; discourteously treated, K. i. 167; sold up for small debts, K. i. 178.
Native attendants, their faithfulness, K. ii. 604; instance of faithfulness, M. i. 279 *n.*; essential nature of their services, K. ii. 603; dread resentment of the English, K. ii. 631 *n.*
Native newspaper comments on Persian proclamation at Dehlí (March), K. ii. 41.

Native officials, instance of faithfulness, K. iii. 262 *n.*; take service under rebel leaders, K. iii. 304; those of Farrukhábád take service under the upstart Nawáb, K. iii. 305 *n.*
Native officers lose rank in Army, K. i. 211; further loss of rank in Army, K. i. 215.
Native opinion, against the annexation of Sitárá, K. i. 80 *n.*; on conflicts among English authorities, K. i. 320; on paucity of British troops in India, K. i. 344; on general service enlistment, K. i. 469; of enlistment of Sikhs, K. i. 471; excited by missionary manifesto, K. i. 472.
Native Press, hostility of, K. iii. 13; highly injurious effect of, K. iii. 13; the tone of, changes after mutiny at Mírat, M. i. 18.
Native rumours of intended pollution of caste, K. ii. 118.
Native version of beginning of the Mutiny, K. i. 651.
Natives, warn the English of coming danger (1856), K. i. 484; more alarmed than the Christians, K. iii. 56; generally worshippers of success, K. ii. 151.
Naushíra, mutiny at (May 21), K. ii. 476.
Naval Brigade, suggested by Gen. Ashburnham, K. iii. 186, M. i. 141; its constitution, M. i. 142; starts for Alláhábád (Aug. 18), M. i. 142; starts from Lakhnau for Calcutta (April 1, '58), M. ii. 545.
Nawábganj, on Faizábád road, strong body of rebels at, M. iii. 267; Gen. Hope Grant's

Nawábgang—*cont.*
attack on rebels at (June 13, '58), M. iii. 268; gallantry of zamíndárs at, M. iii. 268; defeat of the rebels at (June 13, '58), M. iii. 269; important consequences of victory at, M. iii. 269.

Nawáb Nazím, his troops disarmed at Barhámpúr (Aug. 2), M. ii. 139.

Nayler, Telegraph boy, his coolness at action of Alígarh (Aug. 24), K. iii. 413.

Naylor, Col., pursues Tántiá Topí from the Banás (Aug. 14, '58), M. iii. 323.

Nazarána to Emperor of Dehlí, abolished by Lord Ellenborough, K. ii. 12.

Nazím Mír Muhammad Husain Khán, protects Col. Lennox and family, M. i. 403.

Neave, Lieut., killed in attack on Morár (June 16, '58), M. iii. 217.

Need, Capt., pursues Firoz Sháh from Ránod (Dec. 17, '58), M. iii. 363.

Neglected heroism, K. ii. 347.

Neill, Col. James George, arrives at Calcutta with Madras Fusiliers, K. ii. 128; his character, K. ii. 129, M. i. 497, 538.

Arrests railway train on landing at Calcutta, K. ii. 132; arrives at Banáras (June 4), K. ii. 216; suppresses mutiny at Banáras, M. i. 12; receives command of Banáras (June 4), K. ii. 225.

One of the four who preserved Mr. Beadon's line of six hundred miles, M. i. 143.

Appointed to command of Alláhábád, K. ii. 263; arrives at Alláhábád (June 11), M. iii. 439; his physical pros-

Neill, Col.—*cont.*
tration on reaching Alláhábád, K. ii. 263; begins offensive operations at Alláhábád (June 12), K. ii. 264; urged to caution in advancing from Alláhábád, K. ii. 285 *n.*; attacks villages near Fort of Alláhábád (June 17), K. ii. 266; recovers city of Alláhábád (June 18), K. ii. 267; his excutions at Alláhábád not exceptionally severe, K. ii. 269 *n.*; prepares to advance from Alláhábád, K. ii. 271; stopped at Alláhábád for want of transport, &c., K. ii. 272; outbreak of cholera in his force (June), K. ii. 273; leaves admirable instructions to his successor on leaving Alláhábád, K. ii. 394.

Appointed Brigadier-General (July 15), K. ii. 396.

Advances towards Káhnpúr (June 30), K. ii. 274; receives news of fall of Káhnpúr (July 3), K. ii. 284; differs with Col. Havelock as to prudent course after fall of Káhnpúr, K. ii. 286; joins Gen. Havelock at Káhnpúr (July 20), K. ii. 397, M. i. 489; on the state of Káhnpúr (July 22), K. ii. 405 *n.*; resolves on punishing fearfully the Káhnpúr massacres, K. ii. 398 and *n.*; his order for punishing Káhnpúr mutineers (July 25), K. ii. 399; comment on his punishment of Káhnpúr mutineers, K. ii. 400.

Nobly prepares the column for Havelock to command, K. ii. 276; agrees to hold Káhnpúr with a few sick and wounded men, M. i. 490; reorganises police and esta-

Neill, Gen.—*cont.*
blishes order in Káhnpúr (July 25), M. i. 498; sends river party against Bithúr (July 31), M. i. 499; is ready to hold Káhnpúr against any odds, M. i. 499; sends party to Jájaman, which destroys and captures Náná Sáhib's boats (July 31), M. i. 499.
His fury at retrograde movement of Gen. Havelock, M. i. 500; his letter to Gen. Havelock (July 31), M. i. 501 n.; Gen. Havelock's reply to his letter, M. i. 502 n.
Sends second river party against Bithúr (Aug. 5), M. i. 507; sends third river party against Bithúr, M. i. 508; parades his troops with excellent effect, M. i. 509; advises Gen. Havelock to attack Bithúr (Aug. 16), M. i. 510.
Appointed to command right wing of Lakhnau relieving force, M. i. 518; killed at Lakhnau (Sept. 25), K. iii. 543, M. i. 538.
Neville, Capt., killed in attack on rebels near the Bína (Jan. 30, '58), M. iii. 143.
Newberry, Capt., killed in attack on Shorápúr (Feb. 8, '58), M. iii. 128.
Newbery, Capt., killed at Nasírábád (May 28), M. i. 253.
News, rapidity of transmission of, by natives, K. i. 491.
Ni'amat-ulláh Khán, Nawáb, his treason at Murádábád, K. iii. 253 n.
Nicholson, Gen. John, Assistant Commissioner at Peshawar, K. ii. 452; his early services, K. ii. 450–452; his personal appearance, K. ii. 649 n.; his character, K. ii. 452, iii. 658–660 M. ii. 83; his disclaimer

Nicholson, Gen.—*cont.*
of over-much praise, K. ii. 488 n.; his promptitude of action causes offence to superiors, K. ii. 646; strongly opposes Sir J. Lawrence's suggestion to cede Pesháwar, K. ii. 616; ruffles Sir J. Lawrence, K. ii. 647; his impetuosity, K. iii. 548; his apology for brusqueness, K. ii. 648 n.; his views on the punishment of murderous mutineers, K. ii. 401; counsels moderation in punishment, K. ii. 488.
He and Herbert Edwardes prudently exalt Gen. Reed into a useless position, K. ii. 458–460; attacks and destroys mutinous regiment at Mardán (May 25), K. ii. 485, 486; counsels further disarmament of Sepoys, K. ii. 496; returns to Pesháwar (June 10), K. ii. 498.
Selected to command Panjáb Movable Column, with rank of Brigadier-General, K. ii. 512; his popularity with the Movable Column, K. ii 633; disarms 33rd and 35th Regiments at Phillaur (June 25), K. ii. 634; disarms 59th Regiment (July 9), K. ii. 635; disarms wing of 9th Cavalry at Amritsar, K. ii. 637; defeats the Syálkot mutineers at Trimmu Ghát (July 12), K. ii. 640.
Ordered to take his Movable Column to Dehlí (July 22), K. ii. 644; his victory at Najafgarh, M. ii. 1; contemplates wresting the command from Gen. Wilson, K. iii. 550; chosen to lead the assault on Dehlí, K. iii. 580, M. ii. 27; mortally wounded in assault of Dehlí, K. iii. 599;

10

Nicholson, Gen.—*cont.*
his last days, K. iii. 657; his death (Sept. 23), K. iii. 656, M. ii. 83.

Nicholson, Major, commands Outram's first battery on the Gúmtí (March 9, '58), M. ii. 375.

Nímach, mutiny at (June 4), K. iii. 315, M. i. 33; description of, K. iii. 320; Native troops at, K. iii. 321, M. i. 253; garrisoned entirely by Sepoys, M. i. 251; mutiny at (June 3), K. iii. 322, M. i. 254; British officers escape to Udaipúr, M. i. 254; mutiny stopped by Col. Jackson (Aug. 12), M. ii. 554.

Mutineers resolve to march upon A'grá, K. iii. 322; their composition when before A'grá, K. iii. 383.

Party of fugitives from, rescued by Capt. Showers, K. iii. 356.

Rebels from, hasten to support Mandíswar (Nov. 22), M. iii. 79; they meet. Col. Durand at Goráriá, and fight desperately (Nov. 24), M. iii. 80.

Nipál, description of frontier, M. iii. 295; Bálá Ráo and his following driven into (Dec. '58), M. iii. 294; the Begam of Oudh and Náná Sáhib driven into (Dec. '58), M. iii. 294; Jang Bahádur permits English to pursue rebels in, M. iii. 295.

Nipálese troops, their marching, baggage and loot, M. ii. 497; they enter Gorakhpúr (July), M. ii. 316; they occupy A'zamgarh (Aug. 13), M. ii. 317; and Jánpúr (Aug. 15), M. ii. 317; they beat the rebels at Kudúa (Oct. 19), M. ii.

Nipalese troops—*cont.*
319; and again at Chánda (Oct. 30), M. ii. 319; they capture Gorakhpúr (Jan. 5, '58), M. ii. 323; and the fort of Ambarpúr (Feb. 25, '58), M. ii. 324; they arrive at Lakhnau (March 11, '58), M. ii. 388.

Nipání, description of fort, M. iii. 28; the Desáís of, discontented sufferers under Inám Commission, M. iii. 28.

Niraiyan Singh, *see* Náráyan Singh.

Niraulí, Rájá of Bánpúr entrenches himself at, M. iii. 106; and repulses Col. Dalyell (Sept. 15), M. iii. 107.

Nisbán Singh, joins Kunwar Singh, on the Son, M. ii. 444.

Nixon, Major, agent at Bharatpúr, M. i. 257.

Nizám, the, Nasír-ud-Daula (up to May), M. iii. 118; Afzul-ud-Daula (May 18), M. iii. 118; cordially supports the English, M. iii. 124; Sálar Jang, chief minister of, M. iii. 118; Major C. Davidson, Resident with, M. iii. 119; authorises formation of Haidarábád column, for service in Central India (Aug.), M. iii. 124; description of his dominions, M. iii. 117.

Nizám Alí Khán, threatens Pílíbhít (Aug. '58), M. iii. 274.

Nonádí, Major H. Havelock cuts off rear-guard of rebels at (Oct. 20, '58), M. ii. 488.

Norman, Capt., Assistant Adjutant-General of the Army, K. iii. 672; justly estimates the political danger of delay in advancing on Dehlí, K. ii. 167.

Northern India, defenceless condition of, K. ii. 111; general condition of, in July, K. ii. 411.

North-West Provinces, extent and description, M. i. 144, 145, K. iii. 193; administrative divisions of, K. iii. 195, M. i. 146; nature of population, K. iii. 194; settlement of district, K. i. 173; Mr. Thomason emancipates the cultivators from serfdom, M. i. 145; British rule benefits cultivators, M. i. 145.

Mr. John Colvin, Lieut.-Governor of, K. iii. 195; defenceless condition of, at outbreak of Mutiny, K. ii. 197; three central points of attack in, M. i. 178; efforts to strengthen the central line of communication in, M. i. 29; communication with Calcutta interrupted (June), K. iii. 5.

Character of the outbreak in, K. iii. 305; extent of disorganization in (June), K. ii. 126, iii. 2; utter disorganisation of, K. iii. 245; state of, in July, K. iii. 89; for the moment, lost, K. ii. 413.

Nowshera, *see* Naushíra.
Nundydroog, *see* Nandídurg.
Nunny Newab, *see* Nanní Nawáb.
Núrganj, Brig. Jones defeats the rebels at, M. ii. 529.
Núriá, near Pílíbhít, Rohilkhand rebels advance on (Aug. '58), M. iii. 275; Lieut. Craigie sent to protect (Aug. 28, '58), M. iii. 275; Capt. S. Browne sent to reinforce Lieut. Craigie (Aug. 29, '58), M. iii. 276; Lieut. Craigie repulses Rohilkhand rebels at (Aug. 29, '58), M. iii. 276.

O.

Obduracy of British character, K. ii. 606.

O'Brien, Col., conducts his boat in safety from Faizábád to Dánápúr, K. iii. 468.
O'Brien, Dr., escapes from Lallatpúr mutiny, M. iii. 98.
Observatory, the ancient, *see* Dehlí.
Obstructive character of Staff Departments of the Army (May), K. ii. 146.
Officers of Army, reduced by half-batta order (1830), K. i. 271; interest in their men (1809-22), K. i. 257; receive power of life and death in all places, K. iii. 661.
Official correspondence, the bar to rapidity of action, K. i. 510.
Olpherts, Major William, suggests retreat from Banáras (May), K. ii. 202; exonerated from blame for firing into Sikhs at Banáras (June 4), K. ii. 228; he defeats the Maulaví (Jan. 14, '58), M. ii. 351; beats off rebel attack (Feb. 21, '58), M. ii. 355; beats off rebel attack at A'lambágh (March 16, '58), M. ii. 402.
Ommaney, Mr., Judicial Commissioner of Oudh (1856), K. i. 399; his death at Lakhnau, K. iii. 523.
Ommaney's post, a post at Lakhnau Residency, M. i. 444.
Onáo, *see* Unáo.
Oodeypore, *see* Udaipúr.
Opium eating, drinking, and smoking, common in Oudh, K. iii. 426.
Orai, Capt. Alexander commands at (May), M. iii. 466; Lieut. Tomkinson on duty at, M. iii. 466; Lieut. Tomkinson starts from with treasure (June 4), M. iii. 466; Capt. and Mrs. Alexander sent by Sepoys to A'grá (June 8), M. iii. 467.

Oráon, a tribe in Chutiá Nágpúr, M. ii. 134.
Orr, Capt. Adolphus, of the Oudh Military Police, M. i. 383 n.
Orr, Capt. Alexander, Assistant Commissioner in Oudh, M. i. 383 n.
Orr, Capt. Patrick, Assistant Commissioner in Oudh, M. i. 383 n.; induces Sítápúr escort to swear to protect fugitives from Mohamdí, M. i. 386; describes the murder of Mohamdí fugitives, M. i. 387 n.; escapes the massacre of Mohamdí fugitives (June 4), M. i. 388 n.; rejoins his wife at Kachiání, in Maithaulí ráj, K. iii. 482, M. i. 388; he and his wife forced to live in the jungle, K. iii. 483, M. i. 388; remains for five months at Maithaulí, K. iii. 484; he and the other English ordered to leave Maithaulí (Oct. 25), K. iii. 485; he is brought to Lakhnau, with every indignity, K. iii. 487; he and other officers of Sítápúr party, shot at Lakhnau (Nov. 16), K. iii. 489.
Orr, Major, his gallantry in the Málwá campaign, M. iii. 87; pursues Mahídpúr plunderers (Nov.), M. iii. 74; catches up to rebels at Ráwal, M. iii. 75; defeats rebels at Ráwal, with severe loss (Nov.), M. iii. 76; sent to watch the Betwá (April 23, '58), M. iii. 173; attacks and defeats Rájás of Bánpúr and Sháhgarh (April 30, '58), M. iii. 174; marches on Kúnch (May '58), M. iii. 174; moves on Paniar (June '58), M. iii. 214.
Orr, Mrs., her rescue at Lakh-

Orr, Mrs.—cont.
nau (March 17, '58), M. ii. 403 n.
Osborne, Lieut. Willoughby, political agent at Rewá, M. iii. 110; his character, M. iii. 110; wins the support of the Rájá of Rewá (June), M. iii. 111; posts the troops of Rájá of Rewá so as to intercept rebels, M. iii. 111; storms and captures Maihír (Dec. 29), M. iii. 112; captures Jakhání (Dec. 31), M. iii. 112; captures Bíjerájugarh (Jan. '58), M. iii. 112; defeats rebels at Kanchanpúr and Zorah, M. iii. 112; restrains rebellion in Bandelkhand, M. iii. 112.
Oude, see Oudh.
Oudh, the home of the Sepoys, K. ii. 407; early history of, K. i. 113; profligacy of the Court, K. i. 114; subsidy raised (1801), K. i. 116; effects of the subsidy, K. i. 114; annexation of, threatened (1831), K. i. 122; methods of ameliorating condition of, suggested (1832), K. i. 122; Court of Directors' despatch concerning (1834), Lord Bentinck's proposal for amelioration of, K. i. 123; his proposal adopted by Court of Directors, K. i. 124; treaty of 1837, K. i. 126; the treaty disallowed by Home Government, K. i. 127; Lord Hardinge threatens annexation of (1847), K. i. 131; generally anticipated in 1849 that its abominations could no longer be endured, K. i. 133; treaty of 1837, considered valid by Col. Sleeman (1853), K. i. 129 n.
James Outram appointed Resident (1854), K. i. 139;

Oudh—*cont.*
his report on the district, K. i. 141; English officials warned of agitation, but disregard it (1855), M. iii. 481; tranquil condition of, in 1856, K. i. 395; annexation of, K. i. 148; annexation approved by Lord Canning, K. i. 381; but carried out in a headstrong manner, M. iii. 484; bad effects of annexation, M. i. 348; advantages to Sepoys from, before annexation, M. iii. 478; its bad effects on the Sepoys and their privileges, K. i. 346, M. i. 349, iii. 479, 481.

Mr. Coverley Jackson becomes Chief Commissioner, K. i. 398; contention between chief officials in (1856), K. i. 400; disbandment of old army of (1856), K. iii. 423; arrears paid by British Government to old army of, K. iii. 424; alienation of people from the British, M. i. 349; imposition of new taxes by the English, K. iii. 425; imposition of heavy tax on opium, K. iii. 426; opium largely indulged in, by the people, K. iii. 426; suddenness of English changes, the great defect, K. iii. 427; annexation induces natives to assist schemes of Dhundu Pant, K. i. 579 *n.*; held by few British troops after annexation, K. i. 345.

Revenue settlement in, K. i. 157; rough settlement of talúqdárs' claims in, K. i. 160, iii. 421; heavy losses of Faizábád talúqdárs, M. i. 351; the provincial talúqdárs feel no loyalty for the King, M. iii. 264; the talúqdárs

Oudh—*cont.*
hate the British rule, M. iii. 264; they want a common leader, M. iii. 265. Stories of British cruelty in (1856), K. i. 405; beggary of Court parasites after annexation, K. iii. 419; grievances of the ex-King of, K. i. 404; the Oudh Mission of 1856, K. i. 403; the capital devoted to the King, M. iii. 263.

Annexation of Oudh major cause of the Mutiny, K. ii. 496 *n.*, M. i. 352, iii. 388.

Disastrous personal wrangles among English officials in, K. iii. 420; Mr. C. Jackson fails to aid Lord Canning in rebutting charges of British cruelty in, K. i. 406; administration of, in 1856, K. iii. 418.

Mr. C. Wingfield's views on administration of, M. i. 390; condition of, in 1857, K. iii. 417; Sir H. Lawrence, Chief Commissioner in (March 20), M. i. 349; troops occupying district, K. iii. 430, M. i. 357; disposition of troops in Lakhnau, M. i. 360.

Sinister rumours about destruction of caste long in circulation, M. i. 353; Sir H. Lawrence redresses wrongs of Court parasites, K. iii. 421; his Darbár in Lakhnau (May 12), K. iii. 431; he reasons with Sepoy officers, M. i. 358; his proposition to raise pay of Sepoys in, K. iii. 441; disarmament of, a delusion, K. iii. 423.

General rising in (June), K. iii. 451; the general rising gives evidence of pre-concerted design, K. iii. 452; every station except Lakhnau lost to the British (June 12),

Oudh—cont.
M. i. 410; complete collapse of English authority in, K. iii. 481; state of, in July, K. ii. 407; state of, described by Mr. M. Gubbins, K. ii. 408–410; number and distribution of rebel forces in (July '58), M. iii. 270; Gen. Havelock enters (July 25), K. ii. 414.
Lord Canning's impolitic proclamation to (March 20, '58), M. ii. 409; nature of the proclamation, M. iii. 247, 248; Lord Canning excludes from mercy those who had murdered English men and women, M. iii. 249; the proclamation condemned by Gen. Outram, M. iii. 250; his reasons for objecting to it, M. iii. 251; Gen. Outram gets qualifying clause added to Lord Canning's impolitic proclamation, M. ii. 410, iii. 252; Dr. Russell's remark on Lord Canning's proclamation, M. ii. 410; Lord Canning takes credit for the leniency of his proclamation, M. iii. 250; apparent severity, but real leniency, of the proclamation, M. iii. 253.
Mr. Robert Montgomery succeeds Gen. Outram as Commissioner of, M. iii. 262; Brig. Berkeley clears forts in (July '58), M. iii. 281; river steamers watch the Ganges frontier of (July to Sept. '58), M. iii. 285; rebels in, lead a wandering life, M. iii. 273; strange position of English in (Oct. '58), M. iii. 285; becomes British by right of conquest (April '59), M. iii. 297.
See also Lakhnau.

Oudh Auxiliary Force raised, K. i. 128.
Oudh, Begam of, evacuates Bithaulí on approach of Sir Hope Grant (April '58), M. ii. 497; joins the Maulaví at Sháhjahánpúr (May 11, '58), M. ii. 536; her head-quarters at Chauká Ghát, near Faizábád, M. iii. 270; driven into Nipál (Dec. '58), M. iii. 294.
Oudh, King of, difference in feeling for him in his capital and the provinces, M. iii. 263; starts on his journey to England (1856), K. i. 401; reaches Calcutta, K. i. 402; at Calcutta, loses desire to go to England, K. i. 402; he is suspected of complicity in Mutiny, K. iii. 35 and *n.*; evidence of his complicity, K. i. 573 *n.*; his arrest in Calcutta (June 15), K. iii. 38–41, M. i. 27; his behaviour under arrest, M. i. 28.
Oudh, Nawáb of, minister of the Mughál Emperors, K. i. 113; nature of administration, K. i. 114; subsidy granted ¦by him, K. i. 113; he cedes territory to the British (1801), K. i. 117; treaty with (1801), K. i. 117; he is created Rájá, K. i. 119; purchases part of the *tirái*, K. i. 119; receives two years of grace for amendment (1847), K. i. 131; character and administration, K. i. 120; long-suffering of the British with respect to, K. i. 120; irregular troops disbanded (1801), K. i. 116.
Oudh, Queen-Mother of, starts from Calcutta on voyage to England, K. i. 403; her death and burial, K. i. 403.

Oudh, Sa,ádat Alí, Nawáb of (1817), K. i. 118.
Oudh Talúqdárs, their fearful atrocities, K. i. 135 n.
Oudh, Wájid Alí Sháh's amusements, K. i. 132; his army a mere banditti, K. iii. 424; his passionate grief on his dethronement, K. i. 150.
.Outbreak in North-West Provinces, more political than military, K. iii. 305, 306.
Outram, Gen. James, his early acts and character, K. i. 139; his noble character, M. i. 519; his capacity as a general, M. ii. 413; his opinion of sanguinary counsellors, K. iii. 7.

Becomes Resident at Lakhnau, K. i. 139; reports on corrupt state of Oudh, K. i. 141; opposed to annexation, K. i. 396; but ultimately annexes Oudh, K. i. 149; his health breaks down in 1856, K. i. 396; resigns Chief Commissionership of Oudh (1856), K. i. 396.

Appointed to command Persian expedition of 1856, K. i. 422; returns from Persia to Bombay, M. i. 132; telegraphs to Lord Canning for orders (July 9), K. iii. 187; starts for Calcutta, M. i. 132; lands at Calcutta (Aug. 1), M. i. 131, 133; gloomy prospects at Calcutta on his arrival, M. i. 133; his arrival there coincides with Lord Canning's latest wish, M. i. 133; he is appointed Chief Commissioner of Oudh, and to command of Dánápúr and Káhnpúr divisions (Aug. 1), K. iii. 188, M. i. 133, 519; has to improvise an artillery force, K. iii. 189; embarks

Outram, Gen.—cont.
for Dánápur (Aug. 6), K. iii. 189, M. i. 133; specially solicitous for the safety of Alláhábád, K. ii. 242; supersedes Gen. Havelock (Aug. 16), M. i. 512.; reaches Alláhábád (Sept. 2), M. i. 520; sends Major Eyre to Kúdanpati to attack party of insurgents (Sept. 10), M. i. 520; relieved by victory of Major Eyre at Kúdanpati (Sept. 11), M. i. 522; marches into Káhnpúr (Sept. 16), M. i. 518, 522; his appreciation of Major Eyre's victory at Kúdanpati, M. i. 522 n.

His order to the Army (Sept. 16), M. i. 523; nobly leaves the command of relieving force to Gen. Havelock, M. i. 523; his order of Sept. 16, confirmed and extolled by Sir Colin Campbell, M. i. 524; assumes command of troops (Sept. 26), M. i. 542; the shutting up of his troops in Lakhnau leaves central line of communication exposed, M. ii. 125.

Extends the position occupied in Lakhnau, M. ii. 151; tries to send his Cavalry from Lakhnau at night, but fails, M. ii. 153; his description of mining at Lakhnau, M. ii. 159 n.; conveys to A'lambágh plan of city of Lakhnau, M. ii. 162; his directions to the officer relieving Lakhnau, M. ii. 596; establishes semaphore telegraph with A'lambágh (Nov.), M. ii. 162; kept informed of stages of attack by signals, M. ii. 205; resigns to Gen. Havelock the advance from the Residency (Nov. 16), M. ii. 205; joins

Outram, Gen.—*cont.*
Sir Colin Campbell (Nov. 17), M. ii. 204.
Left in charge of the A'lambágh (Nov. 26), M. ii. 222, 342; his position at the A'lambágh (Nov.), M. ii. 343; the Maulaví's plan for driving him from the A'lambágh (Dec.), M. ii. 344; attacked by the Maulaví (Dec. 22), M. ii. 345; defeats the Maulaví, M. ii. 346; attacked by Lakhnau rebels (Jan. 12, '58), M. ii. 347; repulses attack, M. ii. 348; renewed attack upon (Jan. 16, '58), M. ii. 351; defeats renewed attack, M. ii. 352; another attack upon him (Feb. 15, '58), M. ii. 353; a determined attack upon him repulsed (Feb. 21, '58), M. ii. 354; despairing attack of rebels on (Feb. 25, '58), M. ii. 356; again repulses attack, M. ii. 358; his important services at the A'lambágh (Nov. to Feb.), M. ii. 359.

Crosses the Gúmtí to assail Lakhnau (March 6, '58), M. ii. 371; moves along the Gúmtí (March 6, 7, '58), M. ii. 373; Sir Colin Campbell sends him siege guns (March 8, '58), M. ii. 373; enfilades first line of rebel works at Lakhnau (March 9, '58), M. ii. 375; strengthens his position on the Gúmtí (March 10, '58), M. ii. 378; advances to cover Lakhnau bridges (March 11, '58), M. ii. 380; plants batteries against Qaisar Bágh and Mess House (March 11, '58), M. ii. 380; plants a battery at iron bridge, Lakhnau (March 11, '58), M. ii. 381; his admirable work

Outram, Gen.—*cont.*
on the Gúmtí, M. ii. 382!; enfilades rebel second line of defence at Lakhnau (Mar. 11–15, '58), M. ii. 382; Sir Colin Campbell's extraordinary order to him (Mar. 14, '58), M. ii. 397, 413; disastrous consequences of Sir Colin Campbell's order to him, M. ii. 398; ordered to cross Gúmtí at Sikandar Bágh (March 16, '58), M. ii. 399; Sir Colin Campbell's final instructions to, M. ii. 399; storms and carries the Residency at Lakhnau, M. ii. 400; captures remaining positions in Lakhnau (March 17, '58), M. ii. 404; marches against the Músá Bágh (March 19, '58), M. ii. 405; pursues rebels from Músa Bágh, M. ii. 408.

Condemns Lord Canning's Oudh proclamation, M. iii. 250; his reasons for dissenting from this proclamation, M. iii. 251; authorised to amend the proclamation to Oudh, M. iii. 252; gets a qualifying clause inserted in Lord Canning's impolitic Oudh proclamation, M. ii. 410; desires excessive leniency to Oudh talúqdárs, M. iii. 253; raised to the Supreme Council, M. iii. 262.

On the causes of the Mutiny, K. ii. 36 *n.*; he is succeeded by Mr. Montgomery in Commissionership of Oudh, M. iii. 262.

Outram, Sir James, *see* Outram, Gen. J.

Outram, Lady, her pleasant cheerfulness in Fort of A'grá, K. iii. 401.

P.

Paget, Sir Edward, suppresses the mutiny at Bárákpúr (1824), K. i. 269.
Pahlwán Singh, leads the Gorkha advance column into India (Aug.), M. iii. 454.
Paláman, Lieut. Graham blockaded in, M. ii. 437; relieved from blockade (Dec. 8), M. ii. 438; he seizes Debí Bakkas Ráí, and the rebellion collapses, M. ii. 438.
Pallamcottah, mutiny at, threatened (1806), K. i. 239.
Palmer, Mr. G., attacks and disperses marauders at Mandáwar (May), M. iii. 405.
Palmerston, Lord, sends Sir Colin Campbell to command in India, M. i. 142.
Pálí, Rájá of Jodhpúr's troops entrench themselves in (Aug.), M. ii. 563; defeat of Rájá of Jodhpúr's troops at (Sept. 8), M. ii. 565.
Pálpa, Gorkhas from, enter Gorakhpúr (June 28), M. iii. 452.
Pándí, Mangal, the first mutineer, K. i. 538.
Pandit, prophecy of a, M. ii. 350.
Panhat, the indecisive engagement at (May 18, '58), M. ii. 539.
Panic in Calcutta (May), K. ii. 114; at Patná (June 7), K. iii. 74; in Calcutta (June 14), K. iii. 29, M. i. 25; again in Calcutta (March 3, '58), M. ii. 418.
"Panic Sunday," in Calcutta (June 14), K. iii. 29; described by "Friend of India," K. iii. 35 n.; Dr. Mouat's de-

Panic Sunday—*cont.*
scription of, M. i. 25 n.; disgraceful scenes at Calcutta during, M. i. 25; courage of mercantile and trading community at, M. i. 26 n.; probable exaggeration in account of, K. iii. 34; its commencement (June 14), M. i. 23; caused by fear of mutiny of Bárákpúr Sepoys, M. i. 24, 26.
Pánipat, occupation of, by Jhínd Contingent, K. ii. 163.
Panjáb, extent and population (1849), K. i. 48; mixed character of the population, K. ii. 420; advantages of garrisoning, with strong British force, K. i. 344; character of Ranjít Singh's administration, K. i. 54; efforts to establish a good native government, K. i. 2 *et seq.*; council of regency instituted (1846), K. i. 7; Henry Lawrence appointed Resident in, K i. 7; administration of Henry Lawrence as Resident in, K. i. 12, 13; the battle of Rámnagar (1848), K. i. 37; siege of Múltán (1848–49), K. i. 39; battle of Chilliánwálá (1849), K. i. 41; battle of Gujrát (1849), K. i. 45; Afgháns driven from district by Sir Walter Gilbert (1849), K. i. 45; conquest of (1849), K. i. 46; its conquest stopped the mutinous tendencies of Sepoy army, K. i. 309; annexation of (1849), K. i. 47, M. i. 152; effect of annexation on Sepoy allowances, M. iii. 474; Sepoy regiments in, refuse to take reduced pay (1849), K. i. 311.
Placed under a Board of Administration (1849), K. i.

Panjab—cont.
50; divided into seven Commissionerships, K. i. 53; Sikh Sirdárs conciliated, K. i. 59; becomes a Chief Commissionership (1853), K. i. 61. State of, in May 1857, K. ii. 417–419; list of officers administering, K. ii. 421, 422; inhabitants losing confidence in the English, K. ii. 476; cheerful demeanour of defenders of, K. ii. 462, 487; critical condition of, K. i. 612; first appearance of revolt in, checked, K. ii. 430–436; Movable Column formed (June), K. ii. 633; the troops sent to Dehlí (July 22), K. ii. 644; Movable Column moves towards Dehlí (July 24), K. ii. 645; garrison of, after Nicholson's departure (Sept.), M. iii. 302; condition of province (Sept.), M. iii. 300; Sir J. Lawrence forms small movable column (Sept.), M. iii. 303.
Threatened rising at Derá Ismáíl Khán (July '58), M. iii. 305.
Panjáb system, the, K. i. 60; introduced into Oudh (1856), K. i. 152.
Panjábí races, inimical to Sepoys, K. ii. 472 n.; their admiration of English money, K. ii. 492; enlisted by John Lawrence in the Panjáb, K. ii. 472.
Pannú, Brig. Barker defeats rebels at, after desperate battle (Oct. 8, '58), M. iii. 287.
Paramount power assumed by the British in India, K. ii. 9.
Parke, Brig., ordered to continue pursuit of Tántiá Topí (Aug. '58), M. iii. 325; deceived by false reasoning

Parke, Brig.—cont.
allows Tántiá Topí to cross the Chambal and escape, M. iii. 325; pursues Tántiá Topí to Barodá (Nov. '58), M. iii. 352; catches Tántiá Topí at Chhotá Udaipúr (Dec. 1, '58), M. iii. 352; defeats him there, M. iii. 354; himself marches 2,000 miles in pursuit of Tántiá Topí, M. iii. 384.
Paron, Tántiá Topí rejoins Mán Singh at (Feb. '59), M. iii. 368.
Pársís, dispute between them and Muhammadans, at Barúch (May), M. iii. 8.
Partábgarh, one of Rájpút states, M. i. 245 n.; Thákur of, attacks and puts to flight a party of Mandíswar rebels, M. iii. 81; Tántiá Topí marches on (Dec. '58), M. iii. 356; Tántiá Topí baffles Major Rocke and escapes (Dec. '58), M. iii. 357.
Parúliá, Sepoy garrison of (July), M. ii. 134; mutiny at (Aug. 5), M. ii. 136.
Paterson, Mr., Magistrate and Collector of Gorakhpúr (May), M. iii. 447.
Patiálá, Mahárájá of, supports the English K. ii. 162, M. iii. 307; he holds Tháníswar, K. ii. 163.
Pattíálí, battle of (Dec. 17), M. ii. 291.
Patná, district of Patná Division, K. iii. 71 n.; its peculiarities, M. i. 41; its importance, M. i. 40; out-stations of the district of, K. iii. 71; fanaticism at, K. iii. 78; head-quarters of the Wahábís, M. i. 40; its population, M. i. 39; census of population at (1845), K. i. 305;

THE HISTORIES OF THE INDIAN MUTINY. 155

Patná—*cont.*
dangerous character of population of, K. iii. 63, 69 ; conspiracy (1845), K. i. 303 ; the price for defection actually paid to some Sepoys, K. i. 307 ; conspiracy divulged by Jamádár Mótí Misra, K. i. 307.
Mr. W. Tayler, Commissioner at, M. i. 42 ; Industrial Institution at, a cause of dissension between Mr. Halliday and Mr. Tayler, K. iii. 71 ; state of the district in June, K. iii. 64 ; increasing excitement at, K. iii. 68 ; Mr. W. Tayler calls a council of Europeans (June 7), M. i. 43 ; the Judge counsels flight to Dánápúr, M. i. 43 ; the Europeans resolve to support Mr. W. Tayler, M. i. 44 ; opium godown at, protected, K. iii. 66 ; crisis at (June 7), K. iii. 74, M. i. 44 ; the Judge takes refuge in opium godown, M. i. 48 ; panic subsides, K. iii. 76.
Outrageous attempts to corrupt fidelity of Sikhs, M. i. 47 ; Mr. W. Tayler discovers secret societies at (June 7–11), M. i. 48 ; gradual subsidence of confidence in Native gentry, K. iii. 72 ; treasure conveyed to, a source of danger (June 8), K. iii. 67 ; Sepoys at Dánápúr a great source of danger, M. i. 50 ; the grave responsibilities of Mr. Tayler at, M. i. 51, 105 ; Mr. Tayler resolves to strike the first blow at the conspirators, M. i. 51.
The Wahábí Maulavís at, M. i. 52 ; arrest of the three Maulavís at (June 19), K. iii. 82, 681, M. i. 52 ; power to

Patná—*cont.*
work mischief taken from Wahábí Maulavís, M. i. 53 ; seizure of Maulavís at, criticised, K. iii. 83.
Arrest of the patrolling magistrate, M. i. 54 ; Mr. W. Tayler disarms citizens of (June 20), K. iii. 84, M. i. 54 ; tranquillity restored (June 21), M. i. 54 ; Alí Karím implicated in plots at, M. i. 54 ; arrest of Wáris Alí (June 23), M. i. 54.
Rising at (July 3), K. iii. 84, M. i. 55 ; murder of Dr. Lyall by rioters, M. i. 56 ; Rattray's Sikhs put down rising at, M. i. 56 ; capture of ringleaders of rioters, M. i. 57 ; arrest of Pír Alí at, K. iii. 85 ; Wáris Alí, Pír Alí, and Shaikh Ghasíta, hanged at, M. i. 57 ; arrest and release of Lutf Alí Khán (July 5), K. iii. 87, M. i. 57.
Dánápúr Sepoys mutiny (July 25), M. i. 73 ; Mr. W. Tayler rallies the Europeans at his house, M. i. 73 ; small party improvised to cut off some Dánápúr mutineers, K. iii. 102, M. i. 74 ; detachment recalled on revolt of 12th Irregulars, M. i. 74 ; critical position of Mr. Tayler on defeat of Capt. Dunbar, M. i. 104 ; peculiar danger at Gayá and Mozaffarpúr out-stations, M. i. 106.
Splendid conduct of Mr. W. Tayler, M. i. 48 ; Lord Canning's Private Secretary exonerates Mr. Tayler from all blame, M. i. 121 *n.* ; Sir John Low recants his adverse decision against Mr. Tayler's conduct, M. i. 121 ; Mr. Dorin also recants his adverse opi-

Patná—*cont.*
nion against Mr. Tayler, M. i. 121.
Mr. Samuells succeeds Mr. Tayler, M. ii. 443; the town partly fortified (Aug.), M. ii. 443.
Paton, Sergeant, his brave exploit at Sháh Najíf (Nov. 16), M. ii. 194 n., 197, 383.
Patwardhan family, dependants of the Peshwá, M. iii. 28.
Paurí, Rájá of Narwár seizes fort of (Aug. 2, '58), M. iii. 332; Brig. Smith appears before (Aug. 7, '58), M. iii. 332; Brig. Napier joins Brig. Smith before (Aug. 19, '58), M. iii. 334; evacuated by Rájá (Aug. 23, '58), M. iii. 335.
Pay, reductions of, as viewed by the Sepoy, K. i. 302.
Peacock, Mr. Barnes, Member of Supreme Council (1856), K. i. 387; his character, K. i. 390.
Pearson, Capt., fights his guns till they are wrecked at Sháhganj, M. i. 275; heroically strives to save his disabled guns, M. i. 276; his cool courage at Hátrás (July 3), M. i. 295.
Pearl brigade, its strength, M. ii. 128; employed at Patná (Sept.), M. ii. 128.
Peel, Capt. William, his character, M. ii. 127; reaches Calcutta in the *Shannon* (Aug. 8), K. iii. 185, M. i. 141; starts for Alláhábád with Naval Brigade (Aug. 18), M. i. 142, ii. 126; reaches Alláhábád (Sept. 2), M. ii. 128; assumes command of troops at Kajwá (Nov. 2), M. ii. 145; defeats [mutineers at Kajwá, M. ii. 146; leads his

Peel, Capt.—*cont.*
detachment on to Káhnpúr after victory at Kajwá, M. ii. 146; commands Naval Brigade at attack on Lakhnau, M. ii. 171; bombards the Qaisar Bágh (Nov. 19–22), M. ii. 215; his splendid deed at Káhnpúr (Dec. 6), M. ii. 271; wounded at Lakhnau (March 9, '58), M. ii. 378; created Aide-de-Camp to the Queen and K.C.B. (March 2, '58), M. ii. 545; starts for Calcutta (April 1, '58), M. ii. 545; dies of small-pox (April 27, '58), M. ii. 546; Lord Canning's general order on his death, M. ii. 547; statue to his memory in Eden Gardens, Calcutta, M. ii. 547.
Pegu, annexation of, K. i. 66; military defence of, K. i. 459; difficulty of procuring reliefs for garrison of, K. i. 462.
Penny, Gen., commands at Dehlí after Gen. Wilson, M. ii. 105; marches from Balandshahr (April '58), M. ii. 501; deluded into false security, M. ii. 501; attacked and killed at Kakraulí (April 30, '58), M. ii. 501; his column joins Sir Colin Campbell (May 3, '58), M. ii. 502.
Peshwá, the, his supporters in the Marátha country, M. iii. 28; Bájí Ráo accepts a pension (1818), K. i. 99; retires to Bithúr, K. i. 99.
Peshawar, conference at (1856), K. i. 434–442; expected to be surrendered to the Afghans (1856), K. i. 483.
Its garrison in May, K. ii. 447, 475 n.; dread of Afghán irruption (May), K. ii. 448;

Peshawar—*cont.*
opinion of a Sikh Sardár on importance of its tranquillity, K. ii. 449 n.; council at (May 13), K. ii. 457. Formation of Movable Column at, K. ii. 460; Neville Chamberlain selected to command the Movable Column, K. ii. 461; resolution to disarm Sepoys at, K. ii. 477; disarmament effected (May 22), K. ii. 479; punishment of deserters at, K. ii. 481; hanging of Súbádár Major at (May 28), K. ii. 482.
Recruiting at (June), K. ii. 677; critical condition of, K. ii. 607.
Question of abandonment of (June), K. ii. 608; proposal to cede, to Dost Muhammad, K. ii. 608; Capt. Hugo James protests against cession of Peshawar, K. ii. 609; Nicholson, Edwardes, and Cotton, oppose cession of, K. ii. 609, 610; John Lawrence again urges cession of, K. iii. 611; John Lawrence renews his desire to cede (June 25), K. ii. 612; Edwardes, Cotton, and James, entreat Sir John Lawrence not to cede, K. ii. 613; John Nicholson opposes cession of, K. ii. 616; Lord Canning forbids Sir J. Lawrence to cede, K. ii. 619; review of question of cession of, K. ii. 621.
Persia, covets Afghánistán, K. i. 413; rumour of success over English in spring of 1857, K. ii. 35; intrigues during the Crimean War, K. i. 412; war with, threatened (1856), K. i. 409; the Persians again march on Hirát

Persia—*cont.*
(1856), K. i. 414; instigated to seize Hirát by Russia (1856), K. i. 448 n.; dissension excited by Persia in North-West of India (1856), K. i. 482; war with, decided upon, K. i. 416; rupture with (1855), K. i. 412; expedition against starts, K. i. 417; the Persians try to awaken sedition in Dehlí, K. i. 483; admit attempting a diversion in India, K. ii. 40 n.; war with Persia ended, K. i. 599.
Phayre, Capt. (now Sir Arthur), created Commissioner of Pegu, K. i. 67.
Philibít, *see* Pílíbhít.
Phillipps, Mr. Alfred, magistrate of Ítá, rides into Badáon for help, K. iii. 283, M. i. 322; his gallant charge while going to Badáon, K. iii. 284 n.
Phillipps, Mr., and party of fugitives from Sítápúr, lie concealed for ten months, M. i. 381.
Phillaur, its situation and importance, K. ii. 443; Fort manfully held by Lieut. Griffith (May 12), K. ii. 445; the Fort saved (May 13), K. ii. 446; inscrutable conduct of Sepoys at, K. ii. 500.
Phillour, *see* Phillaur.
Phúlpúr, Col. Rowcroft defeats the rebels at (Jan. 19, '58), M. ii. 324.
Pílíbhít, Capt. Larkins commands at (Aug. '58), M. iii. 275; Khán Bahádur Khán falls back upon (May 5, '58), M. ii. 529; station threatened by Nizám Alí Khán (Aug. '58), M. iii. 274; threatened by Alí Khán Mewátí and Nizám Alí Khán (Aug. '58), M. iii. 275.

Pinickney, Brig., ordered to move in concert with Gen. Hope Grant (Oct. '58), M. iii. 289.
Píplia, zamíndár of, subdued by Haidarábád Contingent (Oct.), M. iii. 74.
Pír Alí, leads the rioters at Patná (July 3), M. i. 55; arrest of, at Patná, K. iii. 85, M. i. 57; execution of, K. iii. 86, M. i. 57.
Pírú, Col. Turner defeats rebels at (Oct. 17, '58), M. ii. 486.
Plan of—
Dehlí, K. ii. 513.
Operations of British Army before Dehlí, M. ii. 68.
The final attack of Dehlí (as proposed), K. iii. 545.
Káhnpúr, K. ii. 286.
City of Káhnpúr, M. ii. 276.
City of Lakhnau, K. iii. 417.
Intrenched position covering Lakhnau Residency, M. i. 432.
Operations for relief and withdrawal of Lakhnau garrison, M. ii. 224.
Operations of British Army before Lakhnau in March 1858, M. ii. 400.
Platt, Col., command at Máú, M. i. 206; murdered at Máú (July 1), M. i. 235.
Plowden, Mr., Commissioner of Nágpúr, M. iii. 113; his character and services, M. iii. 115; counsels abandoning line of the Narbadá (July), M. i. 242; Col. Durand opposes his wish to abandon line of the Narbadá, M. i. 243; his injudicious advice counteracted by Col. Durand, M. iii. 85.
Policy of unpreparedness, K. ii. 105.

Pollock, Mr. Archibald, energetically provides for re-inforcements passing through Banáras, K. ii. 239.
Pollution of caste, Native rumours of intended, K. ii. 118.
Polwhele, Brig., a commissioner during temporary illness of Mr. Colvin at A´grá, M. i. 266; officers at A´grá beg him to go out against mutineers, K. iii. 382; he resolves to advance against Nímach mutineers (July 5), K. iii. 379, M. i. 270; his vacillation enables the approaching mutineers to secure best position, K. iii. 383; hesitates to order a charge at Sháhganj, M. i. 272; attempts to fight artillery of mutineers, M. i. 272; Sepoy cavalry charge his guns, M. i. 273; orders advance when too late, M. i. 274; captures village at Sháhganj, M. i. 275; cannot hold village, M. i. 275; retreats from Sháhganj, M. i. 276; returns defeated to A´grá Fort, M. i. 277; removed from command by Governor-General, K. iii. 410, M. i. 285.
Ponsonby, Brig. George, commands at Banáras, K. ii. 201; gives up command at Banáras (June 4), K. ii. 225.
Porahát, Rájá of, proclaimed ruler of Singhbhúm (Dec.), M. ii. 438.
Portuguese Viceroy, places his troops under British command (Nov. '58), M. iii. 246.
Powáin, Rájá of, his unfavourable reception of English fugitives, M. i. 321; refuses shelter to fugitives from

Powáin, Rájá of—*cont.*
Sháhjahánpúr, M. i. 384;
closes his gates on the Maulaví (June 5, '58), M. ii.
543; the Maulaví slain by
his brother (June 5, '58), M.
iii. 544; attacked by rebels for
killing the Maulaví (Aug.
'58), M. iii. 274; protected
by De Kantzow, M. iii. 275;
repulses attack (Oct. 8, '58),
M. iii. 288.
Powell, Col., the strength of his
detachment (Nov. 1), M. ii.
144; starts from Alláhábád
with detachment (Oct. 28),
M. ii. 143; finds the Bihár
mutineers at Kajwá near
Fathpúr (Oct. 31), M. ii.
143; attacks Kajwá (Nov.
2), M. ii. 145; his death
during attack, M. ii. 145.
Powell, Mr., and others, become
Mussulmans to save their
lives, M. i. 332.
Pratt, Lieut.-Col., plants a battery at iron bridge, Lakhnau
(March 11, '58), M. ii. 381.
Prayág, or Alláhábád, its sanctity, K. ii. 260.
Prendergast, Capt., his gallant
charge at Sháhganj (July 5),
M. i. 274.
Press, European and Native
compared, M. i. 16; impolicy
of distinguishing between
European and Native, K. iii.
19; Government freely communicate information to, K.
iii. 21 *n.*; Sir H. Lawrence on
danger of, K. iii. 19; the dangers in India of a free press,
K. iii. 664; the unguarded
utterances of, K. iii. 12; its
dangerous craving for news,
K. iii. 14; offends officials by
criticism, M. i. 17; warns
Government after the Barhámpúr outbreak, M. i. 17;

Press—*cont.*
re-imposition of restraints
upon, always contemplated,
K. iii. 17; restraints upon,
proposed, K. iii. 17; outcry
against restrictions on, K. iii.
18; restraint of, for one year,
K. iii. 18; private letter commending restraint of, K. iii.
19; Lord Canning defends
his restraint of, K. iii. 20,
21; restraint of, justified, K.
iii. 22; argument against
censorship, K. iii. 23; the
"Friend of India" warned,
K. iii. 43.
Press, Native, its circulation and
effect, K. iii. 13; its tone
changes after Mutiny at Mírat, M. i. 18.
Prettijohn, Capt., attacks and
defeats Tántiá Topí's right
at Jhánsí (April 1, '58), M.
iii. 163; leads decisive charge
at Jaurá-Alípúr (June 22,
'58), M. iii. 230; his gallant
charge at Ránod (Dec. 17,
'58), M. iii. 363.
Prichard,Lieut. Iltudus Thomas,
abandons the army for literature, M. ii. 559 *n.*
Prior, Brig. H., commands Nágpúr subsidiary force, M. iii.
114.
Privileges of the Sepoys, K. i.
619.
Probyn, Mr., destroys rebel
boats on the Son (Oct. 14,
'58), M. ii. 484.
Proclamation of May 16, text of
the, K. i. 654; the Queen's
(1858), M. iii. 386, 391; the
principles on which Her Majesty desired it to be based,
M. iii. 390; its enthusiastic
reception in India, M. iii.
396.
Proclamations, probably of slight
utility, K. i. 609 *n.*

Promptitude in suppressing signs of mutiny in 1806, disapproved of, K. i. 241.
Prophecy of the downfall of the English power in India, K. ii. 36 n.
Protected Sikh States, fidelity of, K. ii. 161.
Pryag, see Prayág.
Public Works stopped by Lord Canning, K. iii. 50.
Púchh, Major Gall arrives at, and is joined by Sir H. Rose (May 1, '58), M. iii. 174.
Púna, Gen. Woodburn returns to, in bad health, M. i. 243.
Punjab, see Panjáb.
Punishment of Deserters at Pesháwar, K. ii. 481; of mutineers at Hot-Mardán (June 10), K. ii. 290; at Káhnpúr by Gen. Neill, K. ii. 399; Sir J. Lawrence and J. Nicholson counsel discrimination in, K. ii. 488; the punishment suggested by Col. J. Nicholson, K. ii. 401; opinion of the devout concerning, K. ii. 402.
Purnell, Col., commands 90th Regiment advancing from Lakhnau Residency (Nov. 16), M. ii. 206; secures possession of Chíní Bázár, at Lakhnau (March 14, '58), M. ii. 393; joins Gen. Hope Grant at Chinhat (June 11, '58), M. iii. 267.
Púrniá, district of Bhágalpúr, M. ii. 129; Mr. Yule marches with troops to (Dec. 1), M. ii. 426; Mr. Yule defeats the mutinous Cavalry at, M. ii. 429.
Púrwá, Capt. Evans, Deputy Commissioner at, M. i. 409; Capt. Evans stays at his post until surrender of Gen. Wheeler at Kánhpúr, M. i.

Púrwá—cont.
409; then retires on Lakhnau, M. i. 409.
Puteealah, see Patíálá.

Q.

Qaddam Rasúl, see Lakhnau.
Qaisar Bágh, see Lakhnau.
Queen's birthday at Calcutta, observance of (May 24), K. ii. 119.
Queen's Proclamation, text of the, M. iii. 391; places at which it was read with ceremony (Nov. 1, '58), M. iii. 395; its enthusiastic reception in India, M. iii. 396.

R.

Race and caste of Sepoy Army, in 1857, K. i. 621–626.
Radcliffe, Capt., his gallant charge with Volunteers, M. i. 426; his death at Lakhnau (Sept. 25), K. iii. 542.
Rádhava Govind, Díwán of Kirwí (May '58), M. iii. 199.
Radho Govind, see Rádhava Govind.
Raghugarh, zamíndár of, subdued by Haidarábád Contingent (Oct.), M. iii. 74.
Raghunáth, succeeds to the Ráj of Jhánsí (1840), K. i. 90.
Raghunáth Ráo, Peshwá, his descendants rule at Kirwí (May '58), M. iii. 199.
Ragonáth Ráo, see Raghunáth and Raghunáth Ráo.
Rágugarh, see Raghugarh.

Raikes, Mr., his testimony to devotion of ladies in A'grá Fort, M. i. 284 n.
Railways, introduced into India by Lord Dalhousie, K. i. 193.
Railways and telegraphs, heavy blows to Bráhmanism, K. i. 193.
Raines, Col., drives rebels from hills beyond Kotá-kí-saráí (June 17, '58), M. iii. 219.
Ráípúr, garrison of, M. iii. 113.
Rajab A'lí, Munshí, Native agent, his character, M. ii. 74.
Rájá Rám, assists the English in restoring order in A'grá, M. i. 278.
Rájgarh, Gen. Michel meets Tántiá Topí at, M. iii. 329; Tántiá Topí completely defeated near (Sept. '58), M. iii. 330.
Rájmahal, district of Bhágalpúr, M. ii. 129.
Rájpúr, Tántiá Topí defeated at (Nov. 24, '58), M. iii. 350.
Rájpút Princes, uneasy feeling among, caused by annexations, K. i. 96.
Rájpút States, their antiquity and dignity, K. i. 93; they dread absorption, K. i. 97.
Rájpúra, Tántiá Topí levies contribution from Chief of (Nov. '58), M. iii. 352.
Rájpútáná, the constituent states of, M. i. 245 n.; expected to be annexed by the English (1856), K. i. 483, 484 n.; favourable to British supremacy, M. i. 246; uncertain friendship of, K. iii. 351; popular feeling antagonistic to English, M. iii. 345; chiefs of, co-operate with the British, K. iii. 358; Mahárájá of Jodhpúr, anticipates

Rájpútáná—cont.
request for assistance, K. iii. 352; effect of British rule upon, M. ii. 551; reasons for tranquillity of, during Mutiny, M. ii. 576; military occupation of, M. i. 248.
Principal British officers in, K. iii. 353; Col. G. St. P. Lawrence, political chief of, M. i. 245; Col. Lawrence ordered to abandon, K. iii. 352; and refuses, K. iii. 353; condition of district (May), M. i. 247; Col. G. Lawrence comprehends full significance of Mírat outbreak, M. i. 247; exposed condition of A'jmír arsenal in May, M. i. 248; fort of A'jmír occupied by Mairs and arsenal saved, M. i. 250; Col. G. Lawrence repairs and provisions fort of A'jmír, M. i. 255; and summons British troops from Dísá (May), M. i. 249; proclamation to Native states of, M. i. 251; Col. G. Lawrence goes to Bíáor (June 1), M. i. 254; rising of Sepoys (June), M. i. 12; arrival of troops from Dísá (June 12), M. i. 255; Col. G. Lawrence strictly preserves routine of civil duties in, M. i. 256 n.; Lord Elphinstone sends a column of troops to (July), M. iii. 19; admirable results of Col. G. Lawrence's far-seeing policy, M. i. 261.
Mutiny at I'rinpúra (Aug. 22), M. ii. 558; Thákur of A'wah forced to join the rebels, M. ii. 564; Gen. G. Lawrence makes an attempt on A'wah, but retires, M. ii. 567; defeat of Rájá of Jodhpúr's army (Sept. 8), M. ii. 565; mutiny at Kotá (Oct.

11

Rájpútáná—cont.
15), M. ii. 569; Col. Holmes captures and destroys A'wah (Jan. 24, '58), M. ii. 573; re-inforcements under Major-Gen. H. G. Roberts arrive (March '58), M. ii. 573; Gen. Roberts commands field force in (June '58), M. iii. 319; Gen. Michel succeeds to command in (Aug. '58), M. iii. 328.

Raleigh, Cornet, murdered at Lakhnau (May 30), M. i. 376.

Rámbakkas, rebel leader in Oudh, M. iii. 271.

Rám Chand, created ruler of Jhánsí (1822), K. i. 89, M. i. 180.

Rámchandra Bápají, minister of Dhár, M. iii. 68; acts antagonistically to wishes of the English (May), M. iii. 68.

Rámdurg, Chief of, proves to Mr. Manson the defection of Nargúnd (May '58), M. iii. 242.

Rámgarh, Rájá of, loyally assists the English, M. ii. 136.

Rámkot, Zamindár of, assists party of fugitives from Sítápúr, M. i. 381.

Rám Mohan Ráe, agent of Akbar Sháh in England, K. ii. 11.

Rammohun Roy, see Rám Mohan Ráe.

Rámnagar, battle of (1848), K. i. 37.

Rámnáráyan Pánde, a gallant Sepoy at Lakhnau, M. ii. 157 n.

Ramnuggur, see Rámnagar.

Rámparshád Singh, Bábú, captured, and his house burned by Oudh rebels (July '58), M. iii. 279.

Rámpúr, Col. Walters defeats rebels at (Sept. 9, '58), M.

Rámpúr—cont.
ii. 484; Firoz Sháh seizes part of Lieut. Stack's convoy near (Dec. '58), M. iii. 364; Nawáb of, his steadfast loyalty to the British, K. iii. 260, M. ii. 520.

Rámpúr Kussiá, description of, M. iii. 290; Oudh rebels occupy (Sept. '58), M. iii. 273; captured by Brig. Wetherall (Nov. 3, '58), M. iii. 290.

Rám Ráo Govind, created minister of Náná Sáhib at Gwáliár (June 1, '58), M. iii. 210.

Ramsey, Brig., commands contingent at Gwáliár, K. iii. 313; objects to families of Contingent officers removing to Residency, K. iii. 314; distrusts Sindhiá, K. iii. 314 n.

Ramsay, Major H., brings his Gorkhas from Pálpa into Gorakhpúr (June 28), M. iii. 452.

Rám Singh, Mahárao of Kotá, M. ii. 568; causes the Mutiny to break out (Oct. 15), M. ii. 569.

Rám Singh, Rájá of Jaipúr, thoroughly devoted to the English, M. i. 257.

Ráná of Udaipúr, see Udaipúr.

Ránchí, Sepoy garrison of (July), M. ii. 134; mutiny at (July 31), M. ii. 135; Capt. Dalton forced to abandon, M. ii. 135.

Raneegauge, see Raníganj.

Ranga Bápají, agent of Sitárá in England (1853), K. i. 110.

Rangpúr, Mr. Macdonald saves Government treasure at (Dec.), M. ii. 427; party of seamen arrive at, from Calcutta (Dec. 15), M. ii. 430.

Rángún, the Queen's proclamation read with ceremony at (Nov. 1, '58), M. iii. 395.

Raníganj, ominous fires at, early in 1857, K. i. 497.
Rání of Jhánsí, *see* Jhánsí.
Ránod, Gen. R. Napier arrives at (Dec. 17, '58), M. iii. 362.
Ráo Bháwaní Singh, his loyalty and calm courage, M. i. 158, 159.
Ráo Rágonáth Ráo, Rája of Jhánsí, M. i. 180.
Ráo Sáhib, nephew of Náná Sáhib, K. ii. 312; sends Tántiá Topí with a fresh army against English (May '58), M. iii. 174; orders Tántiá Topí to attack Kálpí and Chárkhárí, M. iii. 161; attacks English left at Kálpí (May 22, '58), M. iii. 184; flies from Gulaulí to Gopálpúr (May '58), M. iii. 203; created Governor of Gwáliár (June 1, '58), M. iii. 209; demands a contribution from Ráná of Jhálrá Pátan (Aug. '58), M. iii. 326; joins in attempt on Indor (Aug. '58), M. iii. 327; occupies Lalatpúr (Sept. '58), M. iii. 338; defeated at Sindhwáo (Oct. '58), M. iii. 340; after his defeat rejoins Tántiá Topí at Lalatpúr, M. iii. 340; grave importance of his presence in Nágpúr territory, M. iii. 343; escapes with Tántiá Topí from defeat at Khorai (Oct. 25, '58), M. iii. 342; Tántiá Topí's only companion (Dec. '58), M. iii. 354; quarrels with Tántiá Topí (Jan. '59), M. iii. 367; abandoned by Tántiá Topí (Feb. '59), M. iii. 367; with 3,000 followers marches on Kosháni (Feb. '59), M. iii. 368; defeated by Brig. Honner at Kosháni (Feb. 10, '59), M. iii. 368;

Ráo Sáhib—*cont.*
escapes through Chattarbhuj pass (Feb. 15, '59), M. iii. 368; his army melts away completely, M. iii. 369; disappears into obscurity (Feb. '59), M. iii. 369.
Ráptí, danger of fording, M. iii. 295.
Rathgarh, description of, M. iii. 139; Sir Hugh Rose invests (Jan. 24, '58), M. iii. 139; the rebels make sorties from, M. iii. 140; Sir Hugh Rose opens breaching batteries against (Jan. 27, '58), M. iii. 141; Rájá of Bánpúr attempts to raise the siege of (Jan. 28, '58), M. iii. 141; rebels evacuate fort (Jan. 28, '58), M. iii. 142.
Rattan Mán Singh, of Nipál, ordered to co-operate with English against Dákhá mutineers, M. ii. 434.
Rattray, Capt., raises a body of Sikhs, M. i. 44; reports outrageous attempts to corrupt his Sikhs, M. i. 47; puts down rising at Patná (July 3), M. i. 56; guards treasure into Patná (June 8), K. iii. 67; left in charge of Chutiá Nágpúr (Oct.), M. ii. 141; led into a false position by Mr. Alonzo Money, M. ii. 445; defeats a body of rebels at Akbarpúr (Oct. 7), M. ii. 445; fights the rebels at Dhanchuá (Nov. 6), M. ii. 446.
Ráwal, fierce contest of rebels with Major Orr's force (Nov.), M. iii. 76.
Ráwalpindí, mutiny at, K. i. 310; council at (May 16), K. ii. 461.
Rawul Pindee, *see* Ráwalpindí.
Read, Lieut., killed at attack on Jíran (Oct. 23), M. ii. 571.

11 *

Reade, Mr. E. A., a commissioner during temporary illness of Mr. Colvin at A'grá, M. i. 266; on the prophecy of the downfall of the English ráj, K. i. 486; saves the revenue records, M. i. 277; his noble unselfishness at A'grá, K. iii. 396 n.; his cheerful assistance to all in Fort of Agrá, K. iii. 404; becomes chief civil officer at A'grá (Sept. 9), M. ii. 94; prepares for defence of station at A'grá, K. iii. 229, M. ii. 96; recommends to Government military rule at A'grá (Sept. 9), M. ii. 94.

Rebellion or Mutiny, which is it? K. i. 617.

Redan battery, a post at Lakhnau Residency, M. i. 442.

"Red Pamphlet," extract from, as to "Panic Sunday" in Calcutta, M. i. 24, 25.

Reductions of pay, dangerous, K. i. 302.

Reed, Gen., counsels delay in assault of Dehlí (June 16), K. ii. 534; assumes command of Dehlí Field Force on death of Gen. Anson (July 6), K. ii. 530, 573; resigns command of Dehlí Field Force to Brig. A. Wilson (July 17), K. ii. 586.

Reed, Lieut., pursues rebels from Garhákot, M. iii. 146.

Regular and Irregular military systems discussed, K. i. 337.

Reid, Major Charles, commands Gorkha regiment at Dehrá Dún (May), M. iii. 419; marches from Dehrá Dún to Mírat (May), M. iii. 420. Commands at Hindú Ráo's House, Dehlí, K. ii. 545; his remarks on this position, K. iii. 672; attacked by muti-

Reid, Major—*cont.* neers (June 12), K. ii. 545; and again attacked (June 13, 15), K. ii. 547; bears the brunt of the affray for months, K. ii. 545 ; Brig. Wilson disregards his pencil notes during siege of Dehlí as "unofficial," M. ii. 17 n.; commands fourth column of assault at Dehlí, M. ii. 28; his plan of attack on Kishanganj, M. ii. 579; wounded while leading fourth column of attack on Dehlí, K. iii. 608.

Re-inforcements reach Calcutta, K. ii. 130, 135; pushed up country, K. ii. 136.

Re-marriage of Hindú widows, Bill to remove legal obstacles to, K. i. 190 n.; question argued, K. i. 188–190.

Remmington, Capt., commands Reid's battery before Dehlí, M. ii. 12; his splendid conduct at Lakhnau (Nov. 18), M. ii. 214.

Renaud, Major, advances with detachment from Alláhábád (June 30), K. ii. 274, 284; terrible instructions given to his column (June 30), K. ii. 274; severities inflicted by, K. ii. 284 n.; killed at battle of A'on (July 15), K. ii. 369.

Renny, Capt., A. W., his bravery at capture of magazine at Dehlí, K. iii. 700, M. ii. 59; his artillerymen do much execution in street-fighting in Dehlí, M. iii. 502.

Rent-free tenures, K. i. 168; how treated in the North-West, K. i. 172.

Repressive measures passed by Legislative Council, K. ii. 275 n.

Resistance or concesssion, policy of, K. i. 322.
Resources for suppression of Mutiny neglected by Government (June 1), M. i. 5.
Resumption operations, by wholesale, K. i. 169, 170.
Revenue, collected in silver, a source of temptation, K. iii. 246; settlement of, K. i. 156; injurious effect of the system at Badáon, K. iii. 282 n.
Rewá, description of defences of, M. iii. 110; Lieut. Willoughby Osborne political agent at, M. iii. 110; troops of the Rájá of, posted so as to intercept rebels, M. iii. 111; the Rájá of, resolves to support the English cause (June 8), M. iii. 111; he sends some troops to Bándá, M. iii. 112.
Rewakántá, Native state in Bombay Presidency, M. iii. 2.
Rice, Capt. W., scatters Firoz Sháh's followers at Sarpúr (Dec. 22, '58), M. iii. 364.
Richardson, Major J. F., joins Mr. Yule in pursuit of Dákhá mutineers (Jan. 11, '58), M. ii. 433; Dákhá mutineers escape from him (Jan. 19, '58), M. ii. 435.
Ricketts, Mr. George Henry, Deputy Commissioner at Ludhíáná, bravely disputes the passage of the Satlaj, K. ii. 503–505; Brig. Johnstone's timidity leaves him to be overpowered, K. ii. 507; he disarms town of Ludhíáná, K. ii. 509.
Ricketts, Mr. Henry, a Bengal civilian, K. i. 396; engaged on scheme for retrenching salaries, K. i. 397; suggested as

Ricketts, Mr. Henry—cont.
successor to Outram in Oudh, K. i. 396.
Ricketts, Mr. Mordaunt, Magistrate and Collector at Sháhjahánpúr, K. iii. 278; murdered at Sháhjahánpúr (May 31), K. iii. 280, M. i. 319.
Riddell, Col., defeats a body of rebels on the Jamná (May 25, '58), M. iii. 210 n.; moves with siege train on Gwáliár (June '58), M. iii. 215.
Ridge, the, at Dehlí, description of, K. ii. 516; occupied by the British (June 8), K. ii. 193. See Dehlí.
Rifles, ammunition for, K. i. 518, 519; ammunition of two-grooved, its composition, K. i. 655.
Ripley, Col., cut down at the Kashmír Gate of Dehlí (May 11), K. ii. 85.
Riwá, feudatory in Ságar territory, M. iii. 88; arrest of treasonable messenger to Darbár of (April 25), M. i. 204.
Riwárí, captured by Brig. Showers (Oct.), M. ii. 108.
Roberts, Capt., commands detachment from Ságar (Nov.), M. iii. 108.
Roberts, Lieut., his gallantry at Fathgarh (Jan. 2, '58), M. ii. 305.
Roberts, Major-Gen. H. G., leads re-inforcements into Rájpútáná (March), M. ii. 573; captures Kotá (March 30), M. ii. 575; commands Rájpútáná Field Force (June '58), M. iii. 319; occupies Nasírábád, M. iii. 319; forces Tántiá Topí to turn from advance on Jaipúr (June 28, '58), M. iii. 319; discovers Tántiá Topí at Bhilwárá (Aug.

Roberts, Major-Gen.—*cont.*
7, '58), M. iii. 321; attacks
Tántiá Topí and puts him to
flight, M. iii. 322; catches up
to Tántiá Topí at Kankraulí,
near the Banás (Aug. 13, '58),
M. iii. 322; defeats Tántiá
Topí (Aug. 14, '58), M. iii.
323; his method of obtaining
correct and speedy intelligence, M. iii. 323 *n.*; he de-
putes Brig. Parke to continue
pursuit of Tántiá Topí (Aug.
'58), M. iii. 325; he is transferred to command of Gujarát (Aug. '58), M. iii. 328;
prevents Tántiá Topí entering Gujarát, M. iii. 346.
Robertson, Lieut. - Governor,
his views on Edmonstone's
Mainpúrí settlement, K. i.
163 *n.*
Robertson, Major, captures rebel
guns at Dhar, M. iii. 70; his
gallantry in the Malwá campaign, M. iii. 87; beats off
rebel attack at A'lambágh
(March 16, '58), M. ii. 402;
sent to Gopálpúr in pursuit
of rebels (May 25, '58), M.
iii. 211; follows rebels towards Gwáliár, and ascer-
tains its capture by them
(June '58), M. iii. 211; sent
in pursuit of Mán Singh
(Aug. '58), M. iii. 335; overtakes Ajít Singh at Bíjapúr
(Sept. 3, '58), M. iii. 335;
defeats Ajít Singh near Bíjapúr (Sept. 4, '58), M. iii.
336.
Robertson, Mr. Dundas, Assistant Magistrate at Sahíranpúr,
M. i. 299; by boldness and
prudence holds Sahíranpúr to
its allegiance, M. i. 300.
Robertson, Mr. J. C., Assistaut
officer at Dehrá Dún (May),
M. iii. 419.

Robertson, Mr. Thomas Campbell, his dislike of the policy
of weakening influential natives, K. iii. 453 *n.*
Robinson, Capt., leads left of
right attack at storming of
Jhánsí (April 3, '58), M. iii.
166.
Rocke, Major, stops Tántiá
Topí's march on Udaipúr
(Dec. '58), M. iii. 356; Tántiá Topí escapes him at Partábgarh (Dec. '58), M. iii.
357.
Rohilkhand, the Pathán inhabitants of, K. iii. 251; Khán
Bahádur Khán becomes su-
preme in, M. i. 332; the nature of his rule in, M. i.
333; his proclamation for extermination of Christians, K.
iii. 288; he fights with the
Thákurs, M. i. 333; the people sicken of Khán Bahádur
Khán's rule, and long for the
return of the English, M. i.
335; force with which rebels
hold district (May '58), M.
ii. 522; the rebels driven
from (May '58), M. ii. 540;
Capt. Boisragon strikes the
first blow at rebellion in (Jan.
9, '58), M. iii. 416; Lord
Canning insists on immediate
attack of (April '58), M. ii.
498; main posts of the rebels
in (April '58), M. ii. 500;
strength of mutineers from,
which reached Dehlí, K. ii.
565 *n.*; rebels of district
cross Rámgangá and occupy
Shamshábád (Jan. 25, '58),
M. ii. 312; their desperate
courage at Núriá (Aug. 29,
'58), M. iii. 276.
Rohillas, desperate fight with at
Goráris (Nov. 24), M. iii. 81:
Rohiní, murderous attack on
Major Macdonald, Adjutant

Rohiní—*cont.*
Leslie, and Dr. Grant, at (June 12), K. iii. 171, M. i. 37; the murderers are Sepoys of Major Macdonald's own regiment, M. i. 38; they are seized and hung in face of the regiment, M. i. 38.
Rohnee, *see* Rohiní.
Rohtak, mutiny at (June), K. ii. 546; the district brought to submission by Van Cortlandt (Oct.), M. ii. 107.
Rolland, Major, commands Native Infantry at Kolhápúr (May), M. iii. 37.
Roman Catholic community in Fort of A'grá, their reserved conduct, K. iii. 402.
Roorkhee, *see* Rúrkí.
Rose, Lieut., greatly distinguishes himself at attack on Morár (June 16, '58), M. iii. 217; he and Lieut. Waller capture rock-fortress of Gwáliár (June 20, '58), M. iii. 228; killed in capture of Gwáliár fort, M. iii. 228.
Rose, Major-Gen. Sir Hugh, K.C.B., his former services, M. iii. 134–136; his untiring care for his men, M. iii. 189; begins to operate near the Jamná (March '58), M. ii. 450.
Commands Bombay column in Central India (Dec.), M. iii. 136; takes up command at Máu (Dec. 16), M. iii. 134; goes to Sihor (Jan. 8, '58), M. iii. 138; marches from Sihor to Rathgarh (Jan. 16, '58), M. iii. 139; invests Rathgarh (Jan. 24, '58), M. iii. 139; drives rebels from town into fort of Rathgarh (Jan. 25, '58), M. iii. 140; opens breaching batteries against Rathgarh (Jan. 27, '58), M. iii. 141;

Rose Major-Gen.—*cont.*
Rájá of Bánpúr attempts to raise the siege of Rathgarh (Jan. 28, '58), M. iii. 141; rebels evacuate fort of Rathgarh (Jan. 28, '58), M. iii. 142; chases rebels from Rathgarh to the banks of the Bína, and defeats them (Jan. 30, '58), M. iii. 143.
Relieves Ságar (Feb. 3, '58), M. iii. 144; marches against Garhákot (Feb. 11, '58), M. iii. 145; attacks Garhákot, M. iii. 145; the rebels evacuate Garhákot (Feb. 12, '58), M. iii. 146; returns from Garhákot to Ságar (Feb. 17, '58), M. iii. 146.
Equips his force for march on Jhánsí, M. iii. 147; captures fort of Barodiá (Feb. 27, '58), M. iii. 148; threatens front and turns flank of Máltún pass (March 4, '58), M. iii. 148; stoutly resisted at pass of Madanpúr (March 4), M. iii. 149; carries Madanpúr pass by infantry charge, M. iii. 150; marches on Jhánsí (March 19, '58), M. iii. 153; takes ground near Jhánsí (March 20, '58), M. iii. 154; ordered to march on Chárkhárí (March 21, '58), M. iii. 155; Sir R. Hamilton authorises him to disobey order to march on Chárkhárí, M. iii. 156; appears before Jhánsí and reconnoitres (March 21, '58), M. iii. 156; invests Jhánsí (March 22, '58), M. iii. 159; effects breach in walls of Jhánsí (March 29, '58), M. iii. 160; Tántiá Topí advances to drive him from the town (March 31, '58), M. iii. 161; his critical position, M. iii. 162; he

Rose, Major-Gen.—*cont.*
attacks Tántiá Topí (April 1, '58), M. iii. 163; totally defeats Tántiá Topí, and captures every gun, M. iii. 165; he captures Jhánsí (April 4, '58), M. iii. 171; his loss in the capture of Jhánsí (April 3-5, '58), M. iii. 171.

Resolves to attack Kalpí, M. iii. 172; joins Major Gall at Púchh (May 1, '58), M. iii. 174; captures Lohárí near Kúnch (May '58), M. iii. 175; pursues Tántiá Topí to Kálpí (May 58), M. iii. 178; he makes flank march upon Kúnch, M. iii. 176; completely defeats rebels at Kúnch, M. iii. 177; advances from Kúnch to Gulaulí (May 15, '58), M. iii. 180; effects junction with Col. Maxwell at Gulaulí, M. iii. 181; opens attack on Kálpí (May 19, '58), M. iii. 183; defeats rebel attack of May 22, and captures Kálpí, M. iii. 186; occupies fort at Kálpí (May 23, '58), M. iii. 187.

Completely carries out the plan of campaign proposed by Sir R. Hamilton, M. iii. 188; clears the way for Gen. Whitlock, M. iii. 198; encounters the danger, and Gen. Whitlock enjoys the spoils, M. iii. 201.

Sends column in pursuit of rebels to Gopálpúr (May 25, '58), M. iii. 211; sends Brig. Stuart towards Gwáliár in pursuit of rebels, M. iii. 212; resigns command of Central India Field Force (June 3, '58), M. iii. 212.

Reassumes command on emergency (June 4, '58), M. iii. 213; severely reprimanded

Rose, Major-Gen.—*cont.*
by Sir Colin Campbell for assuming command unauthorised, M. iii. 213 *n.*; marches on Gwáliár (June 5, '58), M. iii. 214; joined by Brig. Robert Napier (June 16, '58), M. iii. 215; reaches Bahádurpúr (June 16, '58), M. iii. 215; attacks Morár (June 16, '58), M. iii. 216; captures Morár, M. iii. 218; marches to assist Brig. Smith (June 18, '58), M. iii. 222; captures Gwáliár city (June 19, '58), M. iii. 226; carries the heights near Gwáliár, M. iii. 225; prevents Tántiá Topí crossing into Khandesh (Nov. '58), M. iii. 346.

Recapitulation of his memorable campaign, M. iii. 231; his farewell order to Central India Field Force, M. iii. 232.

Becomes Commander-in-Chief of Bombay Presidency, M. iii. 232.

Rosser, Capt., said to have suggested pursuit of Mírat mutineers along the Dehlí road, K. ii. 67; his offer to cut off mutineers escaping from Mírat to Dehlí, K. ii. 663, 692.

Routine, baneful effects of, K. ii. 147; its oppressive character, M. i. 289; mars effect of punishment of 34th Regiment (April), K. i. 549; causes dangerous delay when excitement begins, K. i. 511; it is the safeguard of sedition, K. i. 510.

Rowcroft, Col., strength of his force in Tirhút, M. ii. 321; organises force at Tirhút (Nov.), M. ii. 321; marches against rebels at Sobanpúr (Dec. 26), M. ii. 322; defeats

THE HISTORIES OF THE INDIAN MUTINY. 169

Rowcroft, Col.—*cont.*
rebels at Sobanpúr, M. ii. 322; marches to Burhat Ghát on the Ghághrá (Dec. 27), M. ii. 322; attacks and defeats Muhammad Husain at Hariyá (June 18, '58), M. iii. 282; joins Jang Bahádur's force at Barárí (Jan. 19, '58), M. ii. 323; defeats the rebels at Phúlpúr (Jan. 19, '58), M. ii. 324; commands in Gorakhpúr (Feb. '58), M. ii. 451; encamps at Ámorhá (March '58), M. ii. 452; marches against entrenched camp at Belwá (March 4, '58), M. ii. 451; Mahndí Husain attacks him and is totally defeated (March 5, '58), M. ii. 452; he occupies Hír (June 25, '58), M. iii. 282; defeats Bálá Ráo at Tulsípúr (Dec. '58), M. iii. 293.

Rúiyá, description of fort of, M. ii. 504; Narpat Singh's desires to evacuate, M. ii. 505; Gen. Walpole attacks (April 15, '58), M. ii. 506; Narpat Singh beats off Gen. Walpole, M. ii. 507; and then evacuates fort (April 15, '58), M. ii. 508; Col. Adrian Hope sacrificed at useless attack of (April 15, '58), M. ii. 508; account of Adrian Hope's death at, M. iii. 513.

Rumours of coming of Persian army to India, in spring of 1857, K. ii. 35.

Rungo Bapojee, *see* Ranga Bápají.

Rúp Singh, escapes from Gwáliár (Jan. '58), M. iii. 308; heads the insurgents around I'táwá (July '58), M. iii. 309; occupies Ajítmál (July '58),

Rúp Singh—*cont.*
M. iii. 309; attacks Capt. Gordon (Aug. '58), M. iii. 309; defeated, and fort of Barhí captured, M. iii. 310; reappears at Kuwárí (Oct. '58), M. iii. 310; completely defeated at Kuwárí, M. iii. 310.

Rúrkí, engineering depôt, K. ii. 174; protection of, arranged by Col. Baird Smith (May 16), K. ii. 176; mutiny of sappers at, K. iii. 258; mutinous sappers disarmed at Murádábád, K. iii. 259; mutineers from plan an attack on Bíjnúr (May), M. iii. 402; Col. Coke organises transport for column at, M. ii. 513; column from, crosses the Ganges (April 17, '58), M. ii. 514.

Russell, Brig., commands fifth brigade at final attack on Lakhnau, M. ii. 172.

Russell, Dr., his remark on Sir Colin Campbell's extraordinary order to Gen. Outram, M. ii. 413 *n.*; his description of the plunder of the Qaisar Bágh (March 14, '58), M. ii. 394; his comment on Lord Canning's Oudh proclamation (March 20, '58), M. ii. 410; describes fury of troops at death of Adrian Hope, M. ii. 509 *n.*; his character of Adrian Hope, M. ii. 509; his eulogy of Capt. W. Peel, M. ii. 127.

Russia instigates Persia to seize Hirát (1856), K. i. 448 *n.*; expected to attack British in India in spring of 1857, K. ii. 36.

Rustam Sáh, shelters and provides for several Europeans, K. iii. 471; protects Lieut. Tucker, M. i. 406.

S.

Sa'ábat Alí, Nawáb of Oudh (1817), K. i. 118.
Sa'adat Khán, heads insurrection at Indor (July 1), M. i. 217; conflicting accounts of his office at Indor, M. i. 217 n.
Sabzí-Mandí, see Dehlí.
Sadasheo Rao, see Sadáshiv Ráo.
Sadáshiv Ráo, invited to rule Jhánsí by mutineers, K. iii. 366, 370.
Ságar, garrison of, M. iii. 96; military positions in, M. iii. 97; party of mistrusted Sepoys sent from against a rájá, M. iii. 96; the Sepoys at, hold the fort and treasury, M. iii. 97; Brig. Sage secures treasury of, M. iii. 99; he seizes fort of (June 30), M. iii. 100; mutiny at (July 1), M. iii. 100; loyalty of 31st N.I., M. iii. 100; fight between 31st and 42nd N.I. (July 7), M. iii. 100; victory of loyal 31st, and flight of 42nd N.I., M. iii. 101; state of country while under native control (Aug.), M. iii. 102; relieved by Sir Hugh Rose (Feb. 3, '58), M. iii. 144; Sir Hugh Rose leads troops against Garhákot (Feb. 11, '58), M. iii. 145; Sir Hugh Rose returns to (Feb. 17, '58), M. iii. 146; town occupied by Gen. Whitlock (March 5, '58), M. iii. 193.
Ságar and Narbadá territories, description of, M. iii. 88; historical sketch of, M. iii. 89; joined to North-West Provinces under Mr. Colvin

Ságar and Narbudá—*cont.*
(1855), M. iii. 89; Mr. Colvin proposes violent changes in, M. iii. 90; Capt. Ternan induces Mr. Colvin to abstain from great interference with, M. iii. 90; fretful condition of district of, in 1857, M. iii. 91.
Sage, Brig., commands at Ságar, M. iii. 96; sends party of mistrusted Sepoys against a rájá, M. iii. 96; sends troops to Lallatpúr (June 13), M. iii. 97; Sepoys hold both fort and treasury at Ságar against him, M. iii. 97; he secures the treasury at Ságar, M. iii. 99; and seizes the fort of Ságar (June 30), M. iii. 100; strengthens Ságar fort, and drills Christian community, M. iii. 101.
Sago's house, a post at Lakhnau Residency, M. i. 442.
Sáh Mall, Zamíndár of Bajrúl, his brigandage about Barauth (July), M. iii. 430; Mr. Dunlop marches against him, M. iii. 431; he evacuates Basaud on approach of Mr. Dunlop's party, M. iii. 431; he is defeated and killed by Mr. Dunlop's party (July), M. iii. 434; his death materially affects tranquillisation of district near Dehlí, M. iii. 434.
Sahúranpúr, description of civil station, M. i. 297; importance of station, M. i. 298; dangerous character of inhabitants, K. iii. 250; Europeans at, and garrison, M. i. 298; women and children sent to Masúrí (May 14), M. i. 299; held to its allegiance by noble exertions of officers, M. i. 300; boldness and prudence of officers at, M. i. 300; energetic conduct of Mr. Spankie

Sahāranpúr—*cont.*
the Magistrate, K. iii. 249;
Mr. Spankie preserves order
at, during May, M. iii. 420;
marauders appear in district
(June), M. iii. 422; Sepoys
accompany English and coerce
rebel villagers, K. iii. 250;
capture and execution of a
gang of marauders (June), M.
iii. 423.
Saharunpore, *see* Sahāranpúr.
Sahasrám, protected by Lieut.
Stanton (Oct.), M. ii. 445;
Col. Corfield fights his way
to (May 11, '58), M. ii. 480.
Sai'ad Ahmad Khán, the loyal
agent of Mr. Shakespear at
Bíjnúr (June), M. iii. 407;
he and Muhammad Rahmat
Khán directed by Mr. Shakespear
to take charge of Bíjnúr
(Aug. 6), M. iii. 411.
Sai'ad Mír Khán, his devoted
conduct at Mírat (May 10),
K. ii. 69 n.; his gallant services,
K. ii. 664.
Saif-ulláh Khán, commands Kiraulí
matchlockmen at A'grá,
M. i. 265; his men surrender
two guns to A'grá magazine,
M. i. 267.
St. George, Capt., death of, at
Lakhnau (March 9, '58), M.
ii. 374.
Sálar Jang, chief minister of the
Nizám, M. iii. 118; his character,
M. iii. 118; supports
Major Davidson fully, M. iii.
120; warns Major Davidson
of intended rising, M. iii.
121; firmly suppresses insurrection
(July 17), M. iii.
122; authorises formation of
Haidarábád column for service
in Central India (Aug.),
M. iii. 124.
Salder, Mr., killed at Kotá
(Oct. 15), M. ii. 569.

Sale, Capt., escapes from Lallatpúr
mutiny, M. iii. 98 n.
Sale Law, K. i. 157.
Sales of estates for small debts,
K. i. 178.
Salia Dahár, Brig. Douglas
overthrows rebels at (Nov.
24, '58), M. ii. 492.
Salkeld, Lieut., one of explosion
party at Kashmír gate, Dehlí,
M. ii. 32.
Saloní, Capt. Barrow, Deputy
Commissioner at, K. iii. 471,
M. i. 407; mutiny at (June
10), K. iii. 472; mutiny at
(June 9), M. i. 407; fugitives
from, rescued by Rájá
Hanmant Singh, K. iii. 472,
M. i. 407.
Salúmbar, Tántiá Topí draws
supplies from (Dec. '58), M.
iii. 356.
Salusbury, Capt., protects Outram's
first battery on the
Gúmtí (March 9, '58), M. ii.
375; distinguishes himself at
capture of Machhí Bháwan
(March 16, '58), M. ii. 401.
Sambalpúr, conferred on native
ruler by the British, K. i. 97;
annexation of, K. i. 98; Capt.
Leigh applies to Katák for
help (Sept.), M. ii. 440;
Commissioner of Katák sends
troops to support Capt.
Leigh, M. ii. 441; rebellion
shows itself in (Sept. 25),
M. ii. 440; Lieut. Hadow arrives
at (Nov. 4), M. ii. 440;
Capt. Knocker storms Shergátí
pass (Nov. 5), M. ii.
440; losses incurred by fever
in (Nov.), M. ii. 440; almost
every officer in, prostrated by
fever, M. ii. 441; race between
English and rebels to secure
the person of Apothecary
Hanson (Dec.), M. ii. 441;
Dr. Moore murdered by rebels

Sambalpúr—*cont.*
(Dec.), M. ii. 441; Sepoys, called Sebandís, raised for service in, M. ii. 441; Mr. Cockburn appointed to superintend (Dec. 19), M. ii. 441 a.; Capt. Wood arrives with reinforcements (Dec. 29), M. ii. 441 a.; Capt. Wood attacks and defeats main body of rebels in, M. ii. 441 a.; Súrandar Sahí, leader of rebellion escapes, M. ii. 441 a.

Sumbhulpore, *see* Sambalpúr.

Samuells, Mr., successor to Mr. W. Tayler at Patná, his character, K. iii. 189.

Sandíla, Hashmat Alí Chaudrí of, capture of his camp at Lakhnau (March 11, '58), M. ii. 380; Mr. Kavanagh proposes the capture of (July '58), M. iii. 284; stormed and captured by Capt. Dawson and Mr. Kavanagh (July 30, '58), M. iii. 284; attacked by rebels under Harichand (Oct. 3, '58), M. iii. 286; Capt. Dawson holds the place till relieved by Major Maynard (Oct. 6, '58), M. iii. 286.

Sánganír, Tántiá Topí takes up position near (Aug. 5, '58), M. iii. 321.

Sánglí, Native state of southern Maráthá country, M. iii. 20.

Sangrámpur, fugitives from Fathgarh reach, M. i. 343.

Sankhola, Chatgáon mutineers stopped at, by Rájá of Tiparah (Dec. 2), M. ii. 422.

Sanoda, Sir Hugh Rose destroys fort of (Feb. 8, '58), M. iii. 145.

Sánsí, mutiny at (July 2), M. i. 294.

Sánthália, district of Bhágalpúr, M. ii. 129; mutiny in (Aug. 12), M. ii. 139.

Sáran, district of Patná division, K. iii. 71 n., M. i. 40.

Sarpúr, Capt. Rice defeats Firoz Sháh at (Dec. 22, '58), M. iii. 364.

Sarun, *see* Sáran.

Sarúp Singh, Ráná of Udaipúr, M. i. 259.

Sassiah, scene of Brig. Polwhele's battle, *see* Sháhganj.

Sattarah, *see* Sitárá.

Saunders, Mr. Charles, collector, destroys Government paper at Murádábád (June 1), K. iii. 263; destroys Government paper at Murádábád (June 2), M. i. 331; escapes from Murádábád (June 3), M. i. 332.

Sávanúr, state of southern Maráthá country, M. iii. 20.

Saviell, Mr., killed at Kotá (Oct. 15), M. ii. 569.

Sáwan Mall, Díwán of Múltán, shot, K. i. 18.

Sáwant rebels, troublesome till they surrender (Nov. 20, '58), M. iii. 246.

Sáwant Wárí, Native state in Bombay Presidency, M. iii. 2.

Scamp, Midshipman, his good service in western Bihár, M. iii. 463.

Schneider, Capt., commands local corps at Kolhápúr (May), M. iii. 37.

Scindiah, *see* Sindhiá.

Scott, Capt., nobly leads fugitives from Náogáon, after death of Major Kirke, K. iii. 375; saves Mrs. Mawe's child on retreat from Náogáon, M. i. 196; an undecorated hero of the siege of Dehlí, K. iii. 579.

Scudamore, Major, threatens the pass of Máltún (March 4, '58), M. iii. 148.

Sealkote, *see* Syúlkot.

THE HISTORIES OF THE INDIAN MUTINY. 173

Seaton, Brig. Thomas, sent from Dehlí to Alígarh with convoy (Dec. 9), M. ii. 286; marches his column to Dehlí to take charge of convoy, M. ii. 118; strength of his party, M. ii. 286; joins Col. Farquhar at Alígarh, M. ii. 287; fights the rebels at Khásganj (Dec. 15), M. ii. 288; scatters the rebels at Khásganj (Dec. 15), M. ii. 289; drives the rebels from Pattiálí (Dec. 17), M. ii. 291; great effect of his victory at Pattiálí, M. ii. 292; marches on Mainpúrí (Dec. 23), M. ii. 293; defeats Tez Singh at Mainpúrí (Dec. 24), M. ii. 294; moves his camp to Bewar (Dec. 31), M. ii. 298.

Joins Sir Colin Campbell at Fathgarh (Jan. 4, '58), M. ii. 306; given command of troops at Fathgarh (Jan. '58), M. ii. 311; strengthens and prepares Fathgarh (Jan. '58), M. ii. 499; is joined at Bewar by Gen. Walpole (Jan. 23, '58), M. ii. 298; his junction with Gen. Walpole's force at Bewar (Feb. 3, '58), M. ii. 286; resolves to attack rebels (April '58), M. ii. 499; advances on Kankar, M. ii. 500; storms and carries the village of Kankar (April 6, '58), M. ii. 500.

Appointed to Sháhjahánpúr (May '58), M. ii. 541; defeats rebels near Sháhjahánpúr (Oct. 8, '58), M. iii. 287; his high opinion of Capt. Hodson's bravery and skill, M. ii. 295; his high opinion of the Maulaví, M. ii. 541.

Secrole, *see* Sikraul.
Secrora, *see* Sikrorá.

Securities, almost no depreciation of, K. iii. 49.
Sedition, routine the safeguard of, K. i. 510.
Segowlie, *see* Suggaulí.
Self-preservation, instinct of, a cause of mutiny, K. iii. 68.
Seniority system, effect of supersession under, K. i. 336 *n*.
Sepoy, the, who originated the greased cartridge story, K. i. 490.
Sepoy [*sipáhí*] Army, its origin, K. i. 204, 205; its extent, K. i. 201; its constitution, K. i. 205; diversity of opinion as to condition of, K. i. 329; its unsoundness denounced, K. i. 324; Lord Ellenborough's views on its control, K. i. 300.

Dangerous changes in dress (1805), K. i. 218; irritating changes in dress, equipment, and drill (1805), K. i. 217; grievances of (1806), K. i. 221; re-organisation of (1824), K. i. 264.

Influences of caste upon, K. i. 330; the policy of admixture of caste in, K. i. 331; castes and races of (in 1857), K. i. 621-626; the policy of admixture of nationalities in, K. i. 332; influence of system of promotion in, K. i. 335; effect of half-batta order upon the mind of (1830), K. i. 272; rate of compensation to, for variable prices of commodities, K. i. 316 *n*.; local and general service discussed, K. i. 333; general service enlistment introduced into Bengal, K. i. 466, 467; the presence or absence of Sepoy's family with, discussed, K. i. 334.

Abolition of corporal punishment in (1832), K. i.

Sepoy Army—*cont.*
272; revival of corporal punishment in (1842), K. i. 273; the troops useless for general purposes, K. i. 462; deteriorated in *morale* (1839), K. i. 273; summary of causes of its deterioration, K. i. 348.

Increase of British officers (1784), K. i. 211; selected officers appointed to command (1784–96), K. i. 213; re-organisation of (1796), K. i. 215; appointment to command in, attained by seniority (1796), K. i. 215; regulations of 1796 occasion a dangerous transition period, K. i. 223.

Denuded of officers for supply of civil posts, K. i. 457; danger of too many British officers with, K. i. 458; number of English officers with (1856), K. i. 337 *n.*; English officers of, their life in cantonment, K. i. 338; detachments of, commanded by boy-ensigns, K. i. 214 *n.*; dangerous proselytising officers in, K. i. 479; native officers lose rank in, K. i. 211; further loss of rank by native officers, K. i. 215.

Its supposed fidelity, K. i. 202, 210 and *n.*; unbounded confidence in, K. i. 328; the policy of confiding in, discussed, K. i. 340; its trust in commanders, K. i. 465 *n.*

First mutiny in Bengal (1764), K. i. 206; effect of annexation on, K. i. 276; excitement in, caused by greased cartridge story, K. i. 491, 497; its outburst expected by Sir Henry Lawence, K. i. 453.

Sepoy and English soldier compared, K. i. 254.
Sepoy and Sikh, enmity between, K. ii. 472.
Sepoy officers, K. i. 213; reduced in dignity, by progress of centralisation, K. i. 259; alienated from their regiments by increase of English society in India, K. i. 259; Staff employ, dissolves connection between officers and Sepoys, K. i. 260.

Sepoys; character of, K. i. 326; dread general service, K. i. 479; refuse to cross the sea (1824), K. i. 268; effect of Afghan war on (1838), K. i. 274; fear to enter Afghanistan (1842), K. i. 275; their opinion of annexation, K. i. 347 and *n.*; civil privileges of, K. i. 255, 619; taught to feel their own strength, K. i. 323; summary of causes weakening his attachment to his colours, K. i. 348; chronic state of fear of, K. iii. 67; object to the cartridge paper, K. i. 523; their suspicions numerous concerning the greased cartridges, K. i. 523; permitted to grease their own cartridges, K. i. 515; dread opinion more than actual pollution, K. ii. 66; often urged to mutiny by instinct of self-preservation, K. iii. 68; fear destruction of caste by overwhelming force of Europeans, K. i. 537; pride in their leaders, K. i. 255; reason for respecting their officer, K. i. 328.

Sepoys and officers, relations between (1809–22), K. i. 257; their disbelief of bad news, M. ii. 132.

Apparent inconsistency in

THE HISTORIES OF THE INDIAN MUTINY. 175

Sepoys—*cont.*
conduct of, K. ii. 189; spare the house and furniture of one European at Bíjagarh, M. ii. 93; daring and crafty reconnoitring by, M. ii. 494; extraordinary instance of personal daring among, M. iii. 79 *n.*; those of the 2nd Regiment endeavour to corrupt a Súbáhdár, K. i. 530; two of them found guilty of treasonable intentions (March), K. i. 531; delay in punishing Sepoys of 34th Regiment (April), K. i. 550.
First defeat of, on the Hindan (May 30), K. ii. 184; second defeat of, on the Hindan (May 31), K. ii. 186; third defeat of, at Badlí-kí-saráí (June 8), K. ii. 192; those at Syálkot offer commands in rebel army to two British officers, K. ii. 630; Lord Canning issues order on treatment of mutinous (July 31), M. i. 135; this order criticised, M. i. 137; Lord Canning's order a statesman-like measure, M. i. 137.
Serwa pass, last remnant of rebels scattered at, M. iii. 297.
Seton, Mr., his deference to the Mughál Emperor (1806), K. ii. 7.
Seton-Karr, Mr. George Berkeley, Collector and Magistrate of Balgáon, M. iii. 20; his character, M. iii. 20; his skill and eminent success, M. iii. 34; discovers and arrests a rebel emissary at Balgáon, M. iii. 27; uses his influence over chiefs to preserve order (July), M. iii. 31; endeavours to allay discontent among Maráthás, M. iii. 25; asks and receives plenary powers,

Seton-Karr, Mr.—*cont.*
M. iii. 30; removes the leader of disaffection from Balgáon, M. iii. 32; arrests a rebel emissary from Jámkhandí (July), M. iii. 32; blows from guns two rebels at Balgáon, M. iii. 33; begins to disarm his district (Aug. 20), M. iii. 33; applies to be relieved by part of his duties (April '58), M. iii. 234; stripped of his political duties, M. iii. 235; anxious about effect of Mr. Manson's appointment, M. iii. 236; induces the chief of Nargund to disarm (May '58), M. iii. 238; specially thanked by Lord Elphinstone and Lord Canning, yet allowed to die without reward, M. iii. 35 *n.*
Settlement, necessity for promptitude, K. i. 167; complicated by rent-free tenures, K. i. 168; settlement operations, K. i. 156; as carried out in the North-West Provinces (1833), K. i. 158, 173; its effect, K. i. 165.
Seymour, Major, his gallantry at Pannú (Oct. 8, '58), M. iii. 287.
Sháh A'lam, rescued from Maráthás by Lord Lake, K. ii. 3; protected by the English, K. ii. 3; succeeded by his son Akbar Sháh (1806), K. ii. 6.
Sháh Mahomed Hussén, *see* Sháh Muhammad Husain.
Sháh Muhammad Husain, leading Wahábí of Patná, M. i. 52.
Sháh Najíf, at Lakhnau, description of, M. ii. 188; the attack on (Nov. 16), M. ii. 189; assault of, M. ii. 192; confusion in bringing up sup-

Sháh Najíf—*cont.*
ports, M. ii. 190; critical position of affairs at, M. ii. 191; entrance to, discovered by Sergeant Paton, M. ii. 194 *n.*; entered by Col. Hope at a crevise, M. ii. 194; its capture (Nov. 16), M. ii. 194.

See also Lakhnau.

Sháhábád, district of Patná Division, K. iii. 71 *n.*, M. i. 40; harried by scattered troops of Amar Singh (May '58), M. ii. 481.

Sháhganj, Nímach mutineers reach, M. i. 269; Brig. Polwhele meets Nímach mutineers at Sassiah near, M. i. 271; battle of (July 5), K. iii. 384; Brig. Polwhele hesitates to charge, M. i. 272; and has an artillery duel with mutineers, M. i. 272; artillery ammunition expended before Infantry advance, K. iii. 386; charge of Sepoy cavalry, M. i. 273; Brig. Polwhele orders advance when too late, M. i. 274; splendid conduct of Capt. D'Oyley, M. i. 274; gallant charge of Capt. Prendergast's volunteers, M. i. 274; bravery of British mounted militiamen, K. iii. 389; the British capture village, M. i. 275; retreat of the English, K. iii. 390, M. i. 276; Capt. Pearson tries to save his disabled guns, M. i. 276; Nímach mutineers march from, to Dehlí, M. i. 276.

The stronghold of Rájá Mán Singh, K. iii. 462, M. i. 398; Mán Singh besieged in, by rebels (July '58), M. iii. 271; rebels raise the siege, M. iii. 271.

Sháhgarh, Rájá of, receives charge of British officers from Lallatpur, M. iii. 98 *n.*; attacked and defeated by Major Orr (April 30, '58), M. iii. 174; ordered to concentrate on Gwáliár (June 1, '58), M. iii. 210.

Sháhjahánpúr, garrison and English residents at, K. iii. 278; mutiny at (May 31), K. iii. 279, M. i. 318; Sepoys attack English in church, K. iii. 279, M. i. 318; the ladies are placed in the turret, M. i. 319; native servants bring arms to English in the church, K. iii. 281, M. i. 319; Sikhs hurry to church to protect English, M. i. 320; escape of English from the church, K. iii. 281.

The massacre at, K. ii. 409; murders committed during mutiny, M. i. 319; murder of Europeans in cantonments, (May 31), M. i. 320; fugitives from, reach Rájá of Powáin, M. i. 320; other fugitives reach Mohamdí (June 4), K. iii. 459, M. i. 321; after leaving Mohamdí fugitives overtaken and butchered, K. iii. 460.

All official buildings in, destoyed by Náná Sáhib (April '58), M. ii. 522; the rebels evacuate (April 30, '58), M. ii. 521; re-occupied by the English, M. ii. 522; the Maulaví enters, and besieges the English garrison (May 3, '58), M. ii. 533; Brig. Jones enters, but cannot drive out the Maulaví's troops (May 11–14, '58), M. ii. 536; reinforcements flock in to the Maulaví in, M. ii. 536.

Head of the Maulaví ex-

Shábjahánpúr—cont.
 posed at (June 6, '58), M. ii.
 544; Sir Thomas Seaton defeats rebels near (Oct. 8 '58),
 M. iii. 287.
Shahjehanpoor, see Shábjahánpúr.
Sháhpúr, Mr. Seton-Karr disarms people at (Aug. 20), M. iii. 33.
Sháhzádas, or Princes of Dehlí, captured by Hodson, K. iii. 648-650.
Shaikh Ghasíta, arrest of, at Patná, M. i. 57; hanged there, M. i. 57.
Shaikh Paltú, saves the life of Lieut. Baugh at Bárákpúr, K. i. 539.
Shakespear, Mr. A., Collector and Magistrate at Bíjnúr (May), M. iii. 400; calls for and receives the assistance of natives in suppressing disorder, M. iii. 402; attacks and stops prisoners escaping from Bíjnúr jail (May 21), M. iii. 403; Hindú zamíndárs and others assist him to restore order in Bíjnúr (May 28), M. iii. 404; secures all the treasure at Bíjnúr in a well, M. iii. 404; he induces Nawáb of Najíbábád to retire from Bíjnúr, M. iii. 405; sends his native infantry to head-quarters (June 3), M. iii. 406; sends the treasure safely from Bíjnúr, M. iii. 406; leaves Bíjnúr for ten days to the care of Nawáb of Najíbábád (June 7), M. iii. 408; retires with officers and ladies to Rúrkí (June 11), M. iii. 409; directs Muhammad Rahmat Khán and Sáyad Ahmad Khán to take charge of Bíjnúr (Aug. 6), M. iii. 611; starts from Rúrkí with troops

Shakespear, Mr. A.—cont.
 and in five days reconquers Bíjnúr (April 17, '58), M. iii. 417; his skill in re-organising Bíjnúr, M. iii. 417-419; his remarkable services left unrewarded, M. iii. 419.
Shakespear, Capt., storms Singhorá pass in Chútiá Nágpúr (Jan. 9, '58), M. ii. 441 b.
Shamsábád, rebels occupy city, M. ii. 312; Col. Adrian Hope advances to attack them (Jan. 26, '58), M. ii. 312; defeat of rebels (Jan. 27, '58), M. ii. 313.
Shamshír Singh, the Nipálese leader, defeats rebels at Mandorí (Sept. 19), M. ii. 318.
Shankarpúr, Bení Mádhava chief of, M. iii. 291; Generals Hope Grant, Wetherall, and Pinckney, march on (Nov. 8, '58), M. iii. 291; rebels delay Col. Evelegh's march on (Nov. 8, 9, '58), M. iii. 291; rebels escape from (Nov. 9, '58), M. iii. 291; occupied by Gen. Hope Grant, M. iii. 292.
Shankar Sháh, Rájá, and son, blown from guns at Jabalpúr (Sept. 18), M. iii. 103.
Shannon brigade, its strength, M. ii. 126, 128; names of officers of, M. ii. 126, 128; reaches Alláhábád (Sept. 2), M. ii. 128.
 See also Peel, Capt. William.
Sheeah, see Shí'ah.
Sheikh Pultoo, see Shaikh Paltú.
Shekh Ghasíta, see Shaikh Ghasíta.
Sheorajpúr, see Sivarájpúr.
Shere Singh, see Shír Singh.
Sherer, Col. George Moyle, commands at Jalpáígorí, K.

Sherer, Col.—*cont.*
iii. 173, M. i. 138; his antecedents, and character, M. i. 138, 139; fears order to disarm his men, K. iii. 169; declares that he will resign his commission rather than disarm his men, K. iii. 174; he boldly allows his excited troops to parade with loaded arms, K. iii. 175; seizes and condemns to death four conspirators in his regiment, M. i. 139; blows the four conspirators from guns, M. i. 140; blows from guns two troopers, at Jalpáígorí (Dec.), M. ii. 430; succeeds in preventing mutiny at Jalpáígorí, K. iii. 177; brings his regiment safely through the crisis, M. i. 140.

Sherer, Lieut., defeats Chatgáon mutineers at Látú (Dec. 18), M ii. 424.

Sherer, Mr., his description of the road from Alláhábád to Fathpúr, K. ii. 368.

Sherghátí, Sir Colin Campbell nearly captured at (Oct. 29), M. ii. 142.

Sherriff, Lieut., defeats Bhijalpúr rebels (May '58), M. iii. 211 *n*.

Shír Singh, sent to assist Edwardes against Múltán, K. i. 32; traitorously goes over to Múlráj, K. i. 33; surrenders to the British (1849), K. i. 46.

Shí'ahs and Sunnís, K. ii. 39.

Shorápúr, situation and history of, M. iii. 125; Major Hughes arrives at (Feb. 8, '58), M. iii. 128.

Shorápúr, the Rájá of, reason for his disaffection, M. iii. 126; Capt. Campbell returns from, M. iii. 127; connives at

Shorápúr—*cont.*
murder of Capt. Campbell, M. iii. 127; attempts to ensnare Capt. Wyndham (Feb. 7), M. iii. 127; attacks Capt. Wyndham, but is repulsed, M. iii. 128; flies from his fort and is captured by Sálar Jang, M. iii. 129; his sentence and suicide, M. iii. 129*n*.

Shortt, Brig.-Gen., commands at Bombay, his character, M. iii. 43; distrusts the police of Bombay (Sept.), M. iii. 47.

Showers, Brig., attacks Ludlow Castle at Dehlí (Aug. 12), K. ii. 650; leads a column to the west of Dehlí (Oct.), M. ii. 107; strength of his column, M. ii. 108; captures Jhájar (Oct. 18), M. ii. 108; result of his expedition in October, M. ii. 109; commands at A'grá (March '58), M. iii. 310; scatters rebels at Báh (March 20, '58), M. iii. 311; captures rebel ringleaders at Kachrú, M. iii. 311; escorts Sindhiá into A'grá (June 2, '58), M. iii. 314; covers Bharatpúr from retreating Tántiá Topí (June 19, '58), M. iii. 315; surprises and scatters Tántiá Topí's troops at Diwásá (Jan. 16, '59), M. iii. 366.

Showers, Capt. Charles, Political Agent at Udaipúr, K. iii. 353, M. i. 259, iii. 325; his views of Rájpútáná affairs, K. iii. 686; wins the Maháráná of Udaipúr to the British cause, K. iii. 356; rescues a party of fugitives from Nímach, K. iii. 356; his disobedience of Col. G. Lawrence's orders, K. iii. 684, M. i. 260; dismissed from political employment, K. iii. 685, M. i. 260.

THE HISTORIES OF THE INDIAN MUTINY. 179

Shute, Capt., leads sortie at Lakhnau (Sept. 29), M. ii. 155; commands 64th Regiment advancing from Lakhnau Residency (Nov. 16), M. ii. 206.
Sibbald, Brig., commands at Barailí, M. i. 302; returns to Barailí (May 19), M. i. 307; murdered at Barailí (May 31), M. i. 311.
Siege of Múltán (1848–49), K. i. 39.
Siege train, preparation of, K. ii. 146.
Signolí, see Suggaulí.
Sihor, Col. Durand's Cavalry demand to retreat on, M. i. 238, 240; Col. Durand and party reach (July 4), M. i. 241.
Sikandar Bágh, its position and strength, M. ii. 180; critical position of English during attack on (Nov. 16), M. ii. 180; Travers knocks a hole in wall of, M. ii. 181; the assault of, M. ii. 182; daring leap of Ensign Cooper, M. ii. 182; main body force the gate, and capture the place, M. ii. 185; the entire rebel garrison slaughtered (Nov. 16), M. ii. 187; splendid daring of Cooper and Ewart at assault of, neglected, M. ii. 186.
  See also Lakhnau.
Sikar, Col. Holmes surprises and defeats Tántiá Topí at (Jan. 21, '59), M. iii. 367.
Sikh army, surrenders (1849), K. i. 46.
Sikh Sirdárs, injured by annexation of the Panjáb, K. i. 58 n.; offer their services to the Commissioner of Banáras (May), K. ii. 205.
Sikh prophecy of the sack of Dehlí, K. ii. 420.

Sikh war, the first, end of, K. i. 2; the second, beginning of, K. i. 22, 35.
Sikh and Sepoy, enmity between, K. ii. 472.
Sikhs, enlisted by Sir John Lawrence in the Panjáb, K. ii. 472; additional enlistment of, K. i. 470; Capt. Rattray's regiment, M. i. 44; their compatriots driven into revolt at Banáras (June 4), K. ii. 224; they revolt at Jánpúr in revenge for attack on their brethren at Banáras, K. ii. 238; they are reviled and taunted while on march to Patná, M. i. 47; put down rising at Patná (July 3), M. i. 56; their faithfulness at Sháhjahánpúr, M. i. 320; they bravely beat off a body Kols in Singhbhúm (Dec.), M. ii. 439.
Sikraul, English quarters at Banáras, K. ii. 201.
Sikrí, defeat of Gújars at, by Mr. Dunlop (July), M. iii. 438.
Sikrorá, troops stationed at, K. iii. 473, M. i. 389; Capt. G. W. Boileau commands at, K. iii. 473; Mr. C. Wingfield removes women and children to Lakhnau, K. iii. 474; Capt. Forbes escorts ladies and children from, M. i. 391; Rájá of Balrámpúr undertakes to protect refugees from, M. i. 391; Mr. C. Wingfield retires to Gondá (June 9), K. iii. 475, M. i. 392; officers ride off to Balrámpúr, M. i. 392; Lieut. Bonham bravely remains alone, K. iii. 476, M. i. 393; mutiny at (June 9), M. i. 392; Lieut. Bonham forced by his own men to fly to Lakhnau, K. iii. 477, M. i. 393.

12 *

Simla, unprotected state of, K. ii. 145 and *n.*; threatened attack of (May), K. ii. 143; the two days' panic at, K. ii. 144.

Simmons, Major, his death in sortie at Lakhnau (Sept. 29), M. ii. 155.

Simpson, Major, his services in Western Bihar, M. ii. 436.

Simpson, Quartermaster Sergeant, his bravery at Rúiyá (April 15, '58), M. ii. 507.

Simrí, Col. Evelegh captures fort of (Nov. 9, '58), M. iii. 291.

Sindh, war with (1843), K. i. 276; annexation of (1843), K. i. 276; how it became a Bombay province, K. i. 297; the difficulty in garrisoning, K. i. 289; garrisoning of, a cause of disunion to English authorities, K. i. 321; effect of annexation on Sepoy allowances, M. iii. 473.

Sindhia, Mahárájá Jaijí Ráo, his territory, M. i. 204; his former history, M. i. 151; his martial instincts, K. iii. 311; his great influence in India, M. iii. 206; advantages of his visit to Calcutta, K. iii. 312; has Dinkar Ráo for Díwán, K. iii. 311.

His military force, K. iii. 309 *n.*; the constitution of his Contingent, M. i. 169; distrusts his own Contingent, M. i. 169; knows of the defection of his Contingent, K. iii. 313.

The difficulties of his position, K. iii. 315; the question of his fidelity, K. iii. 309, 310; his loyalty, M. i. 176; the importance of his loyalty, M. iii. 488; probable reasons for his loyalty, M. iii. 206;

Sindhia, Mahárájá—*cont.*
holds the fate of India in his hands (May-Sept.), M. iii. 488; recognises the friendship and strength of the British, M. i. 152; he accurately gauges the crisis, M. i. 151; warns the Resident of the general character of the revolt, M. i. 153; resolves to support the English cause, M. i. 153.

He is applied to by Mr. Colvin for aid, M. i. 153; sends troops to protect A'grá (May 16), K. iii. 209, M. i. 154; sends his body-guard into A'grá (May 31), K. iii. 313, M. i. 169.

Part of his Contingent mutinies at Hátrás (May 26), M. i. 293; suggests the removal of women and children to Residency, M. i. 170; his Contingent resent the removal of women and children, M. i. 170; he protects English women and children, K. iii. 314; he sends troops to Alígarh, M. i. 292; outbreak of his Contingent (June 14), K. iii. 316, M. i. 173, 174; helps fugitive women and children to A'grá, K. iii. 318; unable to protect Europeans (June 15), K. iii. 319; agrees to keep his revolted troops at Gwáliár, if possible, K. iii. 320; keeps Central Indian mutineers in check during August, M. ii. 95; his joy at fall of Dehlí, M. ii. 147.

Supplies Sir Hugh Rose with forage, &c., during siege of Jhánsí, M. iii. 159; he is attacked by Tántiá Topí (May 30, '58), M. iii. 205; marches out against Tántiá Topí (June 1, '58), M. iii.

Sindhia, Mahárájá—*cont.*
208; his troops desert to Tántiá Topí, M. iii. 209; he flies to A'grá, M. iii. 209; and is escorted honourably into A'grá (June 2, '58), M. iii. 314; marches to Dholpúr to join Sir Hugh Rose (June 16, '58), M. iii. 315; his gratitude to English after defeat of Tántiá Topí (July '58), M. iii. 331.

Sindhwáo, Gen. Michel defeats Ráo Sáhib at (Oct. '58), M. iii. 340.

Sindia, *see* Sindhiá.

Singhbhúm, insurrection at (Dec.), M. ii. 438; Capt. Hale suppresses insurrection, M. ii. 439.

Singhpúr, the rebel Dal Ganjan captured and executed at (Nov.), M. iii. 108.

Silhát, boldness of authorities in, preserves order east of Calcutta (Jan. '58), M. ii. 425.

Siprí, trial and death of Tántiá Topí at (April 18, '59), M. iii. 380.

Siraulí, Col. Christie forces rebels to evacuate (March '58), M. ii. 450.

Sirdárpúr, plundered by mercenaries of Dhár and Amjherá (July), M. iii. 69.

Sirmúr regiment of Gorkhas, garrison Dehrá Dún (May), M. iii. 419; their fidelity proved before Dehlí, K. ii. 194 *n.*

Sioni, *see* Siúní.

Sirohí, one of Rájpút states, M. i. 245 *n.*

Sironj, Tántiá Topí occupies (Sept. '58), M. iii. 337; last hiding place of the rebels in Central India (April '69), M. iii. 376.

Sirpúra, rebels fall back on from Núriá (Aug. 29, '58), M. iii. 276; Capt. S. Browne leads attack on (Aug. 30, '58), M. iii. 277; he gallantly captures a gun there, M. iii. 277; but is severely wounded, M. iii. 278; total defeat of rebels (Aug. 30, '58), M. iii. 279.

Sirsa, Gen. Walpole expels the rebels from (April 22, '58), M. ii. 510.

Sítábaldí, at Nágpúr, its description, M. iii. 113; strengthened as a place of refuge, M. iii. 114.

Sítápúr, Mr. G. J. Christian, Commissioner at, K. iii. 452, M. i. 377; incendiarism at (May 27), M. i. 377; Sepoys act loyally (June 1), M. i. 378; Mr. G. J. Christian secures the women and children in his own house (June 1), K. iii. 454, M. i. 379.

Sepoys of the 10th Irreg. Cavalry refuse the flour served out (June 2), M. i. 378; mutiny at (June 3), K. iii. 455, M. i. 379; murder of Col. Birch (June 3), K. iii. 456; murder of Mr. Christian and family (June 3), K. iii. 456, M. i. 380; murder of twenty-four English people during mutiny, M. i. 382; list of victims, and of the few who escaped, K. iii. 457; fugitives from, reach Maithaulí, M. i. 388; they remain at Maithaulí for five months, K. iii. 484, M. i. 381; they are ordered to leave Maithaulí (Oct. 25), K. iii. 485; and are brought to Lakhnau in chains, K. iii. 486; they are lodged in Qaisar Bágh, Lakhnau, K. iii. 487; and are at last shot

Sítápúr—*cont.*
at Lakhnau (Nov. 16), M. i. 389; one child escapes from the Qaisar Bágh, K. iii. 490; the two surviving women are rescued during storming of Lakhnau (March 19, '58), K. iii. 492, M. i. 389 *n.*, ii. 438 *n.*

Narrative of flight of Mr. M. Jackson's party from, K. iii. 482; Lieut. Lester's party of fugitives reach Lakhnau in safety, M. i. 381; Mr. Phillips's party lie concealed for ten months, till rescued by Lord Clyde's army, M. i. 381; one party of fugitives assisted by zamíndár of Rámkot, M. i. 381; one party of fugitives reach the Dhaurerá Rájá, but are taken prisoners to Lakhnau, M. i. 382.

Sitárá, Rájá Appá Sáhib dies (1848), K. i. 48; the status of the Princes of, K. i. 71; annexation of, its justice discussed, K. i. 87; annexed by the Court of Directors (1849), K. i. 74; sovereignty of, assumed by right of lapse, K. i. 71.

Síuní, part of Ságar territory, M. iii. 88.

Sivarájpúr, battle of (Dec. 9), M. ii. 278.

Sivaráj Singh, gallant Sepoy at Lakhnau, M. ii. 157 *n.*

Skene, Capt. Alexander, Commissioner at Jhánsí, K. iii. 362, M. i. 183, iii. 90; has perfect confidence in troops at Jhánsí (June 3), K. iii. 363; retires to Fort of Jhánsí (June 6), K. iii. 364; tries to obtain safe-conduct from Rání of Jhánsí, K. iii. 367; he and the rest of the garrison are massacred (June 8), K. iii. 369.

See also Jhánsí.

Sleeman, Col., his character, K. i. 134; sent to Ságar and Narbadá territories by Lord Ellenborough, M. iii. 89; suppresses *Thugí*, K. i. 139; afterwards becomes Resident at Lakhnau, M. iii. 89; his description of Oudh Talúqdárs, K. iii. 422; report on the fearful corruption in Oudh (1850), K. i. 135; extracts from his diary, K. i. 135 *n.*; he is opposed to annexation policy, K. i. 136 *n.*; but in favour of assuming the Government of Oudh, K. i. 136; and urges that no pecuniary profit should be derived therefrom, K. i. 138.

Sleeman, Sir William, in favour of promotion by selection, K. i. 336; his anecdote of Metcalfe House, Dehlí, K. ii. 543.

Smith, Capt., arrests mutinous Sikhs at Derá Ismáíl Khán (July 20, '58), M. iii. 306.

Smith, Brig., moves on Kotá-kisaráí, M. iii. 214; occupies Kotá-kí-saráí (June 17, '58), M. iii. 218; bravely carries the defile near Kotá-kí-saráí M. iii. 220; reinforced by Sir H. Rose (June 18, '58), M. iii. 222; captures Phúl Bágh, at Gwáliár (June 19, '58), M. iii. 226; occupies Siprí (June '58), M. iii. 318.

Rejects Mán Singh's plea, and attacks him (Aug. 7, '58), M. iii. 334; sends to Gwáliár for reinforcements, M. iii. 334.

Smith, Col., commands at Fathgarh, M. i. 335; sends women and children from Fathgarh to Káhnpúr (June 4), M. i. 335; induces Sepoys to destroy bridge of boats at Fath-

Smith, Col.—*cont.*
garh, M. i. 336; prepares fort at Fathgarh for defence, M. i. 338; takes shelter in fort at Fathgarh, M. i. 337; gallantly defends fort at Fathgarh, K. iii. 298; evacuates fort at Fathgarh, K. iii. 300.

Smith, Major Baird, his character, M. ii. 4; exhaustless energy of his character, K. iii. 547; provides for defence of Rúrkí (May), K. ii. 175; despatches troops from Rúrkí to Mírat, K. ii. 175; saves Rúrkí, K. ii. 177.
Appointed to command Engineers at Dehlí, and flies thither (July 3), K. ii. 563; his opinion of Gen. Barnard, K. ii. 568; describes Gen. Anson's plan of campaign, K. ii. 149; counsels assault of Dehlí (July 6), K. ii. 573; urges Gen. Wilson to immediate action, K. iii. 553, M. ii. 5; works on, in despite of wounds and sickness, M. ii. 5.
Desponding letter of Brig. Wilson to (Aug. 20), M. ii. 2 n.; his answer to the letter, M. ii. 5; Brig. Wilson yields to his opinion as to the necessity for assaulting Dehlí, M. ii. 6; but throws responsibility of assault on him, M. ii. 6; his intimate knowledge of the interior of Dehlí, K. iii. 588; his plan for attacking Dehlí (Sept. 1), M. ii. 10; insists on continuing assault of Dehlí after first day (Sept. 14), K. iii. 618, M. ii. 55.

Smith, Major Percy, death of, at Lakhnau (March 6, '58), M. ii. 373.

Smith, Sergeant, one of explo-

Smith, Sergeant—*cont.*
sion party at Kashmír gate, Dehlí, M. ii. 32.

Smyth, Col. Carmichael, commands 3rd Cavalry at Mírat (May), K. ii. 43; his character, K. ii. 43, 44; informs Gen. Anson of dangerous condition of the army (April), K. ii. 44; orders the parade at Mírat which occasioned the Mutiny (April 24), K. i. 567; his conduct during revolt at Mírat (May 10), K. ii. 63; believes he saves India by provoking mutiny at Mírat, K. ii. 108.

Soane, *see* Son.

Sobanpúr, Col. Rowcroft defeats rebels at (Dec. 26), M. ii. 322.

Soháwal, feudatory in Ságar territory, M. iii. 88.

Soláuu, the people of, release Toráb Alí from captivity in Dhauláua, M. iii. 435; Mr. Dunlop gives Dhauláua land to people of, as reward of loyalty, M. iii. 436.

Somerset, Sir Henry, Commander-in-Chief of Bombay Presidency, M. iii. 13; supports Major Follett's objection to move from Aurangábád (June), M. iii. 16; at length authorises advance from Aurangábád (July 10), M. iii. 17.

Son, the river dividing Patná from Shábábád, M. i. 75.
Dánápúr mutineers allowed to cross, K. iii. 107.
Capt. French destroys rebel boats on the (Sept. 20, '58), M. ii. 484; Mr. Probyn destroys rebel boats on the (Oct. 14, '58), M. ii. 484.

Soonee, *see* Sunní.

Soorut Singh, *see* Súrat Singh.

Sorai, rebels evacuate fort of, M. iii. 150.
Soráou, sacked by Oudh rebels (July '58), M. iii. 279; Lord Canning sends field force to clear district around, M. iii. 280.
Sotheby, Capt., reaches Calcutta in the *Pearl* (Aug. 8), K. iii. 185, M. i. 141; commands *Pearl* brigade, M. ii. 128; attacks and captures fort of Chandípúr (Feb. '58), M. ii. 451.
Souter, Mr. Frank, tracks and captures chief of Nargúnd (June 3, '58), M. iii. 245.
Spankie, Mr. Robert, Magistrate at Saháraupúr, M. i. 299; sends women and children to Masúrí (May 14), M. i. 299; preserves order at Saháraupúr during, M. iii. 420.
Special legislation, after outbreak of Mutiny, K. ii. 133.
Spence, Private, his bravery at Rúiyá (April 15, '58), M. ii. 507.
Speke, Capt., killed at the storming of Dehlí (Sept.), M. iii. 425 n.
Spens, Ensign, killed at capture of Bálábet fort, M. iii. 99 n.
Spottiswoode, Capt., killed at Nasírábád (May 28), M. i. 253.
Spottiswoode, Col. Henry, shoots himself on mutiny of his regiment, K. ii. 485.
Stack, Lieut., his gallantry in defence of his convoy, near Rámpúr (Dec. '58), M. iii. 364.
Stalker, Gen., appointed to commands Persian expedition of 1856, K. i. 422.
Stanton, Lieut., his services in Western Bihár, M. ii. 436; protects Sahasrám (Oct.), M. ii. 445.

Steel, Capt., commands 17th N.I. at Gorakhpúr, M. iii. 449; his Sepoys refuse to obey orders (June 6), M. iii. 450; he and Mr. Wynward prevent attempt of Sepoys to mutiny (June 7), M. iii. 450.
Stephenson, Major, leads sortie at Lakhnau (Sept. 27), M. ii. 154; killed at Lakhnau (Oct. 5), M. ii. 158.
Sterling, Major, leads the 64th Regiment right upon Náná Sáhib's guns, K. ii. 381; killed at Káhnpúr (Nov. 28), M. ii. 251.
Steuart, Brig., commands Sihor column of Central India Field Force, M. iii. 137; commands reserve of right attack at storming of Jhánsí (April 3, '58), M. iii. 166.
Stevens, Capt., surprises camp of Chatgáon mutineers, and captures their arms, M. ii. 425; defeats Chatgáon mutineers near Manipúr (Jan. 12, '58), M. ii. 425.
Stewart, Capt., and wife murdered at Gwáliár (June 14), K. iii. 317, M. i. 174; his distinguished conduct at capture of the Barracks, Lakhnau (Nov. 16), M. ii. 188; his daring capture of two guns, M. ii. 197.
Stewart, Lieut., severely wounded in attack on Shorápúr (Feb. 8, '58), M. iii. 128.
Stockley, Col., commands Bhíls at Indor, M. i. 209.
Stuart, Col. C. S., succeeds Gen. Woodburn in command of Central Indian column (June), M. i. 243, iii. 16; arrives at Aurangábád, and leads his troops to Asírgarh (July 12), M. iii. 17; arrives at Asírgarh, and joins Col. Durand (July 22), M. iii. 60; joined

Stuart, Col.—*cont.*
by Capt. S. Orr and part of Haidarábád Contingent (July 28), M. iii. 61; marches his column to Máú (Aug. 2), M. i. 243, iii. 61.
Commands Máú column of Central India Field Force, M. iii. 137; marches on Chandairí (March 5), M. iii. 151; drives the rebels from Khúkwásás (March 5, '58), M. iii. 152; storms and captures Chandairí (March 17, '58), M. iii. 153; outflanks Tántiá Topí's right at Jhánsí (April 1, '58), M. iii. 164.
Commands reserve of left attack at storming of Jhánsí, M. iii. 167; forces his way into Jhánsí (April 3, '58), M. iii. 167; leads right of left attack at storming of Jhánsí, M. iii. 167; his gallantry at Kálpí (May 22, '58), M. iii. 185; sent towards Gwáliár in pursuit of rebels, M. iii. 212; attacks rebel left at Kotá-kísaráí (June 19, '58), M. iii. 223.

Strutt, Lieut, his gallantry in the Málwá campaign, M. iii. 87; his accurate artillery fire causes rebels to evacuate Garhákot, M. iii. 146.

Subsidiary system, its effects, K. iii. 310.

Subzee-mundee, *see* Sabzí-Mandí.

Succession to property, interference with native views concerning, K. i. 189; native memorials concerning interference with, K. i. 189 *n*.

Suggaulí, Major J. Holmes commands Irregulars at, K. iii. 102; he prevents outbreak at, M. i. 58; mutiny at (July 25), K. iii. 106, M. i. 72, 73; murder of Major Holmes and

Suggaulí—*cont.*
wife, M. i. 73; murder of European residents generally, K. iii. 107.

Sultánpúr, officers and troops stationed at, K. iii. 470, M. i. 405; Col. Fisher commands at, K. iii. 469; Mr. Block, principal civil officer at, M. i. 405.
Mr. Block induces Col. Fisher to send the ladies to Alláhábád (June 6), M. i. 405; mutiny of military police (June 8), M. i. 406; general mutiny at (June 9), K. iii. 470; murder of Col. Fisher, K. iii. 470, M. i. 406; murder of Capt. Gibbings, M. i. 406; murder of Mr. Block and Mr. Stroyan, M. i. 406; Lieut. Tucker escapes from, and reaches Banáras, M. i. 406; Yazín Khán slaughters civilians he had engaged to protect, K. iii. 471; Rustam Sáh protects fugitives from, K. iii. 471.
Battle of (Feb. 23, '58), M. ii. 334; rebels retreat to (July '58), M. iii. 271; Brig. Horsford appears against (Aug. 12, '58), M. iii. 272; rebels attack Gen. Hope Grant, are defeated and fly (Aug. 28, '58), M. iii. 273.

Sultánpúr, Názim of, *see* Mahndí Husain.

Supreme Council, Members of, in 1856, K. i. 387; Commander-in-Chief has a seat at, but seldom occupies his place, K. i. 392; the Council of 1856, lacking in military knowledge, K. i. 392; opinion of, as to removal of Mughál sovereigns from Dehlí, K. ii. 25; its members awake to the great danger, K. i. 594.

Supremacy of the British in India, declared by Lord Hastings, K. ii. 8.
Sunnís and Shí'ahs, K. ii. 39.
Súrandar Sahí, defeated and almost captured, M. ii. 441 a.
Súrat Singh (Sardár), nobly aids the English at Banáras (June 4), K. ii. 230.
Sutherland, Major, watches the fords at Akbarpúr, M. iii. 348; overtakes and defeats Tántiá Topí at Rájpúr (Nov. 24, '58), M. iii. 350.
Sweny, Lieut., his excellent service on the Bombay coast, M. iii. 464.
Syálkot, mutiny at (July 9), K. ii. 627; murders on outbreak of mutiny at, K. ii. 629; mutineers from, defeated by Nicholson at Trimmu Ghát (July 12), K. ii. 640; and completely scattered (July 16), K. ii. 643.
Syfoollah Khán, see Zá,if-ullah Khán.
Sykes, Col., selects Outram to command Persian expedition of 1856, K. i. 423.

T.

Tafazzal Hussain Khán becomes supreme at Farakhábád, M. i. 346; murders forty Europeans at Farakhábád, M. i. 346; his unauthorised pardon, but miserable life, M. i. 347.
   See also Farrukhábád, Nawáb of.
Taimúr, house of, *see* Bahádur Sháh; Dehlí, King of; *and* Mughál Emperors.
Takht Singh, Rájá of Jodhpúr, his misgovernment, M. i. 258;

Takht Singh—*cont.*
   places a contingent at service of the English, M. i. 259.
Tál-Bahat, rebels evacuate fort of, M. iii. 150.
Talookdars, *see* Talúqdárs.
Talúqdárs, their status, K. i. 160; their rights, K. i. 159; those of Oudh have evil reputation, K. iii. 422; their fearful atrocities, K. i. 135 *n.*; rough settlement of their claims in Oudh, K. iii. 421; dispersion of their retainers, K. iii. 423; discourtesy shown towards, K. i. 167; they are antagonistic to English in Oudh, K. iii. 462; and aid in attack of Lakhnau Residency, K. iii. 529.
Tándá, on the Ghághrá, rebels retreat to (July '58), M. iii. 271.
Tanjor, Ráj of, extinguished (1855), K. i. 111.
Tánk, one of Rájpút states, M. i. 245 *n.*; Col. Holmes pursues Tántiá Topí into (June '58), M. iii. 319; Tántiá Topí raids on, M. iii. 319; Nawáb of, resists Tántiá Topí, M. iii. 319; but the mass of the Nawáb's troops join with Tántiá Topí, M. iii. 320.
Tántiá Topí, counsellor and guide of Náná Sáhib, K. ii. 312; his defective generalship, M. iii. 382; orders that all attacks on the English should be after 10 A.M., M. iii. 181.
   His version of the Káhnpúr rising, K. ii. 310 *n.*; his account of occupation of Káhnpúr Treasury by Náná Sáhib, K. ii. 299 *n.*; he is the executive agent in the Káhnpúr massacre, K. ii. 341 *n.*; his account of the massacre at

Tántiá Topí—*cont.*
Káhnpúr, K. ii. 340 *n.*, M. iii. 515; his own account of his general operations, M. iii. 514.
Assumes command of Gwáliár Contingent (Nov. 4), M. ii. 148; marches southwards to threaten Káhnpúr, M. ii. 148; reaches Kálpí (Nov. 9), M. ii. 228; cuts off supplies of Káhnpúr from W. and N.W., M. ii. 229; crosses the Jamná (Nov. 10), M. ii. 229; Gen. Windham's plan for defeating him (Nov. 17), M. ii. 233; severs communications of Sir Colin Campbell (Nov. 19), M. ii. 232; gradually closes round Káhnpúr (Nov. 23), M. ii. 234; Gen. Windham defeats his troops at Pándu rivulet (Nov. 26), M. ii. 236; but he presses on Gen. Windham's retiring troops (Nov. 26), M. ii. 237; and attacks Gen. Windham (Nov. 27), M. ii. 238; his great superiority in artillery, M. ii. 240; Gen. Windham's dispositions for resisting him (Nov. 28), M. ii. 246; he attempts to break bridge at Káhnpúr (Nov. 29), M. ii. 259; he destroys stores at Káhnpúr, M. ii. 260.
His strong position at Káhnpúr (Nov. 30), M. ii. 261; attacks British position (Dec. 2), M. ii. 263; Sir Colin Campbell's plan for driving him from the town, M. ii. 265; he renews his attack on British position (Dec. 4), M. ii. 265; strength of his force at Káhnpúr, M. ii. 266; he is defeated by Sir Colin Campbell (Dec. 6), M. ii. 271; pursuit of his flying

Tántiá Topí—*cont.*
troops for fourteen miles, M. ii. 272; caught in a trap by Sir Colin Campbell, M. ii. 273; but allowed to escape by Gen. Mansfield, M. ii. 275; he is again defeated by Gen. Hope Grant at Sivarájpúr (Dec. 9), M. ii. 278.
Invades Rájpútáná, M. ii. 576; captures Chárkhárí (March '58), M. iii. 161; advances to relief of Jhánsí, M. iii. 161; he is attacked by Sir Hugh Rose (April 1, '58), M. iii. 163; and totally defeated before Jhánsí, M. iii. 164; he retreats across the Betwá, but loses every gun, M. iii. 165; his own account of his attempt to relieve Jhánsí, M. iii. 518.
Entrenches himself at Kúnch, M. iii. 174; completely defeated at Kúnch (May '58), M. iii. 177; his troops retreat in masterly manner on Kálpí, M. iii. 178; flies from Kúnch to Charkí, near Jalaur, M. iii. 180; leaves Charkí for Gopálpúr, M. iii. 203; Sindhia marches against him at Morár (June 1, '58), M. iii. 208; Sindhiá's troops desert to him, M. iii. 209; he defeats Sindhiá, M. iii. 314; and enters Gwáliár (June 1, '58), M. iii. 209.
He is defeated at Morár near Gwáliár (June 16, '58), M. iii. 218; flies southward from Gwáliár (June 19, '58), M. iii. 315; he is defeated with entire loss of *matériel* at Jaurá-Alípúr (June 22, '58), M. iii. 230; his account of his defeat at Jaurá-Alípúr, M. iii. 230 *n.*; he moves to-

Tántiá Topí—*cont.*
wards Jaipúr, M. iii. 317; but is forced to turn from advance on that place, M. iii. 319; he is unable to cross the swollen Chambal, M. iii. 320; he turns towards Búndí (July '58), M. iii. 320; and again turns from Búndí to Nasírábád, M. iii. 320; takes up position near Sánganír and Bhilwárá (Aug. '58), M. iii. 321; Gen. Roberts follows him there, M. iii. 321; caught at Kankraulí near the Banás by Gen. Roberts (Aug. 13, '58), M. iii. 322; he visits shrine at Náthdwárá, M. iii. 323; he is defeated on the Banás, and chased by Col. Naylor (Aug. 14, '58), M. iii. 323; flees towards the Chambal, M. iii. 325; crosses the Chambal and eludes Brig. Parke, M. iii. 325; he gains possession of Jhálrá Pátan, M. iii. 326; and resolves to strike for Indor, M. iii. 327; he is stopped at Rájgarh by Gen. Michel (Sept. '58), M. iii. 329; completely defeated by Gen. Michel, near Rájgarh, M. iii. 330; the demoralised condition of his troops, M. iii. 330 *n.*; retreats from Rájgarh to Sironj, M. iii. 331, 337; he attacks and plunders I'sáogarh (Sept. '58), M. iii. 337; position of the English forces around him at that time, M. iii. 338; he marches from I'sáogarh to Chandairí, and is there repulsed, M. iii. 338; he marches from Chandairí on Mangraulí, M. iii. 338; he is defeated by Gen. Michel at Mangraulí (Oct. 9, '58), M. iii. 339; he flies from Maugraulí to Lalatpúr, and

Tántiá Topí—*cont.*
rejoins Ráo Sáhib, M. iii. 340; he endeavours to march to the south, M. iii. 341; but is attacked at Khorai, and loses half his army (Oct. 25, '58), M. iii. 342.

He crosses the Narbadá and enters Nágpúr (Oct. '58), M. iii. 342; grave importance of his invasion of Nágpúr, M. iii. 343; his fruitless efforts to penetrate far into the Marátha country, M. iii. 346; endeavours, but fails, to cross the Sátpúra range, M. iii. 346; he plunders an English convoy at Thán (Nov. 23, '58), M. iii. 347; he is caught by Major Sutherland near Rájpúr and defeated (Nov. 24, '58), M. iii. 350; he recrosses the Narbadá (Nov. 25, '58), M. iii. 350; and marches on Barodá (Nov. 26, '58), M. iii. 351; levies a contribution from the chief of Rájpúra on his way, M. iii. 352; he is overtaken at Chhotá Udaipúr by Brig. Parke, M. iii. 352; and defeated (Dec. 1, '58), M. iii. 354.

His desperate condition after defeat, M. iii. 354; he enters Bánswára, M. iii. 355; and receives supplies from Salúmbar, M. iii. 356; but deliberates on surrender, M. iii. 356; he marches on Partábgarh (Dec. 16, '58), M. iii. 357; baffles Major Rocke at Partábgarh, and escapes, M. iii. 357; he reaches Zírapúr, and is put to flight by Brig. Benson (Dec. 26, '58), M. iii. 358; put to flight again at Barod (Dec. 28, '58), M. iii. 358; he joins Mán Singh

Tántiá Topí—*cont.*
(Jan. '59), M. iii. 358; and is joined by Firoz Sháh at Indragarh (Jan. 13, '59), M. iii. 359; positions of British columns around, M. iii. 365; he is surprised and his troops scattered by Brig. Showers at Diwásá (Jan. 16, '59), M. iii. 366; escapes from the British cordon of troops towards Márwár (Jan. 18, '59), M. iii. 367; he is again surprised and defeated at Sikar, by Col. Holmes (Jan. 21, '59), M. iii. 367; abandoned by Firoz Sháh (Jan. 21, '59), M. iii. 367; quarrels with Ráo Sáhib, M. iii. 367; six hundred of his troops surrender to Rájá of Bikanír (Jan. 26, '59), M. iii. 367; abandons his troops and joins Mán Singh at Paron (Feb. '59), M. iii. 368; his capture at Paron (April 8, '59), M. iii. 379; his trial and defence, at Siprí, M. iii. 379; hanged at Siprí (April 18, '59), M. iii. 380.

Strictures on his heavy punishment, M. iii. 380; parallel between his acts and those of Hofer, M. iii. 381.

Skill of British Generals in his pursuit, M. iii. 383; extraordinary marches in pursuit of him, M. iii. 383.

Tayler, Mr. Skipwith, saves Gayá from plunder (Sept. 8), M. ii. 445.

Tayler, Mr. William, Commissioner of Patná, M. i. 42; reports native dread of forcible conversion to Christianity, K. i. 473; warns Secretary Beadon, K. iii. 64; warns Government two years before Mutiny, K. iii. 70.

Tayler, Mr. Wm.—*cont.*
His character, K. iii. 69, M. i. 42; his responsibilities, M. i. 51, 105; his confidence in Kunwar Singh, K. iii. 98; pursues the true policy of vigilant confidence, K. iii. 76; disliked for his vigilance, K. iii. 70; his active measures distasteful to Government of Bengal, M. i. 50; his policy of intimidation, K. iii. 81; he supports Major Holmes in his active measures, M. i. 72; but is not always supported with the courage he displayed, K. iii. 77; he receives support of European community (June 7), M. i. 44, 60; his policy compared with that of Mr. F. Halliday, M. i. 59; his splendid conduct at Patná, M. i. 48.

He guages accurately the significance of the first outbreak, M. i. 43; concentrates European residents at his house (June 7), K. iii. 74; calls a council of Europeans at Patná, M. i. 43; he brings Rattray's Sikhs to Patná, M. i. 44; urges Capt. Rattray's rapid advance (June 7), K. iii. 75; makes his house a rallying point, M. i. 44.

Combats first crisis at Patná (June 7), M. i. 44; discovers secret societies there (June 7–11), M. i. 48; resolves to strike the first blow, M. i. 51; arrests the three Maulavís (June 19), K. iii. 82, 681, M. i. 52, 54, 549; his seizure of the Maulavís criticised, K. iii. 83; Sir J. Kaye's criticism contested, M. i. 53; arrest of Ahmadulláh, the Wahábí suspected by him, K. iii. 168; Ahmad-

Tayler, Mr. Wm.—*cont.*
ulláh condemned and transported, K. iii. 169.
Removes treasure from Chaprá and Á'rá to Patná, M. i. 49; presses for disarmament of Sepoys at Dánápúr, M. i. 50; he disarms Patná (June 20), K. iii. 84, M. i. 54; sends Mr. Lowis to arrest Alí Karím (June 23), M. i. 55; suppresses rising (July 3), K. iii. 84, M. i. 56; arrests Pír Alí, K. iii. 85; unfairly blamed for arrest of Lulf Alí Khán, K. iii. 88.
Rallies Europeans at his house (July 25), M. i. 73; sends volunteers and Sikhs to Phúlwárí to chase Dánápúr mutineers, M. i. 74; instance of his efforts to get troops sent after mutineers, K. iii. 109 *n.*; receives intelligence of Major Holmes' murder, K. iii. 102; on revolt of 12th Irregulars, withdraws his detachment from Phúlwárí, M. i. 74; urges Gen. Lloyd to pursue Dánápúr mutineers, K. iii. 101, M. i. 77; again induces Gen. Lloyd to send troops after mutineers, M. i. 79; his prescience provides Á'rá with a garrison, M. i. 81.
His critical position on defeat of Capt. Dunbar, M. i. 104; orders withdrawal of officers from out-stations (July 31), K. iii. 148, M. i. 107; his order to abandon Mozaffarpúr faithfully obeyed, M. i. 109; the extraordinary way in which his order to abandon Gayá was carried out, M. i. 109-115; Mr. Halliday's comments on his order to retire from out-stations, K.

Tayler, Mr. Wm.—*cont.*
iii. 159; charged with panic by Mr. F. Halliday, M. i. 117; the danger of not issuing the order to concentrate, K. iii. 163; essential importance of saving European life, after Dunbar's defeat, K. iii. 162.
Unjustly dismissed from his post, K. iii. 160, M. i. 117; he is personally distasteful to Mr. F. Halliday, M. i. 116; he contests the justice of his dismissal, K. iii. 160; not deserving of punishment, K. iii. 163; routine occasions his downfall, K. iii. 164; ruined by intrigue, M. i. 124; the victim of Mr. F. Halliday's revenge, M. i. 116; disapproval of him imprudently marked by successor appointed, K. iii. 190; his services more valuable than those of Mr. Halliday, M. i. 120; justification of his conduct, K. iii. 161; his great services to Government, M. i. 117; charges against him trumped up by Mr. F. Halliday, M. i. 118 *n.*; Sir John Kaye's manly vindication of his conduct, M. i. 118 *n.*; the reality of the Wahábí conspiracy, K. iii. 165; his views of the Wahábí conspiracy, supported by Sir H. Edwardes, K. iii. 166; and by Mr. A. Roberts, K. iii. 167; his suspicions of Wahábís justified in recent years, M. i. 120; the confirmation of all his suspicions, M. i. 553; he is proved by subsequent events to have been in every respect right, M. i. 554.
Sir John Low recants his adverse decision against, M. i. 121; Mr. Dorin recants his

Tayler, Mr. Wm.—*cont.*
adverse decision against, M. i. 121; Lord Canning's Private Secretary exonerates him from all blame, M. i. 121 *n.*; Mr. Halliday's charge of panic against, everywhere recognised as untrue, M. i. 121; he is one of the four, who preserved Mr. Beadon's line of six hundred miles, M. i. 143; he and Major Eyre save Bihár, M. i. 103; his treatment like that of M. Dupleix, and a reproach to England, M. i. 123.

Taylor, Capt. Alex., his inexhaustible fertility of resource at Dehlí, K. iii. 573; prepares plan for assault of Dehlí (Sept. 1), M. ii. 7; his project for worming through the houses of Dehlí, K. iii. 626; captures the Burn bastion, Dehlí, M. ii. 65.

Tehrí, Rájá of Bánpúr confines British officers in, M. iii. 98.

Tej Singh, *see* Tez Singh.

Telegraphs introduced into India by Lord Dalhousie, K. i. 193.

Telegraphs and Railways, heavy blows to Bráhmanism, K. i. 193.

Ternan, Capt. A. H., Deputy Commissioner at Narsinghpúr, M. iii. 90, 91; he induces Mr. Colvin to abstain from great interference with Ságar and Narbadá territories, M. iii. 90; he has mysterious *chapátís* brought to him (Jan.), M. iii. 91; reports his suspicions about the *chapátís*, M. iii. 92; his report disregarded, M. iii. 92; ordered by Government to disgrace Rájá of Dilherí, M. iii. 94; befriends

Ternan, Capt.—*cont.*
Rájá of Dilherí in his difficulties, M. iii. 94; the Rájá gratefully stands by him when mutiny breaks out, M. iii. 95; he surprises and defeats rebels at Chírápúr (Nov.), M. iii. 108; he captures and executes Dal Ganjan, M. iii. 108; he defeats rebels at Maddanpúr (Jan. '58), M. iii. 109.

Tez Alí Khán, his faithful adherence to fugitives from Faizábád, M. i. 401.

Tez Singh, Rájá of Mainpúrí, attempts to stop Brig. Seaton's advance (Dec. 23), M. ii. 294; he is defeated by Brig. Seaton (Dec. 24), M. ii. 294; he enters Rohilkhand, M. ii. 499.

Thackwell, Gen., crosses the Chináb (1848), K. i. 37.

Thákur Singh, the leader of disaffection at Belgáon, M. iii. 32; sent to command at Badámí (July), M. iii. 32.

Thákurs, many are troublesome subjects of the Rájpút chiefs, K. iii. 350.

Thán, Major Sutherland marches through (Nov. 22, '58), M. iii. 348; Tántiá Topí plunders English convoy at (Nov. 23, '58), M. iii. 346.

Therí, the Rání of, supplies Sir Hugh Rose with forage, &c., during siege of Jhánsí, M. iii. 159.

Thomas, Major, mortally wounded at Sháhganj, M. i. 275.

Thomason, Mr., his character, K. i. 164; his settlement views, K. i. 164 and *n.*; emancipates the cultivators from serfdom, M. i. 145; resists the claim of Náná Sáhib, K. i. 102.

Thompson, Capt., pursues rebels from Morár (June 16, '58), M. iii. 217.

Thompson, Mr. George, appointed agent in England of Bahádur Sháh, K. ii. 12.

Thomson, Lance-Corporal, his bravery at Rúiyá (April 15, '58), M. ii. 507.

Thornton, Mr., a competition-wala, cuts away the bridge of boats at Phillaur, K. ii. 503.

Thornton, Mr. Edward, arrests Hazárá conspirators (Sept.), M. iii. 303.

Thynne, Capt., death of, at Lakhnau (March 11, '58), M. ii. 381.

Tíká Singh, Súbádár of Cavalry, invites Náná Sáhib to sedition, K. ii. 306.

Timmins, Major, attacked and defeated at Mahídpúr (Nov. 8), M. iii. 73.

Timmins, Mrs., her life saved at Mahídpúr by a native tailor (Nov.), M. iii. 75.

Tiparah, Rájá of, called on to cut off mutineers escaping from Chatgáon, M. ii. 421; stops Chatgáon mutineers at Sankhola (Dec. 2), M. ii. 422.

Tirhoot, see Tirhút.

Tirhút, district of Patná division, K. iii. 71 n., M. i. 40; placed under martial-law by Major J. Holmes (June 19), K. iii. 103; arrest of Wáris Alí at, K. iii. 79; force under Col. Rowcroft organised at (Nov.), M. ii. 321.

Tirohan, old name of Kirwí, M. iii. 199.

Tírul, rebels driven from by Brig. Berkeley (July 16, '58), M. iii. 281.

Todd, D'Arcy, and his Sepoys at Hirát, M. iii. 473.

Tombs, Major, scatters mutineers on the Hindan (May 30), K. ii. 184; commands No. 4 battery at Dehlí, M. ii. 20; he and Lieut. Hills, win the Victoria Cross (July 9), K. ii. 577–579.

Tomkinson, Lieut., on duty at Orai (May), M. iii. 466; starts from Orai with treasure (June 4), M. iii. 466; not permitted to enter Gwáliár (June 12), M. iii. 467; not permitted to enter A'grá (June 20), M. iii. 467; his troops mutiny and dismiss him, M. iii. 467; he is concealed by a poor Muhammadan till October, M. iii. 467; he attempts to explode ammunition of rebels (Oct.), M. iii. 468; is discovered and killed in his brave attempt (Oct. 23), M. iii. 468.

Tonnochy, a young volunteer, kills Sáh Mall in battle (July), M. iii. 434.

Tonk, see Tánk.

Topham, Capt., recovers two guns from the Maulaví's troopers (April '58), M. ii. 496.

Toráb Alí, a loyal Muhammadan, taken prisoner by Dhaulána villagers, M. iii. 435; released by inhabitants of Solána, M. iii. 435.

Torábáz Khán, leading insurgent, shot at Haidarábád (July 17), M. iii. 122.

Tottenham, Capt., killed in fight with rebels, near Jabalpúr (Nov.), M. iii. 107.

Townshend, Lieut., shot by bandits during retreat from Naogáon, M. i. 195.

Trades' Association, Calcutta, Government declines their offer to raise volunteers (May), M. i. 2.

THE HISTORIES OF THE INDIAN MUTINY. 193

Transport for reinforcements miserably deficient, K. ii. 135.
Travers, Col., arrives at I'ndor with Cavalry (June), M. i. 210; he receives command of troops at Residency, M. i. 210; conversing at orderly-room when mutiny breaks out (July 1), M. i. 217; he orders out the Cavalry, M. i. 219; with five men he charges the rebel guns, K. iii. 331, M. i. 220; wounds Sa'adat Khán, M. i. 220; forwards Col. Durand's demand for Hungerford's battery, M. i. 221; fights the rebel guns, and disables one, M. i. 221; again endeavours to form men for a charge, M. i. 222; his explanation of retreat from the Residency, M. i. 226 n.
Treachery of Native troops at Mardán, K. ii. 486 n.
Treasurers, their extraordinary duties during Mutiny, M. iii. 444.
Treaty with Nawáb of Oudh (1801), K. i. 117.
Treaty of 1837 with Oudh, disallowed, K. i. 127.
Troup, Col. Colin, in temporary chief command at Brailí (May 14), M. i. 304; tries persuasive measures with Sepoys, M. i. 305; has especial confidence in 8th Irreg. Cavalry, M. i. 305; sends women and children to Náiní Tál (May 15), M. i. 306; he doubles the strength of 8th Irreg. Cavalry, M. i. 306; he attempts to lead Irregular Cavalry from Barailí (May 31), K. iii. 272; he counsels Mr. Colvin to issue proclamation of indemnity to Sepoys, K. iii. 230.

Troup, Col.—*cont.*
Captures Maithaulí (Oct. 8, '58), M. iii. 293.
Tucker, Capt., attacks Jíran, but is repulsed and killed (Oct. 23), M. ii. 571.
Tucker, Col. Henry, warns Government concerning greased cartridges in 1853, K. i. 517.
Tucker, Lieut., stands by Col. Fisher in his last moments, M. i. 406; escapes from Saltánpúr and reaches Banáras, M. i. 406.
Tucker, Mr., member of Court of Directors, strongly opposes removal of Mughál sovereigns from Dehlí, K. ii. 23 n.; his views on settlements, K. i. 165.
Tucker, Mr. Henry Carre, Commissioner of Banáras, his character, K. ii. 209; he labours to preserve tranquillity (May), K. ii. 204; Lord Canning's letter of thanks to him, K. ii. 212; his expectation of speedy suppression of the Mutiny, M. iii. 448; skilfully causes reduction of price of grain at Banáras, K. ii. 204; holds Banáras by moral force, K. ii. 205; he pushes on every soldier who reaches Banáras to Káhnpúr, K. ii. 207; rewards fidelity of Sikh treasure guard (June 5), K. ii. 230 n.; deprecates publication of martial law at Banáras, K. ii. 235; brings in treasure from Mirzápúr and Gházípúr, K. ii. 240; places Mr. Wynward in full charge of Gorakhpúr district, with unlimited power, M. iii. 449; exerts himself actively to prevent the acceptance of assistance from Jang Bahádur, M. iii. 452.

13

Tucker, Mr. Robert Tudor, Commissioner of Fathpúr, his character, K. ii. 363; he refuses to quit Fathpúr after outbreak, K. ii. 365; his heroic death (June 9), K. ii. 367.
Tuffoozul Hoosein Khan=Tafazzul Husain Khán, see Farrukhábád, Nawáb of.
Túkají Ráo Holkár, ruler of Indor, M. iii. 132. See Holkár.
Tulsípúr, Col. Rowcroft defeats Bálá Ráo at (Dec. '58), M. iii. 293.
Turner, Col., secures the Grand Trunk Road in Bihár (June–Sept. '58), M. ii. 484; he defeats rebels at Pírú (Oct. 17, '58), M. ii. 486; annihilates rebel rear-guard at Nonádí (Oct. 20, '58), M. ii. 489.

U.

Ucherá, feudatory in Ságar territory, M. iii. 88.
Udaipúr, one of Rájpút states, M. i. 245 n.; Capt. Showers, Agent at, K. iii. 353, M. i. 259, iii. 325; Major Rocke stops Tántiá Topí's march on (Dec. '58), M. iii. 356; Sarúp Singh, Ráná of, M. i. 259.
Udaipúr, Maháráná of, the most influential Rájpút, K. iii. 355; Gen. G. St. P. Lawrence's alleged dispute with, K. iii. 683; he boldly declares for the British, K. iii. 356; he is on ill terms with his nobles, M. i. 259.
Umballah, see Ambálá.
Umritsur, see Amritsar.
Unáo, battle of (July 29), M. i. 492; cleared of rebels (July '58), M. iii. 284 n.

Ungud, see Angad.
Unpreparedness of the English for the Mutiny, K. ii. 104; the policy of, pursued by Lord Canning, K. ii. 123 n.
Urchah, see Urchhá.
Urchhá, Rájá of, loyal, M. iii. 193.
Ushait, Gen. Penny occupies (April '58), M. ii. 501.

V.

Vans Agnew, Mr., sent to Múltán, K. i. 20; murdered in Múltán, K. i. 21.
Van Cortlandt, reduces the Rohtak district to submission (Oct.), M. ii. 107.
Vaughan, Lieut., skilfully destroys a rebel gun (Jan. 2, '58), M. ii. 302 n.
Vazír Muhammad Khán, Nawáb of Tánk, resists Tántiá Topí (June '58), M. iii. 319.
Venables, Mr., repulses the rebels at A'zamgarh (July 16), M. ii. 316; forced to retreat to Gházípúr (July 30), M. ii. 316; his gallantry at Mandorí (Sept. 19), M. ii. 318; rebels offer 500 rupees for his head, M. ii. 318 n.; nobly assists Gen. Franks during his campaign, M. ii. 340; his untimely death near A'zamgarh (April '58), M. ii. 471; his great services to his country, M. ii. 547–549.
Vengeance, begets vengeance, K. ii. 270.
Vellore (Velúr), Mutiny of, see Mutiny of Vellore, K. i. 224.
Vibart, Major, bravely defends the Ridan at Káhnpúr, K. ii. 319.

Victor Hugo on Revolt, K. iii. 450.
Vindictiveness against natives reprobated, K. iii. 8.
Volunteer cavalry, glorious charge of the Eighteen at Káhnpúr (July 16), K. ii. 378.
Volunteer corps, from Sepoy regiments, for foreign service, K. i. 460.
Volunteer force, Lord Canning declines to organise a, in May, K. ii. 117; probable advantage of, K. ii. 123; doubtful value of, in May, K. ii. 125.
Volunteers, rebuff administered to Calcutta citizens offering to become, M. i. 1; their useful services, K. iii. 42.
Volunteers, Alláhábád, exuberant energy of, K. ii. 266 n.
Volunteer hanging parties, K. ii. 236.

W.

Wahábí, head-quarters at Patná, K. iii. 166, M. i. 40; the conspiracy proved to be real, K. iii. 165; Mr. A. Roberts shows the existence of, for forty years previously, K. iii. 167; the history and establishment at Patná, proved by Dr. Hunter, M. i. 547; Mr. Halliday refuses to believe in traitorousness of Wahábís, M. i. 549.
Wahábí Maulavís at Patná, M. i. 52; power to work mischief taken from (June 19), M. i. 52, 53; their arrest, trial, and condemnation, M. i. 552; Mr. Tayler's suspicions of justified in recent years, M. i. 20;

Wahábí Maulavís—cont.
the leaders convicted by Sir Herbert Edwardes in 1864, K. iii. 166.
Wahábí-ism at Patná, K. iii. 63.
Waiz-ul-Haqq, leading Wahábí of Patná, M. i. 52.
Wájid Alí Sháh, his passionate grief on dethronement, K. i. 150; pension of twelve lákhs of rupees allotted to, K. i. 152; proclaimed king at Dariábád (June 9), M. i. 409.
See Oudh, King of.
Wallahájábád, mutiny suspected at (1806), K. i. 242.
Wake, Mr., Magistrate of Sháhábád, warns Government against harsh treatment of Kunwar Singh, K. iii. 100; reports desertion of A'rá by railway officials (June 11), M. i. 48; takes command of the Sikhs at A'rá, K. iii. 127; associate of the four who saved Mr. Beadon's line of six hundred miles, M. i. 143.
Walker, Col., completely defeats Gújádar Singh and his fragment of rebels (April '59), M. iii. 296.
Waller, Lieut., and Lieut. Rose capture rock-fortress of Gwáliár (June 20, '58), M. iii. 228.
Walpole, Gen., his character, M. ii. 503; his disastrous incapacity, M. ii. 508; rage of his troops against him for his incompetence, M. ii. 509; created K.C.B. for his incompetence, M. ii. 509.
Protects left of Káhnpúr (Nov. 28), M. ii. 246; beats off Tántiá Topí's attack on his position (Nov. 28), M. ii. 249; commands 6th Brigade at attack on Tántiá

13 *

Walpole, Col.—*cont.*
Topí (Dec. 5), M. ii. 267; marches his column to I'táwá (Dec. 18), M. ii. 285; his column annoyed by a few fanatics at I'táwá (Dec. 29), M. ii. 285; joins Sir Colin Campbell at Fathgarh (Jan. 4, '58), M. ii. 306; sent against Alláhganj, M. ii. 311; his junction with Brig. Seaton's force at Bewar (Feb. 3, '58), M. ii. 286; commands right wing of Outram's force on Gúmtí (March '58), M. ii. 374; commands moveable column at Lakhnau, M. ii. 468; leads his column from Lakhnau (April 7, '58), M. ii. 502; nature of his task, M. ii. 502; marches to Rúiyá (April 15, '58), M. ii. 504; description of fort of Rúiyá, M. ii. 504; hears of Narpat Singh's intention to evacuate Rúiyá, M. ii. 505; but disbelieves intention to evacuate Rúiya, M. ii. 505; attacks Rúiyá, M. ii. 506; retreats from Rúiyá (April 15, '58), M. ii. 507; expels the rebels from Sirsa (April 22, '58), M. ii. 510; joins Sir Colin Campbell (April 27, '58), M. ii. 510; made divisional commander in Rohilkhand (May '58), M. ii. 537.

Walter, Col., allows Amar Singh to escape from Jagadíspúr (Oct. '58), M. ii. 487.

Walters, Col., defeats rebels at Rámpúr (Sept. 9, '58), M. ii. 484.

Wantmúrí, the Desáí of, a discontented chief, M. iii. 29.

War with Afghanistan (1838), K. i. 274.

War with Birmá, the first (1824), K. i. 265.

War with Sindh (1843), K. i. 276.

Ward, Sir Thomas, sends half his force from Ceylon to Lord Canning, K. iii. 182.

Wardlaw, Ensign, operates in Chútiá Nágpúr (Jan. '58), M. ii. 441 *b*.

Wáris Alí, arrest of, at Patná (June 23), K. iii. 79, M. i. 54; hanged at Patná, M. i. 57.

Warnings of treachery disregarded, K. ii. 37.

Watson, Capt., suggests retreat from Banáras (May), K. ii. 202.

Watson, Lieut., cuts his way through surrounding Sepoys at Katanjí, M. iii. 105; slays the rebel leader at the Martinière, Lakhnau (Nov. 14), M. ii. 174.

Waugh, Col. Scott, fixes headquarters of Trigonometrical Survey at Dehrá Dún (May), M. iii. 419.

Wellesley, Lord, his character, K. i. 115; his policy, K. ii. 3; his political paradox, K. ii. 5; his policy towards the Rájpúts, M. ii. 576.

Wellington, Duke of, on conflicts of authority between high officials, K. ii. 459 *n*.

Wells, Capt., commands 84th Regiment advancing from Lakhnau Residency (Nov. 16), M. ii. 206.

Weston, Capt. Gould, commands Oudh police, M. i. 357 *n*.; sent to pacify the Malhíábád district, M. i. 370; attempts and fails to stop mutiny of his military police, M. i. 417; gallops five miles after mutinous police to persuade them to return to duty, M. i. 418; his miraculous escape from death, M. i. 419; his services

Weston, Capt.—*cont.*
at Lakhnau and the Álambágh, M. ii. 362; cuts off fugitives from Makkaganj (March 11, '58), M. ii. 381; his services as guide in attacks, M. ii. 400 *n.*

Wetherall, Brig., ordered to move in concert with Gen. Hope Grant (Oct. '58), M. iii. 289; attacks and captures Rámpúr Kussiá (Nov. 3, '58), M. iii. 290.

Wheatley, Capt., his death in attack on Lakhnau (Nov. 14), M. ii. 177 *n.*

Wheeler, Gen. Sir Hugh, commands at Káhnpúr, K. ii. 289; his former services, K. ii. 289; greatly respected by Natives, K. ii. 304; doubts the Sepoy, K. ii. 290.

Resolves to entrench a rallying point at Káhnpúr, K. ii. 293; reason for not choosing the Magazine as rallying point, K. ii. 294; asks help from Lakhnau (May), K. ii. 295; wishes to blow up the Káhnpúr magazine, K. ii. 308 *n.*; believes Káhnpúr safe (June 1), K. ii. 303; sends help to Lakhnau (June 3), K. ii. 304; he is informed by Nána Sáhib that he intends to attack entrenchment, K. ii. 313; opposed to capitulation, K. ii. 333; capitulates, K. ii. 334; massacred at Káhnpúr, K. ii. 341.

Wheler, Col. S. G., commands 34th Regiment at Barákpúr (1857), K. i. 495.

Whiting, Capt., stoutly defends north-east corner of entrenchment at Káhnpúr, K. ii. 319.

Whitlock, Brig.-Gen., appointed to command Jabalpúr column (Nov. 16), M. iii. 190; arrives

Whitlock, Brig.-Gen.—*cont.*
at Jabalpúr (Feb. 6, '58), M. iii. 192; commands Madras column in Central India (Dec.), M. iii. 136; occupies Kámptí (Jan. 10, '58), M. iii. 192; marches on Ságar (Feb. 17, '58), M. iii. 193; refuses to reduce small places on his route, M. iii. 193; occupies Damoh (March 4, '58), M. iii. 193; occupies Ságar (March 5, '58), M. iii. 193; ordered to subdue Bandelkhand (Mar.17,'58),M.iii.194; his movements too slow and cautious, M. iii. 194; marches on Márwá Ghát (April 2,'58), M. iii. 194; occupies Mandalá (April 3, '58), M. iii. 195; occupies Chattarpúr (April 9, '58), M. iii. 195; catches some rebels evacuating Jhigan fort (April 9, '58), M. iii. 195; Nawáb of Bándá lays a trap for him, M. iii. 195; falls into trap of Nawáb of Bándá, M. iii. 196; captures Bándá (April 19, '58), M. iii. 197; orders Brig. McDuff to march on Nagod (May 27), M. iii. 198; resolves to march on Kálpí (May 29, '58), M. iii. 198; ordered to march against Kirwí (May 30, '58), M. iii. 199; the Ráos of Kirwí surrender to him (June 2, '58), M. iii. 200; enters Kirwí (June 6, '58), M. iii. 201; break up of his column after entrance into Kirwí, M. iii. 202; has the path prepared by Sir H. Rose, M. iii. 198; enjoys the spoils while Sir H. Rose encounters the danger, M. iii. 201.

Whish, Capt., forces a large party of mutineers to surrender (May 23), M. i. 329.

Whish, Gen. Samson, sent against Múltán with Edwardes (1848), K. i. 33.

Widdowson, Mrs. Bridget, stands guard over a batch of prisoners at Káhnpúr, K. ii. 323.

Wiláyat Sháh, threatens Powáin (Aug. '58), M. iii. 274.

Wilkin, Capt., his distinguished bravery at the Músá Bágh, M. iii. 509.

Willoughby, Lieut. Edward, his gallantry and death at Rúiyá (April 15, '58), M. ii. 506.

Willoughby, Lieut. George, prepares to defend or to blow up the Magazine at Dehlí (May 11), K. ii. 89; blows up the Dehlí magazine (May 11), K. ii. 90; wounded at capture of Bálábet fort, M. iii. 99 n.; murdered on road from Dehlí, K. ii. 173 n.

Wilson, Brig. Archdale, his prompt conduct on outbreak of mutiny at Mírat (May 10), K. ii. 65; reasons for his inaction at Mírat (May 10), K. ii. 101, 102; hesitates to move from Mírat (May 15), K. ii. 180; defeats mutineers on the Hindan (May 30, 31), K. ii. 184–186; reinforced by Gorkhás (June 1), K. ii. 187; crosses the Jamná (June 4), K. ii. 188.

Counsels delay in assault of Dehlí (June 16), K. ii. 533; receives command of Dehlí Field Force (July 17), K. ii. 586; his desponding letter to Major Baird Smith (Aug. 20), M. ii. 2 n.; asks reinforcement from Panjáb (Sept.), M. iii. 301; his order of the day (Sept. 7), M. ii. 11; yields to Major Baird Smith's opinion, M. ii. 6; but throws

Wilson, Brig. A.—cont.
responsibility of assault on Major Baird Smith, M. ii. 6.

His address to the Army before assault of Dehlí, K. iii. 555; lacks confidence in his men at assault of Dehlí, K. iii. 589; inclined to retire after first day's assault of Dehlí, K. iii. 617, M. ii. 55; his great dejection during assault of Dehlí, K. iii. 622, M. ii. 60 n.; he stops drunkeness by destroying liquors at Dehlí, K. iii. 620; mournful letter (Sept. 18), K. iii. 630, M. ii. 63; remarks on his conduct of the siege of Dehlí, K. iii. 654.

Sends Col. Greathed after Sepoys from Dehlí, M. ii. 87; commends Hodson's shooting the Princes of Dehlí, K. iii. 654; proceeds on sick certificate to Himálayas, M. ii. 105.

Wilson, Brig. N., commands intrenchment at Káhnpúr (Nov. 28), M. ii. 247; ordered to cover Brig. Carthew's advance, M. ii. 250; failure of his attack, M. ii. 251; killed at Káhnpúr (Nov. 28), M. ii. 251.

Wilson, Capt., his military character, M. i. 482; Brig. Inglis's testimony to his bravery and devotion, M. i. 482; his account of Sir H. Lawrence's death stroke, M. i. 434.

Wilson, Mr. Cracroft, Judge at Murádábád, K. iii. 252.

Wilson, Sir Cracroft, reports officially that a general rising of Sepoys had been arranged, K. ii. 109; leads Sepoys against mutineers from Muzaffarnagar, K. iii. 254; recaptures many escaped pri-

Wilson, Sir C.—*cont.*
soners, K. iii. 256; he bravely faces the pointed guns of nascent mutineers, K. iii. 257; restores confidence at Murádábád, K. iii. 257.
Defeats rebellious party from Rámpúr (May 20), K. iii. 258; attacks and disperses Muhammadan fanatics at Murádábád (May 21), M. i. 328; his bold proposal to Sepoy officers, K. iii. 261; places treasure under Sepoy guard while stamped paper is being destroyed (June 1), K. iii. 263; escapes from Murádábád (June 3), M. i. 332; induces Gen. Penny to march without caution (April 30, '58), M. ii. 501.
Windham, Gen. Charles A., left in command of Káhnpúr (Nov. 9), M. ii. 149; his instructions for holding Káhnpúr, M. ii. 149, 226; secures the intrenchment at Káhnpúr, M. ii. 227; guesses Tántiá Topí's design on Káhnpúr, M. ii. 230; obtains permission to detain troops in Káhnpúr (Nov. 14), M. ii. 230; advances beyond town to the west (Nov. 17), M. ii. 231; asks permission to attack Tántiá Topí (Nov. 17), M. ii. 233; his plan for defeating Tántiá Topí, M. ii. 233; Tántiá Topí severs his communications with Sir Colin Campbell (Nov. 19), M. ii. 232; he attempts to re-open communications with Sir Colin Campbell (Nov. 23), M. ii. 232; advances six miles nearer to Tántiá Topí (Nov. 24), M. ii. 234; feels that Tántiá Topí is closing round Káhnpúr, M. ii. 234; his dis-

Windham, Gen.—*cont.*
positions for meeting advance of Tántiá Topí, M. ii. 235; attacks and defeats Tántiá Topí's troops at Pándu rivulet (Nov. 26), M. ii. 236; marches back towards Káhnpúr (Nov. 26), M. ii. 236; Tántiá Topí presses on his retiring troops, M. ii. 237; he is attacked by Tántiá Topí (Nov. 27), M. ii. 238; overborne by Tántiá Topí's superiority in artillery, M. ii. 240; retires on brick-kilns at Káhnpúr, M. ii. 241; orders Brig. Carthew to fall back on brick-kilns, M. ii. 242; abandons tents and kits, M. ii. 243; reasons for his defeat on Nov. 27, M. ii. 245.
His dispositions for resisting Tántiá Topí (Nov. 28), M. ii. 246; protects the Ganges side of Káhnpúr, M. ii. 247; orders Brig. Carthew to advance again (Nov. 28), M. ii. 249; fails to support Brig. Carthew, M. ii. 253; fails to support the key of his position, M. ii. 254; criticisms on his generalship (Nov. 28), M. ii. 249; his bold attack saves Káhnpúr, M. ii. 256.
His ungenerous conduct, M. ii. 254; he is forced to acknowledge that he ordered Brig. Carthew to retire, M. ii. 255.
Again commands intrenchment at Káhnpúr (Dec. 5), M. ii. 267.
Windus, Lieut., his good service in Chutiá Nágpúr, M. iii. 463.
Wingfield, Mr. Charles, Commissioner of Bahráich, K. iii. 472, M. i. 389; his views on Oudh administration, M. i.

Wingfield, Mr. C.—*cont.*
390; disapproves of the Thomasonian revenue system, K. iii. 473; removes women and children from Sikrorá to Lakhnau, K. iii. 474; rides from Sikrorá to Gondá (June 9), K. iii. 475, M. i. 392; leaves Gondá for Balrámpúr (June 10), K. iii. 476.

Woodburn, Gen., Lord Elphinstone organises his column for offensive defence (May), M. iii. 9; composition of his column, M. iii. 9; his column the one hope of Indor, M. i. 212; ordered to march on Máú (June), M. iii. 10; his column diverted to Aurangábád (June 13), M. i. 212, iii. 11; enters Aurangábád and disarms Sepoys (June 23), M. iii. 13; his column halts at Aurangábád, M. i. 213; he is a second time urged to advance to Máú by Lord Elphinstone (June 22), M. iii. 13; excuses himself from advancing (June 25), M. iii. 14; he is almost peremptorily ordered to advance by Lord Elphinstone (June 27), M. iii. 15; a fourth time ordered to advance to Máú (June 29), M. iii. 16; he is urged by Mr. Plowden to march on Nágpúr (July), M. i. 243; dissuaded from marching on Nágpúr by Col. Durand, M. i. 243; he falls ill, and is superseded by Col. Stuart, M. iii. 16; returns to Puná in bad health, M. i. 243; he is succeeded at Aurangábád by Brig. Stuart, M. i. 243.

Woollcombe, Capt., his gallantry in the Málwá campaign, M. iii. 87.

Woolley, Capt., commands at Narsinghpúr, M. iii. 91, 108; defeats and slays Ganjan Singh (Nov.), M. iii. 108; captures and executes the rebel Dal Ganjan at Singhpúr (Nov.), M. iii. 108; clears Narbadá district of rebels (Nov.), M. iii. 108.

Women, their heroism and sufferings at Káhnpúr, K. ii. 322; Amazonian conduct of some, K. ii. 323.

Wolseley, Capt. Garnet, storms the Mess House, Lakhnau (Nov. 17), M. ii. 201, 202; captures the Motí Mahal without orders, M. ii. 203; censured but admired by Sir Colin Campbell for exceeding instructions, M. ii. 204 *n.*

Wray, Midshipman, his good service in Western Bihár, M. iii. 463.

Wroughton, Col., commands at Jánpúr (Sept.), M. ii. 317; captures and hangs Irádat Khán (Sept. 27), M. ii. 319.

Wyndham, Capt., occupies Linsúgúr (Jan. '58), M. iii. 127; marches on Shorápúr (Feb. 7), M. iii. 127; avoids the snare of Rájá of Shorápúr, M. iii. 127; he is attacked, but drives off assailants (Feb. 7, '58), M. iii. 128; Rájá of Shorápúr flies from his fort, M. iii. 129.

Wynyard, Mr. William, ;judge of Gorakhpúr (May), M. iii. 447; his character, M. iii. 447; defers Mr. Paterson's departure on leave on outbreak of Mutiny, M. iii. 448; he receives unlimited power in Gorakhpúr, M. iii. 449; raises volunteers for defence of Gorakhpúr (June), M. iii. 449;

THE HISTORIES OF THE INDIAN EMPIRE. 201

Wynyard, Mr. W.—*cont.*
he and Capt. Steel prevent attempt of Sepoys to mutiny (June 7), M. iii. 450; proclaims martial law in Gorakhpúr, M. iii. 451; receives the thanks of Lord Canning (June 28), M. iii. 453; disarms his detachment of 17th N.I. (Aug. 1), M. iii. 455; leaves Gorakhpúr to charge of loyal landowners (Aug. 31), M. iii. 456; receives no reward for his eminent services, M. iii. 457; arrives at Azamgarh and is made chief civil officer there, M. iii. 457.

Y.

Yár Muhammad, ruler of Hirát, sides with Persia, K. i. 410.
Yule, Mr. George, Commissioner of Bhágalpúr, M. ii. 129; his character, M. ii. 129; tries to maintain order without British troops, M. ii. 130; detains 140 British soldiers for protection in July, M. ii. 131; prepares active demonstration against Mutiny, M. ii. 131.
Secures the towns of Bhágalpúr and Manghír (July), M. ii. 131; secures the navigation of the Ganges, M. ii. 131; severs the disaffected of eastern from western Bihár, M. ii. 132; warns Col. Burney and saves Báosí, M. ii. 133; marches with troops to Púrniá (Dec. 1), M. ii. 426; and defeats mutinous cavalry, M. ii. 429; drives mutineers into Nipál, M. ii. 429.

Yule, Mr. G.—*cont.*
Marches on Cháwa Ghát, M. ii. 431; finds mutineers in strong position there (Dec. 26), M. ii. 431; mutineers out-manœuvre him (Dec. 28), M. ii. 432; tries but fails to intercept mutineers on Dárjíling road (Dec. 29), M. ii. 432; drives the mutineers into Nipál (Jan. '58), M. ii. 433.
He is joined by Major Richardson (Jan. 11, '58), M. ii. 433; Dákhá mutineers escape from him (Jan. 19, '58), M. ii. 435; becomes Commissioner in Eastern Bihár (Jan. '58), M. ii. 425; offers himself and twenty mounted gentlemen to act against Western Bihár (May '58), M. ii. 436 *n.*

Z.

Zá,if-ulláh Khán, Nawáb, offers to co-operate with the British (July), K. iii. 380.
Zamíndárí rights, K. i. 159.
Zeenut Mehat, *see* Zínat Mahal.
Zemindaree, *see* Zamíndárí.
Zínat Mahal, wife of Bahádur Sháh, K. ii. 13, 24; she interferes with succession to sovereignty, K. ii. 24; her schemes and ambition, K. ii. 32.
Zírapúr, Brig. Benson puts Tántiá Topí to flight from (Dec. 26, '58), M. iii. 358.
Zorah, Lieut. W. Osborne defeats rebels at, M. iii. 112.
Zuhúr-ul-Hassan, returns Capt. Orr's unusual kindness by brutality, K. iii. 486.

LONDON:
PRINTED BY W. H. ALLEN AND CO., 13 WATERLOO PLACE.

W. H. ALLEN & CO.'S WORKS RELATING TO AFGHANISTAN.

COLONEL GRODEKOFF'S RIDE from SAMARCAND to HERAT, through BALKH and the UZBEC STATES of AFGHAN TURKESTAN; with his own March-Route from the Oxus to Herat. By CHARLES MARVIN, author of "The Disastrous Russian Campaign against the Akhal Tekke Turcomans," &c. Crown 8vo., with Portrait, 8s.

"Mr. Marvin's translation is issued very opportunely, when public interest is turned in the direction of Candahar and Herat . . . he supplements his excellent translation of this interesting narrative by some observations which throw light on what is obscure, and by others which contest some of the conclusions of the Russian officer."—*Globe.*

"'Colonel Grodekoff's Ride to Herat' ought to enjoy a popularity scarcely inferior to that of the celebrated 'Ride to Khiva.' To Mr. Marvin belongs the credit of having placed this work at the service of the English reader, and the manner in which he has performed his task leaves nothing to be desired.—*The Pen.*

THE EYE-WITNESSES' ACCOUNT of the DISASTROUS RUSSIAN CAMPAIGN against the AKHAL TEKKE TURCOMANS: Describing the March across the Burning Desert, the Storming of Dengeel Tépé, and the Disastrous Retreat to the Caspian. By CHARLES MARVIN. 8vo., with numerous Maps and Plans, 18s.

"To all who wish to study the policy and progress of Russia in the Trans-Caspian district, and to appreciate the serious difficulty of an advance, this book will be acceptable. It is illustrated by some very clear sketch maps and plans."—*Athenæum.*

"Mr. Marvin's workmanship shows the touch of a true artist. A thorough master of both languages, his transla-

Selection from W. H. Allen & Co.'s New Works.

tion has all the vigour of an original work, while the numerous plans and sketches with which his handsome volume is enriched, are as useful to his readers as they are creditable to himself and his publishers.—*United Service Gazette.*

KANDAHAR IN 1879 : Being the Diary of Major LE MESSURIER, R.E., Brigade Major, R.E., with the Quetta Column. Crown 8vo., 8s. This day.

OUR SCIENTIFIC FRONTIER.—By W. P. ANDREW, Author of "India and Her Neighbours," "The Indus and Its Provinces," "Memoir on the Euphrates Route," &c., &c., &c. With Sketch Map and Appendix, 8vo., 6s.

HISTORY OF AFGHANISTAN, from the Earliest Period to the Outbreak of the War in 1878. By Colonel G. B. MALLESON, C.S.I., Author of "History of the Indian Mutiny." Second Edition, 8vo., with Map, 18s.

HISTORY OF THE WAR IN AFGHANISTAN. By Sir J. KAYE. New Edition, three vols., 26s.

THE RUSSIAN OFFICIAL MAP OF CENTRAL ASIA. Compiled in accordance with the Discoveries and Surveys of Russian Staff Officers up to the the close of the year 1877. In cloth cases, 14s.

THE CABUL INSURRECTION OF 1841–42. Revised and corrected from Liet. EYRE's original Manuscript. By Major General Sir VINCENT EYRE, K.C.S.I., C.B. Edited by Colonel G. B. MALLESON, C.S.I. Crown 8vo., with Map and Illustrations, 9s.

WITH THE KURRUM VALLEY FORCE in the Cabul Campaign of 1878–79. By Major J. A. S. COLQUHOUN, R.A. *In the Press.*

January, 1881.

BOOKS, &c.,

ISSUED BY

MESSRS. W. H. ALLEN & Co.,

Publishers & Literary Agents to the India Office,

COMPRISING

MISCELLANEOUS PUBLICATIONS IN GENERAL LITERATURE.

DICTIONARIES, GRAMMARS, AND TEXT BOOKS IN EASTERN LANGUAGES.

MILITARY WORKS, INCLUDING THOSE ISSUED BY THE GOVERNMENT.

INDIAN AND MILITARY LAW.

MAPS OF INDIA, &c.

13, WATERLOO PLACE, LONDON, S.W.

Works issued from the India Office, and Sold by Wm. H. ALLEN & Co.

Tree and Serpent Worship;
Or, Illustrations of Mythology and Art in India in the First and Fourth Centuries after Christ, from the Sculptures of the Buddhist Topes at Sanchi and Amravati. Prepared at the India Museum, under the authority of the Secretary of State for India in Council. Second edition, Revised, Corrected, and in great part Re-written. By JAMES FERGUSSON, Esq., F.R.S., F.R.A.S. Super-royal 4to. 100 plates and 31 engravings, pp. 270. Price £5 5s.

Illustrations of Ancient Buildings in Kashmir.
Prepared at the Indian Museum under the authority of the Secretary of State for India in Council. From Photographs, Plans, and Drawings taken by Order of the Government of India. By HENRY HARDY COLE, LIEUT. R.E., Superintendent Archæological Survey of India, North-West Provinces. In One vol.; half-bound, Quarto. Fifty-eight plates. £3 10s.

The Illustrations in this work have been produced in Carbon from the original negatives, and are therefore permanent.

Pharmacopœia of India.
Prepared under the Authority of the Secretary of State for India. By EDWARD JOHN WARING, M.D. Assisted by a Committee appointed for the Purpose. 8vo. 6s.

The Stupa of Bharhut. A Buddhist Monument.
Ornamented with numerous Sculptures illustrative of Buddhist Legend and History in the Third Century B.C. By ALEXANDER CUNNINGHAM, C.S.I., C.I.E., Major-General, Royal Engineers (Bengal Retired); Director-General Archæological Survey of India. 4to. Fifty-seven Plates. Cloth gilt. £3 3s.

Archæological Survey of Western India.
Report of the First Season's Operations in the Belgâm and Kaladgi Districts. January to May, 1874. Prepared at the India Museum and Published under the Authority of the Secretary of State for India in Council. By JAMES BURGESS, Author of the " Rock Temples of Elephanta," &c , &c., and Editor of " The Indian Antiquary." Half-bound. Quarto. 58 Plates and Woodcuts. £2 2s.

Archæological Survey of Western India. Vol. II.
Report on the Antiquities of Kâthiâwâd and Kachh, being the result of the Second Season's Operations of the Archæological Survey of Western India. 1874–75. By JAMES BURGESS, F.R.G.S., M.R.A.S., &c., Archæological Surveyor and Reporter to Government, Western India. 1876. Half-bound. Quarto. Seventy-four Plates and Woodcuts. £3 3s.

Archæological Survey of Western India. Vol. III.
Report on the Antiquities in the Bidar and Aurungabad Districts in the Territory of H.H. the Nizam of Haidarabad, being the result of the Third Season's Operations of the Archæological Survey of Western India. 1875–1876. By JAMES BURGESS, F.R.G.S., M.R.A.S., Membre de la Societé Asiatique, &c., Archæological Surveyor and Reporter to Government, Western India. Half-bound. Quarto. Sixty-six Plates and Woodcuts. £2 2s.

Illustrations of Buildings near Muttra and Agra,
Showing the Mixed Hindu-Mahomedan Style of Upper India. Prepared at the India Museum under the authority of the Secretary of State for India in Council, from Photographs, Plans, and Drawings taken by Order of the Government of India. By HENRY HARDY COLE, Lieut. R.E., late Superintendent Archæological Survey of India, North-West Provinces. 4to. With Photographs and Plates. £3 10s.

The Cave Temples of India.
By JAMES FERGUSON, D.C.L., F.R.A.S., V.P.R.A.S., and JAMES BURGESS, F.R.G.S., M.R.A.S., &c. Printed and Published by Order of Her Majesty's Secretary of State, &c. Royal 8vo. With Photographs and Woodcuts. £2 2s.

Aberigh-Mackay (G.) Twenty-one Days in India.
Being the Tour of Sir ALI BABA, K.C.B. By GEORGE
ABERIGH-MACKAY. Post 8vo. 4s.

Adam W. (late of Calcutta) Theories of History.
An Inquiry into the Theories of History,—Chance,—Law,—
Will. With Special Reference to the Principle of Positive
Philosophy. By WILLIAM ADAM. 8vo. 15s.

Akbar. An Eastern Romance
By Dr. P. A. S. VAN LIMBURG-BROUWER. Translated from
the Dutch by M. M. With Notes and Introductory Life of
the Emperor Akbar, by CLEMENTS R. MARKHAM, C.B., F.R.S.
Crown 8vo. 10s. 6d.

Allen's Series.
1.—World We Live In. 2s.
2.—Earth's History. 2s.
3.—Geography of India. (See page 9.) 2s.
4.—2000 Examination Questions in Physical Geography. 2s.
5.—Hall's Trigonometry. (See page 10.) 2s.
6.—Wollaston's Elementary Indian Reader. 1s. (See page 30.)
7.—Ansted's Elements of Physiography. 1s. 4d.

Anderson (P.) The English in Western India.
8vo. 14s.

Andrew (W. P.) India and Her Neighbours,
With Two Maps. 8vo. 15s.

Andrew (W. P.) Our Scientific Frontier.
With Sketch-Map and Appendix. 8vo. 6s.

Ansted (D. T.) Physical Geography.
By Professor D. T. ANSTED, M.A., F.R.S., &c. Fifth
Edition. Post 8vo., with Illustrative Maps. 7s.
CONTENTS:—PART I.—INTRODUCTION.—The Earth as a Planet.
—Physical Forces.—The Succession of Rocks. PART II.—
EARTH.—Land.—Mountains.—Hills and Valleys.—Plateaux
and Low Plains. PART III.—WATER.—The Ocean.—Rivers.
—Lakes and Waterfalls.—The Phenomena of Ice.—Springs
PART IV.—AIR.—The Atmosphere. Winds and Storms.—
Dew, Clouds, and Rain.—Climate and Weather. PART V.—
FIRE.—Volcanoes and Volcanic Phenomena.—Earthquakes.

PART VI.—LIFE.—The Distribution of Plants in the different Countries of the Earth.—The Distribution of Animals on the Earth.—The Distribution of Plants and Animals in Time.—Effects of Human Agency on Inanimate Nature.

"The Book is both valuable and comprehensive, and deserves a wide circulation."—*Observer.*

Ansted (D. T.) Elements of Physiography.
For the use of Science Schools. Fcap. 8vo. 1s. 4d.

Ansted (D. T.) The World We Live In.
Or First Lessons in Physical Geography. For the use of Schools and Students. By D. T. ANSTED, M.A., F.R.S., &c. Fcap. 2s. 25th Thousand, with Illustrations.

Ansted (D. T.) The Earth's History.
Or, First Lessons in Geology. For the use of Schools and Students. By D. T. ANSTED. Third Thousand. Fcap. 2s.

Ansted (D. T.)
Two Thousand Examination Questions in Physical Geography. pp. 180. Price 2s.

Ansted (D. T.) and Latham (R. G.) Channel Islands.
Jersey, Guernsey, Alderney, Sark, &c.
THE CHANNEL ISLANDS. Containing: PART I.—Physical Geography. PART II.—Natural History. PART III.—Civil History. PART IV.—Economics and Trade. By DAVID THOMAS ANSTED, M.A., F.R.S., and ROBERT GORDON LATHAM, M.A., M.D., F.R.S. New and Cheaper Edition in one handsome 8vo. Volume, with 72 Illustrations on Wood by Vizetelly, Loudon, Nicholls, and Hart; with Map. 8vo. 16s.

"This is a really valuable work. A book which will long remain the standard authority on the subject. No one who has been to the Channel Islands, or who purposes going there will be insensible of its value."—*Saturday Review.*
"It is the produce of many hands and every hand a good one."

Ansted (D. T.) Water, and Water Supply.
Chiefly with reference to the British Islands. Part I.—Surface Waters. 8vo. With Maps. 18s.

Archer (Capt. J. H. Laurence) Commentaries on the Punjaub Campaign—1848-49, including some additions to the History of the Second Sikh War, from original sources. By Capt. J. H. LAWRENCE-ARCHER, Bengal H. P. Crown 8vo. 8s.

Aynsley (Mrs.) Our Visit to Hindustan, Kashmir, and Ladakh
By Mrs. J. C. MURRAY AYNSLEY. 8vo. 14s.

Bernay (Dr. A. J.) Students' Chemistry.
Being the Seventh Edition of Household Chemistry, or the Science of Home Life. By ALBERT J. BERNAYS, PH. DR. F.C.S., Prof. of Chemistry and Practical Chemistry at St. Thomas' Hospital, Medical, and Surgical College. Crown 8vo. 5s. 6d.

Binning (R. M.) Travels in Persia, &c.
2 vols. 8vo. 16s.

Blanchard (S.) Yesterday and To-day in India.
By SIDNEY LAMAN BLANCHARD. Post 8vo. 6s.

CONTENTS.—Outward Bound.—The Old Times and the New.—Domestic Life.—Houses and Bungalows.—Indian Servants.—The Great Shoe Question.—The Garrison Hack.—The Long Bow in India.—Mrs. Dulcimer's Shipwreck.—A Traveller's Tale, told in a Dark Bungalow.—Punch in India.—Anglo-Indian Literature.—Christmas in India.—The Seasons in Calcutta.—Farmers in Muslin.—Homeward Bound.—India as it Is.

Blenkinsopp (Rev. E. L.) Doctrine of Development in the
Bible and in the Church. By REV. E. L. BLENKINSOPP, M.A., Rector of Springthorp. 2nd edition. 12mo. 6s.

Boileau (Major-General J. T.)
A New and Complete Set of Traverse Tables, showing the Differences of Latitude and the Departures to every Minute of the Quadrant and to Five Places of Decimals. Together with a Table of the lengths of each Degree of Latitude and corresponding Degree of Longitude from the Equator to the Poles; with other Tables useful to the Surveyor and Engineer. Fourth Edition, thoroughly revised and corrected by the Author. Royal 8vo. 12s. London, 1876.

Boulger (D. C.) Central Asian Portraits; or the Celebrities
of the Khanates and the Neighbouring States. By DEMETRIUS CHARLES BOULGER, M.R.A.S. Crown 8vo. 7s. 6d.

Boulger (D. C.) The Life of Yakoob Beg, Athalik Ghazi and
Badaulet, Ameer of Kashgar. By DEMETRIUS CHARLES BOULGER, M.R.A.S. 8vo. With Map and Appendix. 16s.

Boulger (D. C.) England and Russia in Central Asia. With Appendices and Two Maps, one being the latest Russian Official Map of Central Asia. 2 vols. 8vo. 36s.

Bowring (Sir J.) Flowery Scroll.
A Chinese Novel. Translated and Illustrated with Notes by SIR J. BOWRING. late H.B.M. Plenipo. China. Post 8vo. 10s. 6d.

Boyd (R. Nelson). Coal Mines Inspection; Its History and Results. 8vo. 14s.

Bradshaw (John) The Poetical Works of John Milton, with Notes, explanatory and philological. By JOHN BRADSHAW, LL.D., Inspector of Schools, Madras. 2 vols., post 8vo. 12s. 6d.

Brandis' Forest Flora of North-Western and Central India. By DR. BRANDIS, Inspector General of Forests to the Government of India. Text and Plates. £2 18s.

Briggs (Gen. J.) India and Europe Compared.
Post 8vo. 7s.

Bright (W.) Red Book for Sergeants.
Fifth and Revised Edition, 1880. By W. BRIGHT, Colour-Sergeant, 37th Middlesex R.V. Fcap. interleaved. 1s.

Browne (J. W.) Hardware; How to Buy it for Foreign Markets. 8vo. 10s. 6d.

Buckle (the late Capt. E.) Bengal Artillery.
A Memoir of the Services of the Bengal Artillery from the formation of the Corps. By the late CAPT. E. BUCKLE, Assist.-Adjut. Gen. Ben. Art. Edit. by SIR J. W. KAYE. 8vo. Lond. 1852. 10s.

Buckley (R. B.) The Irrigation Works of India, and their Financial Results. Being a brief History and Description of the Irrigation Works of India, and of the Profits and Losses they have caused to the State. By ROBERT B. BUCKLEY, A.M.I.C.E., Executive Engineer of the Public Works Department of India. 8vo. With Map and Appendix. 9s.

Burke (P.) Celebrated Naval and Military Trials.
By PETER BURKE, Serjeant-at-Law. Author of "Celebrated Trials connected with the Aristocracy." Post 8vo. 10s. 6d.

Challenge of Barletta (The).
By MASSIMO D'AZEGLIO. Rendered into English by Lady LOUISA MAGENIS. 2 vols. Crown 8vo. 21s.

Christmas (Rev. H.) Republic of Fools (The).
Being the History of the People of Abdera in Thrace, from the German of C. M. Von Wieland. By Rev. HENRY CHRISTMAS, M.A., F.R.S. 2 Vols. crown 8vo. 12s.

Christmas (Rev. H.) Sin: Its Causes and Consequences.
An attempt to Investigate the Origin, Nature, Extent and Results of Moral Evil. A Series of Lent Lectures. By the REV. HENRY CHRISTMAS, M.A., F.R.S. Post 8vo. 5s.

Cochrane, (John) Hindu Law. 20s. (See page 12.)

Collette (C. H.) Henry VIII.
An Historical Sketch as affecting the Reformation in England. By CHARLES HASTINGS COLLETTE. Post 8vo 6s.

Collette (C. H.) The Roman Breviary.
A Critical and Historical Review, with Copious Classified Extracts. By CHARLES HASTINGS COLLETTE. 2nd Edition. Revised and enlarged. 8vo. 5s.

Cooper's Hill College. Calendar of the Royal Indian Engineering College, Cooper's Hill. Published by authority in January each year. 6s.

CONTENTS.—Staff of the College; Prospectus for the Year; Table of Marks; Syllabus of Course of Study; Leave and Pension Rules of Indian Service; Class and Prize Lists; Past Students serving in India; Entrance Examination Papers, &c.

Corbet (M. E.) A Pleasure Trip to India, during the Visit of H.R.H. the Prince of Wales, and afterwards to Ceylon. By Mrs. CORBET. Illustrated with Photos. Crown 8vo. 7s. 6d.

Cruise of H.M.S. "Galatea,"
Captain H.R.H. the Duke of Edinburgh, K.G., in 1867—1868. By the REV. JOHN MILNER, B.A., Chaplain; and OSWALD W. BRIERLY. Illustrated by a Photograph of H.R.H. the Duke of Edinburgh; and by Chromo-Lithographs and Graphotypes from Sketches taken on the spot by O. W. BRIERLY. 8vo. 16s.

Danvers (Fred. Chas.) On Coal.
With Reference to Screening, Transport, &c. 8vo. 10s. 6d.

Daumas (E.) Horses of the Sahara, and the Manners of the Desert. By E. DAUMAS, General of the Division Commanding at Bordeaux, Senator, &c., &c. With Commentaries by the Emir Abd-el-Kadir (Authorized Edition). 8vo. 6s.

"We have rarely read a work giving a more picturesque and, at the same time, practical account of the manners and customs of a people, than this book on the Arabs and their horses."—*Edinburgh Courant*.

Deighton (K.) Shakespeare's King Henry the Fifth.
With Notes and an Introduction. By K. DEIGHTON, Principal of Agra College. Crown 8vo. 5s.

Destruction of Life by Snakes, Hydrophobia, &c., in Western India. By an EX-COMMISSIONER. Fcap. 2s. 6d.

Dickins, (F. V.) Chiushingura: or the Loyal League.
A Japanese Romance. Translated by FREDERICK V. DICKINS, Sc.B., of the Middle Temple, Barrister-at-Law. With Notes and an Appendix containing a Metrical Version of the Ballad of Takasako, and a specimen of the Original Text in Japanese character. Illustrated by numerous Engravings on Wood, drawn and executed by Japanese artists and printed on Japanese paper. 8vo. 10s. 6d.

Doran (Dr. J.) "Their Majesties Servants":
Annals of the English Stage. Actors, Authors, and Audiences. From Thomas Betterton to Edmund Kean. By Dr. DORAN, F.S.A., Author of "Table Traits," "Lives of the Queens of England of the House of Hanover." &c. Post 8vo. 6s.

"Every page of the work is barbed with wit, and will make its way point foremost. . . . . provides entertainment for the most diverse tastes."—*Daily News*.

Drury (Col. H.) The Useful Plants of India,
With Notices of their chief value in Commerce, Medicine, and the Arts. By COLONEL HEBER DRURY. Second Edition, with Additions and Corrections. Royal 8vo. 16s.

Edwards (G. Sutherland) A Female Nihilist.
By ERNEST LAVIGNE. Translated from the French by G. SUTHERLAND EDWARDS. Crown 8vo. 9s.

Edwards' (H. S.) The Russians At Home and the Russians Abroad. Sketches, Unpolitical and Political, of Russian Life under Alexander II. By H. SUTHERLAND EDWARDS. 2 vols., Crown 8vo. 21s.

Eyre, Major-General (Sir V.), K.C.S.I., C.B. The Kabul Insurrection of 1841–42. Revised and corrected from Lieut. Eyre's Original Manuscript. Edited by Colonel G. B. MALLESON, C.S.I. Crown 8vo., with Map and Illustrations. 9s.

Fearon (A.) Kenneth Trelawny.
By ALEC FEARON. Author of "Touch not the Nettle." 2 vols. Crown 8vo. 21s.

Forbes (Dr. Duncan) History of Chess.
From the time of the Early Invention of the Game in India, till the period of its establishment in Western and Central Europe. By DUNCAN FORBES, LL.D. 8vo. 7s. 6d.

Gazetteers of India.
Thornton, 4 vols., 8vo. £2 16s.
" 8vo. 21s.
" (N.W.P., &c.) 2 vols., 8vo. 25s.

Gazetteer of Southern India.
With the Tenasserim Provinces and Singapore. Compiled from original and authentic sources. Accompanied by an Atlas, including plans of all the principal towns and cantonments. Royal 8vo. with 4to. Atlas. £3 3s.

Geography of India.
Comprising an account of British India, and the various states enclosed and adjoining. Fcap. pp. 250. 2s.

Geological Papers on Western India.
Including Cutch, Scinde, and the south-east coast of Arabia. To which is added a Summary of the Geology of India generally. Edited for the Government by HENRY J. CARTER, Assistant Surgeon, Bombay Army. Royal 8vo. with folio Atlas of maps and plates; half-bound. £2 2s.

Glyn (A. C.) History of Civilization in the Fifth Century.
Translated by permission from the French of A. Frederic Ozanam, late Professor of Foreign Literature to the Faculty of Letters at Paris. By ASHBY C. GLYN, B.A., of the Inner Temple, Barrister-at-Law. 2 vols., post 8vo. £1 1s.

Goldstucker (Prof. Theodore), The late. The Literary Remains of. With a Memoir. 2 vols. 8vo. 21s.

Grady (S. G.) Mohamedan Law of Inheritance & Contract.
8vo. 14s. (See page 11.)

Grady (S.G.) Institutes of Menu.
8vo. 12s. (See page 11.)

Graham (Alex.) Genealogical and Chronological Tables, illustrative of Indian History. 4to. 5s.

Greene (F. V.) The Russian Army and its Campaigns in Turkey in 1877–1878. By F. V. GREENE, First Lieutenant in the Corps of Engineers, U.S. Army, and lately Military Attaché to the United States Legation at St. Petersburg. 8vo. With Atlas. 32s. Second Edition.

Greene (F. V.) Sketches of Army Life in Russia.
Crown 8vo. 9s.

Griffith (Ralph T. H.) Birth of the War God.
A Poem. By KALIDASA. Translated from the Sanscrit into English Verse. By RALPH T. H. GRIFFITH. 8vo. 5s.

Hall (E. H.) Lands of Plenty, for Health, Sport, and Profit.
British North America. A Book for all Travellers and Settlers. By E. HEPPLE HALL, F.S.S. Crown 8vo., with Maps. 6s.

Hall's Trigonometry.
The Elements of Plane and Spherical Trigonometry. With an Appendix, containing the solution of the Problems in Nautical Astronomy. For the use of Schools. By the REV. T. G. HALL, M.A., Professor of Mathematics in King's College, London. 12mo. 2s.

Hamilton's Hedaya.
A new edition, with the obsolete passages omitted, and a copious Index added by S. G. Grady. 8vo. £1 15s. (See page 11.)

Handbook of Reference to the Maps of India.
Giving the Lat. and Long. of places of note. 18mo. 3s. 6d.
⁎ *This will be found c valuable Companion to Messrs. Allen & Co.'s Maps of India.*

Harcourt (Maj. A. F. P.) Down by the Drawle.
By MAJOR A. F. P. HARCOURT, Bengal Staff Corps, author of "Kooloo, Lahoul, and Spiti," "The Shakespeare Argosy," &c. 2 Vols. crown 8vo. 21s.

Holland.
By Edmondo de Amicis. Translated from the Italian by CAROLINE TILTON. Crown 8vo. 10s. 6d.

Hough (Lieut.-Col. W.) Precedents in Military Law.
8vo. cloth. 25s

Hughes (Rev. T. P.) Notes on Muhammadanism.
Second Edition, Revised and Enlarged. Fcap. 8vo. 6s.

Hutton (J.) Thugs and Dacoits of India.
A Popular Account of the Thugs and Dacoits, the Hereditary Garotters and Gang Robbers of India. By JAMES HUTTON. Post 8vo. 5s.

India Directory (The).
For the Guidance of Commanders of Steamers and Sailing Vessels. Founded upon the Work of the late CAPTAIN JAMES HORSBURGH, F.R.S.

PART I.—The East Indies, and Interjacent Ports of Africa and South America. Revised, Extended, and Illustrated with Charts of Winds, Currents, Passages, Variation, and Tides. By COMMANDER ALFRED DUNDAS TAYLOR, F.R.G.S., Superintendent of Marine Surveys to the Government of India. £1 18s.

PART II.—The China Sea, with the Ports of Java, Australia and Japan and the Indian Archipelago Harbours, as well as those of New Zealand. Illustrated with Charts of the Winds, Currents, Passages, &c. By the same. (*In preparation.*)

Indian and Military Law.
Mahommedan Law of Inheritance, &c. A Manual of the Mahommedan Law of Inheritance and Contract; comprising the Doctrine of the Soonee and Sheea Schools, and based upon the text of Sir H. W. MACNAGHTEN's Principles and Precedents, together with the Decisions of the Privy Council and High Courts of the Presidencies in India. For the use of Schools and Students. By STANDISH GROVE GRADY, Barrister-at-Law, Reader of Hindoo, Mahommedan, and Indian Law to the Inns of Court. 8vo. 14s.

Hedaya, or Guide, a Commentary on the Mussulman Laws, translated by order of the Governor-General and Council of Bengal. By CHARLES HAMILTON. Second Edition, with Preface and Index by STANDISH GROVE GRADY. 8vo. £1 15s.

Institutes of Menu in English. The Institutes of Hindu Law or the Ordinances of Menu, according to Gloss of Collucca. Comprising the Indian System of Duties, Religious and Civil, verbally translated from the Original, with a Preface by SIR WILLIAM JONES, and collated with the Sanscrit Text by GRAVES CHAMNEY HAUGHTON, M.A., F.R.S., Professor of Hindu Literature in the East India College. New edition, with Preface and Index by STANDISH G. GRADY, Barrister-at-Law, and Reader of Hindu, Mahommedan, and Indian Law to the Inns of Court. 8vo., cloth. 12s.

Indian Code of Criminal Procedure. Being Act X. of 1872, Passed by the Governor-General of India in Council on the 25th of April, 1872. 8vo. 12s.

Indian Code of Civil Procedure. Being Act X. of 1877. 8vo. 10s.

Indian Code of Civil Procedure. In the form of Questions and Answers, with Explanatory and Illustrative Notes. By ANGELO J. LEWIS, Barrister-at-law. 12mo. 12s. 6d.

Indian Penal Code. In the Form of Questions and Answers. With Explanatory and Illustrative Notes. By ANGELO J. LEWIS, Barrister-at-Law. Post 8vo. 7s. 6d.

Hindu Law. Principally with reference to such portions of it as concern the Administration of Justice in the Courts in India. By SIR THOMAS STRANGE, late Chief Justice of Madras. 2 vols. Royal 8vo., 1830. 24s.

Hindu Law. Defence of the Daya-Bhaga. Notice of the Case on Prosoono Coomar Tajore's Will. Judgment of the Judicial Committee of the Privy Council. Examination of such Judgment. By JOHN COCHRANE, Barrister-at-Law. Royal 8vo. 20s.

Law and Customs of Hindu Castes, within the Dekhan Provinces subject to the Presidency of Bombay, chiefly affecting Civil Suits. By ARTHUR STEELE. Royal 8vo. £1 1s.

Moohummudan Law of Inheritance. (See page 25.)

Chart of Hindu Inheritance. With an Explanatory Treatise, By ALMARIC RUMSEY. 8vo. 6s. 6d.

Manual of Military Law. For all ranks of the Army, Militia and Volunteer Services. By Colonel J. K. PIPON, Assist. Adjutant General at Head Quarters, & J. F. COLLIER, Esq., of the Inner Temple, Barrister-at-Law. Third and Revised Edition. Pocket size. 5s.

Precedents in Military Law; including the Practice of Courts-Martial; the Mode of Conducting Trials; the Duties of Officers at Military Courts of Inquests, Courts of Inquiry, Courts of Requests, &c., &c. The following are a portion of the Contents:—
1. Military Law. 2. Martial Law. 3. Courts-Martial. 4. Courts of Inquiry. 5. Courts of Inquest. 6. Courts of Request. 7. Forms of Courts-Martial. 8. Precedents of Military Law. 9. Trials of Arson to Rape (Alphabetically arranged.) 10. Rebellions. 11. Riots. 12. Miscellaneous. By Lieut.-Col. W. HOUGH, late Deputy Judge-Advocate-General, Bengal Army, and Author of several Works on Courts-Martial. One thick 8vo. vol. 25s.

The Practice of Courts Martial. By HOUGH & LONG. Thick 8vo. London, 1825. 26s.

Indian Criminal Law and Procedure,

Including the Procedure in the High Courts, as well as that in the Courts not established by Royal Charter; with Forms of Charges and Notes on Evidence, illustrated by a large number of English Cases, and Cases decided in the High Courts of India; and an APPENDIX of selected Acts passed by the Legislative Council relating to Criminal matters. By M. H. STARLING, ESQ., LL.B. & F. B. CONSTABLE, M.A. Third edition. 8vo. £2 2s.

Indian Infanticide.
Its Origin, Progress, and Suppression. By JOHN CAVE-BROWN, M.A. 8vo. 5s.

Irwin (H. C.) The Garden of India; or Chapters on Oudh
History and Affairs. By H. C. IRWIN, B.A. Oxon., Bengal Civil Service. 8vo. 12s.

Jackson (Lt.-Col. B.) Military Surveying, &c. 8vo. 14s.
(See page 20).

Jackson (Lowis D'A.) Hydraulic Manual and Working Tables, Hydraulic and Indian Meteorological Statistics.
Published under the patronage of the Right Honourable the Secretary of State for India. By LOWIS D'A. JACKSON. 8vo. 28s.

Jackson (Lowis D'A.) Canal and Culvert Tables.
Based on the Formula of Kutter, under a Modified Classification, with Explanatory Text and Examples. By LOWIS D'A. JACKSON, A.M.I.C.E., author of "Hydraulic Manual and Statistics," &c. Roy. 8vo. 28s.

Jackson (L. D'A.) Pocket Logarithms and other Tables for
Ordinary Calculations of Quantity, Cost, Interest, Annuities, Assurance, and Angular Functions, obtaining Results correct in the Fourth figure. By LOWIS D'A. JACKSON.

James (A. G. F. Eliot) Indian Industries.
By A. G. F. ELIOT JAMES, Author of "A Guide to Indian Household Management," &c. Crown 8vo. 9s.

CONTENTS:—Indian Agriculture; Beer; Cacao; Carpets; Cereals; Chemicals; Cinchona; Coffee; Cotton; Drugs; Dyeing and Colouring Materials; Fibrous Substances; Forestry; Hides; Skins and Horns; Gums and Resins; Irrigation; Ivory; Mining; Oils; Opium; Paper; Pottery; Ryots; Seeds; Silk; Spices; Sugar; Tea; Tobacco; Wood; Wool. Table of Exports. Index.

Jerrold (Blanchard) at Home in Paris.
2 Vols. Post 8vo. 16s.

Joyner (Mrs.) Cyprus: Historical and Descriptive.
Adapted from the German of Herr FRANZ VON LÖHER. With much additional matter. By Mrs. A. BATSON JOYNER. Crown 8vo. With 2 Maps. 10s. 6d.

Kaye (Sir J. W.) The Sepoy War in India.
A History of the Sepoy War in India, 1857—1858. By Sir JOHN WILLIAM KAYE, Author of "The History of the War in Afghanistan." Vol. I., 8vo. 18s. Vol. II. £1. Vol. III. £1.

CONTENTS OF VOL. I.:—BOOK I.—INTRODUCTORY.—The Conquest of the Punjab and Pegu.—The "Right of Lapse."—The Annexation of Oude.—Progress of Englishism. BOOK II.—The SEPOY ARMY: ITS RISE, PROGRESS, AND DECLINE.—Early History of the Native Army.—Deteriorating Influences.—The Sindh Mutinies.—The Punjaub Mutinies. Discipline of the Bengal Army. BOOK III.—THE OUTBREAK OF THE MUTINY.—Lord Canning and his Council.—The Oude Administration and the Persian War.—The Rising of the Storm.—The First Mutiny.—Progress of Mutiny.—Excitement in Upper India.—Bursting of the Storm.—APPENDIX.

CONTENTS OF VOL II.:—BOOK IV.—THE RISING IN THE NORTH-WEST.—The Delhi History.—The Outbreak at Meerut.—The Seizure of Delhi.—Calcutta in May.—Last Days of General Anson.—The March upon Delhi. BOOK V.—PROGRESS OF REBELLION IN UPPER INDIA.—Benares and Allahabad.—Cawnpore.—The March to Cawnpore.—Re-occupation of Cawnpore. BOOK VI.—THE PUNJAB AND DELHI.—First Conflicts in the Punjab.—Peshawur and Rawul Pinder.—Progress of Events in the Punjab.—Delhi.—First Weeks of the Siege.—Progress of the Siege.—The Last Succours from the Punjab.

CONTENTS OF VOL III.:—BOOK VII.—BENGAL, BEHAR, AND THE NORTH-WEST PROVINCES.—At the Seat of Government.—The Insurrection in Behar.—The Siege of Arrah.—Behar and Bengal. BOOK VIII.—MUTINY AND REBELLION IN THE NORTH-WEST PROVINCES.—Agra in May.—Insurrection in the Districts.—Bearing of the Native Chiefs.—Agra in June, July, August and September. BOOK IX.—LUCKNOW AND DELHI.—Rebellion in Oude.—Revolt in the Districts.—Lucknow in June and July.—The siege and Capture of Delhi.

Kaye (Sir J. W.) History of the War in Afghanistan.
New edition. 3 Vols. Crown 8vo. £1. 6s.

Kaye (Sir J. W.) H. St. G. Tucker's Life and Correspondence.
8vo. 10s.

Kaye (Sir J. W.) Memorials of Indian Governments.
By H. ST. GEORGE TUCKER. 8vo. 10s.

Keatinge (Mrs.) English Homes in India.
By MRS. KEATINGE. Part I.—The Three Loves. Part II.—The Wrong Turning. Two vols., Post 8vo. 16s.

Keene (H. G.) Mogul Empire.
From the death of Aurungzeb to the overthrow of the Mahratta Power, by HENRY GEORGE KEENE, B.C.S. Second edition. With Map. 8vo. 10s. 6d.
This Work fills up a blank between the ending of Elphinstone's and the commencement of Thornton's Histories.

Keene (H. G.) Administration in India.
Post 8vo. 5s.

Keene (H. G.) Peepul Leaves.
Poems written in India. Post 8vo. 5s.

Keene (H. G.). The Turks in India.
Historical Chapters on the Administration of Hindostan by the Chugtai Tartar, Babar, and his Descendants. 12s. 6d.

Latham (Dr. R. G.) Russian and Turk,
From a Geographical, Ethnological, and Historical Point of View. 8vo. 18s.

Laurie (Col. W. F. B.) Our Burmese Wars and Relations
with Burma. With a Summary of Events from 1826 to 1879, including a Sketch of King Theebau's Progress. With various Local, Statistical, and Commercial Information. By Colonel W. F. B. LAURIE, Author of "Rangoon," "Narrative of the Second Burmese War," &c. 8vo. With Plans and Map. 16s.

Lee (F. G.) The Church under Queen Elizabeth.
An Historical Sketch. By the Rev. F. G. LEE, D.D. Two Vols., Crown 8vo. 21s.

Lee (F. G.) The Words from the Cross: Seven Sermons
for Lent, Passion-Tide, and Holy Week. By the Rev. F. G. LEE, D.D. Third edition revised. Fcap. 3s. 6d.

Lee's (Dr. W. N.) Drain of Silver to the East.
Post 8vo. 8s.

Le Messurier (Maj. A.) Kandahar in 1879.
Being the Diary of Major LE MESSURIER, R.E., Brigade Major R.E. with the Quetta Column. Crown 8vo. 8s.

Lewin (T. H.) Wild Races of the South Eastern Frontier of India. Including an Account of the Loshai Country. By Capt. T. H. LEWIN, Dep. Comm. of Hill Tracts. Post 8vo. 10s. 6d.

Lewis (A. J.) Indian Penal Code.
In the Form of Questions and Answers. With Explanatory and Illustrative Notes. By ANGELO J. LEWIS. Post 8vo. 7s. 6d.

Lewis (A. J.) Indian Code of Civil Procedure.
In the Form of Questions and Answers. With Explanatory and Illustrative Notes. By ANGELO J. LEWIS. Post 8vo. 12s. 6d.

Leyden and Erskine's Baber.
MEMOIRS OF ZEHIR-ED-DIN MUHAMMED BABER, EMPEROR OF HINDUSTAN, written by himself in the Jaghatai Turki, and translated partly by the late JOHN LEYDEN, Esq., M.D., and partly by WILLIAM ERSKINE, Esq., with Notes and a Geographical and Historical Introduction, together with a Map of the Countries between the Oxus and Jaxartes, and a Memoir regarding its construction. By CHARLES WADDINGTON, of the East India Company's Engineers. 4to. Lond. 1826. £1 5s.

Liancourt's and Pincott's Primitive and Universal Laws of the Formation and development of language; a Rational and Inductive System founded on the Natural Basis of Onomatops. 8vo. 12s. 6d.

Lockwood (Ed.) Natural History, Sport and Travel.
By EDWARD LOCKWOOD, Bengal Civil Service, late Magistrate of Monghyr. Crown 8vo. With numerous Illustrations. 9s.

Lovell (Vice-Adm.) Personal Narrative of Events from 1799 to 1815. With Anecdotes. By the late Vice-Adm. WM. STANHOPE LOVELL, R.N., K.H. Second edition. Crown 8vo. 4s.

McBean (S.) England, Egypt, Palestine & India by Railway.
Popularly Explained. Crown 8vo., with a coloured Map. 4s.

MacGregor (Col. C. M.) Narrative of a Journey through the Province of Khorassan and on the N. W. Frontier of Afghanistan in 1875. By Colonel C. M. MACGREGOR, C.S.I., C.I.E., Bengal Staff Corps. 2 vols. 8vo. With map and numerous illustrations. 30s.

Maggs (J.) Round Europe with the Crowd.
Crown 8vo. 5s.

Magenis (Lady Louisa) The Challenge of Barletta. By Massimo D'Azeglio. Rendered into English by Lady LOUISA MAGENIS. 2 vols., crown 8vo. 21s.

Malleson (Col. G. B.) Final French Struggles in India and on the Indian Seas. Including an Account of the Capture of the Isles of France and Bourbon, and Sketches of the most eminent Foreign Adventurers in India up to the period of that Capture. With an Appendix containing an Account of the Expedition from India to Egypt in 1801. By Colonel G. B. MALLESON, C.S.I. Crown 8vo. 10s. 6d.

Malleson (Col. G. B.) History of the Indian Mutiny, 1857-1858, commencing from the close of the Second Volume of Sir John Kaye's History of the Sepoy War. Vol. I. 8vo. With Map. 20s.

CONTENTS. BOOK VII.—Calcutta in May and June.—William Tayler and Vincent Eyre.—How Bihar and Calcutta were saved. BOOK VIII.—Mr. Colvin and Agra.—Jhansi and Bandalkhand.—Colonel Durand and Holkar.—Sir George Lawrence and Rajputana.—Brigadier Polwhele's great battle and its results.—Baroli, Rohilkhand, and Farakhabad. BOOK IX.—The relation of the annexation of Oudh to the Mutiny.—Sir Henry Lawrence and the Mutiny in Oudh.—The siege of Lakhnao.—The first relief of Lakhnao.

VOL. II.—Including the Storming of Delhi, the Relief of Lucknow, the Two Battles of Cawnpore, the Campaign in Rohilkhand, and the movements of the several Columns in the N.W. Provinces, the Azimgurh District, and on the Eastern and South-Eastern Frontiers. 8vo. With 4 Plans. 20s.

VOL. III.

BOOK XIII.—Bombay in 1857. Lord Elphinstone. March of Woodburn's Column. Mr. Seton-Karr and the Southern Maratha Country. Mr. Forjett and Bombay. Asirgarh. Sir Henry Durand. March of Stuart's Column. Holkar and Durand. Malwa Campaign. Haidurabad. Major C. Davidson and Salar Jang. Sagar and Narbadi Territory.

BOOK XIV.—Sir Robert Hamilton and Sir Hugh Rose. Central India Campaign. Whitlock and Kirwi. Sir Hugh Rose and Gwaliar. Le Grand Jacob and Western India.

Book XV.—Lord Canning's Oudh policy. Last Campaign in, and pacification of, Oudh. Sir Robert Napier, Smith, Michell, and Tantia Topi.
Book XVI.—Civil Districts during the Mutiny. Minor Actions at Out-stations.
Book XVII.—Conclusion. 8vo. With Plans. 20s.

Malleson (Col. G. B.) History of Afghanistan, from the Earliest Period to the Outbreak of the War of 1878. 8vo. 2nd Edition. With Map. 18s.

Malleson (Col. G. B.) Herat: The Garden and Granary of Central Asia. With Map and Index. 8vo. 8s.

Manning (Mrs.) Ancient and Mediæval India.
Being the History, Religion, Laws, Caste, Manners and Customs, Language, Literature, Poetry, Philosophy, Astronomy, Algebra, Medicine, Architecture, Manufactures, Commerce, &c., of the Hindus, taken from their writings. Amongst the works consulted and gleaned from may be named the Rig Veda, Sama Veda, Yajur Veda, Sathapatha Brahmana, Bhagavat Gita, The Puranas, Code of Manu, Code of Yajnavalkya, Mitakshara, Daya Bhaga, Mahabharata, Atriya, Charaka, Susruta, Ramayana, Raghu Vansa, Bhattikavya, Sakuntala, Vikramorvasi, Malati and Madhava, Mudra Rakshasa, Ratnavali, Kumara Sambhava, Prabodha, Chandrodaya, Megha Duta, Gita Govinda, Panchatantra, Hitopadesa, Katha Sarit, Sagara, Ketala, Panchaviusati, Dasa Kumara Charita, &c. By Mrs. MANNING, with Illustrations. 2 vols., 8vo. 30s.

Marvin (Chas.) Colonel Grodekoff's Ride from Samarcand to Herat, through Balkh and the Uzbek States of Afghan Turkestan. With his own March-route from the Oxus to Herat. By CHARLES MARVIN. Crown 8vo. With Portrait. 8s.

Mayhew (Edward) Illustrated Horse Doctor.
Being an Accurate and Detailed Account, accompanied by more than 400 Pictorial Representations, characteristic of the various Diseases to which the Equine Race are subjected; together with the latest Mode of Treatment, and all the requisite Prescriptions written in Plain English. By EDWARD MAYHEW, M.R.C.V.S. 8vo. 18s. 6d.

CONTENTS.—The Brain and Nervous System.—The Eyes.—The Mouth.—The Nostrils.—The Throat.—The Chest and its contents.—The Stomach, Liver, &c.—The Abdomen.—The

Urinary Organs.—The Skin.—Specific Diseases.—Limbs.—
The Feet.—Injuries.—Operations.

"The book contains nearly 600 pages of valuable matter, which reflects great credit on its author, and, owing to its practical details, the result of deep scientific research, deserves a place in the library of medical, veterinary, and non-professional readers."—*Field.*

"The book furnishes at once the bane and the antidote, as the drawings show the horse not only suffering from every kind of disease, but in the different stages of it, while the alphabetical summary at the end gives the cause, symptoms and treatment of each."—*Illustrated London News.*

Mayhew (Edward) Illustrated Horse Management.

Containing descriptive remarks upon Anatomy, Medicine, Shoeing, Teeth, Food, Vices, Stables; likewise a plain account of the situation, nature, and value of the various points; together with comments on grooms, dealers, breeders, breakers, and trainers; Embellished with more than 400 engravings from original designs made expressly for this work. By E. MAYHEW. A new Edition, revised and improved by J. I. LUPTON. M.R.C.V.S. 8vo. 12s.

CONTENTS.—The body of the horse anatomically considered. PHYSIC.—The mode of administering it, and minor operations. SHOEING.—Its origin, its uses, and its varieties. THE TEETH. —Their natural growth, and the abuses to which they are liable.

FOOD.—The fittest time for feeding, and the kind of food which the horse naturally consumes. The evils which are occasioned by modern stables. The faults inseparable from stables. The so-called "incapacitating vices," which are the results of injury or of disease. Stables as they should be. GROOMS.—Their prejudices, their injuries, and their duties. POINTS.—Their relative importance and where to look for their development. BREEDING.—Its inconsistencies and its disappointments. BREAKING AND TRAINING.—Their errors and their results.

Mayhew (Henry) German Life and Manners.

As seen in Saxony. With an account of Town Life—Village Life—Fashionable Life—Married Life—School and University Life, &c. Illustrated with Songs and Pictures of the Student Customs at the University of Jena. By HENRY MAYHEW, 2 vols., 8vo., with numerous illustrations. 18s.

A Popular Edition of the above. With illustrations. Cr. 8vo. 7s.

"Full of original thought and observation, and may be studied with profit by both German and English—especially by the German."*Athenæum.*

McCosh (J.) Advice to Officers in India.
By JOHN McCOSH, M.D. Post 8vo. 8s.

Meadow (T.) Notes on China.
Desultory Notes on the Government and People of China and on the Chinese Language. By T. T. MEADOWS. 8vo. 9s.

Menzies (S.) Turkey Old and New: Historical, Geographical, and Statistical. By SUTHERLAND MENZIES. With Map and numerous Illustrations. 2 vols., 8vo. 32s.

Military Works—chiefly issued by the Government.

Field Exercises and Evolutions of Infantry. Pocket edition, 1s.

Queen's Regulations and Orders for the Army. Corrected to 1874. 8vo. 3s. 6d. Interleaved, 5s. 6d. Pocket Edition, 1s.

Musketry Regulations, as used at Hythe. 1s.

Dress Regulations for the Army. 1875. 1s. 6d.

Infantry Sword Exercise. 1875. 6d.

Infantry Bugle Sounds. 6d.

Handbook of Battalion Drill. By Lieut. H. C. SLACK. 2s; or with Company Drill, 2s. 6d.

Handbook of Brigade Drill. By Lieut. H. C. SLACK. 3s.

Red Book for Sergeants. By WILLIAM BRIGHT, Colour-Sergeant, 37th Middlesex R.V. 1s.

Handbook of Company Drill; also of Skirmishing, Battalion, and Shelter Trench Drill. By Lieut. CHARLES SLACK. 1s.

Elementary and Battalion Drill. Condensed and Illustrated, together with duties of Company Officers, Markers, &c., in Battalion. By Captain MALTON. 2s. 6d.

Cavalry Regulations. For the Instruction, Formations, and Movements of Cavalry. Royal 8vo. 4s. 6d.

Cavalry Sword, Carbine, Pistol and Lance Exercises, together with Field Gun Drill. Pocket Edition. 1s.

Manual of Artillery Exercises, 1873. 8vo. 5s.

Manual of Field Artillery Exercises. 1877. 3s.

Standing Orders for Royal Artillery. 8vo, 3s.

Principles and Practice of Modern Artillery. By Lt.-Col. C. H. OWEN, R.A. 8vo. Illustrated. 15s.

Artillerist's Manual and British Soldiers' Compendium. By Major F. A. GRIFFITHS. 11th Edition. 5s.

Compendium of Artillery Exercises—Smooth Bore, Field, and Garrison Artillery for Reserve Forces. By Captain J. M. McKenzie. 3s. 6d.

Principles of Gunnery. By JOHN T. HYDE, M.A., late Professor of Fortification and Artillery, Royal Indian Military College, Addiscombe. Second edition, revised and enlarged. With many Plates and Cuts, and Photograph of Armstrong Gun. Royal 8vo. 14s.

Notes on Gunnery. By Captain Goodeve. Revised Edition. 1s.

Text Book of the Construction and Manufacture of Rifled Ordnance in the British Service. By STONEY & JONES. Second Edition. Paper, 3s. 6d., Cloth, 4s. 6d.

Handbooks of the 9, 16, and 64-Pounder R. M. L Converted Guns. 6d. each.

Handbook of the 9 and 10-inch R. M. L. Guns. 6d. each.

Handbook of 40-Pounder B. L. Gun. 6d.

Handbooks of 9-inch Rifle Muzzle Loading Guns of 12 tons, and the 10-inch gun of 18 tons. 6d. each.

Treatise on Fortification and Artillery. By Major HECTOR STRAITH. Revised and re-arranged by THOMAS COOK, R.N., by JOHN T. HYDE, M.A. 7th Edition. Royal 8vo. Illustrated and Four Hundred Plans, Cuts, &c. £2 2s.

Military Surveying and Field Sketching. The Various Methods of Contouring, Levelling, Sketching without Instruments, Scale of Shade, Examples in Military Drawing, &c., &c., &c. As at present taught in the Military Colleges. By Major W. H. RICHARDS, 55th Regiment, Chief Garrison Instructor in India, Late Instructor in Military Surveying, Royal Military College, Sandhurst. Second Edition, Revised and Corrected. 12s.

Treatise on Military Surveying; including Sketching in the Field, Plan-Drawing, Levelling, Military Reconnaissance, &c. By Lieut.-Col. BASIL JACKSON, late of the Royal Staff Corps. The Fifth Edition. 8vo. Illustrated by Plans, &c. 14s.

Instruction in Military Engineering. Vol. I., Part III. 4s.

Elementary Principles of Fortification. A Text-Book for Military Examinations. By J. T. HYDE, M.A. Royal 8vo. With numerous Plans and Illustrations. 10s. 6d.

Military Train Manual. 1s.

The Sappers' Manual. Compiled for the use of Engineer Volunteer Corps. By Col. W. A. FRANKLAND, R.E. With numerous Illustrations. 2s.

Ammunition. A descriptive treatise on the different Projectiles Charges, Fuzes, Rockets, &c., at present in use for Land and Sea Service, and on other war stores manufactured in the Royal Laboratory. 6s.

Hand-book on the Manufacture and Proof of Gunpowder. as carried on at the Royal Gunpowder Factory, Waltham Abbey. 5s.

Regulations for the Training of Troops for service in the Field and for the conduct of Peace Manœuvres. 2s.

Hand-book Dictionary for the Militia and Volunteer Services, Containing a variety of useful information, Alphabetically arranged. Pocket size, 3s. 6d.; by post, 3s. 8d.

Gymnastic Exercises, System of Fencing, and Exercises for the Regulation Clubs. In one volume. Crown 8vo. 1877. 2s.

Army Equipment. Prepared at the Topographical and Statistical Department, War Office. By Col. Sir HENRY JAMES, R.E., F.R.S., &c., Director.

PART. 1.—*Cavalry.* Compiled by Lieut. H. M. HOZIER, 2nd Life Guards. Royal 8vo. 4s.

PART 4.—*Military Train.* Compiled by Lieut. H. M. HOZIER, 2nd Life Guards. Royal 8vo. 2s. 6d.

PART 5.—*Infantry.* Compiled by Capt. F. MARTIN PETRIE, Royal 8vo. With Plates. 5s.

PART 6.—*Commissariat.* Compiled by Lieut. H. M. HOZIER, 2nd Life Guards. Royal 8vo. 1s. 6d.

PART 7.—*Hospital Service.* Compiled by Capt. MARTIN PETRIE. Royal 8vo. With Plates. 5s.

Text-Book on the Theory and Motion of Projectiles; the History, Manufacture, and Explosive Force of Gunpowder; the History of Small Arms. For Officers sent to School of Musketry. 1s. 6d.

Notes on Ammunition. 4th Edition. 1877. 2s. 6d.

Regulations and Instructions for Encampments. 6d.

Rules for the Conduct of the War Game. 2s.

Medical Regulations for the Army, Instructions for the Army, Comprising duties of Officers, Attendants, and Nurses, &c. 1s. 6d.

Purveyors' Regulations and Instructions, for Guidance of Officers of Purveyors' Department of the Army. 3s.

Priced Vocabulary of Stores used in Her Majesty's Service. 4s.

Transport of Sick and Wounded Troops. By DR. LONGMORE. 5s.

Precedents in Military Law. By LT-COL. W. HOUGH. 8vo. 25s.

The Practice of Courts-Martial, by HOUGH & LONG. 8vo. 26s.

Manual of Military Law. For all ranks of the Army, Militia, and Volunteer Services. By Colonel J. K. PIPON, and J. F. COLLIER, Esq. Third and Revised Edition. Pocket size. 5s.

Regulations applicable to the European Officer in India. Containing Staff Corps Rules, Staff Salaries, Commands, Furlough and Retirement Regulations, &c. By GEORGE F. COCHRANE, late Assistant Military Secretary, India Office. 1 vol., post 8vo. 7s. 6d.

Reserve Force; Guide to Examinations, for the use of Captains and Subalterns of Infantry, Militia, and Rifle Volunteers, and for Serjeants of Volunteers. By Capt. G. H. GREAVES. 2nd edit. 2s.

The Military Encyclopædia; referring exclusively to the Military Sciences, Memoirs of distinguished Soldiers, and the Narratives of Remarkable Battles. By J. H. STOCQUELER. 8vo. 12s.

The Operations of War Explained and Illustrated. By Col. HAMLEY. New Edition Revised, with Plates. Royal 8vo. 30s.

Lessons of War. As taught by the Great Masters and Others; Selected and Arranged from the various operations in War. By FRANCE JAMES SOADY, Lieut.-Col., R.A. Royal 8vo. 21s.

The Soldiers' Pocket Book for Field Service. By Col. SIR GARNET J. WOLSELEY. 2nd Edition. Revised and Enlarged. 4s. 6d.

The Surgeon's Pocket Book, an Essay on the best Treatment of Wounded in War. By Surgeon Major J. H. PORTER. 7s. 6d.

A Precis of Modern Tactics. By COLONEL HOME. 8vo. 8s. 6d.

Armed Strength of Austria. By Capt. COOKE. 2 pts. £1 2s.

Armed Strength of Denmark. 3s.

Armed Strength of Russia. Translated from the German. 7s.

Armed Strength of Sweden and Norway. 3s. 6d.

Armed Strength of Italy. 5s. 6d.

Armed Strength of Germany. Part I. 8s. 6d.

The Franco-German War of 1870—71. By CAPT. C. H. CLARKE. Vol. I. £1 6s. Sixth Section. 6s. Seventh Section 6s. Eighth Section. 3s. Ninth Section. 4s. 6d. Tenth Section. 6s. Eleventh Section. 5s. 3d. Twelfth Section. 4s. 6d.

The Campaign of 1866 in Germany. Royal 8vo. With Atlas, 21s.

Celebrated Naval and Military Trials. By PETER BURKE. Post 8vo., cloth. 10s. 6d.

Military Sketches. By SIR LASCELLES WRAXALL. Post 8vo. 6s.

Military Life of the Duke of Wellington. By JACKSON and SCOTT. 2 Vols. 8vo. Maps, Plans, &c. 12s.

Single Stick Exercise of the Aldershot Gymnasium. 6d.

Treatise on Military Carriages, and other Manufactures of the Royal Carriage Department. 5s.

Steppe Campaign Lectures. 2s.

Manual of Instructions for Army Surgeons. 1s

Regulations for Army Hospital Corps. 9d.

Manual of Instructions for Non-Commissioned Officers, Army Hospital Corps. 2s.
Handbook for Military Artificers. 3s.
Instructions for the use of Auxiliary Cavalry. 2s. 6d.
Equipment Regulations for the Army. 5s. 6d.
Statute Law relating to the Army. 1s. 3d.
Regulations for Commissariat and Ordnance Department 2s.
Regulations for the Commissariat Department. 1s. 6d.
Regulations for the Ordnance Department. 1s. 6d.
Artillerist's Handbook of Reference for the use of the Royal and Reserve Artillery, by WILL and DALTON. 5s.
An Essay on the Principles and Construction of Military Bridges, by SIR HOWARD DOUGLAS. 1853. 15s.

Mill's History of British India,
With Notes and Continuation. By H. H. WILSON. 9 vols. cr. 8vo. £2 10s.

Mitford (Maj. R. C. W.) To Caubul with the Cavalry Brigade. A Narrative of Personal Experiences with the Force under General Sir F. S. Roberts, G.C.B. With Map and Illustrations from Sketches by the Author. By Major R. C. W. MITFORD, 14th Bengal Lancers. 8vo. 9s.

Muller's (Max) Rig-Veda-Sanhita.
The Sacred Hymns of the Brahmins; together with the Commentary of Sayanacharya. Published under the Patronage of the Right Honourable the Secretary of State for India in Council. 6 vols., 4to. £2 10s. per volume.

Mysteries of the Vatican;
Or Crimes of the Papacy. From the German of DR. THEODORE GREISENGER. 2 Vols. post 8vo. 21s.

Nirgis and Bismillah.
Nirgis; a Tale of the Indian Mutiny, from the Diary of a Slave Girl: and Bismillah; or, Happy Days in Cashmere. By Hafiz Allard. Post 8vo. 10s. 6d.

Notes on the North Western Provinces of India.
By a District Officer. 2nd Edition. Post 8vo., cloth. 5s.
Contents.—Area and Population.—Soils.—Crops.—Irrigation.—Rent.—Rates.—Land Tenures.

Osborne (Mrs. W.) Pilgrimage to Mecca (A).
By the Nawab Sikandar Begum of Bhopal. Translated from the Original Urdu. By Mrs. Willoughby Osborne. Followed by a Sketch of the History of Bhopal. By Col. Willoughby-Osborne, C.B. With Photographs, and dedicated, by permission, to Her Majesty, Queen Victoria. Post 8vo. £1. 1s.

This is a highly important book, not only for its literary merit, and the information it contains, but also from the fact of its being the first work written by an Indian lady, and that lady a Queen.

Owen (Sidney) India on the Eve of the British Conquest.
A Historical Sketch. By Sidney Owen, M.A. Reader in Indian Law and History in the University of Oxford. Formerly Professor of History in the Elphinstone College, Bombay. Post 8vo. 8s.

Oxenham (Rev. H. N.) Catholic Eschatology and Universalism. An Essay on the Doctrine of Future Retribution. Second Edition, revised and enlarged. Crown 8vo. 7s. 6d.

Oxenham (Rev. H. N.) Catholic Doctrine of the Atonement.
An Historical Inquiry into its Development in the Church, with an Introduction on the Principle of Theological Development. By H. Nutcombe Oxenham, M.A. 2nd Edit. 8vo. 10s. 6d.

"It is one of the ablest and probably one of the most charmingly written treatises on the subject which exists in our language."—*Times.*

Oxenham (H. N.) The First Age of Christianity and the Church.
By John Ignatius Döllinger, D.D., Professor of Ecclesiastical History in the University of Munich, &c., &c. Translated from the German by Henry Nutcombe Oxenham, M.A., late Scholar of Baliol College, Oxford. Third Edition. 2 vols. Crown 8vo. 18s.

Ozanam's (A. F.) Civilisation in the Fifth Century. From the French. By The Hon. A. C. GLYN. 2 Vols., post 8vo. 21s.

Pebody (Charles) Authors at Work.
Francis Jeffrey—Sir Walter Scott—Robert Burns—Charles Lamb—R. B. Sheridan—Sydney Smith—Macaulay—Byron Wordsworth—Tom Moore—Sir James Mackintosh. Post 8vo. 10s. 6d.

Pelly (Sir Lewis). The Miracle Play of Hasan and Husain.
Collected from Oral Tradition by Colonel Sir LEWIS PELLY, K.C.B., K.C.S.I., formerly serving in Persia as Secretary of Legation, and Political Resident in the Persian Gulf. Revised, with Explanatory Notes, by ARTHUR N. WOLLASTON, H.M. Indian (Home) Service, Translator of Anwar-i-Suhaili, &c. 2 Vols. royal 8vo. 32s.

Pipon and Collier's Manual of Military Law.
By Colonel J. K. PIPON, and J. F. COLLIER, Esq., of the Inner Temple, Barrister-at-Law. 5s.

Pollock (Field Marshal Sir George) Life & Correspondence.
By C. R. Low. 8vo. With portrait. 18s.

Pope (G. U.) Text-book of Indian History; with Geogra-
phical Notes, Genealogical Tables, Examination Questions, and Chronological, Biographical, Geographical, and General Indexes. For the use of Schools, Colleges, and Private Students. By the Rev. G. U. POPE, D.D., Principal of Bishop Cotton's Grammar School and College, Bangalore; Fellow of the Madras University. Third Edition, thoroughly revised. Fcap. 4to. 12s.

Practice of Courts Martial.
By HOUGH & LONG. 8vo. London. 1825. 26s.

Prichard's Chronicles of Budgepore, &c.
Or Sketches of Life in Upper India. 2 Vols., Foolscap 8vo. 12s

Prinsep (H. T.) Historical Results.
Deducible from Recent Discoveries in Affghanistan. By H. T. PRINSEP. 8vo. Lond. 1844. 15s.

Prinsep (H. T.) Tibet, Tartary, and Mongolia.
By HENRY T. PRINSEP, Esq. Second edition. Post 8vo. 5s.

Prinsep (H. T.) Political and Military Transactions in India.
2 Vols. 8vo. London, 1825. 18s.

Raverty (Major H. G.) The Pus'hto Manual; comprising a Condensed Grammar, with Idiomatic Phrases, Exercises and Dialogues, and Vocabulary. By Major H. G. RAVERTY, Bombay Army, Retired List. Fcap. 5s.

Richards (Major W. H.) Military Surveying, &c.
12s. (See page 20.)

Rowe (R.) Picked up in the Streets; or, Struggles for Life among the London Poor. By RICHARD ROWE, "Good Words" Commissioner, Author of "Jack Afloat and Ashore," &c. Crown 8vo. Illustrated. 6s.

Rumsey (Almaric) Moohummudan Law of Inheritance, and Rights and Relations affecting it. Sunni Doctrine. Comprising, together with much collateral information, the substance, greatly expanded, of the author's "Chart of Family Inheritance." By ALMARIC RUMSEY, of Lincoln's Inn, Barrister-at-Law, Professor of Indian Jurisprudence at King's College, London. Author of "A Chart of Hindu Family Inheritance." 8vo. 12s.

Rumsey (Almaric) A Chart of Hindu Family Inheritance.
Second Edition, much enlarged. 8vo. 6s. 6d.

Sachau (Dr. C. Ed.) The Chronology of Ancient Nations. An English Version of the Arabic Text of the Athar-ut Bâkiya of Albîrûnî, or "Vestiges of the Past." Collected and reduced to writing by the Author in A.H. 390-1, A.D. 1,000. Translated and Edited, with Notes and Index, by Dr. C. EDWARD SACHAU, Professor in the Royal University of Berlin. Published for the Oriental Translation Fund of Great Britain and Ireland. Royal 8vo. 42s.

Sanderson (G. P.) Thirteen Years among the Wild Beasts of India; their Haunts and Habits, from Personal

Observation; with an account of the Modes of Capturing and Taming Wild Elephants. By G. P. SANDERSON, Officer in Charge of the Government Elephant Keddahs at Mysore. With 21 full page Illustrations and three Maps. Second Edition. Fcp. 4to. £1 5s.

Sewell (R.) Analytical History of India.
From the earliest times to the Abolition of the East India Company in 1858. By ROBERT SEWELL, Madras Civil Service. Post 8vo. 8s.

⁎ The object of this work is to supply the want which has been felt by students for a condensed outline of Indian History which would serve at once to recall the memory and guide the eye, while at the same time it has been attempted to render it interesting to the general reader by preserving a medium between a bare analysis and a complete history.

Shadow of a Life (The) A Girl's Story.
By BERYL HOPE. 3 vols., post 8vo. 31s. 6d.

Sherer (J. W.) The Conjuror's Daughter.
A Tale. By J. W. SHERER, C.S.I. With Illustrations by Alf. T. Elwes and J. Jellicose. Cr. 8vo. 6s.

Sherer (J. W.) Who is Mary?
A Cabinet Novel, in one volume. By J. W. SHERER, Esq., C.S.I. 10s. 6d.

Signor Monaldini's Niece.
A Novel of Italian Life. Crown 8vo. 6s.

Simpson (H. T.) Archæologia Adelensis; or a History of the Parish of Adel, in the West Riding of Yorkshire. Being an attempt to delineate its Past and Present Associations, Archæological, Topographical, and Scriptural. By HENRY TRAILL SIMPSON, M.A., late Rector of Adel. With numerous etchings by W. LLOYD FERGUSON. Roy. 8vo. 21s.

Solymos (B.) Desert Life. Recollections of an Expedition in the Soudan. By B. SOLYMOS (B. E. FALKONBERG), Civil Engineer. 8vo. 15s.

Starling (M. H.) Indian Criminal Law and Procedure.
Third edition. 8vo. £2 2s. See page 12.

Steele (A.) Law and Customs of Hindu Castes.
By ARTHUR STEELE. Royal 8vo. £1. 1s. (See page 12.)

Stent (G. C.) Entombed Alive,
And other Songs and Ballads. (From the Chinese.) By GEORGE CARTER STENT, M.R.A.S., of the Chinese Imperial Maritime Customs Service, author of "Chinese and English Vocabulary," "Chinese and English Pocket Dictionary," "The Jade Chaplet," &c. Crown 8vo. With four Illustrations. 9s.

Stothard (R. T.) The A B C of Art.
Being a system of delineating forms and objects in nature necessary for the attainments of a draughtsman. By ROBERT T. STOTHARD, F.S.A., late H.D.S.A. Fcap. 1s.

Strange's (Sir T.) Hindu Law.
2 Vols. Royal 8vo. 1830. 24s. (See page 12.)

Swinnerton (Rev. C.) The Afghan War. Gough's Action at habad. By the Rev. C. SWINNERTON, Chaplain in the with the First Division, Peshawur Valley Field Force. Frontispiece and Two Plans. Crown 8vo. 5s.

Thomson's Lunar and Horary Tables.
For New and Concise Methods of Performing the Calculations necessary for ascertaining the Longitude by Lunar Observations, or Chronometers; with directions for acquiring a knowledge of the Principal Fixed Stars and finding the Latitude of them. By DAVID THOMSON. Sixty-fifth edit. Royal 8vo. 10s.

Thornton's History of India.
The History of the British Empire in India, by Edward Thornton, Esq. Containing a Copious Glossary of Indian Terms, and a Complete Chronological Index of Events, to aid the Aspirant for Public Examinations. Third edition. 1 vol. 8vo. With Map. 12s.

*** *The Library Edition of the above in 6 volumes, 8vo., may be ad, price £2 8s.*

Thornton's Gazetteer of India.
Compiled chiefly from the records at the India Office. By EDWARD THORNTON. 1 vol., 8vo., pp. 1015. With Map. 21s.

₊ *The chief objects in view in compiling this Gazetteer are:—*
1st. To fix the relative position of the various cities, towns, and villages with as much precision as possible, and to exhibit with the greatest practicable brevity all that is known respecting them; and
2ndly. To note the various countries, provinces, or territorial divisions, and to describe the physical characteristics of each, together with their statistical, social, and political circumstances.
To these are added minute descriptions of the principal rivers and chains of mountains; thus presenting to the reader, within a brief compass, a mass of information which cannot otherwise be obtained, except from a multiplicity of volumes and manuscript records.

The Library Edition.
4 vols., 8vo. Notes, Marginal References, and Map. £2 16s.

Thornton (E.) Gazetteer of the Punjaub, Affghanistan, &c.
Gazetteer of the Countries adjacent to India, on the northwest, including Scinde, Affghanistan, Beloochistan, the Punjaub, and the neighbouring States. By EDWARD THORNTON, Esq. 2 vols. 8vo. £1 5s.

Thornton (T.) East India Calculator.
By T. THORNTON. 8vo. London, 1823. 10s.

Thornton (T.) History of the Punjaub,
And of the Rise, Progress, and Present Condition of the Sikhs. By T. THORNTON. 2 Vols. Post 8vo. 8s.

Tilley (H. A.) Japan, the Amoor and the Pacific.
With notices of other Places, comprised in a Voyage of Circumnavigation in the Imperial Russian Corvette *Rynda*, in 1858—1860. By HENRY A. TILLEY. Eight Illustrations. 8vo. 16s.

Tod (Col. Jas.) Travels in Western India.
Embracing a visit to the Sacred Mounts of the Jains, and the most Celebrated Shrines of Hindu Faith between Rajpootana and the Indus, with an account of the Ancient City of Nehrwalla. By the late Lieut.-Col. JAMES TOD, Illustrations. Royal 4to. £3 3s.

₊ *This is a companion volume to Colonel Tod's Rajusthan.*

Trimen (Capt. R.) Regiments of the British Army,
Chronologically arranged. Showing their History, Services, Uniform, &c. By Captain R. TRIMEN, late 35th Regiment. 8vo. 10s. 6d.

Trotter (L. J.) History of India.
The History of the British Empire in India, from the Appointment of Lord Hardinge to the Death of Lord Canning (1844 to 1862). By Captain LIONEL JAMES TROTTER, late Bengal Fusiliers. 2 vols. 8vo. 16s. each.

Trotter (L. J.) Lord Lawrence.
A Sketch of his Career. Fcap. 1s. 6d.

Trotter (L. J.) Warren Hastings, a Biography.
By Captain LIONEL JAMES TROTTER, Bengal H. P., author of a "History of India," "Studies in Biography," &c. Crown 8vo. 9s.

Turkish Cookery Book (The).
A Collection of Receipts from the best Turkish Authorities. Done into English by FARABI EFENDI. 12mo. Cloth. 3s. 6d.

Vambery (A.) Sketches of Central Asia.
Additional Chapters on My Travels and Adventures, and of the Ethnology of Central Asia. By Armenius Vambery. 8vo. 16s.
"A valuable guide on almost untrodden ground."--*Athenæum.*

Victoria Cross (The) An Official Chronicle of Deeds of Personal Valour achieved in the presence of the Enemy during the Crimean and Baltic Campaigns and the Indian, Chinese, New Zealand, and African Wars. From the Institution of the Order in 1856 to 1880. Edited by ROBERT W. O'BYRNE. Crown 8vo. With Plate. 5s.

Waring (E. J.) Pharmacopœia of India.
By EDWARD JOHN WARING, M.D., &c. 8vo. 6s. (See page 2.)

Watson (M.) Money.
By JULES TARDIEU. Translated from the French by MARGARET WATSON. Crown 8vo. 7s. 6d.

Watson (Dr. J. Forbes) Textile Manufactures and Costumes of the People of India. As originally prepared under the Authority of the Secretary of State for India in Council. By J. FORBES WATSON, M.A., M.D., F.R.A.S., Reporter on the Products of India. Folio, half-morocco. With numerous Coloured Photographs. £3. 5s.

This work—by affording a key to the Fashions of the People, and to the Cotton, Silk, and Wool Textiles in actual use in India—is of special interest to Manufacturers, Merchants, and Agents; as also to the Student and lover of ornamental art.

Watson (Dr. J. F.) and J. W. Kaye, Races and Tribes of Hindostan. The People of India. A series of Photographic Illustrations of the Races and Tribes of Hindustan. Prepared under the Authority of the Government of India, by J. FORBES WATSON, and JOHN WILLIAM KAYE. The Work contains about 450 Photographs on mounts, in Eight Volumes, super royal 4to. £2. 5s. per volume.

Webb (Dr. A.) Pathologia Indica.
Based upon Morbid Specimens from all parts of the Indian Empire. By ALLAN WEBB, B.M.S. Second Edit. 8vo. 14s.

Wellesley's Despatches.
The Despatches, Minutes, and Correspondence of the Marquis Wellesley, K.G., during his Administration in India. 5 vols. 8vo. With Portrait, Map, &c. £6. 10s.

This work should be perused by all who proceed to India in the Civil Services.

Wellington in India.
Military History of the Duke of Wellington in India. 1s.

Wilberforce (E.) Franz Schubert.
A Musical Biography, from the German of Dr. Heinrich Kreisle von Hellborn. By EDWARD WILBERFORCE, Esq., Author of "Social Life in Munich." Post 8vo. 6s.

Wilk's South of India.
3 vols. 4to. £5. 5s.

Wilkins (W. N.) Visual Art; or Nature through the Healthy Eye.
With some remarks on Originality and Free Trade, Artistic Copyright, and Durability. By WM. NOY WILKINS, Author of "Art Impressions of Dresden," &c. 8vo. 6s.

Williams (F.) Lives of the English Cardinals.
The Lives of the English Cardinals, from Nicholas Breakspeare (Pope Adrien IV.) to Thomas Wolsey, Cardinal Legate. With Historical Notices of the Papal Court. By FOLKESTONE WILLIAMS. 2 vols., 8vo. 14s.

Williams (F.) Life, &c., of Bishop Atterbury.
The Memoir and Correspondence of Francis Atterbury, Bishop of Rochester, with his distinguished contemporaries. Compiled chiefly from the Atterbury and Stuart Papers. By FOLKESTONE WILLIAMS, Author of "Lives of the English Cardinals," &c., 2 vols. 8vo. 14s.

Williams (Monier) Indian Wisdom.
Or Examples of the Religious, Philosophical and Ethical Doctrines of the Hindus. With a brief History of the Chief Departments of Sanscrit Literature, and some account of the Past and Present Condition of India, Moral and Intellectual. By MONIER WILLIAMS, M.A., Boden Professor of Sanscrit in in the University of Oxford. Third Edition. 8vo. 15s.

Wilson (H. H.) Glossary of Judicial and Revenue Terms, and of useful Words occurring in Official Documents relating to the Administration of the Government of British India. From the Arabic, Persian, Hindustani, Sanskrit, Hindi, Bengali, Uriya, Marathi, Guzarathi, Telugu, Karnata, Tamil, Malayalam, and other Languages. Compiled and published under the authority of the Hon. the Court of Directors of the E. I. Company. 4to., cloth. £1 10s.

White (S. D.) Indian Reminiscences.
By Colonel S. DEWE' WHITE, late Bengal Staff Corps. 8vo. With 10 Photographs. 14s.

Wollaston (Arthur N.) Anwari Suhaili, or Lights of Canopus
Commonly known as Kalilah and Damnah, being an adaptation of the Fables of Bidpai. Translated from the Persian. Royal 8vo., 42s.; also in royal 4to., with illuminated borders, designed specially for the work, cloth, extra gilt. £3 13s. 6d.

Wollaston (Arthur N.) Elementary Indian Reader.
Designed for the use of Students in the Anglo-Vernacular Schools in India. Fcap. 1s.

Woolrych (Serjeant W. H.)
Lives of Eminent Serjeants-at-Law of the English Bar. By HUMPHRY W. WOOLRYCH, Serjeant-at-Law. 2 vols. 8vo. 30s.

Wraxall (Sir L., Bart.) Caroline Matilda.
Queen of Denmark, Sister of George 3rd. From Family and State Papers. By SIR LASCELLES WRAXALL, Bart. 3 vols., 8vo. 18s.

Young (J. R.) Course of Mathematics.
A Course of Elementary Mathematics for the use of candidates for admission into either of the Military Colleges; of applicants for appointments in the Home or Indian Civil Services; and of mathematical students generally. By Professor J. R. YOUNG. In one closely-printed volume. 8vo., pp. 648. 12s.

"In the work before us he has digested a complete Elementary Course, by aid of his long experience as a teacher and writer; and he has produced a very useful book. Mr. Young has not allowed his own taste to rule the distribution, but has adjusted his parts with the skill of a veteran."—*Athenæum*.

Works in the Press.

Merv, the Queen of the World and the Scourge of the Men-stealing Turcomans. By CHARLES MARVIN, author of "The Disastrous Turcoman Campaign," and "Grodekoff's Ride to Herat."

In Zululand with the British, throughout the War of 1879. By CHARLES L. NORRIS-NEWMAN, Special Correspondent of the London "Standard," Cape Town "Standard and Mail," and the "Times" of Natal. 8vo. With Plans and Illustrations.

Sketches from Nipal, Historical and Descriptive; with Anecdotes of the Court Life and Wild Sports of the Country in the time of Maharaja Jang Bahadur, G.C.B.; to which is added an Essay on Nipalese Buddhism. By the late A. A. Oldfield, M.D., many years Resident at Kathmandu. Two vols. Illustrated.

The Lyrical Drama: Essays on Subjects, Composers, and Executants of Modern Opera. By H. SUTHERLAND EDWARDS, Author of "The Russians at Home and Abroad," &c.

Stories of the City of London; Retold for Youthful Readers. By Mrs. NEWTON CROSLAND.

These Stories range from the early days of Old London Bridge and the Settlement of the Knights Templars in England to the time of the Gordon Riots; with incidents in the Life of Brunel in relation to the Thames Tunnel; narrated from Personal recollections.

The Expiring Continent; A Narrative of Travel in Sene-gambia, with Observations on Native Character; Present Condition and Future Prospects of Africa and Colonisation. By ALEX. WILL. MITCHIESON.

Memoirs of a Griffin; or, A Cadet's First Year in India. By Captain BELLEW. Illustrated from Designs by the Author. A New Edition.

A Dictionary of Ethnological and Philological Geography.
By R. G. LATHAM, M.A., M.D., F.R.S., &c.

Incidents of a Journey through Nubia to Darfoor. By
SYDNEY ENSOR, C.E.

The History of China. By DEMETRIUS CHARLES BOULGER,
Author of "England and Russia in Central Asia," &c.

The History of India, as told by its own Historians; the
Local Muhammadan Dynasties. Vol. I. Guzerat. By JOHN
DOWSON, M.R.A.S., late Professor of the Staff College.
Forming a Sequel in two or more volumes to Sir H. M.
Elliott's Original work on the Muhammadan period of the
History of India; already edited, annotated, and amplified by
the same Author. Published under the Patronage of H.M.'s
Secretary of State for India.

With the Kurrum Valley Force in the Caubul Campaign of
1878–79. By Major J. A. S. COLQUHOUN, R.A.

New Editions of Works by PARKER GILMORE ("Ubique.")

A Ride through Hostile Africa. Illustrated.

In the Backwoods. Illustrated.

On the Prairies. Illustrated.

Mansukhi and Sundar Singh; a Hindu Tale. Hindustani
and English. With 24 Illustrations. By H. B. W. GARRICK.

An Integral Calculus. Simplified for Schools. By W. P.
LYNAM, Indian Public Works Department.

Luck, and what came of it. A New Novel. By CHARLES
MACKAY, LL.D.

Catholic Doctrine of the Atonement: an Historical Inquiry
into its Development in the Church, with an Introduction on
the Principle of Theological Development. By H. NUTCOMBE
OXENHAM. A new and enlarged edition.

W. H. ALLEN & Co.,

Analytical Index to Sir JOHN KAYE's History of the Sepoy War, and Col. G. B. MALLESON's History of the Indian Mutiny, combined in one volume. By FREDERIC PINCOTT, M.R.A.S.

Accented Four-Figure Logarithms, and other Tables. For purposes both of Ordinary and of Trigonometrical Calculation, and for the Correction of Altitudes and Lunar Distances. Arranged and accented by LOWIS D'A. JACKSON, A.M.S.C.E., Author of "Canal and Culvert Tables," "Hydraulic Manual," &c.

An Arabic Manual. By Professor E. H. PALMER.

A Hindi Manual. By FREDERIC PINCOTT, M.R.A.S.

An English-Arabic Dictionary. By DR. STEINGASS.

An English-Persian Dictionary. Compiled from Original Sources. By ARTHUR N. WOLLASTON, M.R.A.S., Translator of the "Anwar-i-Suhaili."

An English-Hindi Dictionary. By FREDERIC PINCOTT, M.R.A.S.

Posthumous Papers of C. J. F. S. Forbes relative to the language and races of Burma.

Whisperings in the Wood. From the Swedish of Zacharias Tropelius. By ALBERT ALBERG.

Chili: its People and Resources. Notes of a Visit during the War of 1879–1880. By R. NELSON BOYD, Author of "Coal Mines Inspection."

Foreign Secretaries of the Nineteenth Century: Grenville to Palmerston. By PERCY M. THORNTON.

A SELECTION FROM

MESSRS. ALLEN'S CATALOGUE
OF BOOKS IN THE EASTERN LANGUAGES, &c.

HINDUSTANI, HINDI, &c.

[*Dr. Forbes's Works are used as Class Books in the Colleges and Schools in India.*]

Forbes's Hindustani-English Dictionary in the Persian Character, with the Hindi words in Nagari also; and an English Hindustani Dictionary in the English Character; both in one volume. By DUNCAN FORBES, LL.D. Royal 8vo. 42s.

Forbes's Hindustani-English and English Hindustani Dictionary, in the English Character. Royal 8vo. 36s.

Forbes's Smaller Dictionary, Hindustani and English, in the English Character. 12s.

Forbes's Hindustani Grammar, with Specimens of Writing in the Persian and Nagari Characters, Reading Lessons, and Vocabulary. 8vo. 10s. 6d.

Forbes's Hindustani Manual, containing a Compendious Grammar, Exercises for Translation, Dialogues, and Vocabulary, in the Roman Character. New Edition, entirely revised. By J. T. PLATTS. 18mo. 3s. 6d.

Forbes's Bagh o Bahar, in the Persian Character, with a complete Vocabulary. Royal 8vo. 12s. 6d.

Forbes's Bagh o Bahar in English, with Explanatory Notes, illustrative of Eastern Character. 8vo. 8s.

Forbes's Bagh o Bahar, with Vocaby., English Character. 5s.

Forbes's Tota Kahani; or, "Tales of a Parrot," in the Persian Character, with a complete Vocabulary. Royal 8vo. 8s.

Forbes's Baital Pachisi; or, "Twenty-five Tales of a Demon," in the Nagari Character, with a complete Vocabulary. Royal 8vo. 9s.

Forbes's Ikhwanu s Safa; or, "Brothers of Purity," in the Persian Character. Royal 8vo. 12s. 6d.

[*For the higher standard for military officers' examinations.*]

Forbes's Oriental Penmanship; a Guide to Writing Hindustani in the Persian Character. 4to. 8s.

Platts' Grammar of the Urdu or Hindustani-Language. 8vo. 12s.

Eastwick (Edward B.) The Bagh-o-Bahar—literally translated into English, with copious explanatory notes. 8vo. 10s. 6d.

Small's (Rev. G.) Tota Kahani; or, "Tales of a Parrot." Translated into English. 8vo. 8s.

Platts' J. T., Baital Pachisi; translated into English. 8vo. 8s.

Platts' Ikhwanu S Safa; translated into English. 8vo. 10s. 6d.

Hindustani Selections, with a Vocabulary of the Words. By JAMES R. BALLANTYNE. Second Edition. 1845. 5s.

Singhasan Battisi. Translated into Hindi from the Sanscrit. A New Edition. Revised, Corrected, and Accompanied with Copious Notes. By SYED ABDOOLAH. Royal 8vo. 12s. 6d.

Robertson's Hindustani Vocabulary. 3s. 6d.

Akhlaki Hindi, translated into Urdu, with an Introduction and Notes. By SYED ABDOOLAH. Royal 8vo. 12s. 6d.

Sakuntala. Translated into Hindi from the Bengali recension of the Sanskrit. Critically edited, with grammatical, idiomatical, and exegetical notes, by FREDERIC PINCOTT. 4to. 12s. 6d.

SANSCRIT.

Haughton's Sanscrit and Bengali Dictionary, in the Bengali Character, with Index, serving as a reversed dictionary. 4to. 30s.

Williams's English-Sanscrit Dictionary. 4to., cloth. £3. 3s.

Williams's Sanskrit-English Dictionary. 4to. £4 14s. 6d.

Wilkin's (Sir Charles) Sanscrit Grammar. 4to. 15s.

Williams's (Monier) Sanscrit Grammar. 8vo. 15s.

Williams's (Monier) Sanscrit Manual; to which is added, a Vocabulary, by A. E. GOUGH. 18mo. 7s. 6d.

Gough's (A. E.) Key to the Exercises in Williams's Sanscrit Manual. 18mo. 4s.

Williams's (Monier) Sakuntala, with Literal English Translation of all the Metrical Passages, Schemes of the Metres, and copious Critical and Explanatory Notes. Royal 8vo. 21s.

Williams's (Monier) Sakuntala. Translated into English Prose and Verse. Fourth Edition. 8s.

Williams's (Monier) Vikramorvasi. The Text. 8vo. 5s.

Cowell's (E. B.) Translation of the Vikramorvasi. 8vo. 3s. 6d.

Thompson's (J. C.) Bhagavat Gita. Sanscrit Text. 5s.
Haughton's Menu, with English Translation. 2 vols. 4to. 24s.
Johnson's Hitopadesa, with Vocabulary. 15s.
Hitopadesa. A new literal translation from the Sanskrit Text of Prof. F. Johnson. For the use of Students. By FREDERIC PINCOTT, M.R.A.S. 6s.
Hitopadesa, Sanscrit, with Bengali and English Trans. 10s. 6d.
Wilson's Megha Duta, with Translation into English Verse, Notes, Illustrations, and a Vocabulary. Royal 8vo. 6s.

PERSIAN.

Richardson's Persian, Arabic, and English Dictionary. Edition of 1852. By F. JOHNSON. 4to. £4.
Forbes's Persian Grammar, Reading Lessons, and Vocabulary. Royal 8vo. 12s. 6d.
Ibraheem's Persian Grammar, Dialogues, &c. Royal 8vo. 12s. 6d.
Gulistan. Carefully collated with the original MS., with a full Vocabulary. By JOHN PLATTS, late Inspector of Schools, Central Provinces, India. Royal 8vo. 12s. 6d.
Gulistan. Translated from a revised Text, with Copious Notes. By JOHN PLATTS. 8vo. 12s. 6d.
Ouseley's Anwari Soheili. 4to. 42s.
Wollaston's (Arthur N.) Translation of the Anvari Soheili. Royal 8vo. £2 2s.
Keene's (Rev. H. G.) First Book of The Anwari Soheili. Persian Text. 8vo. 5s.
Ouseley's (Col.) Akhlaki Mushini. Persian Text. 8vo. 5s.
Keene's (Rev. H. G.) Akhlaki Mushini. Translated into English. 8vo. 3s. 6d.
Clarke's (Captain H. Wilberforce, R.E.) The Persian Manual.
A Pocket Companion.
PART I.—A CONCISE GRAMMAR OF THE LANGUAGE, with Exercises on its more Prominent Peculiarities, together with a Selection of Useful Phrases, Dialogues, and Subjects for Translation into Persian.
PART II.—A VOCABULARY OF USEFUL WORDS, ENGLISH AND PERSIAN, showing at the same time the difference of idiom between the two Languages. 18mo. 7s. 6d.
The Bústán. By Shaikh Muslihu-d-Dín Sa'di Shírází. Translated for the first time into Prose, with Explanatory Notes and Index. By Captain H. WILBERFORCE CLARKE, R.E. 8vo. With Portrait. 30s.
A Translation of Robinson Crusoe into the Persián Language. Roman Character. Edited by T. W. H. TOLBORT, Bengal Civil Service. Cr. 8vo. 7s.

BENGALI.

Haughton's Bengali, Sanscrit, and English Dictionary, adapted for Students in either language; to which is added an Index, serving as a reversed dictionary. 4to. 30s.

Forbes's Bengali Grammar, with Phrases and dialogues. Royal 8vo. 12s. 6d.

Forbes's Bengali Reader, with a Translation and Vocabulary Royal 8vo. 12s. 6d.

Nabo Nari. 12mo. 7s.

ARABIC.

Richardson's Arabic, Persian and English Dictionary. Edition of 1852. By F. JOHNSON. 4to., cloth. £4.

Forbes's Arabic Grammar, intended more especially for the use of young men preparing for the East India Civil Service, and also for the use of self instructing students in general. Royal 8vo., cloth. 18s.

Palmer's Arabic Grammar. 8vo. 18s.

Forbes's Arabic Reading Lessons, consisting of Easy Extracts from the best Authors, with Vocabulary. Royal 8vo., cloth. 15s.

An Arabic Manual. By Professor E. H. PALMER. (*In the press.*)

TELOOGOO.

Brown's Dictionary, reversed; with a Dictionary of the Mixed Dialects used in Teloogoo. 3 vols. in 2, royal 8vo. £5.

Campbell's Dictionary. Royal 8vo. 30s.

Bromn's Reader. 8vo. 2 vols. 14s.

Brown's Dialogues, Teloogoo and English. 8vo. 5s. 6d.

Pancha Tantra. 8s.

Percival's English-Teloogoo Dictionary. 10s. 6d.

TAMIL.

Rottler's Dictionary, Tamil and English. 4to. 42s.

Babington's Grammar (High Dialect). 4to. 12s.

Percival's Tamil Dictionary. 2 vols. 10s. 6d.

GUZRATTEE.

Mavor's Spelling, Guzrattee and English. 7s, 6d.
Shapuaji Edalji's Dictionary, Guzrattee and English. 21s.

MAHRATTA.

Molesworth's Dictionary, Mahratta and English. 4to. 42s.
Molesworth's Dictionary, English and Mahratta. 4to. 42s.
Stevenson's Grammar. 8vo., cloth. 17s. 6d.
Esop's Fables. 12mo. 2s. 6d.
Fifth Reading Book. 7s.

MALAY.

Marsden's Grammar. 4to. £1 1s.

CHINESE.

Morrison's Dictionary. 6 vols. 4to. £10.
Marshman's—Clavis Sinica, a Chinese Grammar. 4to. £2 2s.
Morrison's View of China, for Philological purposes; containing a Sketch of Chinese Chronology, Geography, Government, Religion and Customs, designed for those who study the Chinese language. 4to. 6s.

PUS'HTO.

The Pushto Manual. Comprising a Concise Grammar; Exercises and Dialogues; Familiar Phrases, Proverbs, and Vocabulary. By Major H. G. RAVERTY, Bombay Infantry (Retired). Author of the Pus'hto Grammar, Dictionary, Selections Prose and Poetical, Selections from the Poetry of the Afghans (English Translation), Æsop's Fables, &c. &c. Fcap. 5s.

MISCELLANEOUS.

Reeve's English-Carnatica and Carnatica-English Dictionary. 2 vols. (Very slightly damaged). £3.
Collett's Malayalam Reader. 8vo. 12s. 6d.
Esop's Fables in Carnatica. 8vo. bound. 12s. 6d.
A Turkish Manual, comprising a Condensed Grammar with Idiomatic Phrases, Exercises and Dialogues, and Vocabulary. By Captain C. F. MACKENZIE, late of H.M.'s Consular Service. 6s.

A CHRONOLOGICAL AND HISTORICAL

CHART OF INDIA,

Price, fully tinted, mounted on roller or in case, 20s. size, about 40 in. by 50 in.

Showing, at one view, all the principal nations, governments, and empires which have existed in that country from the earliest times to the suppression of the Great Mutiny, A.D. 1858, with the date of each historical event according to the *various eras used in India.*

BY

ARTHUR ALLEN DURTNALL,

Of the High Court of Justice in England.

By this Chart, any person, however ignorant of the subject, may, by an hour's attention, obtain a clear view of the broad lines of Indian History, and of the evolutions which have resulted in the dominion of Her Majesty as EMPRESS OF INDIA. It will be found invaluable for EDUCATIONAL PURPOSES, especially in Colleges and Schools, where an Indian career is in contemplation. It will also be found of PERMANENT UTILITY in all Libraries and Offices as a work of ready reference for the connection of events and dates. Besides the History of India, it includes the contemporaneous histories of AFGHANISTAN, CENTRAL ASIA, and EUROPE.

A RELIEVO MAP OF INDIA.

BY

HENRY F. BRION.

In Frame, 21s.

A map of this kind brings before us such a picture of the surface of a given country as no ordinary map could ever do. To the mind's eye of the average Englishman, India consists of 'the plains' and 'the hills,' chiefly of the former, the hills being limited to the Himalayas and the Nilgiris. The new map will at least enable him to correct his notions of Indian geography. It combines the usual features of a good plain map of the country on a scale of 150 miles to the inch, with a faithful representation of all the uneven surfaces, modelled on a scale thirty-two times the horizontal one; thus bringing out into clear relief the comparative heights and outlines of all the hill-ranges, and showing broad tracts of uneven ground, of intermingled hill and valley, which a common map of the same size would hardly indicate, except to a very practised eye. The plains of Upper India are reduced to their true proportions; the Central Provinces, Malwa, and Western Bengal reveal their actual ruggedness at a glance; and Southern India, from the Vindhyas to Cape Comorin, proclaims its real height above the sea-level. To the historical as well as the geographical student such a map is an obvious and important aid in tracing the course of past campaigns, in realising the conditions under which successive races carried their arms or settlements through the Peninsula, and in comprehending the difference of race, climate, and physical surroundings which make up our Indian Empire. Set in a neat frame of maplewood, the map seems to attract the eye like a prettily-coloured picture, and its price, a guinea, should place it within the reach of all who care to combine the useful with the ornamental."—*Home News.*

MAPS OF INDIA, etc.

Messrs. Allen & Co.'s Maps of India were revised and much improved during 1876, with especial reference to the existing Administrative Divisions, Railways, &c.

District Map of India; corrected to 1876;
Divided into Collectorates with the Telegraphs and Railways from Government surveys. On six sheets—size, 5ft. 6in. high; 5ft. 8in. wide, £2; in a case, £2 12s. 6d.; or, rollers, varn., £3 3s.

A General Map of India; corrected to 1876;
Compiled chiefly from surveys executed by order of the Government of India. On six sheets—size, 5 ft. 3 in. wide; 5 ft. 4 in. high, £2; or, on cloth, in case, £2 12s. 6d.; or, rollers, varn., £3 3s.

Map of India; corrected to 1876;
From the most recent Authorities. On two sheets—size, 2 ft. 10in. wide; 3 ft. 3 in. high, 16s.; or, on cloth, in a case, £1 1s.

Map of the Routes in India; corrected to 1874;
With Tables of Distances between the principal Towns and Military Stations On one sheet—size, 2 ft. 3 in. wide; 2 ft. 9 in. high, 9s.; or, on cloth, in a case, 12s.

Map of the Western Provinces of Hindoostan,
The Punjab, Cabool, Scinde, Bhawulpore, &c., including all the States between Candahar and Allahabad. On four sheets—size, 4 ft. 4in. wide; 4 ft. 2 in. high, 30s.; or, in case, £2; rollers, varnished, £2 10s.

Map of India and China, Burmah, Siam, the Malay Peninsula, and the Empire of Anam. On two sheets—size, 4 ft. 3 in. wide; 3 ft. 4 in. high, 16s.; or, on cloth, in a case, £1 5s.

Map of the Steam Communication and Overland Routes between England, India, China, and Australia. In a case, 14s.; on rollers, and varnished, 18s.

Map of China,
From the most Authentic Sources of Information. One large sheet—size, 2 ft. 7 in. wide; 2 ft. 2 in. high, 6s.; or, on cloth, in case, 8s.

Map of the World;
On Mercator's Projection, showing the Tracts of the Early Navigators, the Currents of the Ocean, the Principal Lines of great Circle Sailing, and the most recent discoveries. On four sheets—size, 6ft. 2 in. wide; 4 ft. 3 in. high, £2; on cloth, in a case, £2 10s; or, with rollers, and varnished, £3.

Handbook of Reference to the Maps of India.
Giving the Latitude and Longitude of places of note. 18mo. 3s. 6d.

Russian Official Map of Central Asia. Compiled in accordance with the Discoveries and Surveys of Russian Staff Officers up to the close of the year 1877. In 2 Sheets. 10s. 6d., or in cloth case, 14s.

In January and July of each year is published in 8vo., price 10s. 6d.,

THE INDIA LIST, CIVIL & MILITARY,
BY PERMISSION OF THE SECRETARY OF STATE FOR INDIA IN COUNCIL.

CONTENTS.

CIVIL.—Gradation Lists of Civil Service, Bengal, Madras and Bombay. Civil Annuitants. Legislative Council, Ecclesiastical Establishments, Educational, Public Works, Judicial, Marine, Medical, Land Revenue, Political, Postal, Police, Customs and Salt, Forest, Registration and Railway and Telegraph Departments, Law Courts, Surveys, &c., &c.

MILITARY.—Gradation List of the General and Field Officers (British and Local) of the three Presidencies, Staff Corps, Adjutants-General's and Quartermasters-General's Offices, Army Commissariat Departments, British Troops Serving in India (including Royal Artillery, Royal Engineers, Cavalry, Infantry, and Medical Department), List of Native Regiments, Commander-in-Chief and Staff, Garrison Instruction Staff, Indian Medical Department, Ordnance Departments, Punjab Frontier Force, Military Departments of the three Presidencies, Veterinary Departments, Tables showing the Distribution of the Army in India, Lists of Retired Officers of the three Presidencies.

HOME.—Departments of the Office of the Secretary of State, Coopers Hill College, List of Selected Candidates for the Civil and Forest Services, Indian Troop Service.

MISCELLANEOUS.—Orders of the Bath, Star of India, and St. Michael and St. George. Order of Precedence in India. Regulations for Admission to Civil Service. Regulations for Admission of Chaplains. Civil Leave Code and Supplements. Civil Service Pension Code—relating to the Covenanted and Uncovenanted Services. Rules for the Indian Medical Service. Furlough and Retirement Regulations of the Indian Army. Family Pension Fund. Staff Corps Regulations. Salaries of Staff Officers. Regulations for Promotion. English Furlough Pay.

THE
ROYAL KALENDAR,
AND COURT AND CITY REGISTER,
FOR ENGLAND, IRELAND, SCOTLAND, AND THE COLONIES,

For the Year 1880.

CONTAINING A CORRECT LIST OF THE TWENTY-FIRST IMPERIAL PARLIAMENT, SUMMONED TO MEET FOR THEIR FIRST SESSION—MARCH 5TH, 1874.

House of Peers—House of Commons—Sovereigns and Rulers of States of Europe—Orders of Knighthood—Science and Art Department—Queen's Household—Government Offices—Mint—Customs—Inland Revenue—Post Office—Foreign Ministers and Consuls—Queen's Consuls Abroad—Naval Department—Navy List—Army Department—Army List—Law Courts—Police—Ecclesiastical Department—Clergy List—Foundation Schools—Literary Institutions—City of London—Banks—Railway Companies—Hospitals and Institutions—Charities—Miscellaneous Institutions—Scotland, Ireland, India, and the Colonies; and other useful information.

Price with Index, 7s.; *without Index,* 5s.

Published on the arrival of every Mail from India. Subscription 26s. per annum, post free, specimen copy, 6d.

ALLEN'S INDIAN MAIL,
AND

Official Gazette

FROM

INDIA, CHINA, AND ALL PARTS OF THE EAST.

ALLEN'S INDIAN MAIL contains the fullest and most authentic Reports of all important Occurrences in the Countries to which it is devoted, compiled chiefly from private and exclusive sources. It has been pronounced by the Press in general to be *indispensable* to all who have Friends or Relatives in the East, as affording the only *correct* information regarding the Services, Movements of Troops, Shipping, and all events of Domestic and individual interest.

The subjoined list of the usual Contents will show the importance and variety of the information concentrated in ALLEN'S INDIAN MAIL.

Summary and Review of Eastern News.

Precis of Public Intelligence	Shipping—Arrival of Ships
Selections from the Indian Press	,, ,, Passengers
Movements of Troops	,, Departure of Ships
The Government Gazette	,, ,, Passengers
Courts Martial	Commercial—State of the Markets
Domestic Intelligence—Births	,, Indian Securities
,, ,, Marriages	,, Freights
,, ,, Deaths	&c. &c. &c.

Home Intelligence relating to India, &c.

Original Articles	Arrival reported in England
Miscellaneous Information	Departures ,, ,,
Appointments, List of Furloughs, Extensions, &c.	Shipping—Arrival of Ships
	,, ,, Passengers
,, Civil	,, Departure of Ships
,, Military	,, ,, Passengers
,, Ecclesiastical and	,, Vessel spoken with
,, Marine	&c. &c. &c.

Review of Works on the East.—And Notices of all affairs connected with India and the Services.

Each year an INDEX is furnished, to enable Subscribers to bind up the Volume which forms a complete

ASIATIC ANNUAL REGISTER AND LIBRARY OF REFERENCE.

LONDON: WM. H. ALLEN & Co., 13, WATERLOO PLACE, S.W.

(PUBLISHERS TO THE INDIA OFFICE),

To whom Communications for the Editor, and Advertisements are requested to be addressed.

Subscription, 32s. per annum. Postage Free. Or in
Monthly Parts, price 3s.

PRÉCIS OF OFFICIAL PAPERS,
BEING
ABSTRACTS OF ALL PARLIAMENTARY RETURNS
DIRECTED TO BE PRINTED BY
BOTH HOUSES OF PARLIAMENT.

SESSION 1880.

"Messrs. Allen have commenced the publication of a most useful work, the need of which has been felt for a long time, though until now no one has had the courage to attempt it. . . . . . The *précis* is very well done."—*Journal of the Statistical Society*, June, 1880.

"There is no doubt as to the value of most parliamentary publications, but few persons have the time or inclination to wade through them, and thus much valuable matter is missed, but in this *précis* Messrs. Allen and Co. give an outline of just what is required."—*Iron Trade Review.*

"Messrs. Allen & Co.'s book is composed of abstracts of all returns directed to be printed by either or both of the Houses of Parliament, and the work has evidently been done by practised *précis* writers who understand how to reach the important features of Government papers."—*Liverpool Daily Courier.*

"This is a publication which supplies a great want. We gladly welcome this work, both for reading and for reference."—*United Service Gazette.*

"The papers are carefully condensed."—*British Mail.*

"In the case of statistical returns it is especially good."—*Cambridge Chronicle.*

"This is not a Blue-book; but none of them can exceed it in value. Every business man will have it upon the desk corner for reference, and it should be found on the table of every public reading room and private library."—*Western Times.*

"A most useful work of reference."—*The Railway News.*

"This is a very important work, and its perusal will place readers on a far higher intellectual level and acquaintance with the parliamentary papers than most embryo members of Parliament possess."—*Finance Chronicle and Insurance Circular.*

"This serial is calculated to be of much service."—*Iron.*

"The above contains a vast amount of valuable information and statistics."—*Sunday Times.*

"We scarcely need add that it is a valuable work."—*Herapath's Railway Journal.*

"As a book of reference, promises to be of inestimable value to public men, journalists, economists, historical students, and, indeed, all who are interested in national progress and contemporary politics."—*The Statist.*

"The difficult work of summarising is extremely well executed. Both paper and type are good."—*Broad Arrow.*

"An excellent publication."—*The Farmer.*

"Messrs. Allen & Co. earn the gratitude of all who require to keep themselves acquainted with the contents of parliamentary papers by the publication of this *précis*. The compilation has been made with discretion, and will be found extremely valuable and useful for reference."—*Dundee Advertiser.*

"As a handy work of reference, and a means of saving time and labour, it will be highly appreciated."—*Allen's Indian Mail.*

"The utility of the *précis* is very considerably heightened by an admirable table of contents numerically and alphabetically arranged."—*The Railway News and Joint Stock Journal.*

"The *précis* of official papers will give new value to the parliamentary returns."—*Liverpool Courier.*

"Nous croyons rendre service au public et à ceux de nos confreres qui ne la connaîtraient pas, en leur signalent cette publication nouvelle."—*Moniteur des Interêts Materiels, Brussels.*

LONDON: W. H. ALLEN & CO., 13, WATERLOO-PLACE.

www.ingramcontent.com/pod-product-compliance
Lightning Source LLC
Chambersburg PA
CBHW021357230426
43666CB00006B/561